Middleware Module

Application Interconnectivity Through Middleware

---

e-Business Applications, Architectures, Integration

MODULE (APPLICATIONS): e-Business Strategies and Applications:
Chapter 1: e-Business - From Strategies to Applications
Chapter 2: e-Business Applications (CRMs, ERPs, eMarkets, SCM, ASPs, Portals)
Chapter 3: From Strategies to Solutions -- A Planning Methodology
Chapter 4: IT Infrastructure -- Overview of Enabling Technologies
Chapter 5: Applications State of the Practice, Market, and Art
MODULE (ARCHITECTURES): Solution Architectures Through Components
Chapter 1: Solution Architecture Overview
Chapter 2: Enterprise Application Architectures -- Component-based Approach
Chapter 3 Enterprise Data Architectures in Web-XML Environments
Chapter 4: Implementing Architectures -- Concepts and Examples
Chapter 5: Architectures State of the Practice, Market, and Art
MODULE (INTEGRATION):Enterprise Application Integration and Migration
Chapter 1: Integration with Existing (Including Legacy) Applications -- An Overview
Chapter 2: Enterprise and Inter-Enterprise Application Integration (EAI/eAI)
Chapter 3: Data Warehouses and Data Mining for Integration
Chapter 4: Migration Strategies and Technologies
Chapter 5: Integration State of the Practice, Market, and Art

The Enabling IT Infrastructure

MODULE (PLATFORMS): Application Servers for Mobile and EC/EB Applications
Chapter 1: Mobile Computing Platforms -- Mobile Application Servers
Chapter 2: e-Commerce Platforms for C2B Trade-- The Commerce Servers
Chapter 3: B2B Platforms and Standards -- The B2B Servers
Chapter 4: Platforms for Multimedia and Collaboration
Chapter 5: Platform State of the Practice, Market, and Art
MODULE (MIDDLEWARE) : Application Connectivity Through Middleware
Chapter 1: Middleware Principles and Basic Middleware Services
Chapter 2: Web, XML, Semantic Web, and Web Services
Chapter 3: Distributed Objects: CORBA, Web Services, J2EE, .NET, SOAP, and EJBs
Chapter 4: Enterprise Data and Transaction Management
Chapter 5: Middleware State of the Practice, Market, and Art
MODULE (NETWORKS): Network Services and Network Architectures
Chapter 1: Principles of Communication Networks
Chapter 2: Network Architectures and Interconnectivity
Chapter 3: Wireless and Broadband Networks -- Next Generation Networks:
Chapter 4: IP-based Networks and the Next Generation Internet
Chapter 5: Networks State of the Practice, Market, and Art

Background and Management

MODULE (OVERVIEW); The Big Picture
Chapter 1: e-Business and 3G Distributed Systems
--From Strategies to Working Solutions
MODULE (EXAMPLES); Case Studies & Examples
Chapter 2: Case Studies and Examples

MODULE (MANAGEMENT): Management and Security
Chapter 1 e-Business Management in Practice
Chapter 2: Management Platforms for Network and Systems
Management
Chapter 3: Security Management - Approaches and
Technologies
Chapter 4: Security Solutions -- Using Technologies to
Secure Systems
Chapter 5: Management State of the Practice, Market, and
Art

MODULE (TUTORIALS): Tutorials and Detailed Discussions on Special Topics

Chapter 1: Network Technologies -- A Tutorial
Chapter 2: Object-Orientation, Java, and UML -- A Tutorial
Chapter 3: Database Technologies and SQL -- A Tutorial
Chapter 4: Web Engineering and XML Processing
-- A Closer Look
Chapter 5: CORBA -- A Closer Look

A Module from
e-Business and Distributed Systems Handbook

Amjad Umar, Ph.D.

Publisher: NGE Solutions, Inc.
(www.ngesolutions.com)

Publication Date: April 2003

Umar, Amjad
  e-Business and Distributed Systems Handbook: Middleware Module ISBN: 0-9727414-8-8

  e-Business and Distributed Systems Handbook: All Modules ISBN: 0-9727414-0-2

Publisher: NGE Solutions, Inc. (www.ngesolutions.com)
       Copyright: 2003 by the Author

This is a module from the "e-Business and Distributed Systems Handbook" by Amjad Umar. The modules of the Handbook include the following:

e-Business and Distributed Systems Handbook: **All Modules** ISBN: 0-9727414-0-2
e-Business and Distributed Systems Handbook: **Overview Module** ISBN: 0-9727414-1-0
e-Business and Distributed Systems Handbook: **Applications Module** ISBN: 0-9727414-2-9
e-Business and Distributed Systems Handbook: **Architecture Module** ISBN: 0-9727414-3-7
e-Business and Distributed Systems Handbook: **Integration Module** ISBN: 0-9727414-4-5
e-Business and Distributed Systems Handbook: **Management Module** ISBN: 0-9727414-5-3
e-Business and Distributed Systems Handbook: **Networks Module** ISBN: 0-9727414-6-1
e-Business and Distributed Systems Handbook: **Middleware Module** ISBN: 0-9727414-8-8
e-Business and Distributed Systems Handbook: **Platforms Module** ISBN: 0-9727414-9-6

See "Handbook at a Glance" and visit www.amjadumar.com for Handbook contents
(overview and detailed).

Editor: Dolorese B. Umar

Handbook at a Glance

This handbook attempts to translate the e-business strategies to working IS solutions by using the latest distributed computing technologies. To accomplish this goal, enough details are provided so that the translation can happen successfully. The handbook consists of several modules, shown on the previous page, that explain different aspects of the subject matter through numerous case studies and examples. These modules can be purchased individually.

Visit the Author Website (www.amjadumar.com) for:

- Additional information about this handbook and updates
- Purchasing options and instructions
- Instructor corner for course outlines, powerpoint slides, sample assignments
- Free Overview Module (PDF only – the printed copy can be purchased separately) that contains:
    - Handbook Preface
    - Suggested Course Usage
    - Detailed Table of Contents
    - Glossary of Terms
    - Chapter 1: e-Business and Distributed Systems – From Strategies to Working Solutions
    - Chapter 2: Case Studies and Examples
- Free Tutorials and Special Topics Module (PDF only) that contains:
    - Chapter 1: Network Technologies -- A Tutorial
    - Chapter 2: Object-Orientation, Java, and UML -- A Tutorial
    - Chapter 3: Database Technologies and SQL -- A Tutorial
    - Chapter 4: Web Engineering and XML Processing -- A Closer Look
    - Chapter 5: CORBA -- A Closer Look
- Free slides (PDF format) of all chapters of the entire handbook that summarize the chapter topics and can be used as lecture notes
- Frequently asked questions
- Feedback and suggestions
- Contacting the author
- Author background

Module Preface

We live in a world where the order processing system of a bookstore in Atlanta can check the inventory stocks in New York, Paris, and Singapore. To accomplish this, network pipes are not enough -- you need interconnectivity software, known as middleware, that enables applications and users to interconnect over a network. As we will see in this module, middleware is the software that handles distributed communications between applications and resides above the network transport layer and below the business-aware application software. This definition excludes "stand alone" system software such as math libraries, operating systems, and file systems. The focus of this module is on the general-purpose and core middleware services that are used in a wide range of applications. These middleware services, as shown in the dark borders in Figure1, reside above the network and can directly support the general-purpose distributed applications or more specialized middleware services.

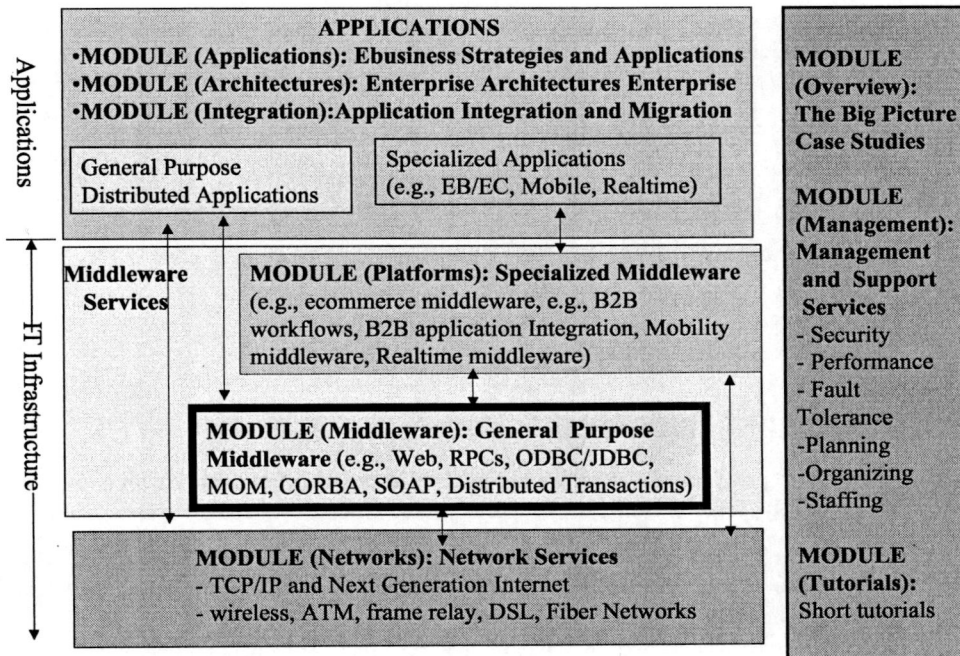

Figure 1: Middleware as Building Block of Modern Systems

Advances in middleware services have enabled rapid and cost effective development of distributed applications ranging from remote database access to large scale B2B systems. Because of their position, these services hide the underlying complexities of networks, operating systems, and computer hardware from the applications. They also manage distributed resources while also leveraging hardware/software technology advances. It is possible, and in some cases desirable[1], to build applications without using any middleware services,. This, however, turns out to be an extremely tedious, error-prone and costly undertaking over the life cycle of a system.

At the same time, currently existing COTS (commercial-off-the-shelf) middleware packages have many problems. In essence, middleware must satisfy the needs of two very demanding masters: applications that reside above the middleware and networks that exist below the middleware (see Figure 2). Both masters are evolving rapidly and impose ever-changing requirements. The chapters of this module, listed below, will introduce you to basic middleware principles and go through details of most popular middleware services such as remote SQL, remote procedure calls, message oriented middleware, Web technologies, distributed object technologies, and distributed

---

[1] Some real-time applications need to be built directly on top of hardware or operating systems.

data and transaction management. The emphasis, as always, is on building blocks and how these building blocks can be used to develop working solutions.

- Chapter 1: Middleware Principles and Basic Middleware Services
- Chapter 2: Web, XML, Semantic Web, and Web Services
- Chapter 3: Distributed Objects, CORBA, J2EE, and .NET
- Chapter 4: Enterprise Data and Transaction Management
- Chapter 5: Middleware State of the Practice, Market, and Art

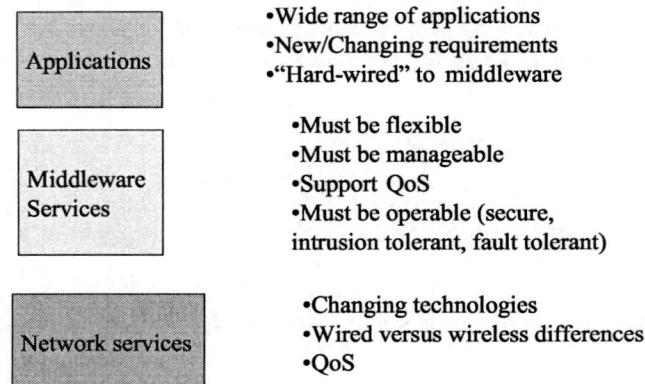

Applications	•Wide range of applications •New/Changing requirements •"Hard-wired" to middleware
Middleware Services	•Must be flexible •Must be manageable •Support QoS •Must be operable (secure, intrusion tolerant, fault tolerant)
Network services	•Changing technologies •Wired versus wireless differences •QoS

Figure 2: Middleware as the "Middle-man"

Reader Background Expected

This module is written for people with basic background in computing. The information contained in the Overview Module is highly recommended as a prerequisite. Specific chapters assume some additional background. For example:

- Chapter 3 assumes some background in object-orientation. This background can be obtained by reviewing the object-orientation chapter of the Tutorials Module.
- Chapter 4 assumes some background in database technologies. This background can be obtained by reviewing the database technologies chapter of the Tutorials Module.

Module Case Studies

XYZCorp Case Study: Middleware for IT Interconnectivity Task

The company has embarked on a major corporate wide interconnectivity effort. The objective is to allow anyone from any part of the company to access any information ("any information, anywhere, anytime"). The customers must be able to do online purchasing over the web and the business partners should be connected for B2B trade. In particular, the corporate center needs to be connected to the regional offices to transfer files and provide corporate wide information sharing. The corporate network must also accommodate a merger with a financial institution (a totally IBM mainframe shop). The management wants to understand the various interconnectivity issues and approaches. The management finally understands at least two levels of IT interconnectivity:

- Network interconnectivity that provides physical paths for the messages to be transported between various computers
- Application interconnectivity so that the users at one site can access applications and databases at other sites of the organization.

The network interconnectivity task was completed in the Network Module. The focus of the XYZCorp case study in this Module is Application Interconnectivity through Middleware (see Figure 3). This task concentrates on the basic middleware architecture. The Platform Module will address the more complex issues involving commercially available "Middleware Platforms" that package several middleware technologies to support mobility and B2B as well as C2B trade. We will develop the Application Interconnectivity Architecture by working through the following projects that will be completed in different chapters of this Module:

Project 1. How the corporate databases (customer, price, inventory) will be accessed from the various purchasing and marketing systems across the corporation by using the network developed in the Network Module (see Chapter 1 for additional details on this project).

Project 2 Choice of a corporate wide Web architecture. The company is interested in moving toward an "Intranet" as soon as possible and wants to develop a customer relationship management portal. We will discuss this project in Chapter 2.

Project 3. Assess the role of distributed object technologies for the corporation with special attention to Web Services, J2EE, and .NET. Project 3: XYZCorp has initiated a technology assessment effort that focuses on distributed object technologies. We will discuss this project in Chapter 3.

Project 4. How the corporate databases will be allocated, accessed, and updated from multiple users from multiple sites. We will discuss this project in Chapter 4. .

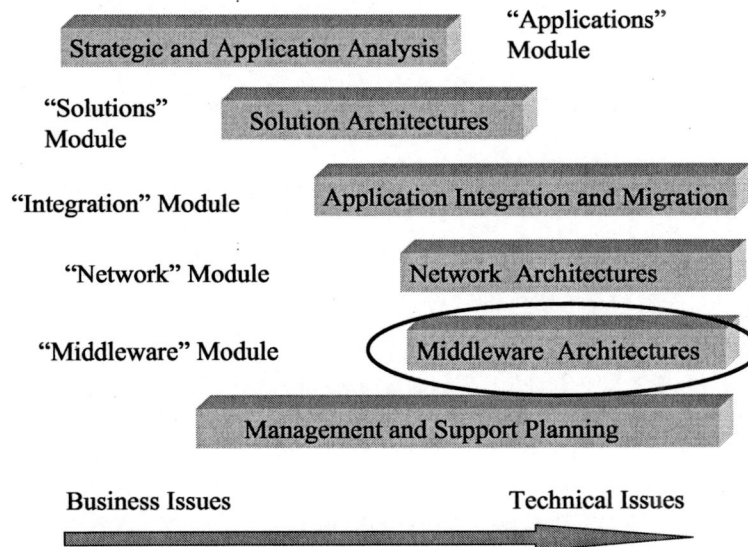

Figure 3: XYZCorp Planning Tasks

Additional Case Studies and Examples

Several additional case studies and examples are discussed in the chapters of this Module. A number of case studies that are relevant to the topics discussed in this Module appear regularly in trade magazines, vendor documents, web sites and books. Chapter 5 of this Module gives a sample of relevant case studies and points to numerous sources for additional case studies and examples.

In addition, several chapters of the Cases Module contain relevant case studies. For example, the following case studies in the first chapter of the Cases Module can be used to illustrate different aspects of the material in this

Module: Section 2.3   Ecommerce/eBusiness Examples: These examples can be used to understand how technical choices were made some time ago and to analyze different interconnectivity options through middleware services for the cases.

Section 2.4   Ecommerce - Online Purchasing Examples. These examples can be used to determine the type of middleware services needed for these systems. You should determine what, why, and where.

Section 2.5   A Financial Marketplace. After reviewing this case study, you can choose the middleware services for application connectivity for this marketplace.

Section 2.8   An Integrated Manufacturing System. A good example to examine how the current and future middleware services (basic middleware, XML-Web Services, .NET, J2EE, distributed data and transaction processors) can be used to integrate in manufacturing environments.

Section 2.9   A Customer Relationship Management Portal. Many technical choices are made in this case study. Can you use XML web services, .NET, or J2EE in this portal? Where and why?

Module Contents

1 Middleware Principles and Basic Middleware Services

1.1   Introduction

This chapter deals with the basic middleware services that are used to interconnect applications, databases, and users located around the network. By using these services, a user in Chicago can access databases in Cleveland and an order processing system in Tokyo can check with an inventory manager in New York. Basic middleware services are the foundation of the "client/server computing wave" that swept the computing industry in the early 1990's. An understanding of this middleware is essential for developing any contemporary distributed application because many higher-level middleware services rely on this middleware. The purpose of this chapter is to explain the basic middleware and answer questions such as the following:

- What are the main services provided by the basic middleware and who provides these services?
- What type of information exchange services are provided by this middleware (e.g., remote procedure call, remote data access, and publish/subscribe)?

The chapter first gives a brief overview of application interconnectivity (Section 1.3) and then discusses the various features of middleware (Section 1.4). The client/server model - the foundation of most Web and Internet-based applications -- is discussed in Section 1.6. Section 1.7 describes how the various pieces (applications, middleware, networks) interact with each other to provide business services. Sections 1.9 through 1.16 describe the basic middleware services in more detail.

Key Points

- Middleware is a set of common business-unaware services that enable applications and end users to interact with each other across a network.
- At a very basic level, middleware supports LOTC:
  - L - Locating the remote partner on the network. This involves a directory or naming service.
  - O - Open a connection with the remote partner and establish a session. This involves authentication of remote partners.
  - T - Transfer information to the remote partner. This means that an agreement as to the format and the rules of exchange have to be established (i.e., an exchange protocol).
  - C - Close the session.
- Web technologies (web browsers, servers, HTTP) are good examples of middleware services.
- Basic C/S middleware services include:
  - Remote communication paradigms such as Remote Procedure Call (RPC), Remote Data Access (RDA), and Message Oriented Middleware (MOM).
  - Management and support services such as security, directories, time, and failure management.
  - Distributed print and file services.
- Ideally, middleware should make the networks irrelevant to the applications and end users. In other words, the users and applications should be able to perform the same operations across a network that they can perform locally.
- Many network operating systems for LANs provide the basic C/S middleware services.
- Many other middleware services are built on top of the basic C/S middleware.
- Each paradigm has its own weaknesses and strengths. Ideally, C/S middleware needs to support RDA, RPC and MOM paradigms to provide application developers maximum flexibility.

1.2 Case Study: XYZCorp Chooses an Interconnectivity Architecture

1.2.1 Middleware for Interconnectivity Project

XYZCorp needs to establish an interconnectivity architecture that goes beyond network connectivity. Figure 1-1 shows a simplified view of XYZCorp in which a variety of applications and databases at various sites (some international) need to be accessed by users. In addition, the applications at one site need to access databases at other sites. The specific issues to be addressed as part of this interconnectivity architecture project are (see Sections 1.8 and 1.17 for hints and partial solutions):

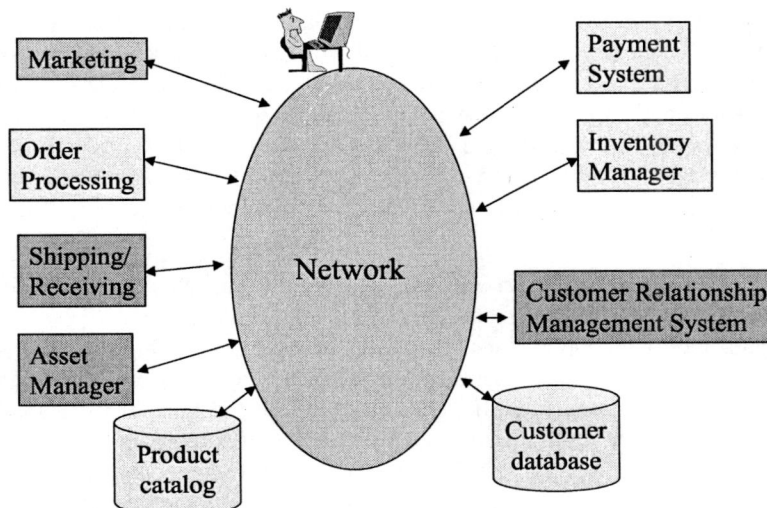

Figure 1-1: XYZCorp Applications and Databases across a Network

1). How can applications at various branch offices access the corporate databases at the headquarters? For example, how can the order processing system in Denver determine available inventory in the corporate inventory database (currently in Chicago)?

2). The business services department has been getting a lot of complaints about their financial report distribution system. The current financial information (personnel costs, materials costs, etc) is stored on the corporate IBM mainframe database. Currently, reports for each local manager are printed once a month on the mainframe printer. These reports are then mailed through office mail to the managers and are usually too late, too rigid and not customizable. What should be done?

3). Technical questions such as the following should also be addressed as part of the project:
- Should a loose versus tightly coupled architecture be adopted to interconnect the large number of users, applications, and databases that reside at different sites?
- How can multiple clients and servers that support different middleware services co-exist in the XYZCorp environment?
- Should a thin client be used everywhere? If not, where can a fat client be used?
- Can a LAN operating system provide interconnectivity within the organization? If yes, which one?
- Should RPC, RDA, MOM, or pub-sub be used as the primary remote communication protocol and why? Which types of protocols are suited for which types of applications?

The Agenda
- Middleware Overview and Principles
- Basic Middleware (RPC, RDA, MOM)
- Comparison and Analysis

1.3 Applications in Distributed Environments

Figure 1-1 shows a typical problem in which a variety of applications and databases at various sites need to be accessed by the users. To support this access, naturally a network connection is needed to transport the messages back and forth. But in addition, a glue is needed that resides above the network and establishes connections to applications and databases across a network. This glue, called middleware, is the main topic of this chapter. For example, if a marketing system in Chicago needs to access a customer database in Seattle, then it is not enough to provide a network pipe – you need to have some middleware services that will connect the marketing system to the customer database, verify security, and then issue a remote database query.

Middleware, defined formally in the next section, is basically the connectivity software that allows applications and users to interact with each other across a network in a distributed computing environment. Basically, every organization with applications that are dispersed across multiple computers is a distributed computing environment. For example, the figure above shows a typical distributed computing environment. Although applications can communicate with each other through file transfer (a really old middleware), client/server (C/S) is the most commonly used model of distributed computing at present. Thus C/S is the foundation of most commercially available middleware packages. Figure 1-2 shows the interrelationships between distributed computing, client/server, and other models of distributed computing. Conceptually, the client/server model is a special case of distributed computing model. Let us discuss these interrelationships in more detail.

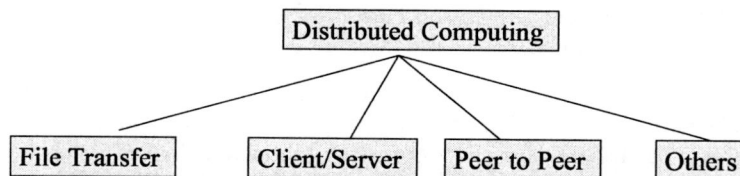

```
                    ┌─────────────────────┐
                    │ Distributed Computing │
                    └─────────────────────┘
         ┌──────────────┬─────────┴──────────┬──────────────┐
   ┌───────────┐  ┌─────────────┐  ┌──────────────┐  ┌──────────┐
   │File Transfer│  │Client/Server│  │ Peer to Peer │  │  Others  │
   └───────────┘  └─────────────┘  └──────────────┘  └──────────┘
```

Figure 1-2: Models of Distributed Computing (Add in – in Peer-to-Peer)

A Distributed Computing System (DCS) is a collection of autonomous computers interconnected through a communication network to achieve business functions. Technically, the computers do not share main memory so that the information cannot be transferred through global variables. The information (knowledge) between the computers is exchanged only through messages over a network.

The restriction of no shared memory and information exchange through messages is of key importance because it distinguishes between DCS and shared memory multiprocessor computing systems. This definition requires that the DCS computers are connected through a network which is responsible for the information exchange between computers. The definition also requires that the computers have to work together and cooperate with each other to satisfy enterprise needs (see [Umar 1993, Chapter 1] for more discussion of DCS).

Distributed computing can be achieved through one or more of the following:

- File transfer model
- Client/server model
- Peer-to-peer model

The file transfer model is one of the oldest models to achieve distributed computing at a very minimal level. Basically, programs at different computers communicate with each other by using file transfer. In fact, email is a special case of file transfer. Although this is a very old and extremely limited model of distributed computing, it is still used to support loosely coupled distributed computers. For example, media clips, news items, and portions of corporate databases are typically exchanged between remote computers through file transfers.

The C/S model allows application processes at different sites to interactively exchange messages and is thus a significant improvement over the file transfer model. Initial versions of the C/S model utilized the remote procedure call paradigm that extends the scope of a local procedure call. A very common example of the C/S model is the World Wide Web where the browsers are the clients that access remote Web servers in real time. At present, the C/S model is increasingly utilizing the distributed objects paradigm that extends the scope of the local object paradigm (i.e., the application processes at different sites are viewed as distributed objects).

The peer-to-peer model allows the processes at different sites to invoke each other. The basic difference between C/S and peer-to-peer is that in a peer-to-peer model the interacting processes can be a client, server or both, while in a C/S model one process assumes the role of a service provider while the other assumes the role of a service consumer. Peer-to-peer middleware is used to build peer-to-peer distributed applications. Many new applications, especially for publishers and subscribers assume the peer-to-peer model.

1.4 Middleware – The Glue Between Applications

1.4.1 What is Middleware?

Although middleware is difficult to define precisely, it basically is the connectivity software that allows applications and users to interact with each other across a network (see Figure 1-3). We will use the following definition in this book (it conforms to [A1999]):

Definition of Middleware: Middleware is a set of common business-unaware services that enable applications and end users to interact with each other across a network. In essence, middleware is the software that resides above the network and below the business-aware application software -- it denotes a reusable, expandable set of services and functions that benefit many applications in a networked environment in terms of scalability, performance, security and interoperability.

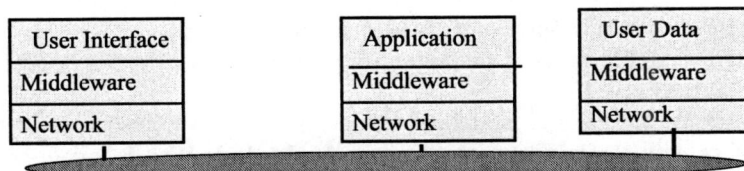

Figure 1-3: Middleware Conceptual View

According to this definition, the key ingredients of middleware are:
- It provides common business-unaware services.
- It enables applications and end users to interact with each other across a network.
- It resides above the network and below the business-aware application software.
- It supports scalability, performance, security and interoperability of applications.

Middleware is business-unaware (i.e., it does not have any business logic) and is available as a common set of routines. The services provided by these routines are available to the applications through application programming interfaces (APIs) and to the human users through commands and/or graphical user interfaces (GUIs). The commonality implies that these routines are available to multiple applications and users. Ideally, middleware should be transparent to end-users -- the end-users should be unaware when it is there and aware only when it is not. Middleware may be embedded within operating systems, or may be separate, and the boundary may change with time.

Middleware is enabling software for applications and end users to exchange information across networks. Ideally, middleware should make the networks irrelevant to the applications and end users. In other words, the users and applications should be able to perform the same operations across a network that they can perform locally. This implies that middleware should also hide the details of computing hardware, operating systems and other software components (e.g., databases) across networks. Thus, SQL middleware can allow users and applications residing on PCs under Windows to access an Oracle database residing on a Sun UNIX computer and a DB2 database on a mainframe MVS computer. We should also point out the significance of end users and applications as the users of middleware (many definitions restrict middleware usage to applications). According to our definition, middleware can support interactions between users to users (e.g., email), users to applications (e.g., Web browsers), and applications to applications (e.g., electronic fund transfer).

Middleware resides above the network and below the business-aware application and database software to provide the needed transparency -- it resides on the client as well as server sides. For example, if you want a customer database on a UNIX machine to be remotely accessed from 100 PCs, then one copy of middleware will need to be purchased/installed for the UNIX machine (e.g., SQL database server) and a copy of the client side middleware will need to be purchased/installed on each one of the 100 PCs. This is why we all have web browsers on our computers because the web browser is a client side middleware that is needed to access web servers over the Internet. In general, middleware can be decomposed into client middleware that resides on every client machine and server middleware that resides on the server machines. There are costs as well as management implications of this.

Middleware services should reinforce and support desirable properties such as scalability, performance, security and interoperability. Any solutions that do not scale with the growth of the application are not very valuable. In addition, connectivity software must not introduce vulnerability such as security exposures. In particular, a system should be more secure and robust *after* using a middleware service than before it. Depending on the application, revenue, profit, operational efficiency, business productivity, and even lives can be at stake in the interconnected digital world of today. Thus middleware services should reinforce and support scalability, performance, security and interoperability of interconnected applications.

These ingredients of our definition can be used to determine if a particular software package qualifies as middleware or not. According to our definition, the following software qualifies as middleware (if you do not know about these, do not worry; the rest of this module is filled with information about many of these software packages):

- Email (it is business unaware and interconnects users at different sites)
- Terminal emulators and file transfer packages (these business-unaware services connect users to resources)
- Web browsers (they are business unaware and support user access to resources on the Internet) As a matter of fact, as we will see in a later chapter, the World Wide Web is a collection of middleware services.
- Database drivers and gateways such as ODBC drivers and Sybase Omni Server (they provide access to remotely located databases)
- Object Management Group's CORBA (Common Object Request Broker Architecture) because it provides services for distributed object applications

Here is a list of software systems that do not qualify as middleware, according to our definition:
- Operating systems such as Windows, Unix, and Linux (they operate only on local resources)

- Airline reservation systems (they are business aware)
- Network routers (they do not reside above the network -- they are part of network services)

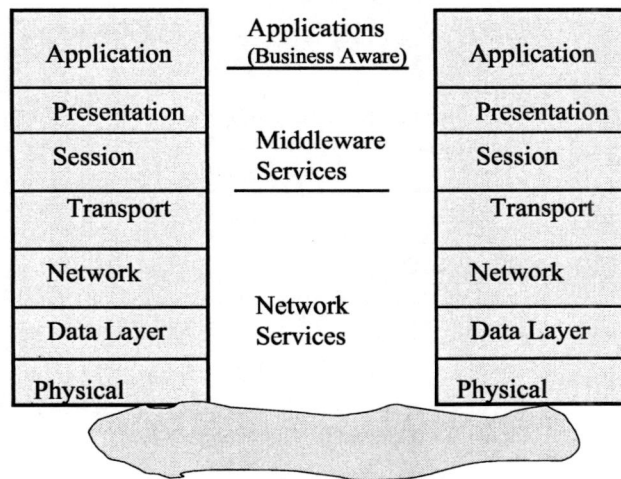

Application	**Applications** (Business Aware)	Application
Presentation		Presentation
Session	**Middleware Services**	Session
Transport		Transport
Network		Network
Data Layer	**Network Services**	Data Layer
Physical		Physical

Figure 1-4: Middleware from an OSI Point of View

1.4.2 Functional View of Middleware

Middleware provides a wide range of functionality such as establishment of sessions between client processes and server processes, security, compression/decompression, and failure handling. At a very basic level, middleware is responsible for **LOTC**:

- L - Locating the remote partner on the network. This involves a directory or naming service.
- O - Open a connection with the remote partner. This means that the clients establish a connection ("open a line") with the server -- just because you know where the partner resides does not mean that he/she actually wants to talk to you. This step involves partner authentication.
- T - Transfer information to the remote partner. This is the actual transfer of information between the two parties (e.g., access a remote database, download an image, etc). It means that an agreement as to the format and the rules of exchange have to be established (i.e., an exchange protocol).
- C - Close the session (and go home!).

Of course, all these operations must be performed securely with attention to performance, scalability, and accounting. Thus, additional middleware services may include:

- Security and robustness (such as identification, authentication, confidentiality, authorization and access control)
- Performance enhancement (such as caching)
- Directory, naming, and location services
- Enhancing reliability and availability
- Support for end-to-end quality-of-service objectives and guarantees
- Support for mobility of devices and users
- Support for standard structured data types (XML, audio, video)
- Support for usage accounting
- Etc.

The main middleware services can be cast into the following broad categories (see Figure 1-5):

- General-purpose middleware services
- Application-specific middleware services
- Management and support services

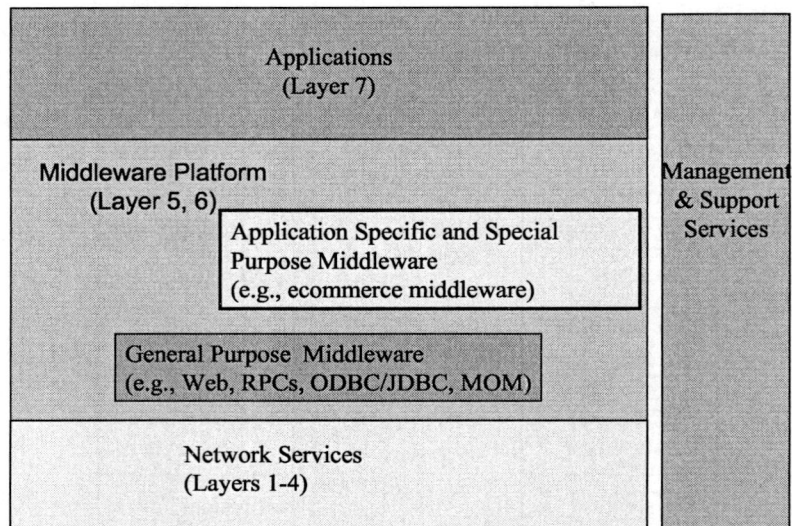

Figure 1-5: Middleware; A Functional View

General-purpose middleware services provide the business value to the end users by sending the needed information across a network in response to a request. In particular, these services may be needed to transfer data, issue commands, receive responses, check a status, resolve deadlocks, and establish/break connections between remotely located application processes and end users. These services typically include synchronous calls (i.e., client sends a request and waits for a response). In many cases, it is desirable to provide asynchronous communication (i.e., keep sending requests without waiting for responses) between remote programs so that the execution of a program is not suspended while waiting for responses. Information exchange must include facility for the servers to handle many concurrent and asynchronous requests simultaneously from many clients. Information exchange services are supported by the middleware through primitive services (e.g., file transfer, terminal emulation, email) and client/server information exchange services (e.g., remote procedure calls). This module is devoted to these middleware services.

Application-specific middleware services provide the services needed by different classes of applications. Examples of these services are groupware services for collaborative processing, workflow services, ecommerce services to support commerce over the Internet, and specialized services needed for mobile computing and distributed multimedia applications. As new classes of applications emerge (such as mobile commerce), more application-specific middleware services are emerging. In some cases, some business-aware logic drifts into these services to support specific applications such as ecommerce. Due to this reason, some people view these middleware services as *"Upperware"* (too many terms!) In many cases, these services are being packaged into "middleware platforms" that provide a set of integrated services for a specific class of applications. An example of these middleware platforms are the eCommerce Platforms such as IBM's WebSphere and Nokia's Mobile Services Platform for mobile applications. The Platform Module looks at these middleware platforms in great detail.

Management and support services are needed to locate distributed resources and administer these resources across networks. These services go across the network, middleware, and application layers. Examples of these services include directory (naming), security, fault, and performance services. In particular, these services include the following:
- Facility for the clients to locate a server (which server to invoke), send the request to a server, receive response from a server, and parse and interpret the response
- Ability to handle security (authentication and journaling)
- Facility to handle failure (timeouts, deadlocks, hardware/software) at the distributed sites (clients as well as servers)

- Ability to monitor and improve the run-time performance of the distributed programs. This should allow measurement of communication traffic, program wait states, deadlocks, etc.

The Management Module studies these issues in some detail.

Figure 1-5 highlights the major functions performed by the middleware. We will further refine this framework in the next section. The application processes are business-aware software and databases that interact with each other through the IT infrastructure. The IT infrastructure (i.e., platform) is needed to develop, deploy, support and manage the applications. At a high level, the IT infrastructure consists of middleware, network services, local services (e.g., database managers, transaction managers), operating systems and computing hardware. Our main interest at present is on the middleware.

Example. To illustrate the middleware functions, consider, for example, that you need to transfer funds from a bank in Chicago to a bank in New York. To accomplish this, you need at least three things: a) a network to connect the two banks, b) application processes on the two banks that will transfer the funds, and c) the middleware that will support the fund transfer application processes. Specifically, the middleware will reside on the Chicago machine (client middleware) and New York machine (server middleware) to provide the following major services:

- General-purpose middleware services that will first establish a connection between the client program (Chicago) and the server program (New York) and then transfer the funds between the two remotely located programs (the program in Chicago will debit one account and the program in New York will credit the other account)
- Application-specific middleware services that will make sure that the transaction is completed successfully. These services will ensure that either the money is transferred completely or not at all
- Management and support services such as directory, security, and administrative support to help locate the resources from authorized users (i.e., make sure no one else starts transferring your funds to Switzerland!)

The services provided by the middleware have evolved, and continue to evolve. This evolution has been driven to satisfy the following objectives:

- Support of newer applications (e.g., World Wide Web applications, mobile computing applications, ecommerce/ebusiness applications, distributed multimedia applications, and computer supported collaborative work)
- Increased transparency for the users (i.e., the user is not aware of what activities are taking place where in the network), developers (i.e., the application developers should be shielded from the details of different systems while developing applications), and managers (i.e., the managers should be able to manage distributed systems as a single system)
- Improved portability and interoperability of applications across computer systems
- Consistency and repeatability of services
- Improved response time and availability of services
- Better management tools and infrastructures

This evolution of middleware is intended to minimize the risks and costs of developing new applications. If continued, this evolution will shape the nature of applications and business practices in the future. We will describe in the next section how the middleware has evolved to meet these goals.

Good Middleware Books

Many books cover different aspects of middleware services. Here are some of my favorites:
- Myerson, J.," The Complete Book of Middleware", Auerbach Publications, 2002

- Lerner, et al, "Middleware Networks: Concept, Design and Deployment of Internet Infrastructure", Kluwer Academic Publishers; 2000

- Serain, D., and Craig, I., "Middleware: Practitioner Series", Springer-Verlag, 1999

- Britton, C., "IT Architectures and Middleware: Strategies for Building Large, Integrated Systems",

---

Addison-Wesley, 2000

The Website **http://www.middleware.org/bookstore.html** lists these and many other books on different aspects of middleware.

1.5 Middleware Examples and a Closer look

Figure 1-6 shows a more detailed view of the middleware stack. The general-purpose middleware itself is further subdivided into Basic Connectivity and Value Added Middleware Services. This subdivision is close to the one suggested by Doug Schmidt [2001]. The **Basic Connectivity Middleware** provides, as the name suggests, very basic services to perform locate, open, transmit, and close operations, Examples of Basic Connectivity Middleware services are:

- Primitive middleware services software such as terminal emulators, email and file transfer packages. These services are not the focus of this book. We discussed these services in the "IP Networks" Chapter of the Networks Module.
- Basic C/S middleware services which include Remote Procedure Call (RPC), Remote Data Access (RDA), and Message Oriented Middleware (MOM). This middleware is typically built on top of the network transport services. We will discuss this middleware in this chapter.
- World Wide Web middleware services to support the dramatically evolving applications over the Internet and Intranets. This includes Web browsers, Web servers, Hypertext Transfer Protocol (HTTP), Hypertext Markup Language (HTML), and Web gateways. We will discuss this middleware in chapter 2 of this module.

The **Value Added Middleware Services** provide, in addition to basic connectivity, other services such as directory and memory management. Examples of these services are:

- Distributed object middleware services that manage distributed object operations. Examples of these services and standards are the Object Management Group's Common Object Request Broker Architecture (OMG CORBA), and Microsoft's DCOM. In particular, CORBA defines a large number of services that include object activation, directory, life cycle support, event management, and security management. Some of these services are built on top of the basic connectivity middleware (e.g., many CORBA implementations are developed on top of RPCs). Similarly, newer distributed object services such as Web Services use Web middleware such as HTTP. We will discuss distributed object middleware services in chapter 3 of this module.
- Distributed data and transaction management middleware services that are responsible for access, manipulation, and update of distributed as well as replicated data. This middleware includes protocols such as two phase commit, transactional RPCs, and XA and "TP Heavy" versus "TP Light" issues. Many of these protocols utilize the basic connectivity middleware (e.g. transactional RPCs use the basic RPCs). In some cases, this type of middleware is also built on top of distributed object services. For example, Object Transaction Management (OTM) systems are built on top of CORBA and DCOM. We will discuss this type of middleware in chapter 4 of this module.

Let us also look at application-specific and special-purpose middleware services that are being developed for emerging applications. We will discuss this middleware in the Platform Module of this book. Examples of this middleware are:

- Middleware for e-commerce and e-business such as e-payment systems, XML-based e-business support such as ebXML, EDI, and electronic catalogs
- Wireless middleware for mobile computing applications. This includes Wireless Application Protocol (WAP), I-Mode, Voice XML, and other emerging middleware services.

- Other special-purpose middleware such as middleware for distributed multimedia applications (e.g., Real-Time Protocols, middleware for groupware (e.g., Lotus Notes), and middleware for legacy application access/integration.

Figure 1-6 is a refinement of the framework presented in Figure 1-5 and serves several purposes. First, it shows the middleware in terms of the components that are commonly used in the industry (this will help in product evaluation). Second, it shows the different application programming interfaces (APIs) that can be invoked from the applications (this illustrates that more middleware components can increase complexity of applications). Third, it shows how different components can be combined together to support different functions and to satisfy the business drivers. (For example, a user may choose Web middleware and distributed objects to support object-oriented information exchange over the Internet). Finally, we will use this figure as a roadmap for discussion in this book (i.e., in which chapter of this book these components are discussed in more detail).

We should clarify that some of the services we describe as middleware (e.g., Web browsers, email) can be viewed as applications from a computing point of view. However, we classify all business- unaware services that reside on top of networks as middleware because from a user and business point of view, these services add no business value.

It is appropriate here to comment about **Homegrown Middleware.** When companies first encounter the need for a middleware layer, they often have a specific problem to address that requires a modest solution. Rather than invest in a middleware package, some firms allow their own development staff to write a middleware-like solution to solve the particular problem. Although initially workable, this approach tends to lack scalability and flexibility as new problems need to be added to the old solution. As a result, supporting the homegrown middleware becomes expensive as it has to be customized and extended constantly—generally by staff members who have never written middleware software before. The final result is an expensive solution that tends to break easily and does not scale well.

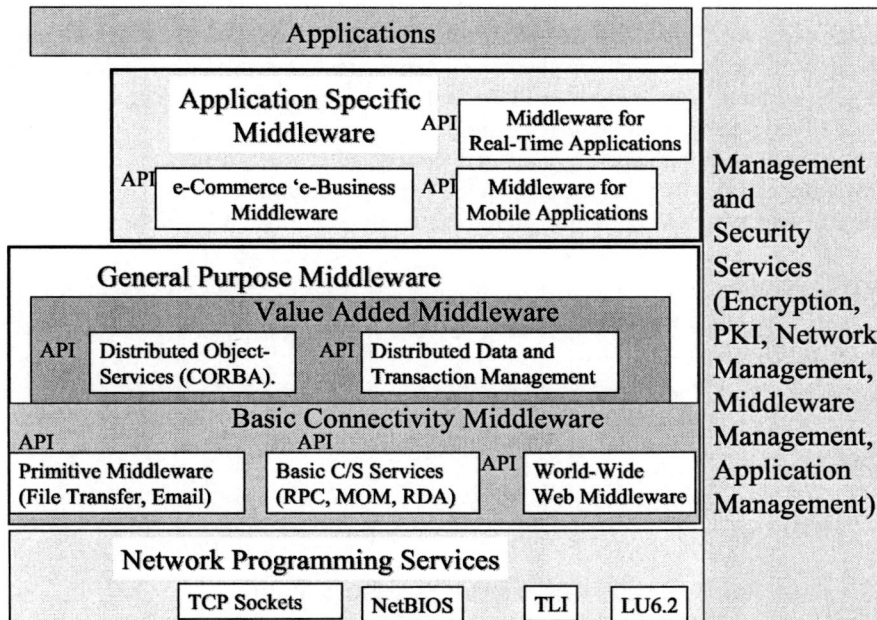

Figure 1-6: More Detailed View of Middleware

1.6 The Client/Server Model – A Closer Look

1.6.1 Overview of Client/Server Model

The term client/server has been used in business for a number of years. For example, in a restaurant the customer is a client and the restaurant owner is the server. In computing, the client/server model is a concept for describing communications between computing processes that are classified as service consumers (clients) and service providers (servers). Figure 1-7 presents a simple C/S model. The basic features of a C/S model are:

- Clients and servers are functional modules with well-defined interfaces (i.e., they hide internal information). The functions performed by a client and a server can be implemented by a set of software modules, hardware components, or a combination thereof. Clients and/or servers may run on dedicated machines, if needed. It is unfortunate that some machines are called "servers". This causes confusion (try explaining to an already bewildered user that a client software is running on a machine called "the server"). We will avoid this usage as much as possible.

- Each client/server relationship is established between two functional modules when one module (client) initiates a service request and the other (server) chooses to respond to the service request. Examples of service requests (SRs) are "retrieve customer name", "produce net income in last year", etc. For a given service request, clients and servers do not reverse roles (i.e., a client stays a client and a server stays a server). However, a server for SR R1 may become a client for SR R2 when it issues requests to another server (see Figure 1-7). For example, a client may issue an SR which may generate other SRs.

- Information exchange between clients and servers is strictly through messages (i.e., no information is exchanged through global variables). The service request and additional information is placed into a message that is sent to the server. The server's response is similarly another message that is sent back to the client.

- Messages exchanged between clients and servers occur in real-time. Conceptually, clients and servers may run on the same machine or on separate machines. In this book, however, our primary interest is in distributed client/server systems where clients and servers reside on separate machines (if it was not for distributed C/S systems, this book would be only ten pages long!). Thus, we will introduce the following additional feature of a client/server model:

- Clients and servers reside on separate machines connected through a network. Thus, all C/S service requests are real-time messages that are exchanged through network services. This restriction introduces several technical issues such as portability, interoperability, security, and performance.

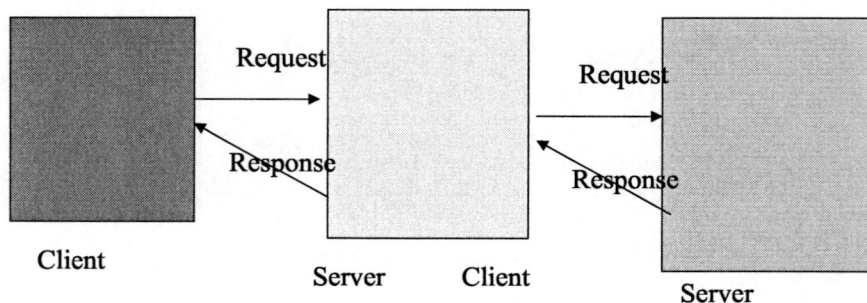

Figure 1-7: Conceptual Client/Server Model

Fundamental Client/Server Properties

- Clients and servers are functional modules that represent a consumer/provider relationship.

- For a given service, clients and servers do not reverse roles (i.e., a client stays a client and a server stays a server).
- All information exchange between clients and servers is through messages (no global variables).
- Message exchange between clients and servers is in real time.
- Clients and servers reside on different machines connected through a network.
- Clients and servers represent business functionality (not machines, not business-unaware software).

1.6.2 Architectural Configurations of C/S Systems

Most applications can be represented in terms of user, processing and data components (we will discuss this topic extensively in later modules of this book). The application can also be physically configured as the following:

- **Single Tiered** (one level of distribution): In this case, all application components (user, application, and data objects) are assigned to one computer (typically a mainframe or a mid-range computer). This configuration represents the traditional terminal-host model.
- **Two Tiered** (two levels of distribution): The application components are split between "front-end" and "back-end" computers. The front-end computer provides the user interface objects (a client machine) and the back-end computer provides the database support.
- **Three and higher (n) Tiered** (several levels of distribution): The application components are split across three types of machines: a front-end machine (usually a desktop), a middle machine (usually a LAN server or a minicomputer) and a back-end machine (usually a mainframe).

In this discussion, tier represents a physical hardware machine. Figure 1-8 shows one- and two-tiered configurations. It shows how the user interfaces, application programs and databases can be distributed between the client and server machines (configuration a is one tiered, all others are two tiered).

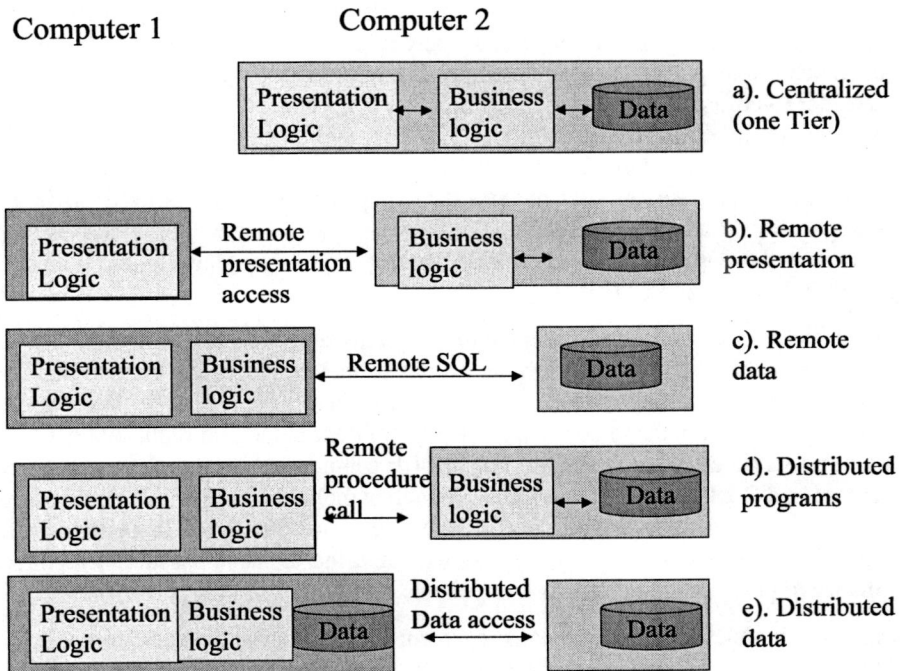

Figure 1-8 Client/Server Application Architectures

Figure 1-8a shows a single tiered application in which all application components are assigned to the same machine. This model represents the classical mainframe model. The architecture shown in Figure 1-8b shows the simplest architecture where the presentation (user interface) is assigned to the client machine, usually a desktop computer. This architecture, used in many presentation intensive applications has the benefit that the user interface processing is parceled out to the end-user sites. It especially fits very well for the situations where different user interfaces for the same application are needed. For example, user interfaces in different languages (e.g., Chinese, Japanese, French) and/or different graphical symbols and tool bars can be easily supported by the remote presentation architecture. This architecture is commonly used in the Web-based applications where the client is the Web browser and everything else (HTML documents, CGI programs, and databases) reside on the Web server site.

Figure 1-8c represents the remote data architecture in which the application programs, in addition to the user interfaces, are fully assigned to the client machines. The remote data is typically stored in an "SQL server" and is accessed through ad hoc SQL statements sent over the network (i.e., the RDA protocol). This "fat client" architecture, used in many management decision support applications (spreadsheets, projections, simulations, etc.) is especially suitable for departmental/group C/S applications (ad hoc SQL over a slow corporate WAN causes "minor discomforts"). This architecture is very popular with the SQL Servers (e.g., Microsoft SQL Server), and is especially appealing for end users who need to perform different application processing on the same shared data (e.g., different users of a subject database need to perform different processing). This architecture also suits the situations where a small amount of remote data is accessed and a great deal of processing time is used in analyzing and presenting the data. However, this architecture can generate unpredictable traffic on the network because ad hoc SQL can result in a large amount of data that is selected and sent back to the client machine. Fast networks (e.g., LANs or Broadband WANs) are a prerequisite for this architecture. In Web-based applications, this architecture supports Java programs and other programs (components in ActiveX) to access remotely located databases through ODBC (Open Database Connectivity) or JDBC (Java Database Connectivity).

Figure 1-8d represents the distributed application program architecture in which the application programs are split between the client and server machines. This architecture, implemented in the very popular remote procedure call (RPC) systems, is based on message exchange between two remote programs. This architecture is especially appealing for the situations where it is not advisable to parcel the entire processing logic to the client machines. In particular, many enterprises have common application logic that is better kept at the corporate center to enforce corporate wide enforcement. Typical exchange protocol used between the client and server program modules is RPC, although CORBA and queued message MOM-based solutions are gaining popularity. This architecture also suits the situations where a small amount of message exchange is needed between clients and servers and a great deal of processing time is used on both sites (e.g., enterprise-wide applications that need to use the relatively slow WAN lines. For Web-based applications, this application supports Java applets on the client side that may invoke programs on the Web server or other servers through RPCs, DCOM, and CORBA.

Figure 1-8e represents the case where data, application programs as well as user interfaces are distributed to many sites. In particular, the data exists at client as well as server machines (distributed data architecture). This architecture has many advantages (e.g., access to local data quickly) but it presents challenges of distributed data and transaction management (e.g., integrity of distributed and replicated data). Typical C/S protocols used for this architecture are the RDA and DTP (distributed transaction processing) protocols such as two phase commit and Replication Servers. Other variations include periodic bulk data transfer to update the client database and usage of a "cache data" at the client side instead of a permanent database. A performance study based on detailed simulations has indicated that a cache-based C/S architecture shows superior performance to other popular configurations [Delis 1993].

In essence, these five architectural configurations represent the continuum between completely centralized (all data, application programs and user interfaces at one computer) and completely decentralized applications (no common data, application programs and user interfaces). These architectures provide the basis for a transition strategy from centralized to distributed applications in which the user interfaces are distributed first, followed by distribution of application programs and data. Table 1-1 shows trade-offs between these five architectures and the single tiered terminal host system in terms of transaction processing needs, flexibility, performance, availability, cost, manageability, and security. For example, Table 1-1 shows that more decentralization leads to improved flexibility, performance, and availability but raises some issues in manageability and security. It should be kept in mind that this table is suggested as a framework for analysis (the factors and the values can be modified if needed).

Table 1-1: Trade-offs Between Single/Two Tiered Architectures

	Terminal Host (Single Tiered)	Remote Presentation	Distributed Programs	Remote Data	Distributed Data
Transaction needs	+3	+2	+1	-2	-2
End user Flexibility and Growth	-3	-2	+2	+2	+3
Performance	-3	-2	+2	+2	+3
Availability	-3	-2	+2	+2	+3
Cost	+3	+2	+1	-1	-3
Manageability					
and Control	+3	+3	-2	-2	-3
Security	+3	+3	-2	-2	-3

Legend: Evaluation factors (-3 to +3) indicate how well the configurations satisfy the requirements

---

Fat Clients Versus Fat Servers

A client or a server is considered "fat" if it provides many functions (i.e., has many objects). The trade-offs between fat clients versus fat servers need to be considered when the application objects are assigned to two or three tiers. The following guidelines and rules of thumb can be used to decide between fat clients versus fat servers:

OLTP (Online Transaction Processing) versus decision support applications: OLTP applications generally require fat servers because more functionality is needed at the database site (commits, logging, rollbacks, etc.) On the other hand, decision support applications generally require fat clients because each user can run his/her own tools (e.g., spreadsheets, data browsers, report writers) that access a back-end database.

Cost, security, and performance considerations: Fat clients can be more expensive to support because more powerful client machines and associated software is needed. Fat servers can be used to enforce corporate wide business rules and security requirements. However, fat servers can become performance bottlenecks.

Location specificity: Some application objects are location specific - they must exist at a specific location. For example, some sensitive information must be kept at the corporate office, manufacturing device status information needs to be kept on the plant floor, etc. Thus, location specific knowledge is used to assign application objects to clients or servers. An object can be location specific due to

- User requirements for some operations and data to be performed at certain sites.
- Security and management restrictions which require some components to be restricted to certain sites such as the corporate office.
- Similarity and natural affinity of certain processes to certain sites (e.g., most manufacturing operations are performed at the plant floor).
- Architecture matching the functionality (e.g., workstations for user interfaces and minicomputers for database servers).
- Financial considerations (e.g., an animation must be performed on the machines which have software

licenses for the animation packages).

Impact of purchased software: A readily available business software package may automatically cluster many objects together and also may determine whether these objects will behave as clients or servers. Thus, a buy versus build decision can make the client or the sever fat. While it is a good idea to buy than to build, you should not buy 20 client application software packages which require 20 different servers and 20 different middleware packages to access the same.

Corporate data: It is better to acquire one server which can support multiple clients from multiple suppliers (this requires open APIs and/or may require some software development).

Clustering: Objects can be grouped together to form "clusters". A cluster is essentially a collection of objects which cannot be subdivided among computers. For example, a purchased product can be considered as a cluster because most purchased products cannot be subdivided into independent modules.

1.7 Putting the Pieces Together

Systems consist of several building blocks (network, computing platforms, middleware, applications). These building blocks interact with each other to support the end users. Figure 1-9 shows a conceptual view of the main IT building blocks: Client and server processes (applications), middleware services, network services, local system software services (e.g., database managers and transaction managers), operating systems, and computing hardware. As shown in this figure, standalone applications only use computing hardware, operating systems, and local system software services because everything resides on one machine. Distributed applications on the other hand use computing hardware + operating systems + local services + middleware + networks because its components can be split and run on multiple computers (the user, business logic, and data components can be spread around 2 or 200 computers). In addition, all building blocks go through a life cycle. Different types of technologies are used in a life cycle (for building, for deploying, etc). Moreover, all layers must be managed and supported. Thus, security, performance, fault tolerance, monitoring, etc are needed for networks, computing platforms, middleware, and applications.

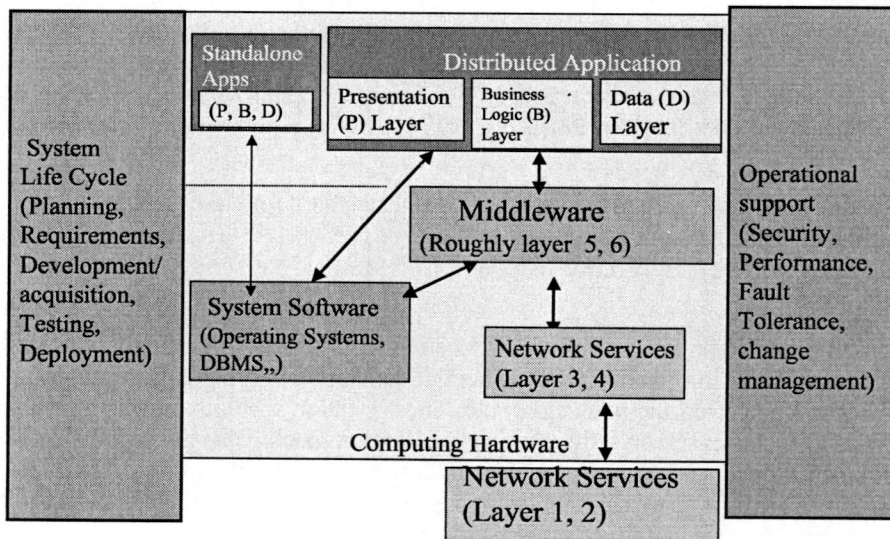

Figure 1-9: Conceptual View of Main IT Building Blocks

Figure 1-10 shows an example of a two machine (two desktops running Microsoft Windows over an Ethernet LAN) system architecture. Let us work through it to illustrate the interactions between the key building blocks. Let us assume that a user on computer 1 (client) needs to find the best customers from the Oracle database on computer 2. To access the Oracle database remotely, an Oracle database server will need to exist at machine 2 and Oracle client software (e.g., Oracle Forms for SQL queries) will need to be installed on computer 1. To enable network communications, Ethernet adapter cards and TCP/IP software will need to be installed on the two machines (recall that IP runs on top of Ethernet). Also, the client and server middleware will have to run on top of TCP (Oracle software does that quite well).

The client process (Oracle Forms) will accept the SQL statement from the user and submit it to the client middleware. The client middleware will accept this SQL statement, establish a connection with the remote database server process, package this SQL statement into a particular format (the Oracle SQL format), and submit this request to the TCP/IP network services. The network services will send the SQL statement as a message over the Ethernet network to the TCP/IP network services on the remote machine. On the remote (computer 2) machine, the SQL statement will be received by the TCP/IP network services and passed on to the SQL server middleware. The server middleware must be able to understand the format in which the SQL statement was sent by the client middleware (i.e., if a non-Oracle SQL server is on the server machine, then a database gateway will be needed). This exchange protocol between the client/server middleware plays a key role in C/S interoperability (in many cases this exchange protocol is proprietary and thus requires clients from vendor X to interoperate with servers from vendor X only). The SQL server middleware will schedule this request for execution by sending it to the customer database manager. After the SQL statement has been processed, the results are passed back by the server middleware to the client middleware in a mutually understandable exchange protocol.

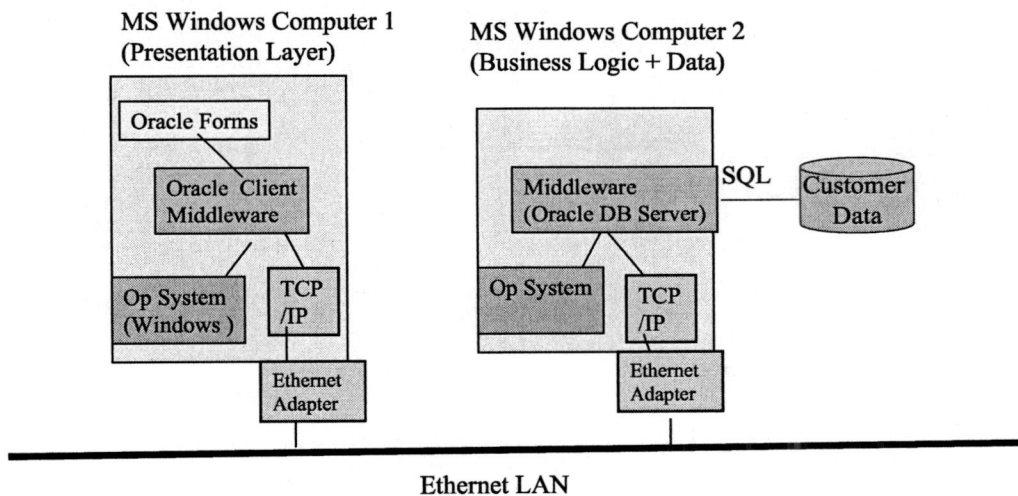

Figure 1-10: System Architecture- Two Machine System View

Figure 1-11 extends the two machine view to a large scale network with a mixture of computing platforms (Windows, Unix, IBM MVS mainframe), physical networks (Ethernet, ATM, FDDI) and network architectures (TCP/IP and IBM SNA)[1]. In this environment, the application is an e-purchasing system that has a master product catalog in DB2 (an IBM database manager) at the mainframe (a business partner machine) and a local Oracle catalog at the Unix minicomputer (a Sun Solaris at the corporate site). The purchasing logic is at the regional office and the client resides at the local site. This is an example of an n-tiered system.

---

[1] TCP/IP is the foundation network technology for the Internet and IBM SNA (System Network Architecture) is an IBM proprietary network technology. See the Network Module for more details on networks.

Let us assume that the user wants to purchase a PC. The user starts with an HTML page that accesses the purchasing system. The client middleware at computer 1 (the browser) will make an HTTP connection to the Web server on machine 2 through the TCP/IP network that runs over Ethernet and ATM networks. The Web server on computer 2 invokes the purchasing system for credit verification by using CGI (Common Gateway Interface) - a protocol for invoking programs from Web servers. The purchasing system first needs to look at the local catalog, so it issues an SQL call in ODBC (Open Database Connectivity) format. The ODBC driver at computer 2 sends this SQL statement to computer 3 through the TCP/IP network over FDDI. This SQL call is handled by the Oracle database server at computer 3 to retrieve the local catalog. The answer is sent back to the purchasing system. Let us now assume that the needed product is in the IBM DB2 catalog. Then, the purchasing system at computer 2 will issue the SQL call to the mainframe. This call will be routed to the mainframe through the Internet gateway (it will have a firewall) that connects to the public Internet. The SNA gateway will convert TCP/IP traffic to SNA and will send it to the IBM DB2 server.

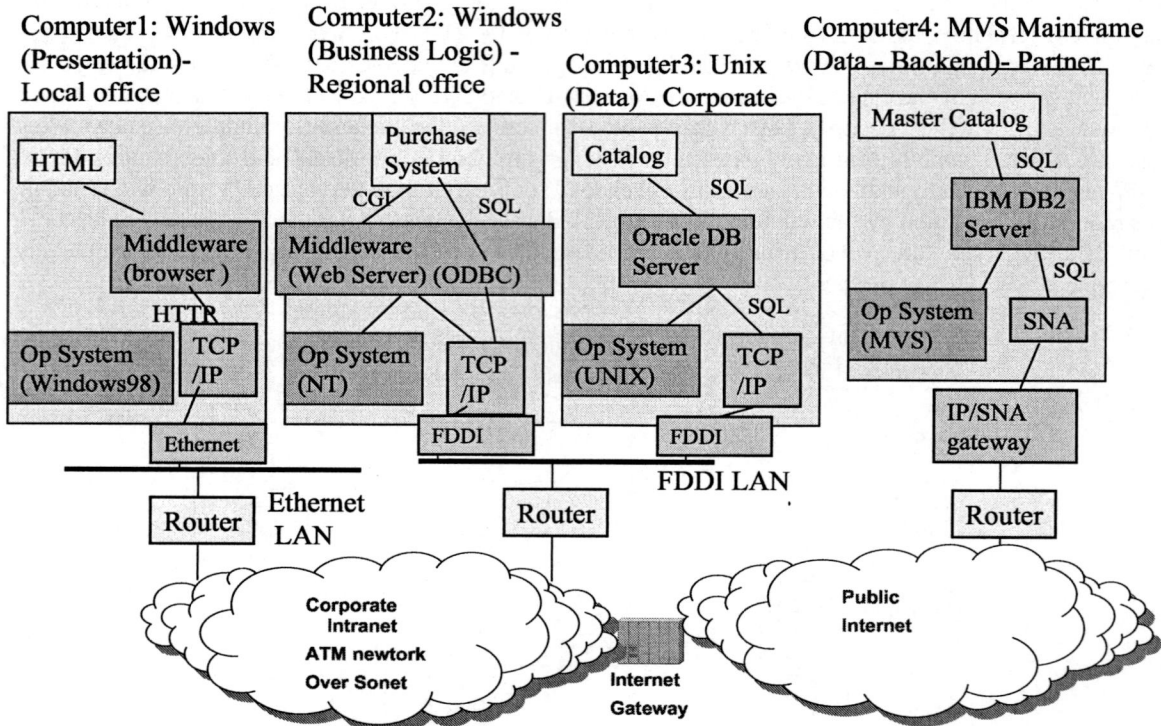

Figure 1-11: A Large Scale Distributed Environment

1.8 XYZCorp Case Study: Partial Solution 1

1.8.1 High Level XYZCorp Application Interconnectivity Architecture

Figure 1-12 shows a general multi-tier interconnectivity architecture that will allow XYZCorp customers, employees, and business partners to access applications and databases at local, regional and corporate levels. This architecture will work across the corporate network with a mixture of computing platforms (Windows, Unix, IBM MVS mainframe), physical networks (Ethernet, ATM, FDDI) and network architectures (TCP/IP and IBM SNA)[2]. In this environment, the regional applications and databases are accessed first (middle tier) and then the master (corporate) applications and databases are accessed at the mainframe. We have explained the various components of this architecture previously.

1.8.2 Business Reporting System

As stated in the problem statement, the current financial information (personnel costs, materials costs, etc) is stored on the IBM mainframe database. The reports are printed on the mainframe printer and are then mailed through office mail to the managers. An analysis of the situation revealed the following problems with this approach:

- The reports are usually too late for the managers to react (the reports for March arrive in April, for example).
- All reports are in a standardized format. Many managers do not like this format.
- The managers cannot get more details about their budgets easily.

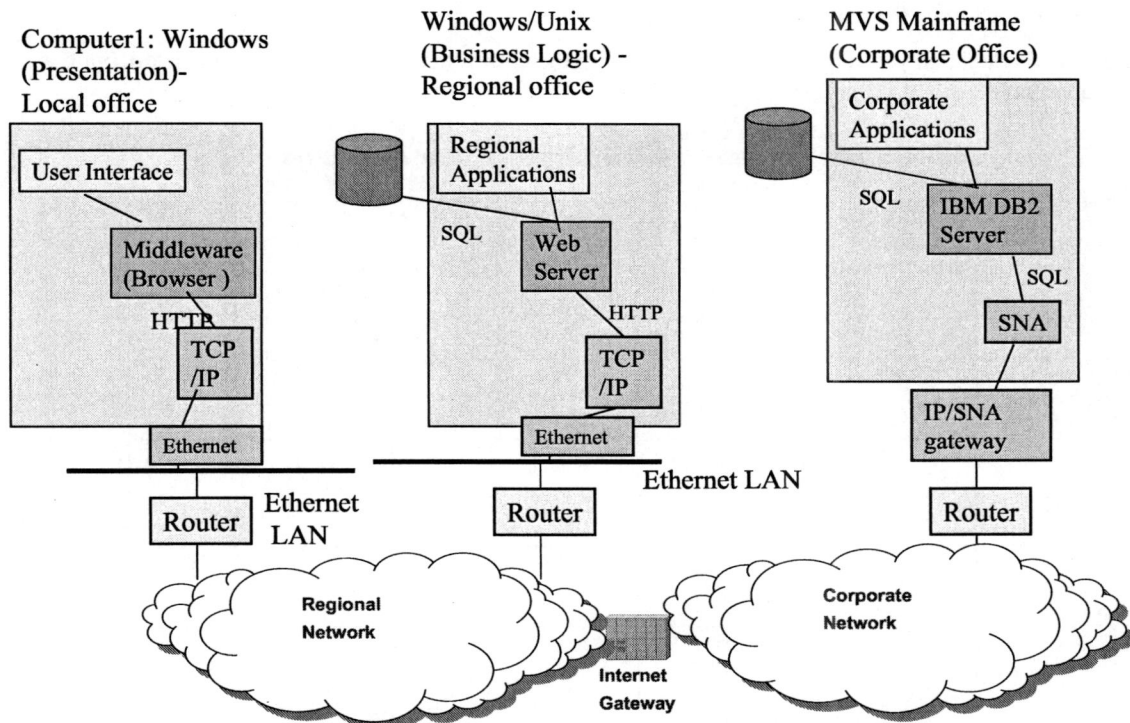

Figure 1-12: XYZCorp Multi-Tier Interconnectivity Architecture

Due to these reasons, the company's budgets are not managed as well as they could be. Many managers maintain their own staff who take the data from the printed reports, type the data into a spreadsheet and produce their own reports. This is simply not acceptable in the current environment for cutting down cycle times and quick response to changing business conditions resulting in the following major requirements:

- Quick Access to Information: Financial information should be available to authorized users to print customized reports, perform spreadsheet analysis and exercise decision support software for greater insight.

---

[2] TCP/IP is the foundation network technology for the Internet and IBM SNA (System Network Architecture) is an IBM proprietary network technology. See the Network Module for more details on networks.

- Facilitate New Applications: New applications and new approaches to existing applications should be easily facilitated.
- Local Application Support: Different local processing (especially at overseas offices) must be provided.
- Cost of Implementation: This cost must be kept to a minimum.
- Security: Financial information must be very secure.

A debate has erupted in the corporation about how to best deal with these requirements. The approaches being discussed are:

- Put printers in the regional offices for the reports (do not re-architect the system).
- Send the financial information through email.
- Keep the database on mainframe and put clients in regions by using some middleware products.
- Move the database to regional servers and then implement C/S architectures.

There has been a great deal of debate about this. Which option should be chosen and why? Let us use an evaluation table that shows these options, along with keeping the current option, against the requirements stated above. We can add additional factors such as management control. Table 1-2 shows the evaluation. According to this analysis, keeping the database at mainframe and using client software to access the database appears to be the best choice.

It should be noted that you may or may not agree with the entries in the table and the conclusion, but this is a good approach to analyze the various options.

Table 1-2: Trade-offs Between Single/Two Tiered Architectures

	Keep current situation	Put Printers in Regional Offices	Use Email to Send Reports	Database at Mainframe, access through Clients	Distributed Data – Move Data to Regional Sites
Quick Access to Information	-3	+2	+1	+3	+3
Facilitate New Applications	-3	-3	+2	+2	+3
Local Application Support.	-3	-3	+2	+2	+3
cost of implementation	+3 (already done)	+1 (minor cost)	-1	-1	-3
Security	+3 (very secure)	+3 (still secure)	+2	+2	-3
Management Control	+3	+3	+3	+3	-1

Legend: Evaluation factors (-3 to +3) indicate how well the configurations satisfy the requirements

Time to Take a Break
✓ • Middleware Overview and Principles
  • Basic Middleware (RPC, RDA, MOM)
  • Comparison and Analysis

Suggested Review Questions Before Proceeding

- What is middleware and what role does it play in application connectivity? Give examples.
- What is the client/server model and how it is implemented as two and three tiered architectures?
- Table 1-1 shows the tradeoffs between various configurations. Expand this table to include other factors used in system design.
- In the 2 tiered configurations (Figure 1-8), where do the following middleware technologies fit: RPC, RDA, MOM, pub/sub (discussed later in this chapter).
- You have been asked to give a one hour talk to managers about middleware. What will you include in this talk, what will you exclude from this talk, and what type of middleware services will you use as examples. .

1.9   Basic Middleware – A Closer Look

Figure 1-13 shows a conceptual view of basic middleware and depicts how a client interacts with a server through the C/S middleware. The C/S middleware is based on a few basic interaction paradigms:
- Remote procedure call (RPC) that accesses a remote program (e.g., a purchasing system at a merchant site).
- Remote data access (RDA), also known as remote SQL, to access remote databases (e.g., an Oracle database at a remote site). ODBC is an example of RDA.
- Message oriented middleware (MOM) that accesses remote systems through queues (also known as queued message processing -QMP).
- Publish/subscribe model that uses channels, very much like TV channels, to push information to subscribers.

These interaction paradigms and supporting middleware technologies are discussed in detail in the next several sections.

RPC

Client → RPC Server → Data base

Application Program   Application Program

RDA

Client —SQL→ SQL Server → Data base

Application Program

QMP/MOM

Client / MOM   Data base / MOM
        Logical Queue

Publish/Subscribe

Push

Publisher —Push→ Channel —Pull→ Subscriber

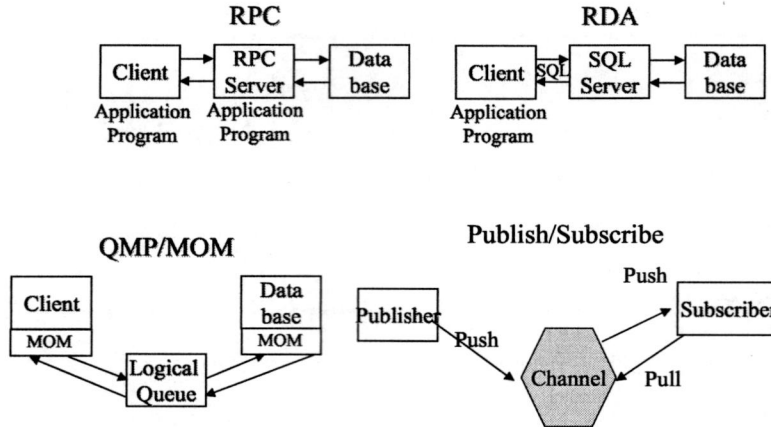

Figure 1-13: Basic Remote Interactions

In all these interactions, the client side of the middleware is typically light-weight (it usually just routes the requests to the servers), but the server side of the middleware is quite sophisticated because it needs to schedule and manage numerous client requests. For example, several clients could request access to the applications, databases, printers and files located at the same server. The C/S middleware relies on network services to transport the messages between sites. The network services may include, if needed, network gateways to convert network protocols (e.g., TCP/IP to SNA).

Network Operating Systems (NOSs) have traditionally provided some of the basic C/S middleware services. An NOS is essentially an operating system that provides the capabilities for transparent access to resources such as printers and files across a network. Historically, NOSs have originated from LANs and have concentrated on directing the user's request to appropriate print and file servers. Novell Netware is one of the oldest NOSs. Other examples are Windows Servers[3], Banyan Vines, and IBM's LAN Manager. However, with time, NOSs have started providing other services needed for distributed C/S applications such as the following:

- Remote communications to access remotely located programs and databases (e.g., RDA and RPC)
- Directory services
- Security
- Time services
- Failure handling
- Task scheduling

Most of the currently available NOSs provide these services within a single LAN - Novell Netware, Windows Servers, Banyan Vines and IBM's LAN Manager. For enterprise-wide C/S computing, available NOSs are glued together through "gateways" that convert protocols from one NOS to another. For mission critical enterprise-wide C/S applications, enterprise-wide directory, security and failure handling capabilities are crucial. In addition, facilities for accessing remotely located programs and databases are essential. Many C/S middleware products provide some of these services on top of the available NOSs. For example, database servers from many vendors are available on Netware and Windows NT. We will first discuss the generic concepts of the basic C/S services needed for enterprise-wide C/S applications and then show how an NOS provides some of these facilities.

---

[3] Windows Servers is used as a generic term here to represent the family of Microsft Windows Servers such as Windows NT Server, Windows 2000 Server, Windows XP Server.

1.10 Connecting to Remote Programs - Remote Procedure Call (RPC)

1.10.1 Overview

Remote Procedure Call (RPC) and its variants are used regularly in accessing remotely located application programs. In ecommerce, for example, customers access purchasing systems at merchant sites by using an RPC type middleware. Examples of RPC-based products are:

- HTTP (Hypertext Transfer Protocol) – the foundation of World wide Web – is a simplified RPC.
- CORBA (Common Object Request Broker Architecture) as well as Microsoft's DCOM uses RPC at its core.
- SUN RPC, Netwise RPC, Novell Netware RPC, and TCP/IP RPC use RPC.

RPC standards are needed because each RPC middleware introduces its own API and exchange protocols. Thus applications based on SUN RPC and Netwise RPC do not interoperate. Another issue in RPC interoperability is the underlying network on which RPC is implemented. Theoretically, RPCs can be built on top of any network protocols and services such as IBM's LU6.2 and TCP/IP Sockets. In practice, most of the available RPCs are built on top of TCP/IP Sockets.

1.10.2 The RPC Paradigm

In this paradigm, the client process invokes a remotely located procedure (a server process), the remote procedure executes, and sends the response back to the client. The remote procedure can be simple (e.g., retrieve time of day) or complex (e.g., retrieve all customers from Detroit who have a good credit rating). Each request/response of an RPC is treated as a separate unit of work, thus each request must carry enough information needed by the server process.

A remote procedure call (RPC) facility allows a language level (local) procedure call by the client to be turned into a language level call at the server. In a remote procedure call, a local process invokes a remote process. RPCs have the main advantage that a programmer issues a call to a remote process in a manner that is very similar to the local calls. The RPC software attempts to hide all the network related details from the client-server developers. The client calls are referred to as requests and the server results being returned are referred to as responses. Figure 1-14 shows a conceptual view of a RPC. Note that the RPC procedure can be called by more than one client (i.e., once you have developed an RPC server, it can be invoked by multiple clients residing on multiple machines). In addition, the database access is optional because the RPC server may or may not need to access a database. For example, the RPC server may produce a graph from given inputs or compute averages without accessing a database).

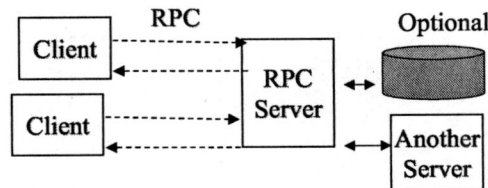

Figure 1-14: Remote Procedure Call (RPC)

RPC is a type-checking mechanism in a manner similar to the local procedure call mechanism. RPC calls may be implemented in a compiler by using the same syntax as the local procedure calls. In many RPC facilities, the synchronization of the client and server are constrained because the client is blocked until the server has responded. In addition, binding between servers and clients is usually one-to-one to reflect the language procedure call primitives (see the discussion on binding later).

Figure 1-15 shows the steps that take place in a remote procedure call. The client and server routines are in two separate processes, usually on two different machines. RPC software creates a dummy procedure with the same name as the server and places it in the client process. This dummy procedure, called a stub, takes the calling parameters and packages them into suitable network transmission messages. Another stub is generated for the server side to perform the reverse processing. Client and server stubs are instances of the client and server middleware we have discussed earlier (RPC introduces new terms, not new concepts). The following steps shown in Figure 1-15 are executed in order:

1). The client issues a call to a local procedure, called a client stub. The client stub appears to the caller as if it is a local procedure. This stub mainly translates the remote procedure call into appropriate network messages in the proper Network Interface Services format (usually TCP/IP Sockets). The stub also determines the actual network address of the server and "binds" to it (sometimes this is done by the runtime libraries).

2). The network messages are prepared and sent to the remote site through network transport services.

3). The messages are sent over the communication media and are received by the network transport services of the server machine. If the network architecture of the client machine is different from the network architecture of the server machine, then a network gateway may be needed (e.g., TCP/IP to SNA gateway).

4). The server network system contacts the server stub that a request has arrived for it.

5). The server stub gets the network message, translates it into a local procedure call format, and executes this call to the server process.

6). The server executes the call and develops a response that is sent to the server stub.

7). The server stub translates the response into one or more network messages which are sent to the network system. The stub may cache many messages before an appropriate response to the client can be developed.

8). The server network system sends the response back to the client network system. Once again, a gateway may be needed if the client and server network architectures are dissimilar.

9). The client network system sends the response messages to the client stub.

10). The client stub receives the response message, translates this message into call responses, and sends the response back to the client. The stub may cache many messages before an appropriate response to the client can be developed.

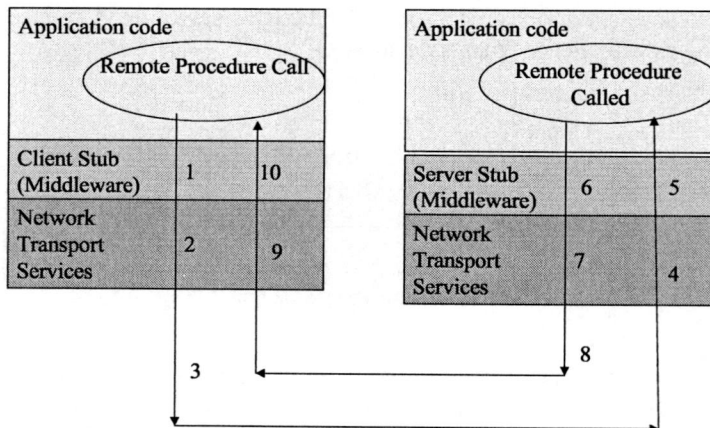

Figure 1-15: Remote Procedure Call (RPC) Flow

1.10.3 RPC Analysis

It can be seen that many decisions are made in various steps of the remote procedure call. Examples of some of these decisions are stub generation, parameter passing, binding, server management, error handling, transport protocols, data representation, performance and security. These issues are briefly discussed next. For a detailed discussion of these issues, the reader is referred to the book on distributed systems by Coulouris et al [Coulouris 2000]. The book, "The Art of Distributed Applications: Programming Techniques for Remote Procedure Calls", by J. R. Corbin [Corbin 1991] gives many technical details.

Stub Generation. Stubs can be generated automatically or by a programmer. For a programmer-generated stub, the RPC system provides a set of functions which can be used to construct a stub. This mechanism has been used by the SUN Microsystem RPC. For automated stub generation, an interface definition language is provided which is compiled by a stub generator to construct client and server stubs.

Parameter Passing. The passing of parameters between remote procedures creates special problems. For example, if the client passes parameters by value, then these values can be copied by the client stub into the network transmission messages. But if a parameter is passed by address, then it is difficult to pass because memory address on one system does not mean much on another system. For this reason, parameter by address in remote procedure calls is not always allowed. Programming details about passing parameters can be found in [Shirley 1993].

Binding. Binding refers to establishing a contact between a client and a server. When a call to a server is received by the client stub, it tries to bind the client with an appropriate server on a remote site. Binding requires two major decisions:
- How to find an appropriate host for a service
- How to find the appropriate server on the chosen host

This is a typical problem in networks. Where should the directory of hosts and servers be located? Some RPC systems use centralized directories to which the servers register when they are started. In other systems, each client system knows the address of the servers. For example, Open Software Foundation's Distributed Computing Environment (OSF DCE) solved this problem by using a distributed directory.

Server Management. In some implementations of RPCs, several instances of a server are installed on the same or different machines for performance or availability reasons. In some implementations of RPC there is a server manager that can create servers on demand and route requests to a duplicate server if one server fails. This is more typical of transaction processing systems.

Data Representation. The data format of the client and server may be different especially when the client and server reside on different computing systems. Data translation may be done at the client or the server site. A common approach used in many RPCs is an intermediate data format which is used by all clients and server stubs in an RPC system. This approach is used in the OSI RPC and the SUN RPC.

Type Consistency. It is important that the number and type of parameters sent by the client are consistent with the server parameters. This happens especially if the clients and servers are implemented in different programming languages supporting different data types. This issue is important in server design because a server must be able to handle corrupt requests.

Call Execution and Call Semantics. In a distributed system, the client and server can fail independently and then be re-started. In such situations, it is not clear how many times a call to a server has been executed. For example, if a server or the transport network failed before the server had a chance to execute the request, then the call was not processed. However, if the server crashed after completing the request, then the request has been executed once. Some procedures do not harm anything if they are executed several times (e.g., time of day, reading a specific record from a file). The call semantics determine how often the remote service might be performed under fault conditions. The following semantics are possible.
- Exactly once means that the server procedure was executed once. This semantic requires extensive checking and is suitable for very reliable distributed systems.

- At most once means that the server procedure is performed once or not at all. The client as well as the server uses a sequenced protocol where a sequence number is attached to each request. This semantic is checked by the server process to make sure that the server process does not execute more than once.
- At least once means that the server process can be executed several times. This semantic allows the client to send the same request for a few times if the server does not respond. This semantic is suitable for read-only servers.

Transport Protocols. Most RPC systems have been built on top of TCP/IP Protocol Suite. Either TCP or UDP is used to transmit the messages across the network. If an RPC system allows UDP as well as TCP protocol, then a parameter may be used in the RPC call for a choice. At present, other than TCP/IP, very few transport protocols are supported by the existing RPC systems. An example of non-TCP/IP RPC protocol is IBM's "AnyNet" feature that supports RPCs over SNA networks, however, the practical use of RPCs over SNA is very sparse.

Error Handling. Many error and exceptional situations can arise in remotely located client-server systems. For example, a server may crash or may go into a loop. In this case, the client may need to recover from the error by using time-outs or may need to stop the server. Similarly, a client may crash before getting response from the server. In this case, the server may hang around and may need to be stopped somehow. In addition, the transport network may fail while the requests and/or responses are being transmitted. Error handling becomes especially difficult when the server communicates with other servers to provide a service (e.g., a server responsible for managing distributed data may need to communicate with other sites where the copies of data exist). A variety of techniques, such as two-phase commit, are used in such cases.

Performance and Security. Implementation of RPCs introduce many performance and security concerns. For example, the network delays need to be taken into account when designing distributed applications. It has been reported that remote procedure calls incur two to three times more overhead than the local calls [Wilbur 1987]. Some performance studies have highlighted the performance impact of number of parameters and the parameter sizes [Birrell 1984]. This is especially serious when parameter data needs to be converted. A common technique in performance improvement is to use an object-oriented approach where the server is called to perform operations instead of sending data structures back and forth. In addition, the impact of starting up a new server process for every client request (perhaps through UNIX forking) needs to be examined. It might be better to keep one reentrant server that is called repetitively every time a client needs the service. It is also important to verify the security of the client before sending the response to it. Multithreaded server environments help this. The Open Software Foundation supports a secure RPC to address the security issues.

1.10.4 Strengths and Weaknesses of RPC

RPCs are well understood, are widely supported and can provide an easy transition from centralized to distributed programs. For example, a centralized program which consists of many procedures to perform specialized tasks can be distributed by simply replacing the procedure calls with the RPC calls to remotely located programs. However, RPC is not a panacea. In many cases, RPCs are awkward especially because the parameter passing can be only through values and not by references.

The currently available RPCs do not support asynchronous queries (most RPCs block the client calls). Another limitation of RPCs is that they are not well suited for ad hoc query processing. For example, an ad hoc SQL query can return many rows with many columns. It is very difficult to set RPC parameters between senders and receivers in this situation. For this reason, a separate data access standard, called Remote Data Access (RDA), is used heavily by the DBMS community (see next section). In a generalized client-server environment, RPC as well as RDA is needed.

In this section, we have primarily discussed the generic RPC paradigm. Many extensions to RPCs have been suggested (see [Couloris 2000]). Of particular interest to us is the extension of RPCs to handle transaction processing. These "transactional" RPCs become a unit of consistency (i.e., the transactional RPC is either committed in total or rolled back). We will review transactional RPCs in a later chapter.

1.11 Accessing Remote Databases Directly - Remote Data Access (RDA)

1.11.1 Overview

Remote data access (RDA), also known as remote SQL, is commonly used to access remote databases (e.g., an Oracle database at a remote site). RDA products are currently heavily supported by the "database server industry". Simply stated, a database server houses a database and controls user access to the database. As stated previously, a large number of vendors are developing SQL database servers that basically handle SQL calls from clients and respond with results.

Many RDA middleware products in the market use proprietary APIs and exchange protocols. Thus a database server from vendor A can only be used by client tools from vendor A or from vendors who are "business partners" of vendor A. Standardizing bodies such as X/Open and ISO have been trying to define standards in this area. However, the best known example is the Microsoft's ODBC (Open Database Connect). ODBC is an API standard based on X/Open and SAG (SQL Access Group) Command Level Interface API. Users of ODBC issue the same API calls to access databases from different vendors. ODBC relies on "drivers" which convert ODBC calls to appropriate database calls. At present, a large number of ODBC drivers for accessing Microsoft, Informix, Oracle, Sybase, and other databases are commercially available. JDBC (Java Database Connectivity) is similar to ODBC but it provides Java support (ODBC provides C support). IBM's DRDA (Distributed Relational Database Architecture) is another de facto standard worth mentioning. DRDA was introduced by IBM to provide an "open" exchange protocol for other DBMS clients to access DB2 data. At present, more than 30 DBMS vendors provide DRDA gateways that translate different vendor DBMS calls to DRDA format for DB2 access. We will discuss DRDA and ODBC/JDBC in a later chapter.

1.11.2 RDA Paradigm

This paradigm allows client programs and/or end-user tools to issue ad hoc queries, usually SQL, against remotely located databases. The key technical difference between RDA and RPC is that in an RDA the size of the result is not known. For example, consider the following SQL statement that is sent to a remotely located database server:

SELECT * FROM CUSTOMER;

The result of this query could be one row or thousands of rows, depending on the number of customers in the customer table. In addition, we do not know how many columns will be returned in each row. In contrast, each parameter for the RPC must be clearly specified. Due to this difference, RDA paradigm supports a dialog between clients and servers so that a client can retrieve one row at a time (through SQL FETCH verb), and process it. Thus each C/S interaction is not a self-contained and independent unit of work. Instead, just like human conversations, the interactions depend on the context of the conversation (this implies that some context related information is kept and used during the conversation). Conversational processing requires both parties to be alive during the conversation. In addition, the exchanges are usually synchronous.

Figure 1-16 shows the steps that take place in a remote data access. The client and server routines are in two separate processes, usually on two different machines. RDA software basically gives an impression to the RDA client that SQL calls are being issued to a local database. The following steps are executed in order:

1). The client issues an SQL call in an API made available by the client middleware (we will discuss the two API formats later). The client API calls can be issued from end user tools or application programs. The client middleware mainly encodes the SQL call into appropriate network messages. As we will see later, the client middleware may support "database procedure" calls in addition to remote SQL calls. The middleware also determines the actual network address of the server and "binds" to it.

2). The network message, containing the SQL statement, is prepared and sent to the remote site through network transport services.

3). The message is sent over the communication media and is received by the network transport services of the server machine. If the network architecture of the client machine is different from the network architecture of the server machine, then a network gateway may be needed (e.g., TCP/IP to SNA gateway).

4). The server network system contacts the server middleware that a request has arrived for it.

5). The server middleware gets the network message and schedules the execution of this call by the database server. As we will discuss later, the middleware may invoke a database procedure consisting of several SQL calls, instead of one SQL call.

6). The database server processes the SQL call and develops a response (selected table rows and columns) which is sent to the server middleware.

7). The server middleware translates the response into one or more network messages which are sent to the network system. The middleware may cache many messages before an appropriate response to the client can be developed. For example, the server middleware may not send the entire selected table back to client as a single response; instead it may send large tables as several blocks (e.g., 4 megabytes) of data.

8). The server network system sends the response back to the client network system. Once again, a gateway may be needed if the client and server network architectures are dissimilar.

9). The client network system sends the response messages to the client middleware.

10). The client middleware receives the response message, translates this message into call responses, and sends the response back to the client. The middleware may supply the response to the client one row at a time based on "FETCH" statements issued by the client process.

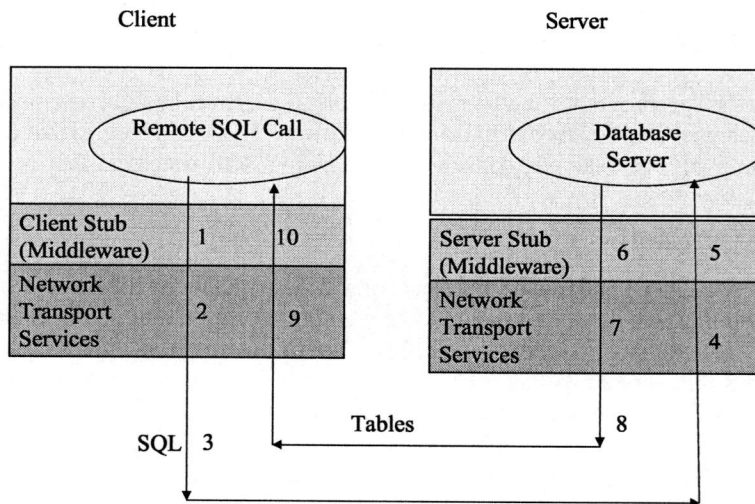

Figure 1-16: Remote Data Access Flow

1.11.3 RDA Analysis

Many decisions are made in various steps of the remote data access paradigm. Examples of some of these decisions are discussed here.

Call Level Versus Embedded API. Call level interface (CLI) and embedded SQL are the two generally accepted application programming interfaces (APIs) for RDA. In CLI, an SQL statement is passed as a character string parameter to the SQL server. For example, the client process may issue the following call to run an SQL statement:

CALL SQLRUN ("SELECT * FROM CUSTOMERS", RESULTS, RC)

After this call, the client process may issue additional calls to fetch rows. A CLI may provide additional calls for connecting to a particular server, breaking the connection, etc. Open Database Connect (ODBC) is an example of a CLI. The embedded SQL API allows client processes to include SQL statements in program code. The embedded SQL statements are distinguished from the other program code through special indicators (e.g., a $ in first column). For example, an embedded SQL query may appear as

$ SELECT * FROM CUSTOMERS

Typically, vendors provide a preprocessor that converts the embedded SQL statements to calls that are sent across the network.

Static Versus Dynamic SQL. Static SQL statements are known and explicitly coded into a program before it is compiled. In contrast, dynamic SQL statements are generated at run time, typically through desktop tools.

Static SQL statements can be optimized and prepared for execution at the time the program is compiled and linked. An "execution plan" can be generated at compile time to efficiently run the SQL statements when invoked. Static SQL, although efficient for local database calls, is not generally suitable for RDA because the data in a network can move around several times between the time the program is compiled and the time it is run. Due to this reason, most RDA middleware products only support dynamic SQL or support dynamic preparation (plan generation) at run time.

Stored (Database) Procedures. Most RDBMS vendors at present support database procedures which contain a collection of SQL statements that can be invoked through a single call (see Figure 1-17). Database procedures, also known as stored procedures, are typically implemented by extending SQL to include programming constructs (e.g., branching and looping). These procedures are compiled and stored for later invocation by authorized programs. For example, a database update that requires modification of several tables can be implemented as a stored procedure and invoked by authorized application programs. The mechanism for invoking these procedures is usually a special call. Stored procedures offer several potential benefits:

- They can enforce data integrity and extra security by requiring updates to be performed only through stored procedures. As a matter of fact, there is currently a debate in the C/S community whether distributed transaction managers can be replaced with stored procedures (see [Schlak 1995]).
- They can improve performance by issuing one message that can generate multiple SQL statements at the SQL server. (see Figure 1-17).
- They can introduce a degree of "object orientation" to a relational database by providing a set of "methods" that can be invoked through messages without having to know the internal table structure.

Many RDA middleware products provide support for remote SQL as well as database procedures. Database procedures allow applications to intermix SQL calls and database procedure calls (e.g., an application can issue an SQL call, invoke a database procedure, and again issue a series of SQL calls). Although database procedures somewhat resemble the RPCs, the primary difference between the two paradigms is that a database procedure returns a table which can be navigated by the application through subsequent fetches; RPCs typically return a fixed number of parameters with virtually no capability for navigating through variable length objects.

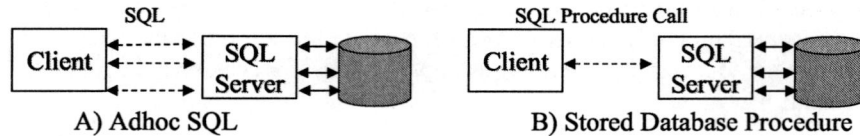

Figure 1-17: Remote Data Access with Ad hoc SQL and Stored Database Procedures

Distributed Query Processing and Distributed Transaction Management. Some applications may need to access data on multiple database servers concurrently. There are two basic approaches to support this:

- Allow programs to explicitly connect with each database server and then issue a remote SQL or database procedure against the database. In this case, a single SQL statement operates on a single database server.
- Employ a distributed query processor that presents a virtual database consisting of data at multiple sites. The distributed query processor receives an SQL statement from client programs against this virtual database and sends requests to multiple servers to access remotely located data. Typically, distributed query processors allow joins between remotely located tables.

A distributed transaction manager is needed if the data at multiple sites needs to be updated by the client programs. The distinction is that query processing is read only, whereas transaction processing supports data writes/updates that require additional capabilities. We will discuss the issues of distributed query processing and distributed transaction management in later chapters.

1.11.4 Strengths and Weaknesses of RDA

RDAs are widely supported by DBMS vendors and an almost unlimited number of RDA-based desktop tools are commercially available. The main strength of RDA (especially remote SQL) is that no server software needs to be developed (the database server is the procedure invoked by remote SQL). In addition, the large number of RDA-based desktop tools facilitate "plug and play" C/S capabilities. In contrast, users of RPC must code a client as well as a server process. However, RDA needs to be carefully evaluated. In many cases, remote SQL can generate a great deal of traffic on the network due to large tables being shipped across the network. At a minimum, this can cause "minor discomfort" to the user community at large. In general, remote SQL is a good paradigm for ad hoc queries while RPCs (and database procedures) work well for database updates.

1.12 Loose Coupling Between Applications – Message Oriented Middleware (MOM)

1.12.1 Overview

In loosely coupled applications, the components in an application send messages through a message service instead of communicating directly with each other. The message service, in turn, delivers messages to the specified recipients. Message oriented middleware (MOM) supports this paradigm. Two different types of MOM have emerged:

- **Message queuing**. In message queuing, program-to-program communications occur via a queue, which is typically a file. It allows programs to send and receive information without having a direct connection established between them.
- **Message passing (Publish-Subscribe)**. This approach differs from message queuing in that rather than oblige applications to retrieve the information they request, the information is pushed to the interested

parties. A popular flavor of message passing is known as publish-subscribe. We will describe publish-subscribe in Section 1.13.

The message service is much like the postal service: we could deliver our own mail, but letting someone else do it greatly simplifies our lives. It is especially suitable for mobile applications (one mobile application can send a series of messages to another application that can respond whenever suitable).

MOM mainly provides asynchronous communication. An application creates a message, labels it with destination information, and hands the message over to the MOM. The application is then relieved from the work of delivering the message to its destination. The common building blocks of the MOM model are:

- Producer: an application producing messages
- Consumer: an application receiving messages
- Client: an application using a messaging service is called a client, irrespective of whether it is a producer or a consumer. In fact, a client can fulfill both roles at the same time, or change its role over time.
- Message: a self-contained unit of information. This can be an XML expression, a WML deck, a text string, an intelligent agent, a user-defined Java object — pretty much anything, as long as both the sender and the recipient can understand it.
- Destination: an abstract entity denoting the destination of a message. In this paper we consider message queues and publish-subscribe topics as the two different kinds of destination.

QMP is supported by MOM (message oriented middleware). MOM products are getting serious vendor attention. Interest in MOM is fueled by the dramatic increase of mobile devices and the application requirements that require asynchronous behavior. The most popular MOM package is the MQSeries from IBM that include a variety of services ranging from database replication to downsizing of mainframe applications. Other products include message-oriented middleware used in Tuxedo and Encina and Pipes Platform from Peer Logics. See the sidebar "MOM Products and Information Services" for more details.

Standards for MOM are needed for APIs to store and retrieve information from the queues. Generally accepted standards for MOM are not available at the time of this writing. In reality, IBM MQseries is becoming the de facto standard. Two main consortia have been formed to promote message-oriented middleware products:

- The **Message-Oriented Middleware Association (MOMA)** both promotes MOM as a middleware solution as well as MOM products. MOMA describes itself as a "worldwide consortium of users, suppliers, consultants and analysts dedicated to enhancing the interoperability of distributed and client/server computing via message oriented middleware."
- **Business Quality Messaging (BQM)** has a more (up-front) commercial purpose. It focuses on promoting a specific subclass of MOM that uses message queuing. BQM's statements describe the advantages of its products, such as "BQM technologies provide messaging reliability for business-critical applications and allow messaging products to reliably extend further across networks and the Internet."

MOM Products and Information Sources

Several companies that are members of MOMA offer MOM products. The following provides the name of the corporation and its MOM product as well as a brief description of the product based primarily on the information provided in the MOMA literature.

IBM UK Laboratories Ltd.: Product: **MQSeries**

MQSeries provides: 1) a single, multiplatform API; 2) insulation from communications programming; 3) time-independent processing; and 4) robust middleware for high-performance distributed application integration. It can be used on over 20 IBM and non-IBM platforms.

Momentum Software Corporation: Product: **XIPC**

XIPC's features include scalability, message tracking, high-performance queuing, automatic data translation,

---

disk and memory queuing, and management tools.

<u>NCR Corporation:</u> Product:: **TOP END**

Features offered by TOP END include: 1) scalability; 2) 7x24x52 high availability; 3) legacy mainframe coexistence; 4) comprehensive security; 5) open systems compliance; 6) application, tool, database, and connectivity options; 7) comprehensive client workstation support; 8) heterogeneous server platform support; and 8) intranet, extranet and internet support.

<u>PeerLogic, Inc:</u> Product:: the **PIPES Platform**

PIPES maintains a logical, real-time view of every application running on a network. Software components can find each other instantly, regardless of physical location and communicate directly through reliable messaging. PIPES achieves this through a dynamic naming service.

<u>Talarian Corporation:</u> Product: **SmartSockets**

SmartSockets offers high-speed interprocess communication, scalability, reliability and fault tolerance. It supports a variety of communication paradigms including publish-subscribe, peer-to-peer and RPC.

<u>Veri-Q Inc.</u> (North American headquarters): Product:: **VCOM**

VCOM enables mission-critical application integration across internet, intranet and extranet boundaries providing reliable and secure process-to-process communication for distributed systems. Features include: 1) Single language independent API supports legacy languages and environments such as IBM's MVS CICS and IMS, OS/400 as well as new IDE's and runtime environments through its Java, OLE and ActiveX controls and classes; 2) Built-in single-seat remote management, monitoring, and problem determination facilities; and 3) Tightly (synchronous) or loosely (asynchronous) coupled process integration designs supported.

<u>CommerceQuest:</u> Product: **Expert/MQ**

Expert/MQ is an operational and configuration management tool that simplifies management of MQ series products. Expert/MQ incorporates a number of facilities such as version control, configuration analysis, operational analysis, configuration management, script generation, reporting, queue browsing, and other management functionality to facilitate the use of MQSeries in heterogeneous environments. Written in Java, it features a highly portable architecture.

1.12.2 MOM with Message Queuing Paradigm

In the queued message processing (QMP) paradigm, the client message is stored in a queue and the server works on it when free (Figure 1-18). The server stores ("puts') the response in another queue and the client actively retrieves ("gets") the responses from this queue. This model, used in many transaction processing systems, allows the clients to asynchronously send requests to the server. Once a request is queued, the request is processed even if the sender is disconnected (intentionally or due to a failure). In queued message processing, arriving messages are first queued and then scheduled for execution. After storing the message in the queue, the client can go back and continue its work. In particular, once execution of a request begins, the client does not interact with the execution process.

MOM (message-oriented middleware) supports the message queuing paradigm in a C/S environment. It provides APIs for getting and putting messages in and out of the queues and supports the queued messaging paradigm. MOM has recently gained industrial attention due to its appeal to "nomadic" computing (e.g., wireless-based detachable computers) that favor the type of asynchronous processing provided by MOM (the detachable computers are not always connected for RPC and RDA type message exchanges).

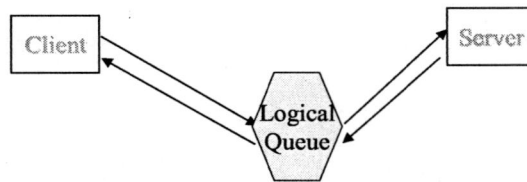

Figure 1-18: Conceptual Views of Queued Message Processing

Figure 1-19 shows the steps that take place in queued message processing. The client and server routines are in two separate processes, usually on two different machines. We are showing two logical queues for the purpose of discussion; Q1 is the input queue upon which the clients store their messages and Q2 is the output queue from which the clients receive their results. Designers and implementers of QMP can choose different number of queues for performance and availability purposes. For conceptual discussion, we will also assume that the queues are located "somewhere" on the network. In practice, the queues may exist at the server machine, at client machines, in a middle machine (e.g., a gateway), or a combination thereof. The following steps are executed in order:

1). The client issues a "Put message on Q1" call in an API made available by the client middleware. The client API calls can be issued from end-user tools or application programs. The client middleware mainly encodes the call into appropriate network messages.

2). The network message, containing the put message, is prepared and sent to the remote site through network transport services.

3). The message is sent over the communication media and is stored in the input queue (Q1). If the network architecture of the client machine is different from the network architecture of the server machine, then a network gateway may be needed (e.g., TCP/IP to SNA gateway). Q1 may be allocated to this gateway.

4). The message is stored in Q1. The server middleware is notified that a request has arrived for it (in some cases, the server middleware scans the queue for any new messages).

5). The server middleware retrieves the message by issuing a "Get Q1" and schedules execution of this call by the database server.

6). The database server processes the message and develops a response message which is sent to the server middleware. The message is sent to the output queue (Q2) through a "put Q2" message.

7). The server middleware translates the response message into one or more network messages. For example, if a very large response is generated, the server middleware may not send the entire message to the output queue.

8). The server network sends the response back to the client network system and stores the message(s) in Q2. Once again, recall that we are assuming that the queues are located somewhere on the network.

9). The client middleware is notified of any responses in Q2.

10). The client middleware sends the response to the client process whenever it receives a "get Q2" statement from the client process.

This model can be easily extended to include client side and server side queues.

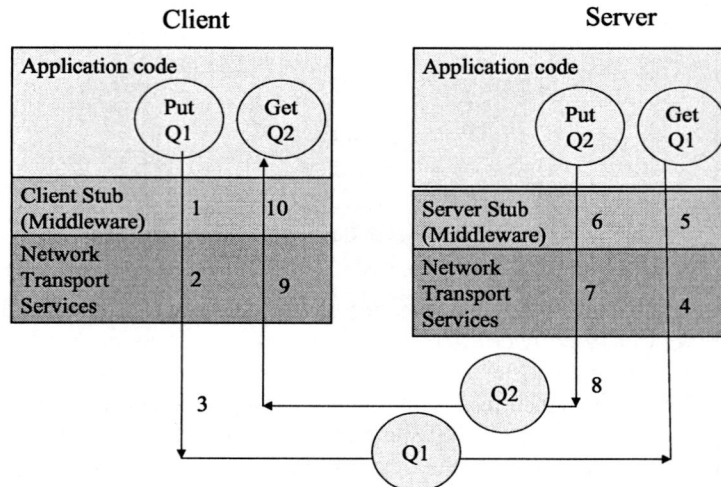

Figure 1-19: Queued Message Processing

1.12.3 QMP Analysis

Many decisions are made in various steps of the queued message paradigm. Examples of some of these decisions are discussed here.

Asynchronous ("non-blocked") paradigm. The clients can put a message on the queue and then continue processing. Another segment of client code can continue to monitor the output queue for any responses and process the outputs received. Asynchronous processing has the following benefits:
- It is suitable for detachable (e.g., wireless) computers that need to access data asynchronously without having to be in constant session with the hosts.
- Failure of server does not stop the clients from continuing to process as much as possible.
- Clients can be more efficient and responsive because they do not have to wait for the server to response.
- Clients and servers can use "deferred message" or call back features if a response is not available.

However, it must be kept in mind that developing good asynchronous code is non-trivial.

Queue considerations. The message queues can be stored on disk (persistent) or in main memory (non-persistent). In most cases, queues are stored on disks for failure recovery. The queues can be at client machines, at server machines, in a middle machine, or replicated on client and server machines. If the queues are replicated, then "data movers" are provided as part of MOM that move queues from one machine to another. A major consideration in QMP is handling of very large messages in the queue. If queries generate large tables with millions of rows as responses to be stored in queues, then very large queue sizes need to be allocated. Queue overflows can be quite dangerous to the health of QMP based C/S environments.

Handling Different Speed Processors. A major advantage of QMP is that the queues can be written into and retrieved from a diverse array of client and server processes. These processes can operate at different speeds on different machines and not cause any interference and/or delays.

1.12.4 Strengths and Weaknesses

The main strength of message-oriented middleware (MOM) is asynchronous processing, i.e., the clients and servers are not blocked while waiting for response from each other. This feature of MOM also allows development of peer-to-peer distributed applications. Another strength of MOM is recoverability from failures because the message queues on disks can be used to recover the system after failures. For example, once a message has been received and queued by MOM, these messages are not lost (the queues are used to restart applications, if needed).

Yet another strength of MOM is that it can be used to link existing legacy applications very easily without modifying any code at either side (i.e., redirect the output of application A to a disk queue and redirect the input of application B from the same disk queue). This approach does not require the additional software development on either side (you do not need a client that issues an RPC and a server that receives, parses and dispatches processes). MOM also provides an appealing solution for distributed transaction processing because the queue messaging can be transactional (i.e., MOM can make sure that only one message is transferred and that automated rollback recovery is available). This is a very familiar territory for mainframe-based transaction managers such as IMS (IMS has been using queued messages since the 1970s). We will discuss the MOM approach to distributed transaction processing in Chapter 6.

The main limitation of MOM is that the overhead of writing/reading from disk queues can slow down a C/S application. In addition, queuing of unpredictably large responses can result in disk overflows.

Ideally, C/S middleware needs to support RDA, RPC and QMP paradigms to provide C/S application developers maximum flexibility.

1.13 Pushing Information to Consumers – Publish-Subscribe Model

1.13.1 Overview

The publish-subscribe model pushes the information to the subscribers without an explicit request from them. As stated previously, publish-subscribe can be viewed as a subset of message-oriented middleware. The main difference between message queuing and publish/subscribe aspect of MOM is that the former implements a one-to-one communication model (much like a postal system), while the latter provides a many-to-many communication model (similar to television/radio transmission).

In pub-sub, consumers subscribe to (register interest in) a channel that represents one or more subjects (Figure 1-20). Publishers push (send) messages to the channel. Once a subject has been subscribed to, the subscriber will receive any messages published to that subject. Subjects are defined by the application developer. In traditional network applications, when two processes must communicate with each other, they need network addresses to begin communicating. If a process wants to send a message to many other processes, it first would need to know the physical network addresses of the other processes and then create a connection to all those processes. This architecture does not scale well because configuration is complicated and tedious.

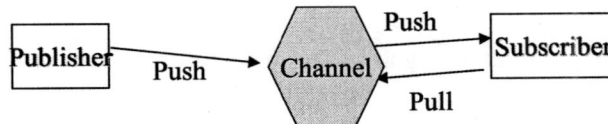

Figure 1-20: Publish/subscribe model

Publish/subscribe is used for delivering real-time information, such as stock quotes, sports news, business alerts, or the events of a distributed gaming application. For example, a publisher could push the message "new customer signed up" to the channel. Then many subscribers such as salesmen, managers, and customer service representatives could automatically get this information.

The pub-sub model is the foundation of "*event-based*" processing where each event is a subject. For example, an event could be "inventory level too low". Many order processing systems and inventory managers can subscribe to this event and take appropriate actions. The main idea is that new subscribers can be added without the publisher knowing anything about the subscribers.

The pub-sub model can be very useful for wireless systems. With this model, it becomes possible to send the same information to thousands or millions of subscribers. It is also the foundation of real-time enterprises that monitor business activities on an on-going basis. See the discussion in Chapter 5, State of the Art Section.

The pub-sub model has been implemented in JMS (Java Messaging Services) from Sun. Another example is the Talarian SmartSockets publish-subscribe middleware. In addition, most EAI (enterprise Application Integration) platforms use the pub-sub model.

1.13.2 Publish/Subscribe Model

Figure 1-19 shows the steps that take place in publish-subscribe, commonly referred to as "pub-sub", processing. In this model, a producer labels a message with its destination topic, and hands it to the channel. A topic is a character string such as `"inventory"`; it denotes a many-to-many transmission channel. The channel middleware delivers the message to all consumers that have registered an interest in receiving messages on that topic. In contrast to message queuing, these messages are typically volatile. A topic subscriber receives only the messages published while the subscriber is active and running:

The publisher and subscriber routines are in two separate processes, usually on two different machines. We are showing only one channel for the purpose of discussion. However, a separate channel can be created for each subject. Designers and implementers of pub-sub can choose a different number of channels for performance and availability purposes. For conceptual discussion, we will also assume that the channels are located "somewhere" on the network. Typically, the channels reside in a middle machine (e.g., a broker). The following steps are executed in order:

1). The publisher issues a "Push message on channel" call in an API made available by the publisher middleware. The API calls can be issued from end-user tools or application programs. The push middleware mainly encodes the call into appropriate network messages.

2). The network message, containing the push message, is prepared and sent to the remote site through network transport services.

3). The message is sent over the communication media and is stored in the channel.

4). The message is pushed to the subscribers of this channel. Only the subscribers who are registered for this channel are sent this information.

5). The subscriber middleware retrieves the message and sends it to the subscriber for processing.

6). The subscriber may choose to "pull" the events posted on the channel on an as needed basis instead of being pushed the information.

7). The subscriber middleware translates the pull request into a network message.

8). The pull request is handled by the channel.

9). The pulled information is routed back to the subscriber.

10). The subscriber middleware sends the response to the subscriber process.

This model can be easily extended to include multiple channels.

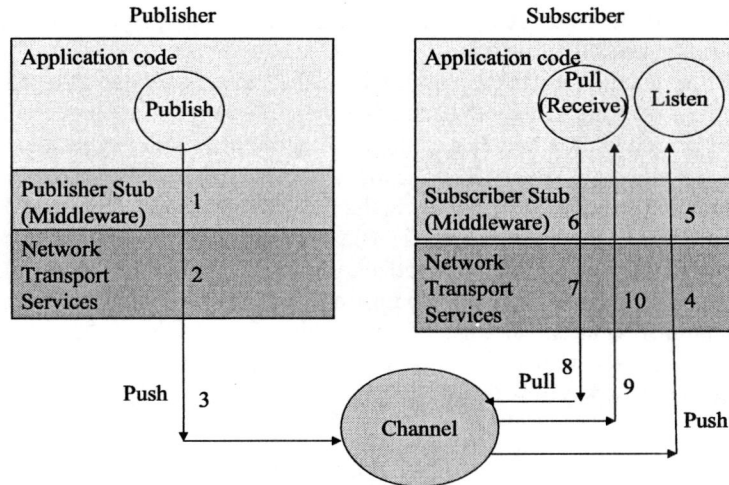

Figure 1-21: Publish-Subscribe Flow

1.13.3 Publish-Subscribe Analysis

Middleware vendors typically implement publish-subscribe with a set of agents that maintain a real-time database, listing which programs are interested in which subjects. A program publishes a message by connecting with one of the agents (it may or may not be on the same machine) and sending the message to it. The agent then routes the message to the appropriate programs. Often, the pub-sub middleware has greater fault tolerance because the agents can perform dynamic routing of the messages as well as provide hot fail over should any system fail.

Many decisions are made in various steps of the publish-subscribe paradigm. Examples of some of these decisions are discussed here.

- **Pull versus Push**. The channel can push the information to the subscribers or the subscriber can pull the information from the channel. The decision is dependent on application, naturally. With pull, the application has some control over when the information is accessed (like watching news at 11 PM). But push is very useful for sending events (triggers) that the application must pay attention to.
- **Number of subjects and channels**. It is not a good idea to have a very large number of subjects (topics) due to performance reasons. For a large number of topics, sophisticated filters are needed.
- **Handling large number of subscribers**. A major advantage of pub-sub is that the participants are isolated from each other. The only commonality is the topic. It is important to determine the topics carefully -- a separate topic per subscriber is not a good idea.

1.13.4 Strengths and Weaknesses

The main strength of pub-sub is the scalability and location transparency of the communicating partners. This is because the publish-subscribe communications model allows a program to send the message with a subject as the destination property while the middleware routes the message to all programs that have subscribed to that subject. This is in contrast to the traditional client/server models where the clients communicate with each other through network addresses. If a process wants to send a message to many other processes, it first would need to know the physical network addresses of the other processes and then create a connection to all those processes. The traditional architectures do not scale well because it is difficult to keep track of network addresses.

Pub-sub is most appropriate for very loosely coupled applications where fault tolerance and high performance are important. It does not work well in situations where processes may be disconnected from the network for long periods of time (the channels may not write the messages on disks). Ideally, pub-sub is another alternative to other middleware needs to support RDA, RPC and queued messaging. The model has found several applications such as the following:

- Enterprise application integration (EAI) platforms use the pub-sub model on a regular basis. Diverse enterprise applications communicate with each other by publishing and subscribing to events posted on the channel, called the integration bus. For example, an order processing application can post the event of order arrival on the integration bus. All applications interested in handling orders can subscribe to this event. EAI platforms are discussed extensively in the Integration Module (naturally!).
- Real-time enterprises that monitor and react to business activities in real-time are also increasingly using the pub-sub model. See the State of the Market discussion in Chapter 5.
- Security systems also use the pub-sub model to raise security alarms. Whenever an intrusion is detected, an alarm event is published to an "alrams" channel. Subscribers to these alarms are different systems that may reconfigure or even shut down a system based on the type of alarm. See the Management Module for a detailed discussion of security.

1.14 The JMS Standard – Combining Messaging into One

The Java Message Service (JMS) API specification was released in Fall 1998 by Sun as a uniform interface addressing both message queuing and publish-subscribe messaging. JMS is a building block of the Sun Java 2 Enterprise Edition (J2EE) platform - a platform for developing enterprise-wide Java applications by using components, specifically the Enterprise Java Bean (EJB) technology. We will discuss J2EE in a later chapter.

JMS combines Java technology with enterprise messaging to support message queuing as well as the pub-sub model. It includes a common API and provider framework for development of portable, message based applications in Java. The JMS API defines a common set of messaging concepts and programming strategies that are supported by JMS technology-compliant messaging systems. The key features of JMS are:

- **Extensions of pub-sub model.** In a pub-sub model, a timing dependency exists between publishers and subscribers. Basically, a client that subscribes to a topic can consume only messages published after the client has created a subscription, and the subscriber must continue to be active in order for it to consume messages. The JMS API relaxes this timing by allowing clients to create *durable subscriptions*. Durable subscriptions can receive messages sent while the subscribers are not active.
- **Integrated with Sun J2EE (Java Enterprise Edition).** The JMS API is part of the J2EE 1.3 platform. In particular, any J2EE component (an Enterprise JavaBeans™ (EJB™) component or a web component) can send or synchronously receive a JMS message. A new kind of enterprise bean, the message-driven bean, enables the asynchronous consumption of messages. In addition, message senders and receivers can participate in Java Transaction API (JTA) transactions.
- **Reliability Support.** The JMS API provides several ways to achieve different kinds and degrees of reliability. For example, with JMS you can:
  - specify different levels of control over message acknowledgment.
  - specify that messages are persistent, meaning that they must not be lost in the event of a provider failure.
  - set different priority levels for messages, which can affect the order in which the messages are delivered.
  - specify an expiration time for messages, so that they will not be delivered if they are obsolete.
  - create temporary destinations that last only for the duration of the connection in which they are created.
  - create durable topic subscriptions, which receive messages published while the subscriber is not active. Durable subscriptions offer the reliability of queues to the publish-subscribe message domain.
  - use local transactions, which allow you to group a series of sends and receives into an atomic unit of work. Transactions are rolled back if they fail at any time.

Since its release, more than twenty vendors have endorsed the specification (including companies like IBM, Oracle, and BEA). For example, IBM has announced JMS support for its very popular MQ Series. JMS was originally intended for business applications running on non-mobile PCs and servers. However, JMS implementation for wireless mobile devices has been offered by some companies such as SoftWired (www.softwired.com).

The JMS API is detailed in the JMS Specification, which can be downloaded from Sun's web site at http://java.sun.com/products/jms. This web site also includes an extensive tutorial on JMS.

1.15 Other Interaction Paradigms

Programs at different machines can interact with each other by using a wide variety of interaction paradigms. The paradigms discussed so far are very popular at present and are supported by many products. However, several other paradigms are also used on a regular basis. Here are some examples:

- Peer-to-peer model in which either remotely located process can initiate an interaction. The basic distinguishing feature of the C/S model is that a client initiates an interaction with a server by sending a message or by invoking an operation. In contrast, either process of a peer-to-peer model can initiate an interaction. A C/S model can be implemented over peer-to-peer protocols as a special case. C/S computing systems at present are based on the C/S model. "Distributed cooperative processing systems" use the peer-to-peer or C/S model for processes at different computers to interactively exchange information with each other (C/S computing is a subcategory of distributed cooperative processing).
- One-way data flow from one process to another. This can be used when response is not expected and is natural for the type of programs that receive streams of input and produce streams of output. This technique minimizes control (handshaking) messages between distributed programs and is simplex (one-way traffic). For example, this technique can be used in file transfers and invocation of remotely located text formatters (e.g., UNIX Troff). Another example is a speech recognition system that constantly monitors an audio port for sound (the sound is transferred one way) and processes speech whenever it arrives.
- Broadcasting. In this paradigm, one program needs to send the same data to several other programs. Broadcasting is a commonly used technique in network technologies and is often implemented as a low level primitive (e.g., in Ethernet). In order to implement broadcasting between application programs (e.g., to notify loss of a critical data file), the application programs have to choose and implement search criteria such as spanning trees.
- Heartbeat and multicasting. The processes send messages to neighbor processes and forward requests to successor processes, respectively. These algorithms are used in many cooperativeprocessing situations where none of the servers have complete information. In these cases, the servers coordinate their work with each other by sending/receiving messages to neighbors and successors.
- Replicated server processing. This is used when many servers at different sites perform same activities. For example, many name servers may be replicated in a network. The replicated servers can either choose one server to perform the task or split a task among many replicated servers for load balancing.

In addition, remote programs can interact with each other by using the paradigms and associated protocols that we will discuss in later chapters (e.g., the distributed object interactions, Web access to remote resources through HTTP, and mobile code applications such as Java applets).

Time to Take a Break
✓ • Middleware Overview and Principles
✓ • Basic Middleware (RPC, RDA, MOM)
• Comparison and Analysis

Suggested Review Questions Before Proceeding

- What is RPC, when should it be used, what are its common examples, and what are its plusses/minuses?
- What is RDA, when should it be used, what are its common examples, and what are its plusses/minuses?
- What is MOM, when should it be used, what are its common examples, and what are its plusses/minuses?
- What is push model, when should it be used, what are its common examples, and what are its plusses/minuses?
- How does JMS combine and support many client/server models?
- Prepare a checklist, in the form of a table, that compares and contrasts the basic client/server middleware services such as RPCs, RDAs, MOMs, etc?

1.16 Comparison and Analysis

Which paradigm should be used when? We have discussed the trade-offs between RPCs, RDA, MOM, and pub-sub. The main consideration is minimization of the communication message traffic and reliability of the products that support the paradigms. However, we need to keep the following factors in mind:

- Application requirements: which paradigm best meets the application needs?
- Time and money constraints: how much time and money is allowed for this project?
- Availability of off-the-shelf middleware: what is commercially available to satisfy application needs within the time and money constraints?

Most of the discussion mainly revolves around loose versus tight coupling between clients and servers. An enterprise application provider is likely to choose a loosely coupled messaging API (such as MOM) over a tightly coupled API (such as RPC) when:

- The application business model allows a component to send information to another and continue to operate without receiving an immediate response.
- The provider wants the components not to depend on information about other components' interfaces, so that components can be easily replaced.
- The provider wants the application to run whether or not all components are up and running simultaneously.

For example, components of an enterprise application for a car manufacturer can use a loosely coupled messaging system in situations like these:

- The business publishes updated catalog items to its sales force and web site.
- The inventory component can send a message to the factory component when the inventory level for a product goes below a certain level, so the factory can make more cars.
- The factory component can send a message to the parts components so that the factory can assemble the parts it needs.
- The parts components in turn can send messages to their own inventory and order components to update their inventories and order new parts from suppliers.
- Both the factory and parts components can send messages to the accounting component to update their budgets.

Using messaging for these tasks allows the different components to interact with each other efficiently, without tying up network or other resources. On the other hand, tightly coupled C/S systems are very effective in highly interactive systems where the two partners have to maintain contexts of conversation as it proceeds.

In addition to the paradigms supported, all middleware packages should support a variety of support features (GUIs, samples, examples, etc). See the sidebar " What Should a Good Middleware Package Have".

What Should a Good Middleware Package Have?

- Graphical, interactive tools to monitor, test, debug and administer applications.
- A solution that is easy to get started "out of the box" and without requiring dozens of consultants to assist in its use.
- Straightforward tuning of parameters to specific application requirements and offer synchronous and asynchronous messaging.
- A rich API that includes class libraries for all leading languages and component architectures, including C, C++, and Java.
- Pre-packaged modules to handle many of the complex, low-level "plumbing" chores.
- Guaranteed message delivery to eliminate the need for customers to write complex error recovery code.
- Extensive sample C, C++, and Java example programs to get off to a fast start.
- Comprehensive, example-rich, easy-to-read documentation.

1.17 XYZCorp Case Study: Partial Solution 2

Let us try to answer the questions raised in the case study (if we cannot answer them now, then when?):

Q: Should a loose versus tightly coupled architecture be adopted to interconnect the large number of users, applications, and databases that reside at different sites?

A: It is better to have a loosely coupled architecture where the clients and servers are not tightly bound to facilitate new users, applications, and databases. This is the reason why MOM and pub-sub architectures are becoming more popular.

Q. How can multiple clients and servers that support different middleware services co-exist in the XYZCorp environment?

A. "Middleware Gateways" are commercially available to convert one type of middleware to another. An example is the database gateways that convert different types of database accesses (e.g., Oracle to MS Access).

Q. Should a thin client be used everywhere? If not, where can a fat client be used?

A. Thick clients are useful when business logic needs to reside at the client site. In XYZCorp, the overseas offices are good candidates for handling local business logic.

Q. Can a LAN operating system provide interconnectivity within the organization? If yes, which one?

A. The typical LAN operating systems are not very well suited for enterprise-wide systems that span several regions of the United States and overseas. It is better to rely on the Internet (public, private) and web technologies for long haul connectivity. For small regional offices, Windows LAN Manager or Novell do OK.

Q. Should RPC, RDA, MOM, or pub-sub be used as the primary remote communication protocol and why? Which types of protocols are suited for which type of applications?

A. The following table can be used to compare and contrast the various protocols. The information discussed in relevant sections can be used to complete this table.

	Strengths	Weaknesses	Sample Applications
RPC			
RDA			
MOM			
Pub-sub			

1.18 State of the Practice, Market, and Art

The basic middleware technologies became state of the practice in the early 1990s in the LAN environments. This is because many C/S applications were initially developed on LAN NOSs such as Novell Netware, Windows NT, IBM LAN Manager, and Banyan Vines. In particular, RPC is very commonly used because many existing products use RPCs. Moreover, RPC is at the heart of Web (http is a simple RPC) - thus any user of Web is automatically using RPCs. RDA is also very popular because ODBC/JDBC is based on RDA. Most of the applications that rely on SQL servers use ODBC/JDBC (i.e., issue remote SQL calls to SQL servers). Thus, the applications using the Oracle SQL Server, Microsoft SQL Server, or any other SQL server heavily use the RDA paradigm. In addition, many off-the-shelf applications such as PeopleSoft's Human Resource Application also uses RDA. The use of MOM and publish-subscribe has grown dramatically due to B2B e-commerce because business partners are typically loosely coupled and asynchronous.

For state of market, C/S middleware to support RPC, RDA, and MOM is commercially available at the time of this writing. In addition, many management and support services are also being included in off-the-shelf products. Here is a brief synopsis of state of the market.

Remote Procedure Call (RPC)-based middleware is widely available in UNIX, MVS and PC environments. Here are some examples of RPC products:
- Open Software Foundation's RPC (this is used in the Microsoft DCOM products)
- SUN RPC system
- Netwise RPC
- Novell Netware RPC
- Information Builder's EDA/SQL RPC
- IBM TCP/IP

RDA products are currently heavily supported by the "database server industry". Simply stated, a database server houses a database and controls user access to the database. As stated previously, a large number of vendors are developing SQL database servers that basically handle SQL calls from clients and respond with results. Most of the database servers were originally developed for LANs (e.g., the Gupta SQL Server for IBM Token Ring LANs). Database servers in mainframe WAN environments are now available from database vendors such as Oracle and IBM. IBM's DRDA (Distributed Relational Database Architecture) has emerged as a popular approach for accessing mainframe DB2 databases from clients operating in UNIX and PC environments.

MOM (message-oriented middleware) products are getting serious vendor attention at present. Interest in MOM is fueled by mobile computing and B2B trade that require asynchronous behavior. In particular, JMS (Java Message Service) specification that supports QMP as well as the publish-subscribe model is quite popular. A partial list of MOM products in the industry is:

- MQSeries of products from IBM that include a variety of services ranging from database replication to downsizing of mainframe applications
- Message-oriented middleware used in Tuxedo and Encina
- Enterprise Messaging Services (EMS) from Sybase for Sybase Open Cleint/Open Server
- MOM-based workflow systems from Momentum, Inc.
- Communications Integrator from Covia Technologies
- X_IPC middleware for MOM
- Pipes Platform from Peer Logics

Standards for the basic middleware have also matured. Unfortunately, there are many RPC implementations with no standards. RPC standards are needed because each RPC middleware introduces its own API and exchange protocols. Thus, applications that are based on SUN RPC and Netwise RPC do not interoperate. However, since RPCs are imbedded in larger systems such as CORBA and DCOM, individual RPC interoperability issues rarely arrive. A new RPC standard, SOAP (Simple Object Access Protocol) is currently under development (we will discuss SOAP in a later chapter). The situation is much better in RDA because ODBC/JDBC and DRDA are de facto industry standards. Standards for MOM are currently gravitating towards JMS.

For a more general discussion of state of the practice, market, and art, see chapter 5 of this Module.

1.19   Summary

In this chapter, we have attempted to define middleware and discussed how it is used to interconnect applications and users located around the network. Most of the chapter has concentrated on the basic middleware services that are essential for developing any contemporary distributed application - many higher-level middleware services rely on the basic middleware services.

Basic C/S middleware services are based on a few interaction paradigms such as Remote Procedure Call (RPC), Remote Data Access (RDA), Queued Messaging, and Publish-Subscribe. We have discussed these paradigms and the protocols/products that support these paradigms in some detail.

1.20   Review Questions and Exercises

Extend the discussion about two tiered architectures to three and N-tiered architectures.

What is the difference between a remote interaction paradigm and a remote communication protocol? Explain through examples. Is RPC a paradigm or a protocol?

Compare and contrast RDA, RPC, MOM, and pub-sub. Show what type of applications can utilize these protocols through real life examples.

Develop a pseudo code for an MS Excell client that accesses an SQL server on a remote site. You may choose any of the protocols and facilities to develop the pseudo code.

Describe the peer-to-peer protocol by utilizing the framework used to describe the RPC, RDA, and MOM paradigms.

List the factors you will use to evaluate off-the-shelf basic client/server middleware products.

Study in detail the JMS specification and discuss its strengths and weaknesses.

1.21 Additional Information

A1999. Network Policy and Services: A Report of a Workshop on Middleware, IETF RFC 2768, 1999 (see http://www.rfc-editor.org/rfc/rfc2768.txt). This IETF RFC, generated following a workshop held December 4-5, 1998, defines a consistent set of terminology surrounding middleware.

A2000. CISE ANIR "Committee of Visitors FY97-00 Report", June 14-15, 2000. This Committee of Visitors report discusses the philosophy and imperative behind the NSF middleware imitative, and makes a number of suggestions on how it should be organized and managed.

Amaru, C., "Building Distributed Applications with MOM", Client/Server Today, November 1994, pp. 83-93.

Andrews, G.R., "Paradigms for Process Interaction in Distributed Programs", ACM Computing Surveys, March 1991, pp. 49-90.

Berson, A., "Client/Server Architectures", McGraw Hill, 1993.

Birrel, A.D. and Nelson, B.J., "Implementing Remote Procedure Call", ACM Trans. on Computer Systems, Vol. 2, pp.39-59.

Britton, C., "IT Architectures and Middleware: Strategies for Building Large, Integrated Systems", Addison-Wesley, 2000

Camara, J. et al, "A message-oriented communication service for the Portuguese Energy Market", ICDP96, Dresden, Feb. 1996.

Corbin, J. R., "The Art of Distributed Applications: Programming Techniques for Remote Procedure Calls", Springer-Verlag, 1991.

Coulouris, G., Dollimore, J., and Kindjberg, T., "Distributed Systems: Concepts and Design", Addison Wesley, third edition, 2000 .

IBM (International Business Machines), ``Advanced Program-to-Program Communication for the IBM Personal Computer, Programming Guide'., .

Johnson, J., "Enterprise NOSs: Now is the Time", Data Communications, May 15, 1995.

Khanna, R., "Distributed Computing: Implementation and Management Strategies", Prentice Hall, 1993.

Kramer, M., "How Message-Oriented Middleware Supports a Managed Care Solution", Distributed Computing Monitor, Patricia Seybold Group, Vol. 10, No. 5, 1995, pp. 23-28.

Lerner, et al, "Middleware Networks: Concept, Design and Deployment of Internet Infrastructure", Kluwer Academic Publishers; 2000

Lewis, T., "Where is Client/Server Software Headed", IEEE Computer Magazine, April 1995, pp. 49-55.

Myerson, J.," The Complete Book of Middleware", Auerbach Publications, 2002

Neuman, B. and Ts'o, T., "Kerberos; An authentication Service for Computer Networks", IEEE Communications Magazine, 1994, pp. 33-37.

Orfali, R., Harkey, D., and Edwards, J., "Client/Server Survival Guide", Van Nostrand Reinholt, 1994.

Schilller, J., "Secure Distributed Computing", Scientific American,, Nov. 1994, pp. 72-76.

Schmidt, D., "Adaptive and Reflective Middleware Systems", Presentation, DARPA/ITO, 2001.

Schmidt, D., et al, "Towards Adaptive and Reflective Middleware for Network-Centric Combat Systems", CrossTalk, Nov. 2001

Serain, D., and Craig, I., "Middleware: Practioner Series", Springer-Verlag, 1999

Stahl, S., "Peer Logic Helps Insurer Access Data", Information Week, Jan. 9, 1995.

Stevens, W., "UNIX Network Programming", Prentice Hall, 1990.

Umar, A., "Object-Oriented Client/Server Internet Environments", Prentice Hall, revised edition, 1997.

Whiting, R.(a), "Getting on the Middleware Express", Client/Server Today, November 1994, pp. 70-75.

Whiting, R.(b), "Turning to MOM for the Answers", Client/Server Today, November 1994, pp. 76-81.

Wilbur, S. and Bacarisse, B., "Building Distributed Systems with Remote Procedure Calls", Software Engineering Journal, Sept. 1987, pp. 148 - 159.

Wood, A., "Predicting Client/Server Availability", IEEE Computer Magazine, April 1995, pp. 41-48.

2 Web, XML, Semantic Web, and Web Services

2.1   Introduction

The growth in the use of Internet is astounding. The origin of Internet is the ARPANET (Advanced Research Projects Agency Network) that was initiated in 1969 to support researchers on DOD (Department of Defense) projects. For many years, Internet was used mainly by scientists and programmers to transfer files and send/receive electronic mail. The users of Internet relied on text-based user interfaces and tedious commands to access remote computing resources. In 1989, this changed with the introduction of World Wide Web (WWW), commonly referred to as the Web. The Web has been a major contributor in turning the Internet, once an obscure tool, into a household word. The Web allows users to access, navigate and share information around the globe through GUI clients ("Web browsers") that are available on almost all computing platforms. The Web browsers allow users to access information that is linked through hypermedia links. Thus, a user transparently browses around, or "surfs" around, different pieces of information that is located on different computers in different cities and even in different countries.

We are living in a time when the Web has become the primary source of accessing the majority of information needed by hobbyists, students, researchers, consumers and corporations. For example, many businesses are using their Web site(s) as their main source of advertising, sales, and customer services. In addition, the Web is being used for a myriad of new applications (e.g., publishing, distribution, and electronic commerce) and is being integrated with traditional business applications to solve business problems. Since its introduction in the early 1990s, Web has evolved through the following phases:

- As the current universal information access and delivery platform thanks to the very large number of Web sites
- As a *Semantic Web* that is transforming the Web from the current human intensive platform to an environment where humans and programs can collaborate with each other through XML and its "family members"
- As an extensive global application development and delivery platform through *Web Services* that allows service providers around the globe to provide applications to the end users in a global virtual environment

The purpose of this chapter is to review the core concepts and technologies that comprise World Wide Web and walk through the evolutionary phases of the Web. The following questions will guide the discussion in this chapter:

- What is Internet and how does it relate to Intranets and the World Wide Web (Section 2.3)?
- What are the key concepts and components of World Wide Web (Section 2.4)?
- What do terms such as HTML, HTTP, Web browsers and Web servers mean in the traditional Web environments (Sections 2.5, 2.1, 2.1, and 2.9)?
- What type of gateways are needed to integrate Web with existing applications and how can corporate information be accessed through the Web (Section 2.8)?
- What is XML and why is it so popular (Section 2.11)?

- What is the Semantic Web and why is it significant (Section 2.12)?
- What are Web Services and why are they important for the future global applications (Section 2.13)?
- What is Java and why is it so hot (Section 2.18)?

A great deal of information about Web and XML is currently available. Naturally, one chapter is not enough. We will take a closer look at this topic in the chapter "Web, XML, and XML Databases -- A Closer Look" in the Tutorials Module. For engineering aspects of Web, see the book "Web Protocols and Practice: HTTP/1.1, Networking Protocols, Caching, and Traffic Measurement" by Balachander Krishnamurthy, Jennifer Rexford, Addison Wesley, 2001.

Key Points

- The World Wide Web is essentially a middleware that operates on top of the Internet to support a community of users and applications.
- Web users can access corporate information by using Web gateways.
- Intranet is a private Internet used by a corporation for its internal use. Intranets use Web technology for corporate services and applications.
- The main appeal of Web for e-business applications is that organizations can standardize on Web browsers for the end-user access to all applications (e.g., marketing, human resources or engineering). In addition, the same Web interface can be used for applications that cross the company, industry, and country boundaries.
- The Web is based on the following concepts and technologies:

  – Web servers

  – Web browsers

  – Uniform Resource Locator (URL)

  – Hypertext Transfer Protocol (HTTP)

  – Hypertext Markup Language (HTML)

  – Extended Markup Language (XML)

  – Web navigation and search tools

  – Gateways to non-Web resources

  – Web automation efforts that focus on metadata and are concentrating on the Document Object Model (DOM) and Resource Definition Framework (RDF)
- XML and its variants are key players in EC/EB because XML allows trading partners to formally specify and enforce the content and format of documents exchanged.
- What makes WWW unique is that it makes hypermedia available on the Internet in what has evolved into a global information system.
- Java is a programming language designed to work on the Web. The main thing is that Java applications (known as Java applets) can run on the Web browser site. Thus, Java applets can be used to execute business logic at the Web browser sites and thus implement the first tier of C/S applications.
- Web access to non-Web resources is provided through Web gateways. For example, Web access to relational databases is provided through "relational gateways" that serve as translators and mediators between Web browsers and relational database managers.
- XML and Web metadata (data bout data) is at the foundation of the Semantic Web for automated agents and business partners to review, understand, and react to the information available on Web sites.
- Web Services are intended to provide global distributed applications where an inventory system in Singapore can be combined with an order processing system in London to handle orders placed by someone in Chicago.

2.2   Case Study: Web Portal for XYZCORP

The company is planning to develop a corporate "Intranet" that will serve the Web users within this organization. In addition, a customer relationship management (CRM) portal will be developed to provide a single point of contact for all customers. The purpose of this CRM portal is to provide a common integrated view of the entire corporation that has acquired several companies, some of them with their own CRM and customer contact centers. The acquired companies are run as "Providers" that collectively provide the overall services of the corporation. Examples of the Providers are an e-shop, a financial institution that issues credit cards, a customer contact center, and several manufacturing plants. Some Providers currently have their own CRM — thus the customers cannot take advantage of any crossover functionality. For example, if a customer buys something from the e-shop, she does not know anything about the financing options available to her from the affiliated finance Provider. Development of this portal includes several decisions such as the following:

- An overall architecture of the portal
- Determination of the Web technologies (e.g., Web browsers, Web servers, Web gateways) support the overall architecture
- Evaluation to see how the Next Generation Web (Semantic Web) will fit within portal architecture. Specifically, how RDF, XML Schema, DOM, and XML variants will fit into this vision
- Evaluate XML Web services for the portal — how can they be used

The Agenda
- Internet and Web
- Web Technologies
- XML and the Semantic Web
- Web Services

2.3   Internet and Intranets: A Quick Refresher[1]

Technically speaking, Internet is a network based on the TCP/IP protocol stack. At present, the term Internet is used to refer to a large collection of TCP/IP networks that are tied together through network interconnectivity devices such as routers and gateways. The term, cyberspace, first introduced through a science fiction book by [Gibson 1984], has been permanently transferred to our vocabulary. It represents thousands of computers and computer resources around the globe interconnected through the Internet. At present, the term Internet is used to symbolize the following two situations:

- **Public Internet,** or just the Internet, that is not owned by any single entity — it consists of many independent TCP/IP networks that are tied together loosely. Initially, the public Internet was used to tie different university networks together. With time, several commercial and private networks have joined the public Internet. The computers on the public Internet have publicly known Internet Protocol (IP) addresses that are used to exchange information over the public Internet (see discussion on addressing below). The public Internet at present consists of thousands of networks.

---

[1] Internet technologies, in particular TCP/IP, are covered in detail in the Network Module of this book. The material here is duplicated from that Module for a quick overview before getting into Web.

- **Private Internets**, or Intranets, are the TCP/IP networks that are used by corporations for their own business, especially by exploiting Web technologies. Technically, an Intranet uses the same technology as the public Internet -- it is only smaller and privately owned and thus hopefully better controlled and more secure. Thus, any applications and services that are available on the public Internet are also available on the Intranets. This is an important point for WWW because many companies are using WWW technologies on their Intranets for internal applications (e.g., employee information systems).
- **Extranets** are the TCP/IP networks that are owned by corporations to conduct business. These networks use the same Internet technologies, however, the physical network is collectivity owned by corporations to meet the security and reliability requirements imposed by the owners. An example of an Extranet is the Exhchange-Net formed by GM, Ford, Chrysler, and other manufacturing organizations to conduct manufacturing b2b transactions.

Unless otherwise indicated, the discussion in this chapter is oriented towards the public Internet although most concepts also apply to the Intranets and Extranets.

Domain Naming Services (DNSs) are used in the Internet to locate different resources. This protocol defines hierarchical naming structures that are much easier to remember than the IP addresses. For example, the machine with an IP address of 135.25.7.82 may have a domain name of shoeshop.com. A user "mills" may have an email address mills@shoeshop.com. The DNS naming structures define the organization type, organization name, etc. The last word in the domain name identifies an organization type or a country. Consider, for example, the following domain names:

        bellcore.com = commercial company Bellcore

        ibm.com = commercial company IBM

        um.edu = educational institution University of Michigan

        omg.org = organization OMG (Object Management Group)

        waterloo.ca = waterloo university in Canada

        lancs.ac.uk = Lancaster University in UK

        ansa.co.uk = ANSA consortium in UK

        iona.ie = Iona Corporation in Ireland

The Internet uses a large number of domain name servers that translate domain names to IP addresses (the IP routers only understand IP addresses). Domain names are used in the Internet as well as the Web.

Figure 2-1 shows a conceptual and partial view of the Internet. This Internet shows three networks (a university network with two computers, a commercial company network, and a network in UK). Each computer ("host") on this network has an IP address and has been assigned a domain name as well. Internet is very heterogeneous (i.e., different computers, different physical networks.) However, to the users of this network, it provides a set of uniform TCP/IP services (TCP/IP hides many details). We will use this simple Internet to illustrate the key Internet capabilities.

Since the Internet is based on TCP/IP, the applications and services provided by TCP are also available on the Internet. From an end-user point-of-view, the following services have been, and still are, used very heavily on the Internet:
- Email
- Telnet
- FTP
- Gopher
- WAIS (Wide Area Information Servers)

Electronic mail on the Internet is based on the **Simple Mail Transfer Protocol (SMTP)**. This TCP based protocol is the Intermet electronic mail exchange mechanism. Email is still one of the most heavily used service in the Internet. Users on the Internet have email addresses such as johnm@cs.um.edu, hevner@sun.com and howard@bank1.co.uk.

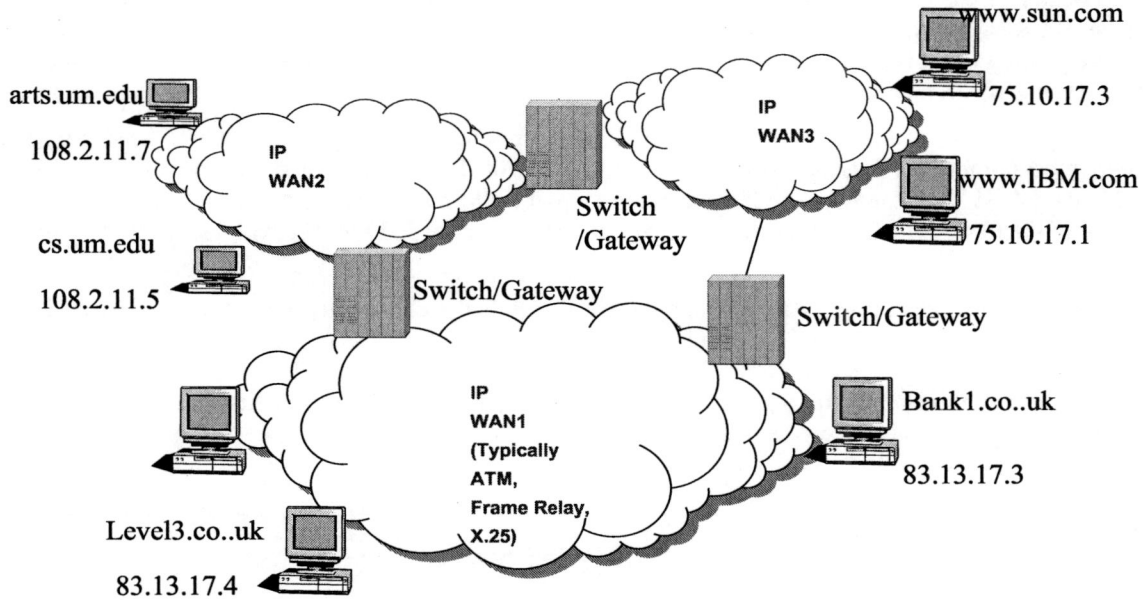

• DNS (Domain Name Services) translates cs.um.edu to 108.2.11.5
• Telnet cs.um.edu = Telnet 108.2.11.5
• FTP cs.um.edu = FTP 108.2.11.5

Figure 2-1: Partial View of Internet

Terminal emulation is used to remotely logon to other machines. **Telnet** provides terminal access to hosts and runs on top of TCP. Let us assume that a user "joe" on cs.um.edu needs to remotely logon to the bank1.co.uk machine to run a program "directory". The user would use the following steps (the steps are explained through comments in /* */):

```
> telnet bank1.co.uk        /* invoke Telnet. Could have typed " telnet 85.13.17.3".*/
bank1> enter logon: joe     /* prompt from bank1 for logon ID. joe is ID */
bank1> password: xxxx       /* prompt from bank1 for password */
bank1> directory        /* run the program "directory" */
bank1> exit            /* quit telnet */
```

File transfer is used for the bulk of data transfer over the Internet. The **File Transfer Protocol (FTP)** provides a way to transfer files between hosts on the Internet. Let us assume that a user "garner" on "sun.com" needs to transfer a file from the host arts.um.edu. The following steps would be used (the steps are explained through comments in /* */):

```
> ftp arts.um.edu           /* invoke FTP. Could have typed " ftp 102.52..10.7"*/
arts> enter logon: garner    /* prompt from arts.um for logon ID. garner is ID */
arts> password: xxxx       /* prompt from arts.um for password */
arts> get file1 file2     /* FTP file transfer command */
arts> exit (or quit)         /* quit FTP */
```

Gopher is a well-known interface for the Internet. Developed at the University of Minnesota, Gopher is very similar to the WWW because it provides a friendly face to tools such as FTP and Telnet, among others. However, Gopher does not support hypertext. Gopher provides a numbered list or, in some cases, icons to represent different files that you can transfer and access over the Internet.

WAIS (Wide Area Information Servers) generates and allows you to search a huge range of databases stored on the Internet based on search keys. These databases contain pointers to locations on the Internet that hold documents containing the search keys. WAIS rates its search results (e.g. a rating of 1000 means direct hit and 100 means marginal hit). WAIS allows you to keep narrowing the search until you find exactly what you are looking for. It is used in WWW for full keyword searching (in most cases, you do not know that the Web is using WAIS internally).

For many years, Internet had been used mainly by researchers, teachers, scientists, students, and programmers to transfer files and send/receive electronic mail. These users relied on text-based commands to do their job. WWW is a set of services that run on top of the Internet. The two main features of WWW are the use of GUI and hypertext to make the life of Internet users easy and fun. We will discuss WWW in the next section in more detail.

We should mention that the users access the Internet either directly or indirectly. *Direct Internet users* reside on the machines that have IP addresses while *indirect Internet users* remotely logon to the machines with IP addresses. For example, America Online is an Internet Access Provider that actually has machines with IP addresses (direct access). If you subscribe to America Online, then you dial into an America Online machine (i.e., you are indirectly accessing the Internet).

Internet Role Players

Different individuals, groups and organizations play different roles in the Internet. To illustrate these roles, let us envision the Internet as an electronic shopping mall. Then we can discuss the following roles:
- **Internet users** are the people who visit the shopping mall (i.e., logon to the Internet). The Internet users are essentially the consumers of the services provided by the Internet.
- **Content providers** are the merchants (individuals, groups or organizations) that provide the products in the shopping mall (i.e., resources available on the Internet). You can think of these content providers as the merchants in the shopping mall.
- **Internet access providers (IAPs)** are the organizations that facilitate your access to the shopping mall (i.e., give you a communication line and an access port on the Internet). You can think of IAPs as the local authorities that provide you with roads and signs to get you to the shopping malls.
- **Internet service providers (ISPs)** are the individuals and organizations that help the content providers set up their shops in the shopping mall (i.e., help in building Web sites). Many small content providers seek the help of ISPs to set up Web servers with appropriate security and backup/recovery.

What are Intranets and why are they so Hot?

Intranets have become a favorite term at present. As we stated previously, an Intranet is a private TCP/IP network used by a corporation for its own business. In particular, Intranets employ Web technologies for corporate use. For example, the employees use Web browsers to perform their routine tasks plus access corporate information. Intranets have been called the Internet's killer application for business. Why? The reasons are: that they are inexpensive (most of the infrastructure is already in place), they require minimum training (many users are already Web literate), they are easy to use and develop (many people know how to develop Web pages), they provide natural access to the outside world (most Intranets are connected to the public Internet), and they move technology away from IS and into the hands of end users (end users can develop and deploy their own applications).

The main idea behind the Intranets is that organizations can standardize on Web browsers for the end-user access to all applications (e.g., finance, marketing, human resources or engineering). In addition, the same Web interface can be used for applications that cross different organizational units of the company. Due to the prevalence of Web technologies, the same user interface can be used to access information that may cross the company, industry, and country boundaries. Also, the users can employ the same user interface when they are accessing information from home (many user interfaces developed for traditional client/server applications at present do not work over dial up lines). The power of mobile code applications by using Java applets also creates very interesting possibilities for corporate applications. For example, each user interface can be reconfigured dynamically based on user profiles and preferences.

Intranets are initiated by first deploying one or more internal Web sites, providing some Web gateways, and encouraging/requiring use of Web browsers. There are several implications of this:

- Web browsers provide a common user interface for all employees, including telecommuters, who use different desktops.
- Web is used for groupware, i.e., for email, document exchange, workflows and collaborative work (we will discuss groupware in a later chapter).
- Java applets can be used to perform a variety of operations on the user desktops.

2.4   Overview of World Wide Web

2.4.1   Brief History

World Wide Web (WWW) was started in 1989 by Tim Berners-Lee at the Geneva European Laboratory for Particle Physics (known as CERN, based on the laboratory's French name) [Berners-Lee 1999, Berners-Lee 1993]. The initial proposal suggested development of a "hypertext system" to enable efficient and easy information-sharing among geographically separated teams of researchers in the High Energy Physics community. The initial proposal had three basic components:

- A common and consistent user interface
- Incorporation of a wide range of technologies and document types
- A "universal readership" to allow anyone sitting anywhere on the network, on a wide variety of computers, to easily read the same document as anyone else

By the end of 1990, a line-browser (called www) was developed to implement the principles of hypertext access and the reading of different document types. In 1991, the line-browser was made available to the CERN community and a gateway for Wide Area Information Servers (WAIS) searches was developed. In 1992, a few more browsers were developed and around 50 Web sites (the machines that house Web documents) were implemented. During 1993, Web took off — the number of Web sites increased to 500, the Web network traffic grew from 0.1 percent of Internet traffic to 1 percent (a 10 fold increase), and the Mosaic browser for X Windows was developed at NCSA (National Center for Supercomputing Applications at University of Illinois). Since 1994, the Web has been gaining popularity dramatically, with increases in the number of browsers, search engines, Web servers, and usage.

The "First Generation of Web", discussed in Section 2.4.2, is based on a few simple concepts and technologies. Due to the popularity of Web, many limitations of the first generation started appearing. Based on this, a great deal of activity has focused on the "Next Generation of Web", discussed in Section 2.4.4. Perhaps the best known activity from this work is XML and what is now being called "the semantic Web".

A good historical view of WWW is presented by Tim Berners-Lee in his book "Weaving the Web" (Harper San Francisco, 1999).

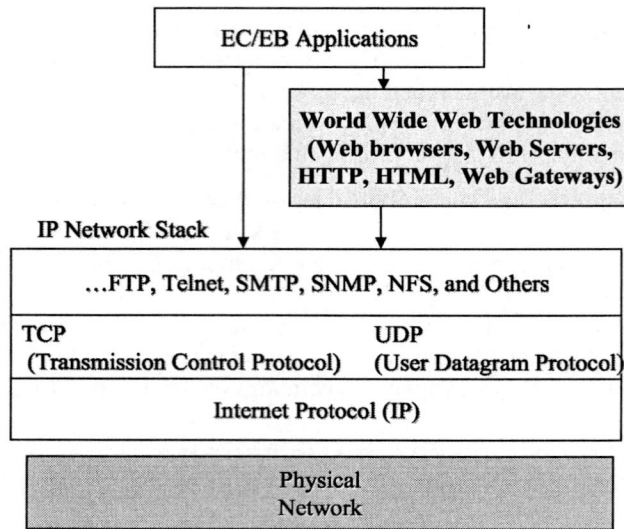

Figure 2-2: Technical View of World Wide Web

2.4.2 World Wide Web Technologies – The First Generation

Technically speaking, WWW is a collection of technologies that operates on top of the IP networks (i.e., the Internet). Figure 2-2 shows this layered view. The purpose of the WWW technologies is to support the growing number of users and applications ranging from entertainment to corporate information systems. Like many other (successful) Internet technologies, the first generation of WWW is based on a few simple concepts and technologies such as the following (see: Figure 2-3):

- Web servers
- Web browsers
- Uniform Resource Locator (URL)
- Hypertext Transfer Protocol (HTTP)
- Hypertext Markup Language (HTML)
- Web navigation and search tools
- Gateways to non-Web resources

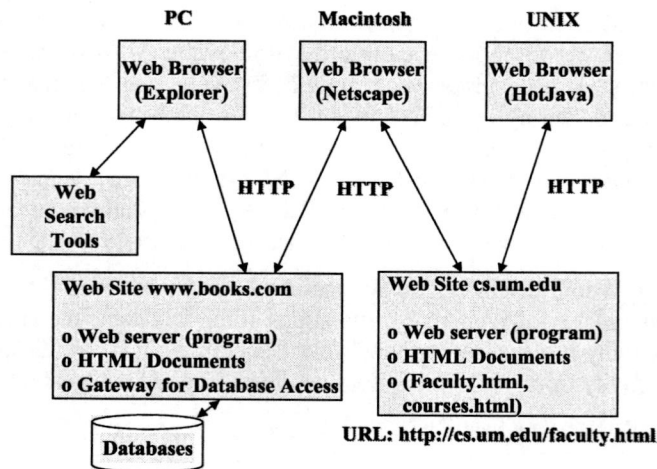

Figure 2-3: Conceptual View of World Wide Web

Let us briefly review these components and show how they tie in with each other through an example. We will discuss these components in more detail later in this chapter

Web sites provide the content accessed by Web users. Web sites are populated and in many cases managed by the content providers. For example, Web sites provide the commercial presence for each of the content providers doing business over the Internet. Conceptually, a Web site is a catalog of information for each content provider over the Web. In reality, a Web site consists of three types of components: a Web server (a program), content files ("Web pages") and/or gateways (programs that access non-Web content). A Web server is a program (technically a server process) that receives calls from Web clients and retrieves Web pages and/or receives information from gateways (we will discuss gateways later). Once again, a Web user views a Web site as a collection of files on a computer, usually a UNIX or Windows NT machine. In many cases, a machine is dedicated/designated as a Web site on which Web accessible contents are stored. As a matter of convention in EC/EB, the entry point to a Web site is a "home page" which advertises a company business. Very much like storefront signs in a shopping mall, the home pages include a company logo, fancy artwork for attention, special deals, overviews, pointers to additional information, etc. The large number of Web sites containing a wide range of information tto be navigated and searched transparently by Web users is the main strength of WWW. Figure 2-3 shows two Web sites -- one for a shoe shop (www.shoes.com) and the other for a computer science department for a university (cs.um.edu). Web sites and Web servers are explained in Section 2.1.

Web browsers are the clients that typically use graphical user interfaces to wander through the Web sites. The first GUI browser, Mosaic, was developed at the National Center for Supercomputer Applications at the University of Illinois. Mosaic ran on PC Windows, Macintosh, UNIX and Xterminals. At present, Web browsers are commercially available from Netscape, Microsoft and many other software/freeware providers. These Web browsers provide an intuitive view of information where hyperlinks (links to other text information) appear as underlined items or highlighted text/images. If a user points and clicks on the highlighted text/images, then the Web browser uses HTTP to fetch the requested document from an appropriate Web site. Web browsers are designed to display information prepared in a markup language, known as HTML. We will discuss HTTP and HTML later. Three different browsers are shown in Figure 2-3. Even though these are different browsers residing on different machines, they all use the same protocol (HTTP) to communicate with the Web servers (HTTP compliance is a basic requirement for Web browsers). The Web browsers are reviewed in Section 2.1.

Most browsers at present are relatively dumb (i.e., they just pass user requests to Web servers and display the results). However, this is changing very quickly because of Java, a programming language developed by Sun Microsystems. Java programs, known as Java applets, can run on Java compatible browsers. This is creating many interesting possibilities where Java applets are downloaded to the Java enabled browsers where they run producing graphs/charts, invoking multimedia applications, and accessing remote databases. We will briefly review Java and Java applets in Section 2.18. For a more detailed discussion of Java, see the tutorial on this topic in the Tutorial Module.

Uniform Resource Locator (URL) is the basis for locating resources in WWW. A URL consists of a string of characters that uniquely identifies a resource. A user can connect to resources by typing the URL in a browser window or by clicking on a hyperlink that implicitly invokes a URL. Perhaps the best way to explain URLs is through an example. Let us look at the URL "http://cs.um.edu/faculty.html" shown in Figure 2-3. The "http" in the URL tells the server that an HTTP request is being initiated (if you substitute http with ftp, then an FTP session is initiated). The "cs.um.edu" is the name of the machine running the Web server (this is actually the domain name used by the Internet to locate machines on the Internet). The "/faculty.html" is the name of a file on the machine cs.um.edu. The "html" suffix indicates that this is an HTML file. When this URL is clicked or typed, the browser initiates a connection to the "cs.um.edu" machine and initiates a "Get" request for the "faculty.html" file. Depending on the type of browser you are using, you can see these requests flying around in an appropriate window spot. Eventually, this document is fetched, transferred to the Web browser and displayed. You can access any information through the Web by issuing a URL (directly or indirectly). As we will see later, the Web search tools return a bunch of URLs in response to a search query. The general format of URL is:

protocol://host:port/path

where

protocol represents the protocol to retrieve or send information. Examples of valid protocols are HTTP, FTP, Telnet, Gopher, and NNTP (Network News Transfer Protocol).

host is the computer host on which the resource resides

port is an optional port number (this is not needed unless you want to override the HTTP default port, port 80)

path is an identification, typically a file name, on the computer host.

Hypertext Markup Language (HTML) is an easy-to-use language that tags the text files for display at Web browsers. HTML also helps in creation of hypertext links, usually called hyperlinks, which provide a path from one document to another. The hyperlinks contain URLs for the needed resources. The main purpose of HTML is to allow users to flip through Web documents in a manner similar to flipping through a book, magazine or a catalog. The Web site "cs.um.edu" shown in Figure 2-3 contains two HTML documents: "faculty.html" and "courses.html". HTML documents can imbed text, images, audio, and video. We will discuss HTML in more detail in Section 2.5.

Hypertext Transfer Protocol (HTTP) is an application-level protocol designed for Web users. It is intended for collaborative, distributed, hypermedia information systems. HTTP uses an extremely simple request/response model that establishes connection with the Web server specified in the URL, retrieves the needed document, and closes the connection. Once the document has been transferred to your Web browser, then the browser takes over. Keep in mind that every time you click on a hyperlink, you are initiating an HTTP session to transfer the needed information to your browser. The Web users shown in Figure 2-3 access the information stored in the two servers by using the HTTP protocol. We will discuss more details of HTTP in Section 2.3.

Web navigation and search services are used to search and surf the vast resources available over the "cyberspace". The term, cyberspace, as stated previously, was first introduced through a science fiction book by [Gibson 1984] but currently refers to the computer-mediated experiences for visualization, communication, and browser/decision support. The general search paradigm used is that each search service contains an index of information available on Web sites. This index is almost always created and updated by "spiders" that crawl around the Web sites chasing hyperlinks for different pieces of information. Search engines support keyword and/or subject-oriented browsing through the index. The result of this browsing is a "hit list" of hyperlinks (URLs) that the user can click on to access the needed information. For example, the Web users in Figure 2-3 can issue a keyword search, say by using a search service for shoe stores in Chicago. This will return a hit list of potential shoe stores that are Web content providers. You, then, point and click until you find a shoe store of your choice. Many search services are currently available on the Web. Examples are Yahoo, Lycos and Alta Vista. At present, many of these tools are being integrated with Web pages and Web browsers. For example, the Netscape Browser automatically invokes the Netscape home page that displays search tools that you can invoke by just pointing and clicking. It is beyond the scope of this book to describe the various Web navigation and search tools. Many books on Internet describe these search tools quite well. For example, the book by [December 1995] has an extensive discussion of Web search and navigation tools with information about how to locate and use them.

Gateways to non-Web resources are used to bridge the gap between Web browsers and the corporate applications and databases. Web gateways are used for accessing information from heterogeneous data sources (e.g., relational databases, indexed files and legacy information sources) and can be used to handle almost anything that is not designed with an HTML interface. The basic issue is that the Web browsers can display HTML information. These gateways are used to access non-HTML information and convert it to HTML format for display at a Web browser. The gateway programs typically run on Web sites and are invoked by the Web servers. At present, Common Gateway Interface (CGI) is used frequently. We will discuss CGI gateways and other types of Web gateways later in this chapter. "Relational gateways" that provide access to relational databases from Web browsers are an area of active work. We will discuss relational gateways in Section 2.8.

2.4.3 A Simple Example

Figure 2-4 illustrates how the Web components can be used for purchasing from a department store, "Clothes.com". This store wants to advertise its products on the Web, (i.e., wants to be a Web content provider). The store first designates a machine, or buys services on a machine, called "clothes.com" as a Web site. It then creates an overview document, "overview.html", that tells the potential customers of the product highlights (think of this as the first few pages of a catalog). In addition, several HTML documents on the Web site for different types of clothes (men.html, women. html, kids.html) are created with pictures of clothes, size information etc. (once again think of this as a catalog). We can assume that the overview page has hyperlinks to the other documents (as a matter of fact, it could have hyperlinks to other branches of Clothes.com). In reality, design of the Web pages would require a richer, deeper tree structure design as well as sequential links for alphabetical and keyword searches needed to support the "flipping through" the catalog behavior.

Once HTML documents have been created on the Web server, an Internet user can browse through them as if he/she is flipping through a catalog. The customers typically supply the URL, directly or indirectly, for the overview (http://clothes.com/overview.html) and then use the hyperlinks to look at different types of clothes. Experienced customers may go directly to the type of clothes needed (e.g., men may directly go to the "men.html" document). As shown in Figure 2-4, the URL consists of three components: the protocol (http), the Web server name (clothes.com), and the needed document (overview.html). HTTP provides the transfer of information between the Web users (the clients) and the Web Servers.

At first, clothes.com is only using Web to store an electronic catalog. After a customer has browsed through the catalog and has selected an item, he/she calls the store and places an order. Let us say that clothes.com also wants the customers to purchase the items over the Internet. In this case, a "Purchasing Gateway" software is developed and installed at the Web site. This gateway program gets into action when a user clicks on the "purchase" button on his screen. It prompts the user with a form (HTML supports forms) that the user fills out. The gateway program uses this form information to interact with a purchasing system that processes the purchase (see Figure 2-4). The purchasing system can be an existing system that is used for traditional purchasing. The role of the gateway is to provide a Web interface to the purchasing system. We will discuss gateways later in this chapter.

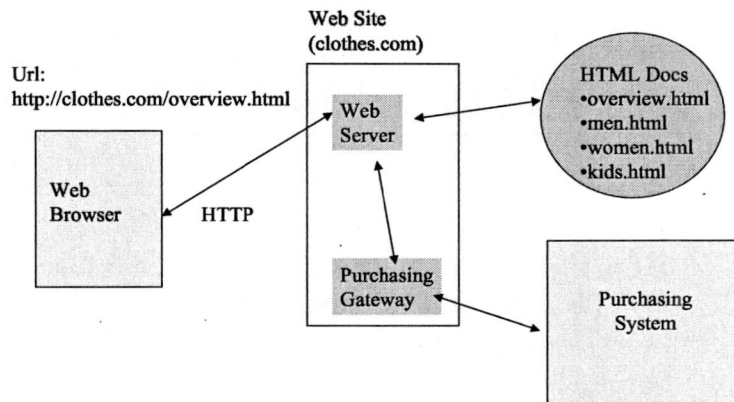

Figure 2-4: Conceptual View of an Internet-based Purchasing System

2.4.4 Evolution of Web Technologies – The Next Generation Web

First Generation Web, needless to say, gained popularity due to its simplicity and ease of use. However, the use of this technology has spread far beyond the initial design goals and imagination of the designers. Thus, some limitations of the initial Web technologies have started to show. In particular, the following limitations are worth noting:

- Suited for human viewing only. The HTML documents can be only used for displays. However, in some cases, the consumer is not a human. For example, if you send an HTML document to a machine, then the machine has to "screen scrape" all the tags to get useful data. This is a major problem in EB because many C2B and B2B operations involve machine-to-machine communications.
- Desktop display oriented. The original Web browser assumed a desktop display. However, the new breed of users want to access and display Web information on Palm Pilots and cellular phones.
- Technical limitations. The first generation Web suffers from many technical problems. For example, the technology for Web gateways (CGI – Common Gateway Interface) does not scale well (i.e., is not suitable for a hundred or more users simultaneously). In addition, the original HTTP was stateless (i.e., you could not keep track of a conversation state during a browsel and drill down application).

The WWW Consortium (known as W3C) has embarked work in several directions to overcome these and other possible limitations. This work, under the general umbrella of Next generation Web, includes the following key developments (see Figure 2-5). :

- XML (Extended Markup Language). Family of standards and services introduced to improve machine-to-machine communications. We will study XML in Section 2.11.
- Variations of markup languages such as HTML, MathML, SVGML, SMIL, etc. for different applications.
- Improvements in the core technologies such as improvement of HTTP and also introduction of more choices for Web gateways.
- Web automation efforts that introduce an object model for Web. These efforts include DOM, RDF, PICS, P3P and others. We will study these technologies in Section 2.12.

It can be seen from Figure 2-5. that XML is at the core of Next Generation Web. An immediate result of this activity is the Semantic Web, discussed in Section 2.12.

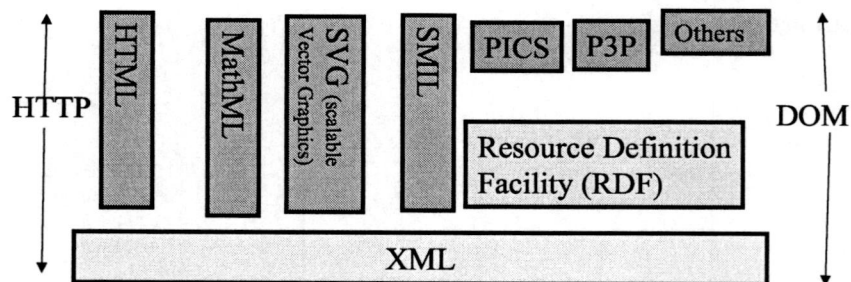

PICS: Platform for Internet Content Specification
P3P: Platform for privacy preferences
SMIL: Synchronous Multimedia Interaction Language
DOM: Document Object Model

Figure 2-5: Next Generation Web

Time to Take a Break
✓• Internet and Web
• Web Technologies
• XML and the Semantic Web
• Web Services

Suggested Review Questions Before Proceeding

▪ Is Web the same as the Internet? Why and why not?
▪ What are the five core Web technologies and what do they do? Explain through an example of a Web site such as Amazon.com.
▪ How has Web evolved? List the main steps and the main developments in each step.

2.5   Hypertext Markup Language (HTML)

HTML prepares the media type that the Web browsers understand. HTML is a cross-platform documentation language -- any computer equipped with a Web browser can read and display your document. HTML is based on the Standard Generalized Markup Language (SGML) that was developed at IBM to make documents readable across a variety of computing platforms. HTML documents are not WYSIWYG (what you see is what you get). You create an HTML document as an ASCII text file by using HTML markup tags (see the sidebar on HTML example). HTML tags are used to indicate headings, italics, bolds, ordered lists, and places where graphics, sound bites, and other pieces of information can be located in the document.

A Simple HTML Example

Suppose you wanted to create a simple home page that looks like the following:

Consulting Group1

Welcome to our consulting group. By using this home page, you can do the following:
▪ Read about our services
▪ Access home pages of our business partners (IBM and Microsoft)

Now choose the connections by pointing and clicking to the following hotlinks:

Our services

IBM Information

Microsoft Information

The following HTML statements can be used to design this home page (we have inserted appropriate URL's for the hot links):

```
<HTML>

<TITLE>Consulting Group1 </TITLE>

<H1>Consulting Group1 </H1>

<P> Welcome to our consulting group. By using this home page, you can do the following:

<UL>

<LI> Read about our services.

<LI> Access home pages of our business partners (IBM and Microsoft)

</UL>

<P> Now choose the connections by pointing and clicking to the following hotlinks:

<a href="http://www.myserver.com/services.html"> Our services</a>

<a href="http://www.IBM.com"> IBM Information </a>

<a href="http://www.microsoft.com"> Microsoft Information </a>

</HTML>
```

Hypertext and hypermedia are at the core of HTML and WWW. A hypertext is a series of documents, each of which displays at least one visible link on the screen, called a hypertext link, to another document in the set. Hypermedia extends hypertext in two ways: it incorporates multimedia into hypertext documents, and it allows graphic, audio and video elements to become links to other documents or multimedia elements. In other words, hypermedia allows you to link multimedia elements by providing multimedia links (i.e., you can click on a graphic instead of just a text link).

What makes HTML and WWW unique is that it makes hypermedia, as defined by the Dexter Model [Halasz 1994], available on the Internet in what has evolved into a powerful global information system. The Dexter Model for multimedia is a result of a multimedia designer's workshop held at the Dexter Inn in Sunapee, New Hampshire, in October 1988. Over subsequent meetings, the "Dexter Group" developed a data and process model that could act as a reference standard against which new hypertext systems could be analyzed, evaluated, and compared. The Dexter Model is considered the foundation of HTML.

For our purpose we need to concentrate on the "hotlinks" that are the main distinguishing feature of hypertext, hypermedia and HTML. These hotlinks are hyperlinks (i.e., hypertext or hypermedia links) that provide a path from one document to another. HTML provides tags so that you can create these hyperlinks anywhere in your document. The hyperlinks are highlighted (usually in color and underlined) when displayed by the Web browsers. Use of HTML allows you to browse through Web documents in a manner similar to, but more powerful than, browsing through a library -- you click on the hotlink and get access to the needed page/document that may be located anywhere on the Web. For example, suppose that you are browsing an "HTML--ized" article that describes various communications products where each product reviewed has a hyperlink to the vendor page. Then, you can directly access additional information about chosen products by simply pointing and clicking. By using hyperlinks, you can start with a home page in Chicago and the next page you read is from New York City and the next from England. The hyperlinks use the URL to locate information. Each click to a hyperlink initiates an HTTP session (connect, request, response, close).

The following sidebar lists the common HTML tags.

Common HTML Tags

```
<H1> Heading </H1>
<P>
<UL>
<LI>
</UL>
<a href="http://www.w3.org"> WWW Information</a>

<IMG SRC="img001.gif" WIDTH=480 HEIGHT=360>

<APPLET CODE=myapplet.class WIDTH=110 HEIGHT=100>
</APPLET>
```

- — Imbeds a Java applet (myapplet) in HTML page

- — The applet code has to reside on the same server as HTML pages

```
<FORM ACTION="/cgi.bin/viewguery"
```

- — Invokes a cgi program (viewguery) on the server

- — cgi programs are typically written in scripting languages (e.g., PERL) but can be written in any language (C, C++, Java)

HTML capabilities include basic features as well as "fill-in forms" for sending search arguments, comments and other pieces of information (e.g., credit card numbers, telephones, and addresses) to the Web servers. The basic features describe how to use the HTML tags to define titles, lists, paragraphs, image placements and the like. The simple HTML example shown in the sidebar illustrates many of these features. The fill-in form capabilities are provided by the FORM statement. FORM is an HTML construct that has been used for developing Web gateways to corporate information systems and relational databases. Basically, a FORM contains some fields where the user enters data in a structured way, a button to submit the form (which simulates submitting a form similar to the real world), and a button to clear the user's input so that the form can be used again. The browser uses the FORM statement to construct a URL and data that is sent to the Web server. The Web server passes this information to a script that performs the needed operations and returns the results back to the client.

A FORM is implemented as follows in HTML:

```
<FORM ACTION="URL" METHOD=GET | POST >
<INPUT TYPE="TEXT"  NAME ="Keyword1" SIZE = "length" <P>
<INPUT TYPE="TEXT"  NAME ="Keyword2" SIZE = "length" <P>

 .....

 .....

<INPUT TYPE="SUBMIT"  VALUE="Submit your form"> <P>
<INPUT TYPE="RESET"  VALUE="Reset your form"> <P>
</FORM>
```

The METHOD keyword specifies the HTTP method to be used to submit the form information to the server. METHOD uses two arguments, GET (this sends the form data as part of URL) and POST (this sends the form data as a separate message to the Web server). Most browsers at present use POST because it is more efficient. The ACTION keyword specifies the URL to which the form data will be sent. This URL is typically a link to an executable script or binary file that can be used as a gateway program. The INPUT statements are used to receive different types of inputs such as text (TYPE = "TEXT"), pressing of submit button (TYPE = "SUBMIT") and clearing of typed inputs (TYPE = "RESET"). Typically a series of TYPE = "TEXT" statements are used to receive customer inputs and assign names to the form input fields (these fields are used by the processing scripts). The following HTML page illustrates a simple form that allows a user to type in a 30 byte long query and push a submit button after typing the statement (the statements are processed by a gateway process "/cgi.bin/userquery"):

```
<TITLE> User Query </TITLE>
<HI> User Query </HI>
Please enter your query:
<FORM METHOD=POST   ACTION="/cgi.bin/userquery"
Enter your query:  <INPUT TYPE = 'TEXT' NAME="query" SIZE "30" <P>
 <INPUT TYPE="SUBMIT"   VALUE="Submit your form"> <P>
 </FORM>
```

Due to the popularity of Web, many new tags and parameters keep appearing in HTML. Like many other active areas in computing, HTML standards lag implementations. There are differences between approved standards, proposed standards and vendor extensions. It seems that every vendor browser introduces a few new twists to HTML. Although browsers usually skip the unrecognized tags, this creates problems for content developers because they have to test their Web pages against a bevy of browsers to make sure that the material developed looks acceptable on different browsers.

Although HTML documents can be developed by using any ASCII text editor, special purpose "HTML editors" are commercially available to assist users in building HTML documents. These editors automatically place HTML tags in the document by simply pointing and clicking icons from the toolbars. Examples of such editors are the Microsoft Internet Assistant for Word, Quarterdeck's Webauthor, HTML Assistant, HTML Editor, etc. In addition, filters are commercially available that convert documents created in popular word processors (e.g., Frame Maker, Microsoft Word, Word Perfect, Latex) to HTML. For example, you can create a document in Microsoft Word and just save HTML or "Web page" – the filters automatically convert from Word to HTML.

It is not our purpose here to give a complete tutorial on HTML. Many books do this quite well. HTML standards and proposals are being promulgated by the World Wide Web Consortium (http://w3.org/) and independent extensions are being proposed by companies such as Netscape Corporation (http://www.netscape.com/).

2.6 Web Browsers

2.6.1 Overview

Web browsers are the end user interface to the Web servers. These browsers, also known as Web clients, typically reside on PCs, Macs and UNIX workstations. From an end users' point of view, the browsers give a GUI and easy to use view of the Internet and provide pull down/pop up menus and buttons for accessing remote servers, scrolling through documents, printing results, downloading code, saving retrieved documents on your local disk, performing searches, and surfing the net. Many browsers have been introduced since 1990. Examples are the Microsoft Internet Explorer, NCSA X-Mosaic, NCSA Mosaic for Windows, Netscape Navigator, Spyglass, Air Mosaic, Win-Tapestry, and Web-Explorer. However, the Microsoft Internet Explorer and Netscape Navigator are most commonly used at present.

Many popular browsers, such as the Netscape Navigator and the Microsoft Internet Explorer run on most platforms (PCs, Macs, UNIX). This is one of the many reasons for the popularity of WWW in the corporate world. While in the past a library system or a customer information system could have been developed by using a specially designed user interface, it seems much more natural for organizations today to use Web browsers for user interfaces. By using the Web browsers, users residing on different machines can use the same browser to interact with the corporate systems. The same browser can also allow the users to use Web for document searches. This makes WWW unique in that it makes hypermedia a key enabler of business as well as non-business information that is becoming available through the Internet and Intranets.

2.6.2 Highlights of Browser Capabilities

Web browsers are designed to display information in HTML format and communicate with the Web servers through HTTP. As a matter of fact, you can develop your own browser if you provide the following two capabilities:

- HTML compliance, i.e., display information on the screen as specified by HTML tags.
- HTTP compliance, i.e., generate HTTP commands to connect to the Web server, initiate needed operations whenever a user clicks on a hyperlink, and receive/interpret the responses.

Web browsers can access resources located in Web servers, FTP servers, Telnet servers, Gopher servers, News server servers, and distributed object servers through CORBA, etc. (see).

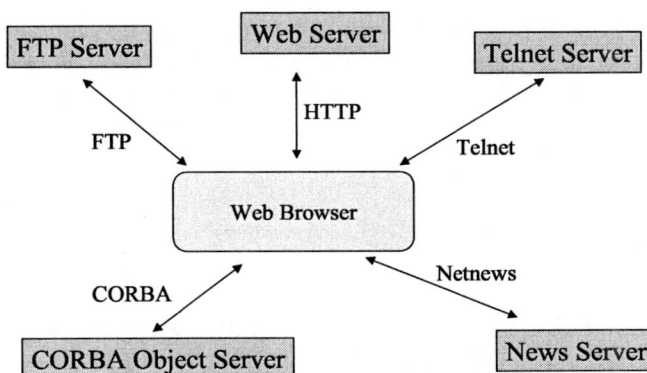

Figure 2-7: Web Browser Interfaces

Two main functions of a browser, as mentioned previously are a): browser request handling that consists of sending HTTP get, put, and post commands to the Web server and b) browser response handling that involves HTML tag processing, applet invocation, and interpretation of HTTP headers. Additional highlights of browser capabilities are:

- Browsers cache information to avoid reloading. The cache can be bypassed by hitting "Reload" button on the browser.
- Browsers can be configured for different fonts, colors, physical appearance, security features and language preferences. For example, browsers can send "accept-language: French" to server for a response in French.
- Helper applications for different (non-HTML) media types (e.g., word, PDF, postscript, etc) are commercially available. Helper applications are represented as MIME (Multipurpose Internet Mail Extensions) types. MIME is used for multimedia files, thus helper applications are treated as different types of multimedia instead of extending the browser to incorporate specific helper application processing.
- Browser security involves establishing an SSL session and also many options to process files. However, Java security is the main concern.

2.6.3 Browsers as Web Clients

Let us look at browsers as Web clients. The two basic functions of a Web client are:

- Navigation to facilitate the travel through cyberspace from one resource to another.
- Browsing to facilitate the perusal of information located by the navigator.

At present, these two functions have been tightly integrated and are commonly referred to as browsers or navigators. Well-designed browsers make Web browsing an enjoyable experience but ill-conceived browsers can result in irritation and frustration. We will refer to Web browsers to include browsing as well as navigation capabilities. Commercially available browsers provide a wide range of features such as the following:
- Compliance
- Performance
- Reconfigurability
- Integration
- Navigation aids

Compliance is related to the degree to which the operational characteristics of the client match the expectations of the connecting server. This reduces to compliance with HTTP and HTML. HTTP compliance is absolutely essential. Most HTTP protocols at present work over TCP/IP. HTTP connectivity may also be needed over other networks in addition to TCP/IP. It is also important to support secure HTTP communications for security reasons. This can be achieved by using Secure HTTP protocol or Secure Socket Layer (you should browse the Internet for extensive information on S-HTTP and SSL). HTML compliance is needed because different versions of HTML exist (HTML 0, 1, 2, and 3) and extensions to HTML from Netscape exist in the industry. Many developers at present are using HTML version 3). In addition to HTTP and HTML, the browsers should be able to connect to popular environments such as Gopher, WAIS, FTP, and email. Proxy client support may also be needed to enable a client to behave as an intermediate server to gain passage through security firewalls.

Performance is an extremely important aspect of navigators/browsers. The limited bandwidth of many Internet communications and the lengthy load times for multimedia resources make client performance crucial. Many Web products use caching to boost performance. Caching retains visited documents or pages at the local host to reduce slow reloads over the Internet. Caching can exist for the session duration (called soft caching) or can be transferred to hard disk (hard caching). Clients may use multi-threading to keep multiple, concurrent Web sessions to improve performance. Web browsers also include special features for document loading (e.g., load abort, enhanced transfer modes, incremental graphics loading).

Reconfigurability is the ability to change the look-and-feel of the Web client to satisfy client-site and/or user needs. For example, you can include user-defined default home pages so that your own home pages appear instead of the vendor home page (e.g., Netscape home page is shown by default whenever you use the Netscape browser but this can be reconfigured). Other configurability options may include font and color changes. Different reconfigurability options are provided by different browsers/navigators. Most of the client software is reconfigured by using menu-driven options.

Integration of the Web client software with the host desktop (i.e., the machine where the Web client resides) may become an important area of future development. For example, you should be able to seamlessly integrate graphics viewers such as GIF (Graphical Interchange Format), multimedia, and audio formats with the search capabilities. In addition, external search engines such as spiders and worms should be integrated with the browsers.

Navigation aids help to reduce the processing time of navigation. The basic problem is that the hyperlinks do not scale well (i.e., if you have to access hundreds of resources over the Internet, then it is difficult to keep track of this information). To aid navigation, "cyberlogs" are used by the Web clients to keep track of recently accessed resources. Cyberlogs keep information by document names instead of URLs and are created during navigation for subsequent displays. Cyberlog entries can be reloaded by pointing and clicking. In addition to cyberlogs, navigators/browsers provide hotlists and bookmarks that are generated by the users when needed. For example, if you access a resource frequently, then you can add it to your hotlist/bookmark for future reference. However, hotlists/bookmarks and cyberlogs do not scale well either (they become awkward after about 100 entries). The scalability problem can be solved by providing multiply nested folders or multiple hotlists.

Current browsers provide many of the features discussed above, For example, Netscape Navigator and Microsoft Internet Explorer bring Web exploring, secure email, newsgroups, chat, and FTP capabilities together in an integrated package. These browsers provide a platform for live online applications, supporting Live Objects and other interactive multimedia content such as Java applets, frames, inline plug-ins, bookmark features, GIF animation, FTP upload, Progressive JPEG support, and support for multiple simultaneous streaming of video, audio, and other data formats.

Additional Web Protocols

– Internet Protocol version 6 (IPv6) is expected to accommodate Internet's growth, boost the real-time multimedia capabilities over the Internet, and provide added security. IPv6 is designed to run well on high bandwidth networks such as ATM. It is also expected to run efficiently on low bandwidth networks such as wireless.

– Virtual Reality Modeling Language (VRML) is used by newer multimedia applications over the Internet.

– Internet Relay Chat (IRC) and Multi-user Object Oriented (MOO) systems are popular for socializing and gaming.

2.7   Web Sites and Web Servers

2.7.1 Overview

A Web site provides the content of the World Wide Web. Having the Web without the Web sites is like having a TV without any TV stations. The growing number of Web sites containing a wide range of information (known as "resources") that can be accessed transparently by Web users is the main strength of WWW. Examples of the Web sites at present are corporate Web sites, university Web sites, publishing/advertising Web sites, travel agency Web sites, and small business Web sites. Web sites can be large (e.g., large corporations may dedicate several machines as Web sites) or small (smaller companies may rent or lease portions of a Web site). Although conceptually, a Web site is a catalog of information for each content provider over the Web, in reality, a Web site consists of three types of components (see Figure 2-8):

- Content files such as the HTML documents
- A Web server (a program) that receives browser calls and accesses contents, and/or
- Gateways that can generate Web content (e.g., generate HTML pages) and provide access to non-Web content (e.g., relational databases).

Many practitioners do not differentiate between Web servers and Web sites. We will attempt to separate Web servers and Web sites by using the following equation:

Web site = Web server + contents + Web gateways

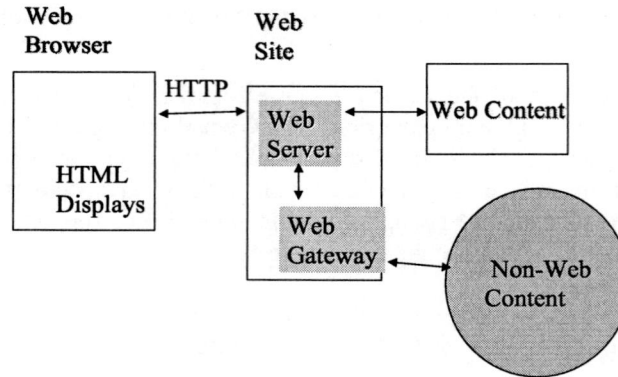

Figure 2-8: A Web Site

2.7.2 Web Server Architectures

A Web server is essentially a scheduler for Web client requests. Specifically, the server software includes schedulers that handle the HTTP calls, (libraries and directories for Web gateways, server configuration files, icons, error and access log files, utility programs, etc.). One of the first, and still popular, server software package, known as the httpd (HTTP Daemon) server, was developed by NCSA (National Center for Supercomputing Applications). Initially developed for UNIX, the NCSA HTTPD server has been ported to other platforms and extended/modified for different environments. A closely related server software is the Windows HTTPD server. Several other servers are also available from vendors such as Netscape, Oracle, and Microsoft. These off-the-shelf servers make it easy to install Web sites.

One server may serve hundreds of clients. To handle the large number of Web clients, Web servers use one of the following approaches [Krishnamurty 2001].

- **Event driven.** The server is a single process that handles requests one at a time. Once the request is completed, then the next request is handled. This architecture can be very slow especially when the Web clients need to access a back-end system. This type of Web servers are usually designed for light workloads and are older.
- **Process-driven.** These servers initiate a separate process per HTTP request (user). Thus each process is completely dedicated to a Web client. This type of server can handle several users simultaneously because each process is independent of the other. The number of processes can increase with number of users. Typically a master process listens for requests and invokes a process, thus the master process acts as a master scheduler.
- **Hybrid architectures.** These architectures combine event-driven and process-driven architectures. For example, each process can use an event driven approach or an event driven process can initiate several threads to handle multiple tasks simultaneously. Most Web servers intended for large scale user communities employ hybrid architectures.

Setting up a Web site involves a large number of issues such as the following:

- Deciding who will develop the Web site, i.e., your own organization or an outside service provider.
- Determining rent versus own issue, i.e., will the site be owned by your organization or will you rent/lease space on an existing Web site (this is called "virtual hosting").
- Choosing a Web site platform, i.e., will the Web server and contents reside on a UNIX or Windows NT platform.
- Choosing a sharing level, i.e., will a machine be dedicated as a Web site or will the Web site software coexist with other software (e.g., LAN software).
- Providing and controlling access to the site, i.e., determine the networking configurations and the security firewalls to be set up.
- Designing the site, i.e., designing home pages, assigning defaults, and server configurations.

- Management and support considerations such as backup/recovery, site security, site administration, hotline support, etc.

2.7.3 Web Server Security

Web servers must be able to enforce security and protect all the resources that are accessed from the Web server (e.g., HTML/XML files and back-end databases and applications that can be accessed through the Web gateways). In particular, the Web server must be able to enforce authentication (are you really Joe?) and authorization (what is Joe authorized to do, i.e., read and/or update a database?).

The main problem in Web security is that HTTP is stateless. Thus each request is a separate "session" that must be authenticated and authorized. To address this problem, a user agent in the browser captures the user ID and password and passes it to server for every request. There are serious security issues in accessing back-end systems from the Web servers. In particular, how to pass the password/ID to multiple back-end systems This is known as single user logon, i.e., a user logs on to a Web server that then logs on to the back-end systems. There are many additional issues in Web security (e.g., role of proxies). For a detailed discussion of Web security, see the two chapters on security in the Management Module.

How to Run Multiple Web Servers on the Same Machine

The issue of running multiple Web servers on a single machine is of interest to many Web hosters. Consider, for example, a Web hoster that wants to provide Web hosting for 2 small businesses (www.joe.com and www.sam.com) on the same machine. A common approach used is to assign multiple IP addresses to the same machine. For example, the hoster could assign 2 IP addresses to one machine and run 2 Web servers on that machine, one for Joe, the for Sam. Thus the requests for www.joe.com and www.sam.com will end up at the same machine because DNS will resolve this domain names to the IP addresses that are on the same machine. The machine operating system will invoke the Joe or Sam server. This approach is fine, but it consumes too many IP addresses. HTTP 1.1 solves this problem by allowing multiple servers on the same IP address. In essence, HTTP 1.1 adds a new header ("host") that can be used to specify multiple hosts on the same site. For details, see the "Web Engineering and XML Processing" chapter in the Tutorials Module.

2.8 Web Gateways: Accessing Non-Web Information

2.8.1 Web Gateway Overview

Web gateways bridge the gap between Web browsers and the corporate applications and databases. These gateways are important because many Web applications at the time of this writing are document browsing applications. There is an urgent need for integration of traditional corporate applications into the World Wide Web. Why? Mainly because most of the corporate data resides in the corporate applications, many of which are legacy applications (The old saying: "why do you rob banks?" The answer: "That is where the money is".). For World Wide Web to truly succeed in the corporate world as the primary user interface to all information, it must provide access to corporate databases and applications.

Web access to corporate databases and applications is a challenging task. A major challenge is that many of the existing applications are stateful (i.e., they keep an ongoing interaction with the user where the answer to one query may depend on how far you are in your conversation). These systems are implemented by using stateful protocols where the meaning of a message depends on previous messages. Unfortunately, Web browsers do not support states (recall that HTTP is a stateless protocol, i.e., it treats each interaction independent of the previous ones). The Web gateways attempt to handle the differences between stateful and stateless protocols by using techniques such as hidden fields in HTML forms that can be used to keep track of states [Schulzrinne 1996]. In addition to handling state translations, Web gateways also generate HTML pages for display at the browsers. For example, if you issue a database query, the Web gateway will format the results of the query to HTML before sending it to the browser. Web gateways can also perform other functions such as accessing and integrating information from heterogeneous data sources.

In general, Web gateways can be used to handle almost anything that is not already adapted to browsers or HTML/XML. At present, the following approaches are commonly used to develop Web gateways:

- Common Gateway Interface (CGI)
- JSP (Java Server Pages)
- Servlets
- Client-side Mobile Code Gateways
- Other gateways such as ASPs

2.8.2 Common Gateway Interface (CGI)

CGI gateways are one of the oldest technologies. A CGI gateway is a program that resides on the Web server. This program can be a script (e.g., a UNIX shell script or a Perl script) or an executable program (e.g., Java, C or C++ programs). After this program has been written, it is prepared for execution by the Web server (this step typically involves placing the gateway program in the /cgi.bin/ directory or other designated library of the server). Hyperlinks to this program can then be included in HTML documents in the same way as hyperlinks to any other resource. For example, if the gateway program is called testgate.pl, the URL for this program is

http://www.myserver.com/cgi.bin/testgate.pl

This URL is included in the HTML page at an appropriate place. For example, we can write the following HTML statement to invoke testgate.pl (Href is used to indicate a hypertex link):

<A Href="http://www.myserver.com/cgi.bin/testgate.pl">

When the user clicks on this hyperlink, the gateway URL is passed to the Web server. The Web server locates the gateway program in the /cgi.bin/ directory and executes it. The output produced by the Gateway program is sent back to the Web browser.

The fundamental difference between a user accessing a regular HTML file and accessing a CGI gateway is that the CGI gateway program is executed on the server to perform some specialized functions instead of just fetching and displaying an existing HTML page. These functions may include creation of HTML pages, if needed (see Figure 2-10).

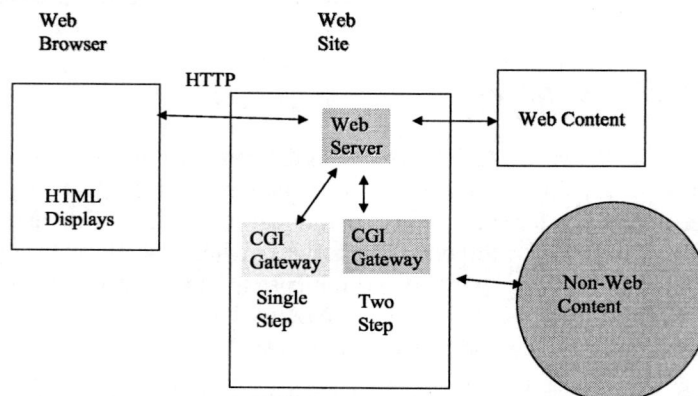

Figure 2-10: CGI Gateways

What type of CGI gateways can be developed? Virtually anything. Examples range from simple time and date retrievals to sophisticated database applications. In general, CGI gateways fall into two categories (see Figure 2-10).:

- Single-Step CGI Gateway - An application program is executed as a CGI executable itself, thereby forking the application process for every request. In this case, the CGI executable contains the application logic invoked by the Web client.
- Two-Step CGI Gateway - An application program runs as a daemon process. A CGI executable just dispatches the request rather than performing any application functions. In this case, the CGI gateway has no business logic and is just used as a dispatcher.

Single-step CGI gateways are typically used for quick and relatively simple functions. The two-step CGI gateways are more useful for large, in many cases, legacy applications. In many cases, two-step CGI gateways are used for connecting existing applications with Web (it is easier to invoke existing programs from CGI scripts than to rewrite them completely as CGI scripts). You may also use a combination, i.e. perform some functions in the CGI executable and then dispatch existing applications where needed. The following example shows a simplified CGI program "viewquery", written in Perl (a scripting language) that issues an SQL query and returns the answers back to the browser.

```
Viewquery: CGI program in Perl:
$perform query =&name
select * from customer where customer-name=&name
/* convert results to HTML */
 echo <HTML>
echo <body>
..
Echo </body>
```

You first put this program in a library "cgi.bin" and then invoke it using a variety of ways. A common approach is to invoke the program by coding it in the action part of an HTML form statement such as the following:

```
<Form Action="/cgi.bin/viewquery"
```

2.8.3 Servlets

Servlets are Java programs that perform the same function as CGI scripts. However, servlets are easier to program and faster to run than CGI. Servlets receive the calls issued by the client (browser), perform some computations, fetch some Web/non-Web content, and generate the response to be sent back to the client. For example, a servlet would receive SQL calls from a Web browser, send the SQL statements to the target databases, receive the results of the SQL query, build HTML pages from the results, and send the results back to the Web browsers. Figure 2-11 shows a conceptual view of servlets.

Basically, servlets are to servers what applets are to browsers. Like applets, servlets cannot run as standalone programs -- they require a container such as the Web server. Servlets are developed by using the Java Servlet API. This API is supported by numerous Web servers including the very popular Apache server. You compile and store the servlet in a specific library (the library name somewhat depends on the Web server) and then invoke it in a manner similar to CGI programs.

2.8.4 Java Server Pages (JSPs)

A JSP is an HTML or XML page that may contain Java code (called JSP elements). Even with no JSP elements, it is a legitimate JSP page (just change the extension, for example, from .html to .jsp and it will display as a normal HTML page). Thus, a JSP page has Java code interspersed with HTML/XML tags. In processing a JSP page, the JSP processor leaves the HTML/XML tags alone and only acts upon the JSP elements. So what are the JSP elements? They are basically Java code (Java expressions and Java statements). The code is evaluated and the results are stored back into the page. Figure 2-12 shows an example of JSP.

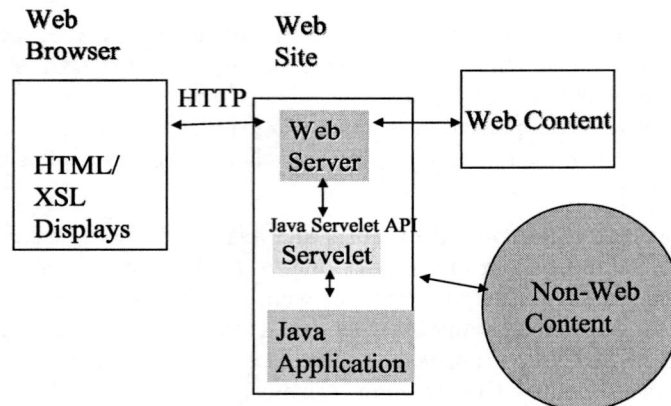

Figure 2-11: Servlets

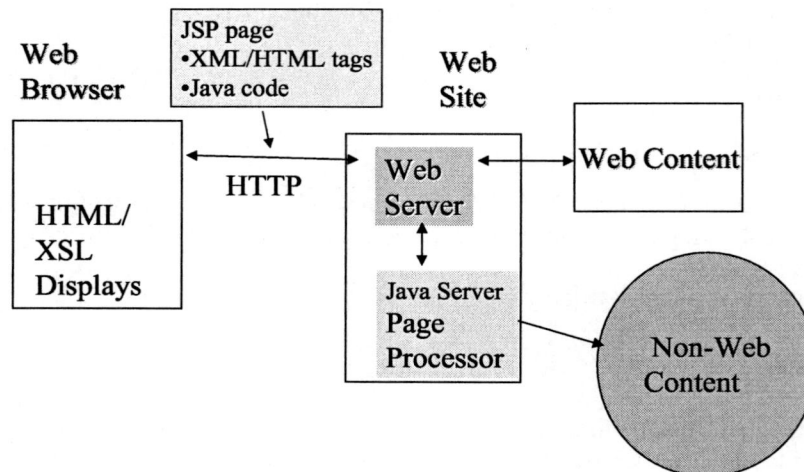

Figure 2-12: Java Server Pages

2.8.5 Client-Side Mobile Code Gateways

The gateways discussed so far operate on the server side. Java applets are changing this. The basic idea is to distribute code of the target application and send it to the Web client where it executes. This approach suits the Java model very well. Java applets, as we will discuss later, can be imbedded in HTML pages and sent to the Web browsers where they execute.

By using this approach, access to remote applications and databases can be invoked directly from the browser. The Java applet can ask the user to issue a query and then send this query to a remote application or database (Figure 2-13). This is especially interesting for database gateways where the database gateway functionality runs on the client side. A standard called JDBC (Java Database Connectivity) is being developed to allow Java programs to issue calls to relational databases.

We should keep in mind that an entire legacy application is difficult to convert into Java applets. However, some aspects of legacy application, perhaps the legacy user interface processing, can be recoded as Java applets and thus used to integrate the legacy applications with WWW.

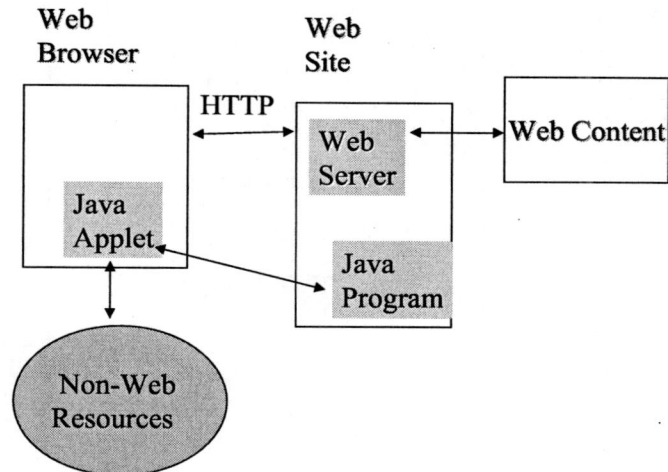

Figure 2-13: A Java-Based Gateway

2.8.6 Other Gateways

We should mention the following gateways also:

- **Active Server Page (ASP) gateways**. These gateways use the Microsoft Active Server Pages (ASPs) and are very similar to the JSPs. Basically, JSPs support Java but ASPs support VBScript.
- **Standalone servers** are dedicated to gateway functionality thus they perform much better than the CGI gateways. Every call received by these servers is assumed to perform gateway functions. For example, a dedicated database gateway would receive SQL calls from a Web browser, send the SQL statements to the target databases, receive the results of the SQL query, build HTML pages from the results, and send the results back to the Web browsers.
- **Legacy Gateways for the Web**. These gateways are dedicated for access to legacy systems and support Web to screen scraping technologies.

2.9 Hypertext Transfer Protocol (HTTP)

The Hypertext Transfer Protocol (HTTP) is at the core of WWW. HTTP is an application-level protocol designed for interactive users who need the lightness and speed necessary for collaborative hypermedia work. Hence, it must accomplish its tasks reasonably fast. HTTP accomplishes this mainly by using an extremely simple model that consists of the following steps (see Figure 2-14):

- Locate - The client finds the server by using DNS (Domain Name Services) that returns the IP address of the Web server for the URL.
- Open - The client establishes a connection with the server that is located at the IP address returned by DNS.
- Transfer that involves a request (the client sends a request message to the server) and a response (the server responds to the client with an answer).
- Close - The closing of the connection by client or server.

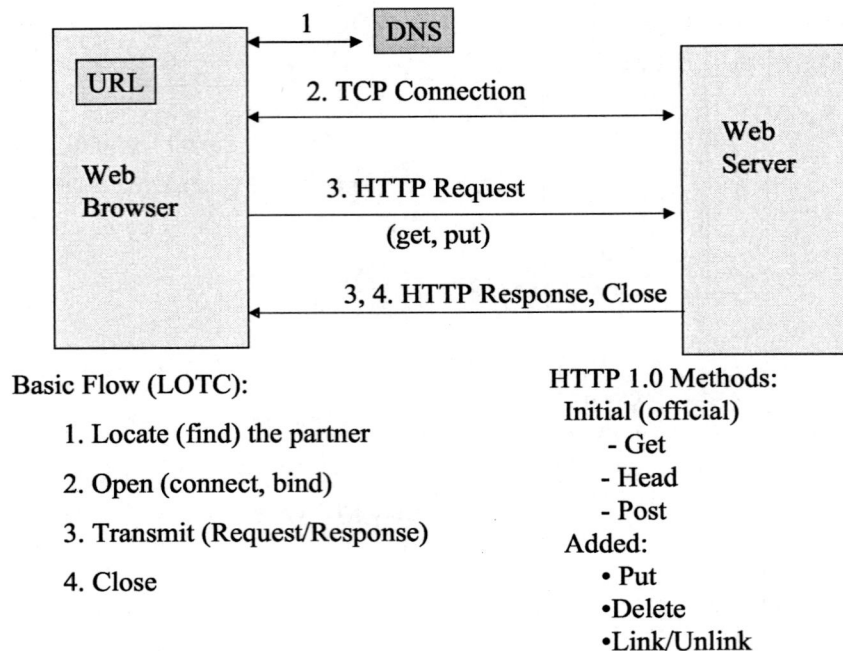

Figure 2-14: A Typical HTTP Session

These LOTC (Locate, Open, Transfer, Close) operations were introduced in the previous chapter. HTTP has gone through several development stages. The first stage (1992-1996) consisted of HTTP/0.9 to HTTP/1.0 developments, the second stage (1996-2001) has saw HTTP/1.0 to HTTP/1.1 developments and the Next Generation HTTP is ongoing work. We first describe HTTP 1.0 to develop the basic conceptual model and then describe HTTP 1.1 to reflect a more recent view. Note that in the following discussion, HTTP refers to HTTP 1.0 (we will explicitly indicate HTTP 1.1). The initial idea of HTTP was to exchange documents for human viewing by using MIME (Multimedia Internet Mail Extensions). The current view is to use HTTP for transport between applications -- this is what Microsoft's Dot Net does.

Information about HTTP is readily available over the Internet. An HTTP Working Group is establishing future directions for HTTP and publishes Internet Drafts to indicate work in progress. Information about HTTP can be found at the WWW Consortium site (www.w3.org).

2.9.1 The Initial Model (HTTP 1.0)

HTTP implements a single interaction consisting of a single request and response pair in a session with a WWW-server. For example, if you need to access a Web page "http://www.sun.com/overview.html", then connect will establish a connection with the Sun Web site "www.sun.com", request will ask for the Web page "overview.html", response will transfer the page to your client, and close will terminate the connection.

HTTP is a stateless protocol, i.e., each connection is handled as a self-contained session (connection, request, response, close is treated as one session). Thus, if you access three different Web documents over the Internet, HTTP treats this as three independent, self-contained, sessions. No information is maintained between these three sessions. This causes some discomforts in developing database applications over the Web because many database applications involve conversational, ongoing interactions that require some state information between sessions.

Let us go through some details (if you are not interested, you can skip the following discussion).

Universal Resource Identifiers (URIs). URLs, discussed earlier, are just one of the names used to designate objects in WWW. The whole family is technically known as universal resource identifiers (URIs), of which URLs name the physical location of objects in WWW. Other main object identifiers in the URI family are universal resource names (URNs) that identify the resource name without regard to location and universal resource citations [URCs) that describe properties of objects. Due to the generality of URI, it is used frequently in the WWW technical documents such as HTTP specifications.

Connection. HTTP is implemented on top of TCP/IP, but it can be implemented on other network stacks. When using TCP/IP, port 80 is the default port for connection, but other non-reserved ports may be specified in the URL. In many cases, you find the Web sites with names such as www.ibm.com, www.bellcore.com, www.transarc.com, www.omg.org, etc. These are not the actual machine names but are convenient aliases (Domain Name Services translates these aliases to physical machine addresses). This allows the companies to designate a general alias name for the outside world and change the physical machines that actually serve as Web servers.

Request. After the requesting program (client) establishes a connection with a receiving program (server), it sends a request to the server. The request message contains the Universal Resource Identifier (URI), a request method, protocol version, request modifiers, client information, and possible body contents. The method is the most important part of this message because it shows the type of operation that needs to be performed. Examples of the methods initially included in HTTP 1.0 are (see Figure 2-14):
- GET - this is most commonly used and indicates that a document needs to be retrieved from the server. This method either retrieves the document specified or a default document. Web servers return a default page if you do not specify a document. For example, if you type a URL (http://www.telcordia.com), then it returns Telcordia's default page). See the side bar "Simple HTTP1.0 GET Request".
- HEAD - this is used just to get meta information (headers) without transferring the entire document. This method is typically used to test hypertext links for validity, recent modifications, and accessibility.
- POST - this method is used for sending messages that can be posted on a bulletin board, newsgroup, or mailing list.

The following methods were added later in HTTP 1.0:
- PUT - this method requests that the enclosed entity be stored on the specified URI. This method is used to transfer documents to the Web server.
- DELETE - this method is used to delete the resources identified in the URI.
- Link/Unlink – these rarely used methods allowed creation of links between URI and other links (these methods were dropped in HTTP1.1 due to their lack of use).

Simple HTTP 1.0 GET Request

GET project.html HTTP 1.0

Response. The server responds, after interpreting the request, with an HTTP response message. The response message consists of a status line (e.g., status codes), server information, meta information, and possible body contents. The server sends the requested information back to the browser in an Internet standard called MIME (Mutipurpose Internet Mail Extension). MIME defines how information other than straight ASCII text is sent between Internet machines. MIME supports exchange of text/HTML, images, video, audio, and application code. The server precedes the returned data with a MIME header containing bits of information, including the content type. The clients (Web browsers) use these headers to interpret the type of information being sent and to display it to the user.

Close. In many cases, the client establishes the connection prior to each request and the server closes the connection after sending the response. However, HTTP does not require this (either client or server can initiate and/or close the connection). HTTP clients and servers must be capable of handling premature connection closing from either side due to time outs, program failures, or user actions. The closing of the connection by either party always terminates the current request, regardless of its status.

Some Comments. HTTP is a generic, stateless and object-oriented protocol which can be used for many different tasks. An important feature of HTTP is the typing and negotiation of data representation at the time of connection (i.e., MIME type requests/response), thus allowing applications to be built independently of the data being transferred. The statelessness and the lightness of HTTP are major advantages of HTTP for retrieving documents. But, this creates serious problems for several applications that require state information. An example of such applications are database applications, applications that maintain a "virtual shopping cart" for a particular visitor, shopping via on-line catalogs, and keeping track of customers who utilize certain Web sites. Different approaches to maintain state have been used such as hidden fields in HTML forms and Netscape "HTTP cookies". In addition to statelessness, HTTP has a few other problems. For example, HTTP is inefficient when you are browsing through a large number of hyperlinks (each time you click on a hyperlink, a separate HTTP session is established). HTTP 1.1 uses a single TCP connection that stays open for several HTTP transfers in certain situations.

As stated previously, HTTP is currently implemented on TCP/IP Sockets because Internet is based on the TCP/IP protocol. The default port is TCP 80, but other ports can be used. However, HTTP can be implemented on top of other protocols on the Internet and other networks. Proposals for making HTTP more generally available have been discussed but not widely implemented.(e.g., support for HTTP on top of Novell LANs and SNA).

2.9.2 New Model – HTTP 1.1

As Web traffic has come to dominate the Internet, remedying the weaknesses of the HTTP protocol has become critical. W3C has worked with the Internet Engineering Task Force (IETF) for refinements to HTTP. This new specification, called HTTP/1.1, has become an IETF Draft Standard.

The focus of the work behind the HTTP/1.1 specification has been to alleviate the most prominent problems in HTTP/1.0 that have led to serious bottlenecks on the Internet. The three main features of interest are as follows[2]:

1) Support for Virtual Hosting. The rapid growth of the Web has produced a frenzy for domain names like mycompany.example.com. Domain names may be infinite in number, but the IP addresses they translate into are not, and IP address depletion has become a serious concern. The HTTP/1.1 **Host header field** allows Web service providers to assign multiple domain names to a single IP address in such a way that a Web server can distinguish the home page for mycompany.example.com from yourcompany.example.com without using more than one IP address.

2) Requests for information handled more efficiently. HTTP uses the Internet TCP/IP protocol stack. To function efficiently, HTTP must take advantage of TCP/IP's strengths and avoid its weaknesses, something that HTTP/1.0 does not do very well. Whenever a client accesses a document, an image, or a sound bite, HTTP/1.0 creates a new TCP connection and as soon as it is done, it is immediately dismissed and never reused. As a result, time and resources are wasted in making/breaking connections.

HTTP/1.1 fixes this in two ways. First, it allows the client to reuse the same TCP connection (**persistent connections**) again and again when talking to the same server. Second, it makes sure that each TCP packet carries as much information as possible (**pipelining**) so that it does not have to run back and forth as much. That is, not only does HTTP/1.1 use less TCP connections, it also makes sure that they are better used. The result is less traffic jam and faster delivery.

3) Efficient Caching. Documents you read on the Web are often read by thousands and even millions of other people at the same time. It is much better to "cache" the needed pages to avoid server accesses. HTTP/1.0 did enable caching, but it did not specify any well-defined rules describing how a cache should interact with clients or with origin servers. A major part of the HTTP/1.1 specification is devoted to

---

[2] This discussion is largely based on the W3C Activity Statement on HTTP 1.1 and other associated documents.

providing a well-defined caching model that allows both servers and clients to control the level of cachability and the conditions under which the cache should update its contents.

4) Digest Authentication. Digest authentication allows users to authenticate themselves to a server without sending their passwords in clear text which can be sniffed by anybody listening on the network. In HTTP/1.0, passwords are sent without being encrypted using so-called basic authentication. Although not providing real security, Digest Authentication is an important step in making the Web a more secure place to live.

The HTTP Extension Framework. A continuing area of interest is how HTTP can be extended according to the needs of specific applications. This Framework provides a simple, yet powerful, mechanism for extending HTTP. The framework enables authors to introduce extensions in a systematic manner. Programmers will be able to specify **which** extensions are introduced along with information about **who** the recipient is, and **how** the recipient should deal with them.

We will take a closer look at HTTP in the chapter "Web Engineering and XML Processing -- A Closer Look" in the Tutorials Module. A great deal of information about HTTP can be found in the book "Web Protocols and Practice: HTTP/1.1, Networking Protocols, Caching, and Traffic Measurement" by B. Krishnamurthy and J. Rexford, Addison Wesley, 2001.

2.10 Web Cookies and Web Proxies

2.10.1 Cookies

A cookie is a small data item that was introduced to maintain HTTP state by Netscape around 1994. A cookie is created by a Web server and sent to a client (Web browser) as a header. It is used subsequently by the server. The client does not interpret cookies. Cookies are kept in browser memory, then written to a file for future communications. Figure 2-15 shows the basic operations of a cookie. The basic operations of cookies are:

- Client (Web browser) contacts a Web server for some information.
- Server responds but also installs a cookie at the client browser by issuing the command

    set-cookie:customer="joe", path="/cars".

- All future interactions with the client browser have the cookie.

    customer="joe", path="/cars"

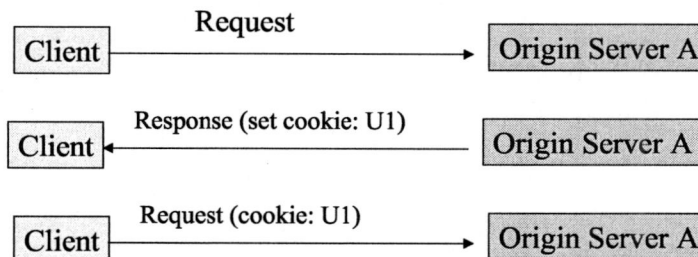

Figure 2-15: Cookies

Technically speaking, the Web server uses the cookies to maintain a session with the browser by noting the pages that the browser has visited. Naturally, this has raised several privacy issues because cookies can tell what Web pages have you visited, how long did you visit them, etc.

Users, however, can control cookies. They can decide to have no cookies, accept cookies from specific sites only, or for a specific session only. There are some tradeoffs involved in these decisions. For example, if a client decides not to have a cookie, then the server may not be able to maintain a session with the client.

Cookies can be client side or server side, although most cookies are client side. For example, the discussion of cookies so far has been on client side. Server side cookies can also be created by a Web server. In this case, a cookie is installed on the server and behaves as the "audit trail". Since the cookie is installed and runs on the server, the clients have no control over this cookie.

The Web site ww.cookiecentral.com has a great deal of information about cookies.

2.10.2 Web Proxies

Proxies sit between clients and servers and act as "standins". For example, a proxy acts as a server to a client and vice versa (see Figure 2-16). Proxies can be used for security, workload balance, etc. Proxy servers are commonly found in Web environments. A proxy server is essentially an intermediate program that behaves as a server but in fact passes the requests to real server(s). In effect, it is a fake server. In most practical cases, the proxy server receives the client calls, does some processing (typically security checking) and then, itself, becomes a client to other servers. Why would anyone want to use proxies? A proxy can:

- Act on behalf of a server to provide anonymity to clients or servers.
- Be a front-end to many clients, i.e., instead of handling calls from all clients, the Web server handles calls from the proxy that is front-ending many clients.
- Handle security because it can sit outside a firewall and then pass information to a server inside the firewall. This does introduce security threats because client not authorized for access may use a proxy to fake authorization.
- Translate requests from Web to non-Web by intercepting calls from a remote program and converting them to Web HTTP calls (i.e., serve as a Web gateway).
- Cache the information so that the clients can access a local proxy instead of remote Web servers for information access.
- Do workload balance by routing work to more than one server.
- Filter requests and responses, if needed, between clients and servers.

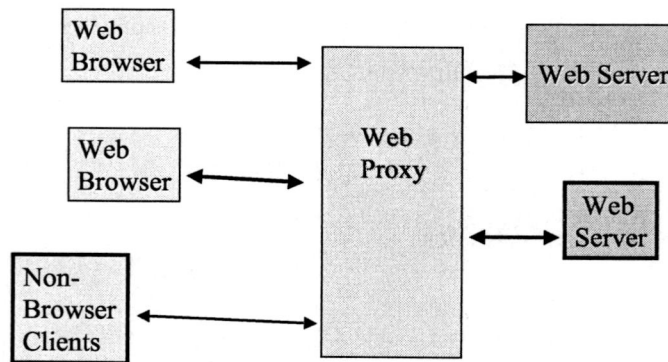

Figure 2-16: Web Proxies

Specific examples of using proxies are:

- A proxy server sits outside the firewall to receive the Public Internet calls, authenticates the clients, and then invokes services inside the firewall for authorized users. In many cases, these proxy servers rewrite packets to hide unneeded information.
- A proxy server, residing on an HTTP server machine, receives Java applet calls (recall that many browsers restrict Java applets to communicate with the HTTP server from where they were loaded) and then establishes connections with remote databases and programs on behalf of the Java applets.

- A proxy server behaves as an application gateway by receiving calls from different clients for different applications and then invoking needed applications.

Figure 2-17 shows how a proxy server is used between a customer and a seller. We are assuming here, for simplicity, that the customers reside entirely on the Public Internet. The Proxy Server sits outside the seller firewall and connects to the seller purchasing system.

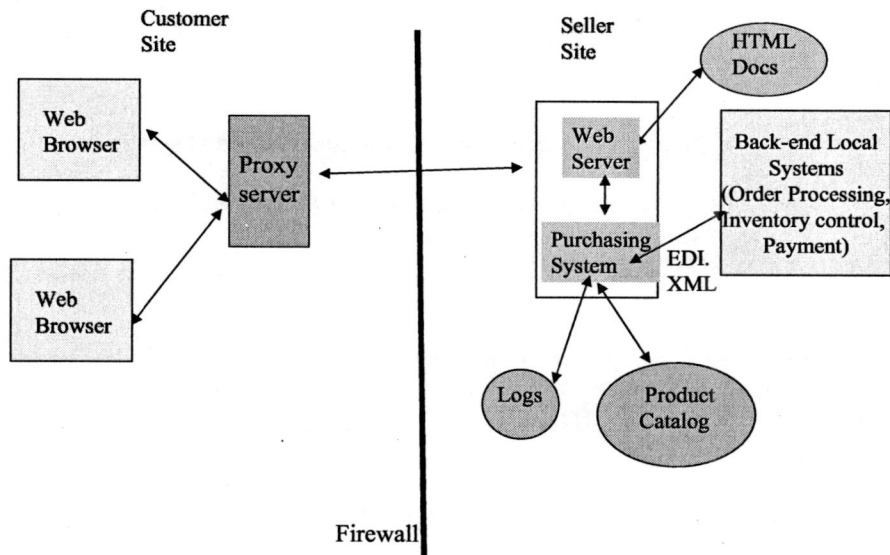

Figure 2-17: A Proxy Server Example

Figure 2-18 shows how proxy servers are used to locate Web servers. The browser uses the URL of the proxy server that responds and establishes a TCP connection to the proxy server through DNS and receives the HTTP request from the browser (steps 1, 2, 3). The main activity is in step 4 where the proxy server once again uses DNS to locate the target Web server. After the connection is made with the Web server (step 5), the proxy server sends the HTTP request received from the Web browser in step 3 to the Web server (step 6). The response is received and also sent back to the browser by the proxy (steps 7 and 8).

As expected, a wide range of proxy design issues need to be addressed:
- Security/privacy – the proxies should not promote/demote clients for their security status (i.e., the client security state must be faithfully carried forward by the proxy).
- Do not promote/demote itself – the proxies must stay at the server level and not assign higher level status.
- Handling large connections – proxies must be able to handle a large number of connections from clients.
- Providing audit trails – proxies must keep good audit trails to support non-repudiation.
- Handling cookies – proxies must know how to handle client as well as server side cookies.

For an extensive discussion of proxy design issues, see the book "Web Protocols and Practice: HTTP/1.1, Networking Protocols, Caching, and Traffic Measurement" by Balachander Krishnamurthy and Jennifer Rexford, Addison Wesley, 2001.

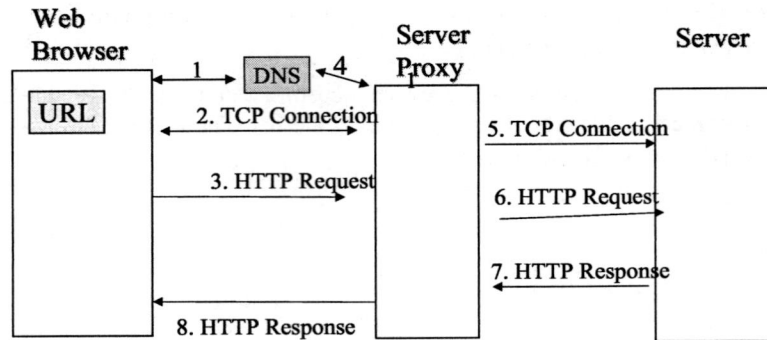

Step 4: The proxy uses DNS to locate the real server

Figure 2-18: How Proxy Servers are Used to Locate Web Servers

Time to Take a Break
- ✓ Internet and Web
- ✓ Web Technologies
- XML and the Semantic Web
- Web Services

Suggested Review Questions Before Proceeding

- What are Web browsers and what are their main functions? Can a browser handle other than html documents? How?
- What is the difference between a Web site and a Web server? What specifically are the functions of a Web Server?
- What are Web gateways and why they are needed? List the main Web gateway technologies and their tradeoffs? Which one is the oldest?
- What does HTTP do? What are the limitations of HTTP?
- What are cookies and why they are needed? What are the issues with cookies and can you get rid of them?
- What are proxies and why they are needed? List some common examples of proxies,

2.11 XML (Extended Markup Language)

2.11.1 What is XML?

XML is a markup language, similar to HTML, for documents containing structured information. The main limitation of HTML is that it only concentrates on presentation (i.e., headers, highlights, etc). If you need to specify, for example, the structure of information (i.e., represent customer name and address), then HTML cannot help. In fact, XML is a simplified version of SGML (Standard Generalized Markup Language) – the first standardized markup language. Unfortunately, SGML is too overbearing to use in tandem with the Web. Thus, XML is a simplified version of SGML and is similar to HTML (in fact, HTML and XML are both simplifications of SGML).

Before going into details, let us quickly show a very simple example of XML. The following statements represent an XML document that contains a customer's name and address:

```
<CUSTOMER>

    <NAME> Joe </NAME>

    <ADDRESS> NY </ADDRESS>

    <AGE> 33 </AGE>

</CUSTOMER>
```

You can see the striking resemblance between HTML and XML, at least at this simple level (i.e., tags in the format <tag> that are terminated by </tag>). As we will see, you can develop XML documents that represent customers, orders, bills, airline schedules, TV programs, bank statements, catalogs, etc by just creating new tags. XML is very popular at present with applications ranging from e-commerce to music.

The term "document" in XML-context refers not only to traditional documents, like articles and books, but also to other XML "data formats" such as e-commerce transactions, mathematical equations, and graphics. XML provides a facility to define tags and the structural relationships between them for documents. There are no preconceived semantics (i.e., meaning) associated with XML because there is no predefined tag set. All of the semantics of an XML document are either defined by the applications that process them or by stylesheets. The XML specification by W3C sets out a set of goals for XML that include ease of use, flexibility, and use over the Internet (see the sidebar "XML Goals"). A great deal of XML activity exists at present in various areas such as Web (new Web browsers support XML), electronic commerce (XML is being considered as a possible replacement for EDI), data management (e.g., XMI, XML Metadata Interchange, used to exchange models between vendor tools), CWM, (Common Warehouse Metadata, for Oracle and other data warehouses), and publishing (XML is often used in place of SGML because of its "lightness").

According to the W3C, XML is intended to:
- Enable internationalized media-independent electronic publishing.
- Allow industries to define platform-independent protocols for the exchange of data, especially the data of electronic commerce.
- Deliver information to user agents in a form that allows automatic processing after receipt.
- Make it easier to develop software to handle specialized information distributed over the Web.
- Make it easy for people to process data using inexpensive software.
- Allow people to display information the way they want it, under style sheet control.
- Make it easier to provide metadata -- data *about* information -- that will help people find information and help information producers and consumers find each other.

The XML Activity (phase 1) was started by the W3C in June 1996. It culminated in the W3C XML 1.0 Specification (issued February 1998, revised Oct 2000). In the second phase, work proceeded in a number of working groups in parallel. In September 1999, W3C began the third phase, continuing the unfinished work from the second phase and introducing a Working Group on XML Query. Since 1996, the work of several W3C working groups and other standards/industrial bodies has resulted in a "family" of XML standards that include (see Figure 2-19):

- Document Type Declarations (DTD) to specify the set of rules for the structure of an XML document. DTDs are used to verify and validate XML documents and are thus central to XML-based e-business exchanges.
- XSL (eXtensible Stylesheet Language) to display information. XSL supports a basic premise of XML – separation of content from presentation. XSL is also useful to translate one XML description to another.
- XML query language to support querying of XML data.
- XML schema to specify the format (e.g., the character lengths) and relationships between XML elements.
- Other developments such as XML Link, XML signature, and XML Path.
- Variants of XML for different application areas. Examples are the Wireless Markup Language (WML), Voice Markup Language (VML), Mathematical Markup Language (MathML), Chemical Markup Language (CML) and others.

We will discuss some of these capabilities of XML in this section. Due to the popularity and growth of XML, W3C has started an XML Coordination Group to coordinate the workflow and dependencies between various working groups. The Group also maintains a liaison inside and outside the W3C and gathers and forwards requests for additional requirements to the appropriate WG(s).

The discussion of XML in this chapter is extremely brief. Our purpose is not to make you an XML expert. Instead, the goal is to give you a quick conceptual overview of XML at a big picture level. Many books on XML are available at bookstores (many more than 800 pages!). The following sidebar on XML Resources lists a few references. For an up-to-date view of XML and its developments, visit the W3C site (www.w3.org).

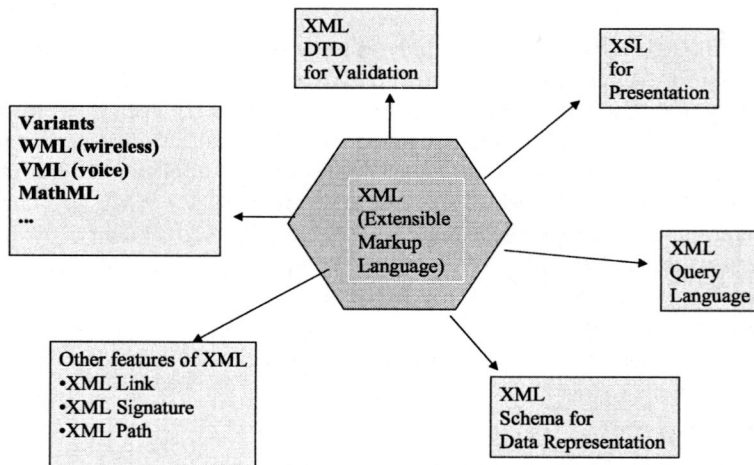

Figure 2-19: The XML Family

XML Resources

Information about XML is growing rapidly. Here is a very small list to get started:
- Extensible Markup Language (XML) 1.0 description at http://www.w3.org/TR/WD-xml.
- www.xml.com, a very useful Web site for a great deal of information about XML.
- ebXML initiative and the XML/EDI group Web sites.

- "Beginning XML", book by David Hunter, Wrox Press, 2000.
- "Xml by Example: Building E-Commerce Applications", Book by Charles F. Goldfarb Series on Open Information Management) by Sean McGrath (Paperback - June 1998).
- "Xml for EDI : Making E-Commerce a Reality" Book by Hussain Chinoy, et al (Paperback - May 2000).
- "Understanding BizTalk", book by John Matranga, et al (Paperback – March 2000).

Goals of XML (as specified by W3C)

1. It shall be straightforward to use XML over the Internet. Users must be able to view XML documents as quickly and easily as HTML documents. In practice, this will only be possible when XML browsers are as robust and widely available as HTML browsers, but the principle remains.

2. XML shall support a wide variety of applications. XML should be beneficial to a wide variety of diverse applications: authoring, browsing, content analysis, etc. Although the initial focus is on serving structured documents over the Web, it is not meant to narrowly define XML.

3. XML shall be compatible with SGML. Most of the people involved in the XML effort come from organizations that have a large, in some cases staggering, amount of material in SGML. XML was designed pragmatically, to be compatible with existing standards while solving the relatively new problem of sending richly structured documents over the Web.

4. It shall be easy to write programs that process XML documents. The colloquial way of expressing this goal while the spec was being developed was that it ought to take about two weeks for a competent computer science graduate student to build a program that can process XML documents.

5. The number of optional features in XML is to be kept to an absolute minimum, ideally zero. Optional features inevitably raise compatibility problems when users want to share documents and sometimes lead to confusion and frustration.

6. XML documents should be human-legible and reasonably clear. If you don't have an XML browser and you've received a hunk of XML from somewhere, you ought to be able to look at it in your favorite text editor and actually figure out what the content means.

7. The XML design should be prepared quickly. Standards efforts are notoriously slow. XML was needed immediately and was developed as quickly as possible.

8. The design of XML shall be formal and concise. In many ways a corollary to rule 4, it essentially means that XML must be expressed in EBNF and must be amenable to modern compiler tools and techniques.
   There are a number of technical reasons why the SGML grammar *cannot* be expressed in EBNF. Writing a proper SGML parser requires handling a variety of rarely used and difficult to parse language features. XML does not.

9. XML documents shall be easy to create. Although there will eventually be sophisticated editors to create and edit XML content, they won't appear immediately. In the interim, it must be possible to create XML documents in other ways: directly in a text editor, with simple shell and Perl scripts, etc.

10. Terseness in XML markup is of minimal importance. Several SGML language features were designed to minimize the amount of typing required to manually key in SGML documents. These features are not supported in XML. From an abstract point of view, these documents are indistinguishable from their more fully specified forms, but supporting these features adds a considerable burden to the SGML parser (or the person writing it, anyway). In addition, most modern editors offer better facilities to define shortcuts when entering text.

2.11.2 A Few XML Details

Let us now go through some details of XML by considering the following XML description.

```
<?xml version="1.0" standalone="yes"?>
< -- customer example -- >
<customer>
        <name>
                <first>Amjad</first>
                <last>Umar</last>
        </name>
        <address>
                <street>MCC-1C337B</street>
                <street>445 South Street</street>
                <city>Morristown</city><state>NJ</state>
                <zip>07960</zip>
        </address>
        <phone>973-829-3114</phone>
</customer>
```

The first statement in XML starts with "<?xml" to indicate an XML document. The XML document consists of elements and sub-elements that define various tags. Each element starts with a <tag> and ends with a </tag>. This example describes the customer element with sub-elements name and phone. The sub-elements of name are first and last, etc. Comments in XML begin with <!-- and end with -->. XML allows definition of optional fields, repeating fields, etc.

XML represents the information as a tree. For example, Figure 2-20 represents the model of the customer information. This model is the foundation of automated processing of XML, as we will see in the discussion of Document Object Model (DOM).

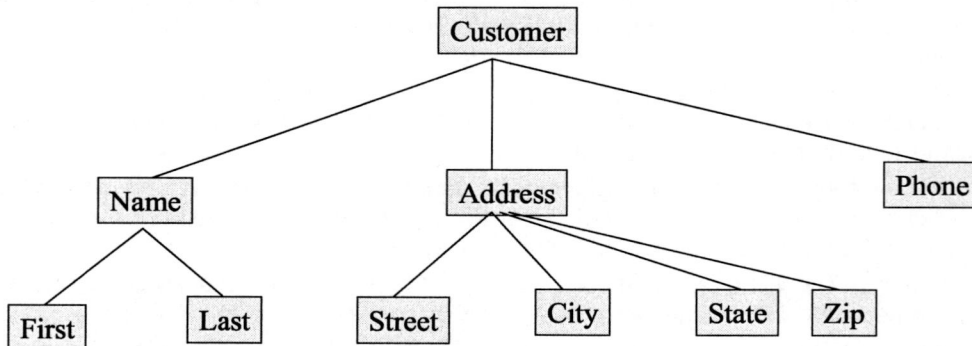

Figure 2-20: Model of Customer

Here is another example of XML – it represents a computer located in Chicago (why not?):

```
<?xml version="1.0" standalone="yes"?>
< -- computer example -- >
<Computer>
<Location city="Chicago">
        <name>
                <Type>Dell</type>
                <ID>IPX-222599</ID>
        </name>
        <Properties>
                <CPU>550 MHZ</CPU>
                <RAM> 56 Meg</RAM>
                <Disk>20 gigabyte </state>
                <Modem>56 Kbps </zip>
        </properties>
        <price>$900</price>
    </Location>
</computer>
```

Once again, the XML syntax uses matching start and end tags, such as `<name>` and `</name>`, to mark up information. A piece of information marked by the presence of tags is called an *element*; elements may be further enriched by attaching name-value pairs (for example, `city="chicago"` in the example above) called *attributes*. Its simple syntax is easy to process by machine, and has the attraction of remaining understandable to humans. XML is based on SGML, and is familiar in look and feel to those accustomed to HTML.

2.11.3 Why XML is So Popular

Although XML is relatively new, it has found applications ranging from e-commerce to music. Here are some examples of where XML is being used:

- **E-Commerce.** XML is being used, of course, in e-commerce for representing the purchase orders and invoices. This is an active area of work with many standards such as Biztalk, Rosettanet and Open Application Group at the forefront.
- **Push technology and Web publishing.** XML is being used to represent the programs (e.g., stocks, news, special offers, events) that the users can subscribe to. The foundation is an XML-based Channel Definition Format (CDF) that describes who subscribes to what (see the Web site www.iechannels.com for a sample).
- **Online banking.** XML is being used to represent financial transactions for online banking. An example is the Open Financial Exchange (OFX) specification. XML documents in OFX specify account information, monthly payments, bank statements, etc.
- **Software distribution.** XML is at the foundation of OSD (Open Software Distribution) specification that allows users to download the software they need, with proper associated and prerequisite software.
- **Web automation.** XML is at the foundation of WIDL (Web Interface Definition Language) to generate programs that can read and react to the Web sites.
- **Scientific publishing.** XML is the foundation of several markup languages for scientific publishing. Examples are the Mathematical Markup Language and Chemical Markup Language.
- **Airline reservation systems.** XML is being used in the airline industry to represent flight information, arrival times, departure times, etc.
- **Music and Theater.** At present, several efforts are underway to use XML to represent some songs (title, singer, year of recording) and also some opera plays (such as Shakespeare's Othello).

Many groups (outside and inside W3C) are defining new formats for information interchange. The number of XML applications is growing rapidly, and the growth appears likely to continue. There are many areas, for example, the healthcare industry, the Inland Revenue, government and finance, where XML applications are used to store and process data.

2.11.4 Document Type Declarations (DTD)

Document Type Declarations (DTD) are an important part of XML. A DTD specifies a set of rules for the structure of the document. For example, the following is a DTD for the customer record defined previously:

```
<!ELEMENT customer (name, address?, phone?)>
<!ATTLIST customer id CDATA #REQUIRED>
<!ELEMENT name (first, middle?, last)>
<!ELEMENT address (street+, city, state, zip)>
<!ELEMENT phone (#PCDATA)>
<!ELEMENT first (#PCDATA)>
<!ELEMENT middle (#PCDATA)>
<!ELEMENT last (#PCDATA)>
<!ELEMENT street (#PCDATA)>
<!ELEMENT city (#PCDATA)>
<!ELEMENT state (#PCDATA)>
<!ELEMENT zip (#PCDATA)>
```

In a DTD, optional fields are suffixed by a "?". For example "address?" and "phone?" indicate that address and phone number are optional, but the name is not. Thus, this DTD will make sure that all XML documents that describe the customer have a name entry. Also, a multi-line entry is suffixed by a "+". (for example "street+" indicates that street address may go over more than one line). The CDATA and PCDATA entries indicate that the element is character data or parsed character data, respectively. CDATA is just string data that is not parsed, while PCDATA is.

We can save this into a file called customer.dtd. DTDs are required in SGML but optional in XML. DTDs are the foundation of well-formed and valid documents:

- A Well-Formed Document adheres to the syntactic rules defined by the XML standard, e.g. Tags are delimited by < and >.
- A Valid Document is a well-formed document that also adheres to the rules of a specified Document Type Definition (DTD).

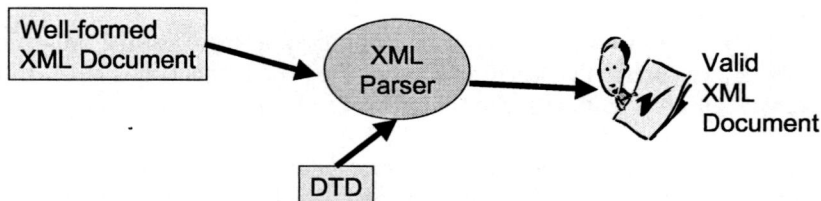

Figure 2-21: The Role of XML

Thus, if you create an XML document without a DTD, then it is well-formed but not valid. By creating a DTD, you make the document well-formed as well as valid because XML parsers compare the document against a DTD to verify if the document adhered to the DTD specifications. In E-commerce, it is always a good idea to define a DTD before creating XML documents.

The following XML definition represents a valid XML document (note that we have specified that this document is not standalone and that customer.dtd is consulted as a DTD):

```
<?xml version="1.0" standalone="no"?>
<!DOCTYPE customer SYSTEM "customer.dtd">
<customer id="12345">
        <name>
                <first>Amjad</first>
                <last>Umar</last>
        </name>
        <address>
                <street>MCC-1C337B</street>
                <street>445 South Street</street>
                <city>Morristown</city><state>NJ</state>
                <zip>07960</zip>
        </address>
        <phone>973-829-3114</phone>
</customer>
```

The following document represents a well-formed but *not* Valid XML document:

```
<?xml version="1.0" standalone="no"?>
<!DOCTYPE customer SYSTEM "customer.dtd">
<foo1 id="12345">
        <foo2>
                <foo3>Amjad</foo3>
                <foo4>Umar</foo4>
        </foo2>
        <foo5>
                <foo6>MCC-1C337B</foo6>
                <foo7>445 South Street</foo7>
```

```
            <foo8>Morristown</foo8><foo9>NJ</foo9>
            <foo10>07960</foo10>
      </foo5>
      <foo11>973-829-3114</foo1>
</foo1>
```

2.11.5 XSL ((XML Stylesheet Language)

XML separates document structure from document display – separation of content from presentation is an important goal of XML. XML supports XSL (eXtensible Stylesheet Language) to display information. XSL is also useful to translate one XML description to another.

The purpose of XSL is to provide a powerful, yet easy-to-use, stylesheet syntax for expressing how XML documents should be rendered. XSL is independent of any one output format -- you can use one XSL stylesheet to format XML for HTML, MS Word documents, or email. In addition, you can create multiple XSL sheets for the same XML document. Figure 2-22 shows this processing.

An XSL stylesheet consists of a set of construction rules that specify how the XML elements will be converted to output. The following XSL statements generate a straightforward HTML document that contains children of the XML customer element.

```
<xsl>
<rule>
<! – pattern to indicate that we want to trigger this rule for element customer – >
<target-element type="customer"/>
<! – Action: generate the HTML document that contains children (sub-elements) of customer – >
<HTML>
          <BODY>
                    <children/>
          </BODY>
</HTML>
</rule>
</xsl>
```

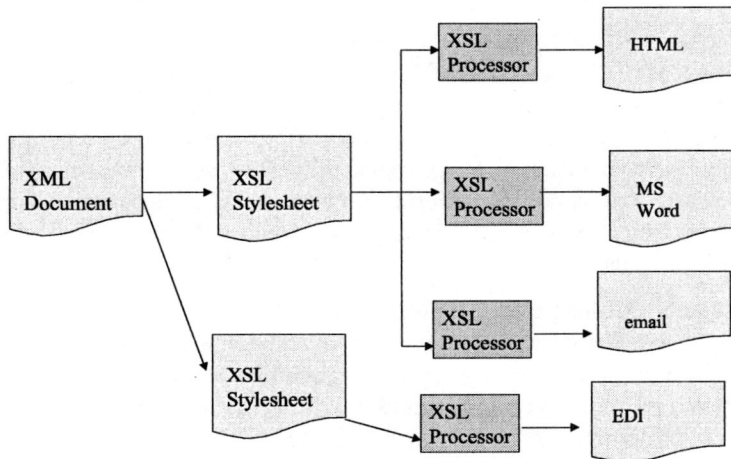

Figure 2-22: XSL Processing .

A wide array of XSLT (XSL Transformation) Processors, such as the following, are commercially available at present:
- Sun's XSLT Compiler creates a Java program that performs the transformation instructions described by a XSLT file.
- XSLTC is an XSLT compiler. It takes as input an XSLT stylesheet, and generates C++ code that is expected to have the same behavior as the source stylesheet.

- <u>LotusXSL</u> is a complete implementation of the W3C Recommendations for XSL Transformations (XSLT) and the XML Path Language (XPath).
- <u>Resin</u> is a servlet/JSP engine with integrated XPath and XSLT support.
- <u>XT</u> from James Clark is a free Java-based implementation of XSLT.

2.11.6 XML Schema

The XML Schema defines the structure, content and semantics of XML documents. How is this different from the Document Type Definition (DTD) that also defines the XML data? XML Schema is more rigorous and comprehensive than DTD. For example (for a detailed technical comparison of XML Schema versus DTDs, see [Hunter 2000]):

- DTD does not specify the attribute lengths while XML Schema does.
- DTDs do not allow inheritance while XML Schema does.
- DTDs support only a few data types while XML Schema supports most.

XML Schema is more comprehensive because it shows how the component parts of an application fit together, the document structure, attributes, data-typing, and so on. However, DTDs are very mature at present while XML schemas are relatively new. Thus, it is envisioned that DTDs will be subsumed by XML Schema.

2.11.7 Other XML Capabilities

XML Query Language. The XML Query working group is trying to provide flexible query facilities to extract data from real and virtual documents on the Web. In addition, several database vendors are trying to support XML directly into their databases. Examples are the Microsoft SQL server 2000 and Oracle Database servers with XSQL servlet support.

XML Namespaces (XMLNS). This specification allows element names to be made unique by adding URL as a prefix. For example, an element named "customer" from a company <u>www.xyzcorp.com</u> becomes <u>www.xyzcorp.com/customer</u>. You would specify XMLNS: ="<u>www.xyzcorp.com/</u>" to assure that the company name is used as a prefix.

Programmed Access to XML: (Simple API for XML -SAX). SAX is an API that allows programmers to read and process XML documents. SAX is event driven, i.e., you can ask for certain events to be raised when something happens while reading the XML document (for example, if an order exceeds $1000). The application program handles the events (i.e., triggers an approval process). Due to this, SAX is quite suitable for extracting and processing small amount of information from the XML documents. The main competition to SAX is the Document Object Model (DOM) that also provides APIs for XML documents. We will discuss this more when we discuss DOM (Section 2.12.4).

Linking XML Documents (XLink: and XPointer). The XML Linking Working Group is defining a standard way to represent links between XML resources. In addition to simple links like HTML's <A> tag, XML has mechanisms for links between multiple resources and links between read-only resources. XPointer describes how to address a resource, XLink describes how to associate two or more resources. These two methods can be used to define links between objects - "external" links, and "internal" links to locations within XML documents.

2.12 The Semantic Web – A Look at the Next Generation of Web

2.12.1 Overview and Motivation

At present, a great deal of information is being advertised by Web sites about the company products, special discounts, business partners, office locations, etc. Consider the situation where you wanted to use the Web to find out how many bookstores offer volume discounts, or what drugstores can fill certain prescriptions, or how many PC stores can repair your laptop in your neighborhood. Your main choice is to sit in front of your Web browser and issue endless queries, review the results manually and then make selections. Anyone who has used a Web search service like AltaVista or HotBot knows that typing in a few keywords and receiving a couple of thousand "hits" is not necessarily very useful. A lot of manual "weeding" of information has to happen after that.

It would be very nice to have an "automated agent" that could go around the Web, do all the work, and return the needed responses. These Web agents, while appealing, are not very easy to implement at present because the Web sites present information to you in a human readable format. So far, the Web is mainly built as a forum for human interaction; because most Web documents are written for human consumption. The only available form of searching on the Web is to simply match words or sentences contained in documents. For example, by just looking at the HTML output, how can a program determine the location of a store. It will have to do "Web scraping", i.e., issue a query to a Web site, store the output received in a local page, search the page for something that *may* sound like a location (e.g., city name). This is where XML and its variants have helped a lot. By using XML elements, the advertisers can define a tag "location" that can be used by agents to search and retrieve Web data. The benefits of structured Web data are not limited to intelligent personal agents. In fact, B2B trade can be greatly improved through automated programs that read, interpret, and react to Web sites of business partners.

Semantic Web, an initiative of the World Wide Web Consortium (W3C) led by Tim Berners-Lee in 1998, is addressing the major problem with World Wide Web as it exists today -- it is really hard to automate any tasks which one has to perform on the Web. A possible solution for the search problem - and for the general issue of letting automated "agents" roam the Web performing useful tasks - is to provide a mechanism that allows a more precise description of things on the Web. This, in turn, could elevate the status of the Web from *machine-readable* to something we might call *machine-understandable, i.e., Semantic Web*. Semantic comes from the Greek words for sign, signify, and significant, and relates to meaning. The Semantic Web, also known as the Next Generation Web, is an extension of the current Web in which information is given well-defined meaning, better enabling computers and people to work in cooperation. It is the idea of having data on the Web defined and linked in a way that it can be used for discovery, automation, and integration across various business and personal applications. The basic components of Semantic Web are:

- XML and its family members to define, store, and exchange structured data
- DOM (Document Object Model) to read, process, and manipulate XML data through programs
- RDF (Resource Description Framework) for defining the metadata (data about data), for the Web.

We have discussed XML previously. Let us now look at DOM and RDF in some detail after a brief discussion of metadata – the foundation of Semantic Web.

2.12.2 Web Metadata and PICS (Platform for Internet Content Selection)

Metadata is "data about data" or specifically in our current context "data describing Web resources." For example, the site map of a Web site shows what Web pages are on the Web site and how they are interlinked. Thus, a site map is a metadata of a Web site. The distinction between "data" and "metadata" is not an absolute one; it is a distinction created primarily by a particular application ("one application's metadata is another application's data").

The history of Web metadata is long at W3C. The history of metadata at W3C began with PICS (Platform for Internet Content Selection). PICS is a mechanism for specifying ratings of Web pages through *rating labels*. These labels are XML tags that contain information about the content of Web pages: for example, whether a particular page contains sex, nudity, violence, foul language etc. These tags can be used to determine, for example, if the page is suitable for viewers under some age. Recall that XML is being used to produce the next generation of TV Guide. Thus, the PICS labels could be used to determine ratings for TV viewers. Similarly, parents worried about their children's Web usage could set their browser to filter out any Web pages not matching their own criteria. PICS development was motivated by the possible restrictions on the Internet through US legislation such as the Communications Decency Act. For more information about PICS, see (www.w3.org/PICS/).

PICS is a limited metadata framework. RDF, described next, is a general metadata framework - and in a way is a general *knowledge representation mechanism* for the Web.

2.12.3 Resource Definition Framework (RDF)

The Resource Description Framework is a foundation for processing metadata (data about data). Let us use the example of site maps once again. Companies have a great deal of information on their Web sites. It contains advertisements, white papers, announcements, job openings, product descriptions, etc. Can you describe what is on your Web site in a systematic fashion so that an agent can understand it? RDF provides the facilities to describe Web sitemaps, privacy practices, digital signatures, device characteristics, etc.

RDF uses XML as its encoding syntax. The resources being described by RDF are, in general, anything that can be named via a URI (Uniform Resource Identifier). URIs are similar to URLs. You can describe the resources in terms of properties such as "author", "publisher", etc. For example, you can describe a book in terms of its title, publisher, author, chapter titles, etc. Some standard vocabularies are available for describing typical resources. The Dublin code (DC) is one of the earliest vocabularies that consists of:

    Title
    date
    subject

Warwick code is another vocabulary.

Here is an example of how a new benefits announcement for personnel document can be defined by using RDF:

```
<RDF xmlns="http://www.w3.org/1999/02/22-rdf-syntax-ns#"

 Xmlns:DC="http://purl.org/dc/elements/1.0/"

<Description about = "http://www.telcordia.com/announcel.html"

<DC:title> Telcordia Personnel  </DC:title>

<DC:date> 2000-10-10 </DC:date>

<DC:subject> New benefits </DC:subject>

</description>

</RDF>
```

XML Namespaces (specified in the xmlns statements) are used for name conflict resolution in RDF. The Dublin code (DC) is used in this example. The statement, "Xmlns:DC=http://purl.org/dc/elements/1.0/" shows that the Dublin Code vocabulary is used in this example.

At the core, RDF data consists of *nodes* and attached *attribute/value pairs*. Nodes can be any Web resources (pages, servers, basically anything for which you can give a URI), even other instances of metadata. Attributes are named properties of the nodes, and their values are either *atomic* (text strings, numbers, etc.) or other resources or metadata instances. In short, this mechanism allows us to build *labeled directed graphs*.

The essence of RDF is the model of nodes, attributes, and their values. In order to store instances of this model into files or to communicate these instances from one agent to another, we need a graph serialization syntax. The particular language used in RDF is XML. RDF and XML are complementary; there will be alternate ways to represent the same RDF data model, some more suitable for direct human authoring.

Examples of RDF usage are *resource discovery* to provide better search engine capabilities; and *cataloging* for describing the content and content relationships available at a particular Web site. RDF with *digital signatures* is a key to building the "Web of Trust" for electronic commerce, collaboration, and other applications.

RDF in itself does not contain any predefined vocabularies. It is expected that standard vocabularies will emerge as we move along. Some of the vocabularies in the foreseeable future are a PICS-like rating architecture, a digital library vocabulary (currently the "Dublin Code"), and a vocabulary for expressing digital signatures. Anyone can design a new vocabulary, the only requirement for using it is that a designating URI is included in the metadata instances using this vocabulary. This use of URIs to name vocabularies is an important design feature of RDF: many previous metadata standardization efforts in other areas have floundered on the issue of establishing a central attribute registry. RDF permits a central registry but does not require one.

The RDF *working group* includes representatives from key browser companies and organizations: Netscape, Microsoft, IBM, Nokia, OCLC, etc. Once the Web has been sufficiently "populated" with rich metadata, what can we expect? First, searching on the Web will become easier as search engines have more information available, and thus searching can be more focused. Doors will also be opened for automated software agents to roam the Web, looking for information for us or transacting business on our behalf. The Web of today, the vast unstructured mass of information, may in the future be transformed into something more manageable - and thus something far more useful.

2.12.4 Document Object Model (DOM)

W3C's Document Object Model (DOM) is a standard internal representation of the document structure and aims to make it easy for programmers to access components and delete, add or edit their content, attributes and style. The goal of DOM is to allow programmers to write applications that work properly on all browsers and servers, and on all platforms. While programmers may need to use different programming languages, they do not need to change their programming model. DOM allows programs and scripts to dynamically access and update the content, structure and style of documents. The document can be further processed and the results of that processing can be incorporated back into the presented page.

Let us go through an example to illustrate the key points. Figure 2-23 shows an "object model" of the following XML document that represents a customer.

```xml
<?xml version="1.0" standalone="no"?>
<!DOCTYPE customer SYSTEM "customer.dtd">
<customer id="12345">
        <name>
                <first>Joe</first>
                <last>Zombie</last>
        </name>
        <address>
                <street>Graveyard Rd</street>
                <city>Horrorville</city><state>NJ</state>
                <zip>99999</zip>
        </address>
        <phone>555-888-1311</phone>
</customer>
```

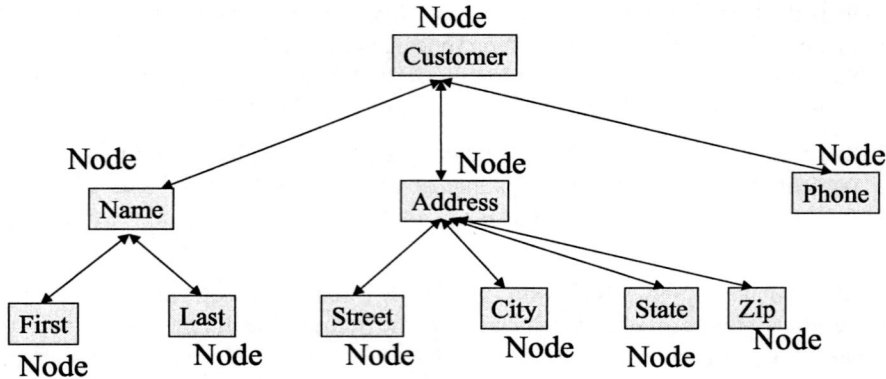

Note: The bidirectional arrow indicates a parent-child relationship

Figure 2-23: Object Model of Customer XML document

If you want to write a program that processes this document, then the program will have to be written for this specific model. The basic idea of DOM is to present a generic model of XML and HTML that can be used by programmers to read and process documents.

DOM attaches behavior to Web documents – the Web documents are viewed as objects with a collection of nodes. Each node scan has attributes and text associated with it. In addition, nodes can be interlinked with a parent-child relationship. For example, each node can represent an XML element that is connected to sub-elements through parent-child relationships. Figure 2-23 shows the DOM view of the customer XML document. A program can now travel through this tree to access and process various elements.

DOM provides an OO API for accessing Web documents and treats document contents as programmable objects. The class hierarchy is accessed by the API that defines standard traversing verbs such as next, child, parent, etc. DOM works in the following manner:

- Processor (browser) reads XML/HTML into an internal format and constructs the DOM tree.
- Client code (typically Java applet) reads the document contents.
- The client can store the document (entirely or part of) in a database, display it in different formats, or do anything else.

Now some more details…

There are various modules of the Document Object Model. The first, the **DOM XML**, relies on an internal tree-like representation of the document (shown above), and enables you to traverse the hierarchy accordingly. The standard model of viewing a document is as a hierarchy of tags, with the computer building up an internal model of the document based on a kind of tree structure.

Meanwhile, the **HTML DOM** provides a set of ways to manipulate HTML documents. The initial HTML DOM merely describes methods for example, for accessing an identifier by name, or a particular link. The HTML DOM is sometimes referred to as **DOM Level 0** but has been imported into **DOM Level 1**.

DOM is being developed at various levels. The HTML and XML DOMs form part of DOM Level 1. DOM Level 2 includes DOM Level 1 but adds a number of new features.

"Dynamic HTML" is a term used by some vendors to describe the combination of HTML, stylesheets and scripts that allows documents to be animated. W3C has received several submissions from member companies on the way in which the object model of HTML documents should be exposed to scripts. These submissions do not propose any new HTML tags or stylesheet technology.

Work on DOM is done at W3C by the Document Object Model Working Group. Work by this group covers:

- Modeling new parts of XML: the DOM is an API to an XML document. As new features are added to XML, the DOM API should model these. Namespaces is an example.
- CSS (Cascading Style Sheet) Object Model: an object model for modifying and attaching a CSS stylesheet to a document.
- Event model: a model for allowing user and application events.
- Traversal interfaces: an interface for selectively processing parts of the document according to user-specified criteria.
- Content Models and Validation: an object model for modifying and attaching a Content Model to a document.
- Load and Save interfaces: loading XML source documents into a DOM representation and for saving a DOM representation as a XML document.
- Views and Formatting Object Model: physical characteristics and state of the presentation.

Time to Take a Break
- ✓ Internet and Web
- ✓ Web Technologies
- ✓ XML and the Semantic Web
- Web Services

Suggested Review Questions Before Proceeding

- What is XML, how is it different from HTML, and why is it so popular?
- Describe 5 different applications of XML.
- Develop an XML document that describes a desktop computer (keep it simple) and then develop a DTD for the computer.
- What is the difference between DTD and XML schema?
- What is XSL and how is it used in processing XML documents?
- What is semantic Web and what are its key components?

2.13 Web Services – Using Web to Build Global Applications

2.13.1 Overview

A development worth noting at this point is the growth and acceptance of the Web and XML as a way to develop and deliver enterprise applications. The main idea is that most of the applications will be developed by using XML and delivered through the Web by using HTTP. An interesting development is the XML

Web Services that is currently at the foundation of Microsoft Dot Net (.NET) and Sun J2EE environments. XML Web Services, also just known as Web Services, provide application components that are accessible via standard Web protocols such as HTTP. Since this is all done over HTTP, an application component (e.g., a payment system) in Atlanta can be combined with an order processing component in Paris to handle a purchase from Tokyo. URLs can be used to locate the application components in a manner similar to locating Web pages. This can lead to globally distributed applications. These services, initially introduced as part of the Microsoft Dot Net initiative, are currently an active area of work at W3C. As mentioned previously, Web Services have been also adopted by Sun as part of the J2EE initiative.

The main idea of Web Services is quite simple -- instead of using Web for document exchange, start using Web for serious corporate applications where all services are delivered by using the Web technologies, especially XML and HTTP. This is dramatically different than using other middleware services such as CORBA, discussed in the next Chapter, for support-distributed applications. Thus, Web is used to support LOTC (locate, open, transfer, close) operations for distributed applications. Specifically, Web Services consist of (see Figure 2-24): .

- **UDDI** (Universal Description, Discovery and Integration) to provide a directory of services on the Internet. UDDI provides yellow pages directory for Web Services so that the potential users (clients/consumers) can *locate* the needed services.
- **WSDL** (XML Web Services Description Language) to define XML Web Services in terms of the formats and ordering of messages. WSDL is an XML document that describes the location and interfaces a particular service support. It is used by the client to *open* a Web Service and is a contract between Web Services clients and servers.
- **SOAP** (Simple Object Access Protocol) through which XML Web Service consumers can send and receive messages (*transfer*) using XML. SOAP provides explicit serialization (HTTP + XML description) protocol used in service exchanges.
- **XML & HTTP** are the core open Internet technologies that are the foundation of XML Web Services.

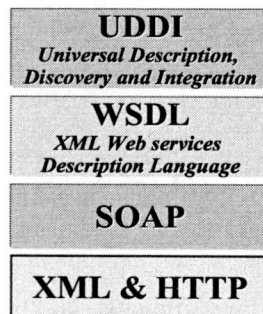

Figure 2-24: XML Web Services

A great deal of information about various aspects of Web Services is available at present over the Web. An example of the source is the Microsoft site (http://msdn.microsoft.com). Another source is the W3C site (www.w3.org). It is beyond the scope of this chapter to discuss technical details of Web Services. A brief example highlights the main ideas. We will revisit this topic on the chapter on Distributed Object Technologies and especially discuss SOAP[3] in some detail along with a treatment of MS Dot Net and J2EE.

2.13.2 A Quick Example

To the outside world, a Web Service is an application that accepts service requests, does some processing, and then returns a response. Suppose that a Web service called "ePayment" is available in Singapore. A

---

[3] We will discuss SOAP in the chapter on Distributed Object Technologies because a background in distributed objects is helpful in understanding SOAP.

consumer in Detroit wants to invoke this service by submitting a purchase order (PO). From a consumer point of view, the following steps take place to use this service (see Figure 2-25):

- Locate the Service: The consumer sends a request to UDDI (www.uddi.org) to find where the ePayment service is located. UDDI returns, say, the ePayment service URL (www.epayment.com). If more than one ePayment service is available, then more than one URLmay be returned. It is possible to search UDDI with selection criteria to minimize the number of URLs returned.
- Learn about the Service so that an appropriate session can be established. The consumer now issues a call to WSDL to learn how to invoke the needed service (i.e., what method to use, what are the input/output parameters needed for submitting a PO). This discovery process is important because different ePayment systems may use different PO formats.
- Invoke the service and transfer information. The consumer prepares a PO as a SOAP message, an XML document, that is sent to www.epayment.com over HTTP. This transfers the PO to ePayment for processing and may respond with another SOAP message.
- After being satisfied with the results, the consumer may close the session.

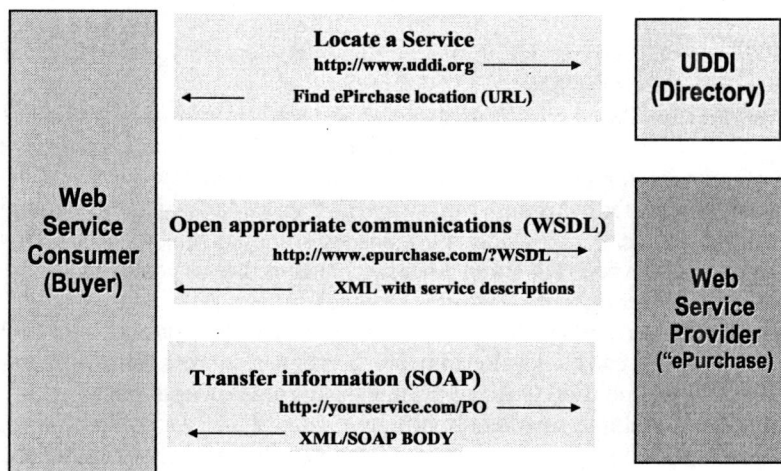

Figure 2-25: Sample Flow of Web Services

2.13.3 Why are XML Web Services Important? What are the Main Activities?

Web has evolved from a platform for exchange and display of HTML documents to a Semantic Web used for searching, comparing, and automation of universally accessible content evolution. In the first phase of Web technologies (initiated in the early 1990s consisting ofHTML, Web Browsers, Web Servers, HTTP, and Web Gateways), the following has been typical practice:

- Fetch and display HTML documents that are stored on the Web server. This is the typical "Web advertising" model, also known as the "C2B Information Delivery Business Pattern" that is the foundation of most Web sites at present.
- Connect to non-Web resources (e.g., relational databases, payment systems) by using Web Gateways such as CGI, Servlets, JSPs, etc. This is the foundation of most e-commerce systems at present.

In the second phase (initiated in the late 1990s), distributed object technologies were integrated with Web technologies primarily due to the popularity of Java. In this phase, the following is typical practice:

- Fetch and display HTML documents containing Java applets that are stored on the Web server.
- The Java applet is activated in the Web browser.
- Connection to the non-Web resources is made by using Java applets that connect to an "object server" through technologies such as RMI/CORBA (we will discuss this in next chapter).

This "Web-OO" approach has its benefits because the Web server is not used for corporate database access, thus reducing the load on the Web server. Thus many large-scale, Web-based enterprise applications have been developed by using this approach.

In the current phase of semantic Web, focus has shifted from human displays to exchange of Web information between programs. At the core of this development is XML because it makes it easier for programs in different environments to exchange information. In addition, XML namespaces and XML schemas serve as useful tools for providing directory type services.

XML Web Services combine many features of the aforementioned developments with focus on delivering global applications over the Web. The directory services (UDDI), the service descriptions (WSDL), and service delivery (SOAP) are all done using XML, HTTP, Web browsers, and Web servers. The need for separate directories and protocols for distributed objects that restrict access to one organization is eliminated. For example, CORBA has its own directory services and its own exchange protocol (IIOP) that we will discuss in the next chapter. Thus, the only people who can use these services have to have CORBA directories. We will discuss the technical tradeoffs in the next chapter, but positioning Web technologies at the core of enterprise applications for global access is the main idea of Web Services. The main advantages of this approach are:

- XML and HTTP basis of Web Services provide great interoperability and extensibility thanks to the widespread use and adoption of XML.
- Use of a universal directory based on Web that can be accessed by anyone, anywhere. Thus, a merchant from Singapore can advertise his services and a buyer from Chicago can access his services by using Web. This type of universal directory access is not part of distributed object systems.
- Provide all information transfer by using XML over HTTP instead of several technologies such as RMI, CORBA, DCOM, MOM, etc. Although other options are still open, this reduces complexity. There are some technical tradeoffs between HTTP and other mechanisms. Let us postpone it to a later chapter (see the Chapter on Web Engineering in the Tutorials Module).
- Use of HTTP has a major advantage due to firewalls. All firewalls at present allow HTTP traffic to go through. Global applications can be developed which combine resources from different corporations ("a virtual corporation") for an end user. Once again, this raises some security issues.
- Simpler operations from multiple suppliers in different parts of the world can be combined to achieve more complex operations. This opens up an interesting possibility of a new marketplace.

The main idea is that just as people are using Web technologies to access information, programs should be able to do something similar to access and combine services from multiple service providers. In order to achieve this goal, the architecture of Web Services needs to be better understood, and several technologies need to be developed. W3C is providing a platform for discussion and for planning and creation of a variety of technologies needed for Web Services. The W3C Web Services Activity is currently composed of the following three Working Groups and a Coordination Group.

- The Web Services Architecture Working Group is identifying the building blocks and how they interact with each other. This Working Group is chartered with producing an architecture document identifying the technologies that the Activity needs to design, their scope and how they relate to each other.
- XML Protocol Working Group is chartered to develop an XML-based protocol, in the form of four deliverables: a) an envelope to encapsulate XML data for transfer in an interoperable manner, b) an operating system-neutral convention for the content of the envelope, c) a mechanism to serialize data based on XML Schema datatypes, and d) in cooperation with the IETF, a non-exclusive mechanism layered (SOAP) on HTTP transport.
- Web Services Description Working Group is chartered with designing WSDL for describing interfaces to Web services and how to interact with them.

The role of the Web Services Coordination Working Group is to ensure coordination between the different groups of the Web Services Activity, as well as with the Semantic Web Activity. Extensive information on the W3C standards activities for Web Services can be found at the W3C Web site (www.w3.org).

In addition to W3C standards activities, several other companies such as IBM and Microsoft (the usual suspects) are developing products around Web Services.

2.14 XYZCorp Case Study: Hints and Suggested Solution

The CRM portal is conceptually shown in Figure 2-26. Development of this portal includes:
- Front-end integration with customers using Web browsers, cellular phones (WAP), and voice recognition systems (Voice markup language).
- Back-end integration with existing partner CRM systems (e.g., e-shop CRM, delivery CRM, credit card CRM, etc).
- Business processing of the CRM Portal.

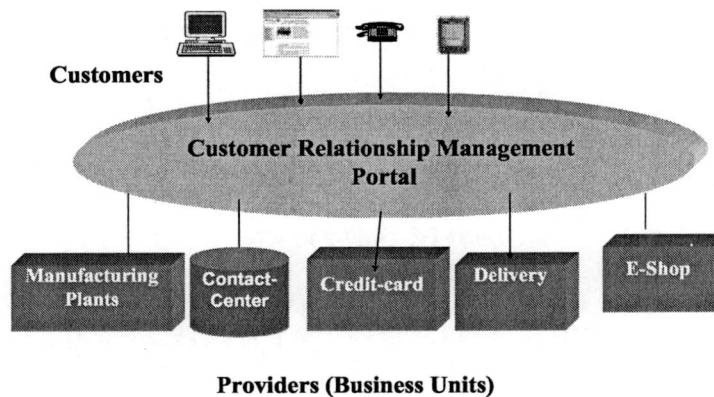

Figure 2-26: Conceptual View of a CRM Portal

The system is accessed by multiple media (phone, Internet, wireless/wireline devices). Even though these access technologies are different from each other, the system should provide the same functionality when being accessed by voice.

Figure 2-27 shows the Web architecture of the portal.
- The data served by the Web server is in XML. The user is presented this data in different formats: XML/XSL for XML-enabled browsers, HTML for browsers that are not XML-enabled, and WML (wireless Markup Language) \for Wireless phones and PDA's.
- The system translates the XML data to HTML or WML before serving it to the users of non-XML enabled browsers or wireless devices.
- The main business logic of the CRM portal is to coordinate between multiple systems. The portal can be developed as a servlet or a JSP.
- Semantic Web can be definitely of value in this portal. Because the information is sent in XML, the various players (internal as well as Providers) can read the XML documents by using DOM.
- XML Web Services can be very useful to this portal because the various players can advertise their services by using WSDL and SOAP to send XML docs.

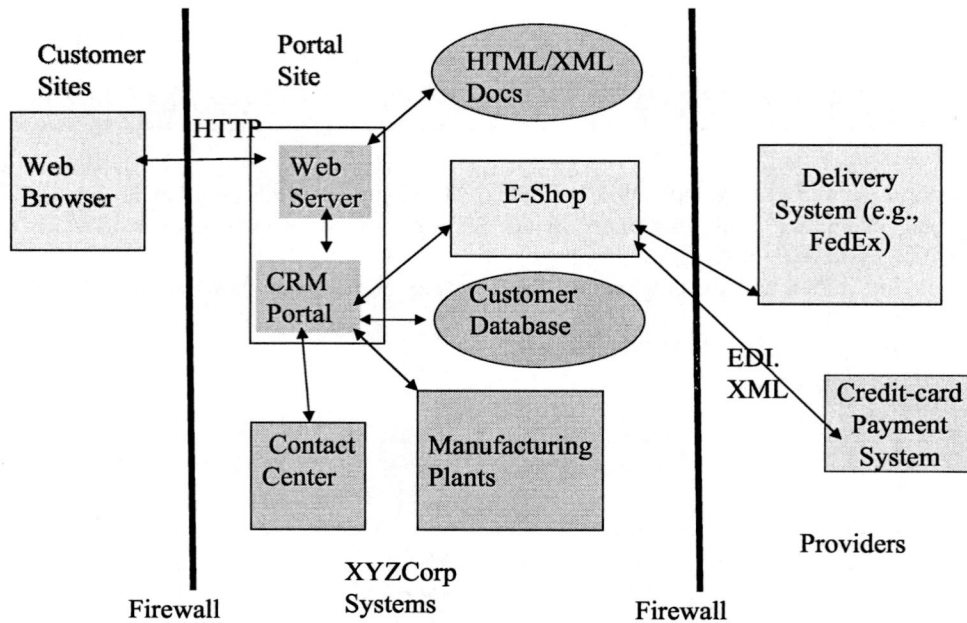

Figure 2-27: XYZCorp Portal

2.15 Summary

The "middleware" for the original World Wide Web started with Web browsers, Web servers, HTTP, HTML, and CGI gateways. This model, shown in Figure 2-1, has moved to new directions that include XML, automation aids, and object orientation.

This evolution of Web is driven by the following limitations of the first generation Web:
- Not suitable for automation. The HTML documents could be only used for displays.
- Desktop display oriented. The original Web browser assumed a desktop display that is not suitable for Palm Pilots and cellular phones.
- Technical limitations of CGI and HTTP.

The WWW Consortium (known as W3C) has embarked work on Next Generation Web that includes the following key developments (see Figure 2-29):
- XML (Extended Markup Language) - Family of standards and services introduced to improve machine-to-machine communications.
- Improvements in the core technologies such as improvement of HTTP and also introduction of more choices for Web gateways.
- Semantic Web for automation of Web that introduces an object model for Web. These efforts include DOM, RDF, PICS, P3P and others.

It can be seen from Figure 2-29 that XML is at the core of Next Generation Web.

In addition to Semantic Web, the developments in Web services that can allow users to discover and use application components around the globe in a manner similar to Web pages is an interesting area of growth.

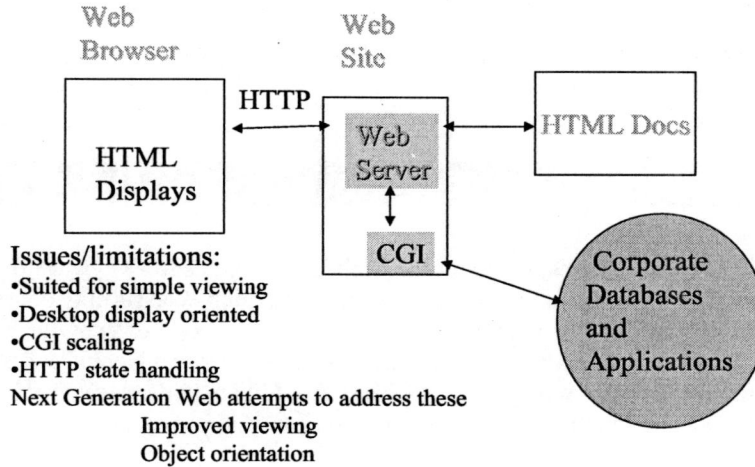

Issues/limitations:
•Suited for simple viewing
•Desktop display oriented
•CGI scaling
•HTTP state handling
Next Generation Web attempts to address these
        Improved viewing
        Object orientation

Figure 2-28: First generation Web and Its Limitations

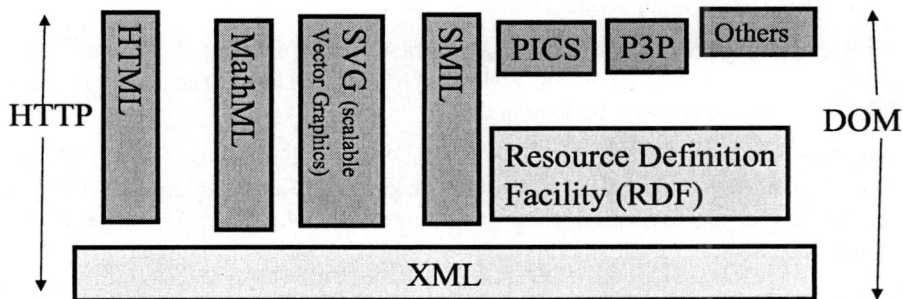

PICS: Platform for Internet Content Specification
P3P: Platform for privacy preferences
SMIL: Synchronous Multimedia Interaction Language
DOM: Document Object Model

Figure 2-29: Next generation Web

2.16   Problems and Exercises

1)   Choose an industrial Web site and analyze it in detail in terms of its Web site, unique features, ease of use, etc.

2)   Compare and contrast HTTP with RPC. Can HTTP be used instead of RPC?

3)   What are the rewards and risks of using Java in Internet?

4) Choose and analyze one Web gateway in detail.

5) Compare and contrast Java-based gateways to CGI-based gateways.

2.17 Additional Information

The best source for additional information about the Web is the W3C site - www.w3.org. You can easily access a great deal of information about various developments by using Web surfing tools such as Google or AltaVista. For people who only like to read paper documents, many good books on the Internet and World Wide Web are available from bookstores such as Amazon.com, Barnes and Nnoble and Borders Bookstore (you can find many racks of books devoted to these topics). In addition, trade magazines such as Web Week, World Wide Web Journal, and Internet Advisor are good sources of information.

A Few Useful Home Pages

http://info.cern.ch/hypertext/WWW/Protocols/HTTP/HTTP2.html - T. Berners-Lee, "HTTP: A Protocol for Networked Information" CERN, IEFT Internet Draft, original version 1991, updated several times.

http://info.cern.ch/hypertext/WWW/MarkUp/HTML.html - T. Berners-Lee, "Hypertext Markup Language (HTML)", version 1.2, IEFT Internet Draft.

http://hoohoo.ncsa.uiuc.edu/cgi/ - R. McCool(1993) "The Common Gateway Interface" NCSA, University of Illinois at Urbana-Champaign, updated severaal times.

http://www.elsevier.nl/cgi-bin/WWW94link/01/overview - D. Eichmann, T. McGregor, D. Danley (1994) "Integrating Structured Databases Into the Web: The MORE System" Proc. of the First Conference on the World Wide Web, CERN, Geneva, Switzerland.

htttp://www1.cern.ch/PapersWWW94/cvarel.ps - C. Varela, C. Hayes (1994) "Zelig: Schema-Based Generation of Soft WWW Database Applications", Proc. of the First International Conference on the World Wide Web, CERN, Geneva, Switzerland.http://dozer.us.oracle.com:8080/ - Home page for the Oracle World Wide Web Interface Kit.

http://info.cern.ch/hypertext/WWW/Addressing/URL/Overview.html - T. Berners-Lee(1994) "Uniform Resource Locators" IEFT Internet Draft.

http://www.netscape.com/ - Homepage for Netscape Communications Corp.

Selected Books and Articles

Barron, B., Ellsworth, J., and Savetz, K., editors, "Internet Unleashed", latest edition, Samsnet book

Berghel, H., "The Client's Side of the World Wide Web", Communications of the ACM, Jan. 1996, pp. 30-40.

Berners-Lee, T., et al, "The Semantic Web", The Scientific American ,special issue May 2001.

Berners-Lee, T., "Weaving the Web", Harper San Francisco, 1999

Berners-Lee, T. and, R. Cailliau, "World Wide Web" Computing in High Energy Physics 92, Anney, France, 1992.

Berners-Lee, T., R. Cailliau, N. Pellow, A. Secret, "The World Wide Web Initiative" Proc. INET '93, Internet Society, San Francisco, USA, 1993.

Berners-Lee, T., and Connolly, D., "Hypertext Markup Language 2.0", RFC 1866, IETF, Nov. 1995.

Bicket, R., "Building Intranet", Internet World, pp. 72-75.

Bjorn, M., "A WWW Gateway for Interactive Relational Database Management", Doctoral Program of Socio-Economic Planning, 1-1-1 Tennodai, Tsukuba, Ibaraki 305, JAPAN, 1995.

Chadwick, D., "A Method for Collecting Case Study Information via the Internet", IEEE Network, March/April 1996, pp. 36-38.

Chandler, D., "Running a Perfect Web", Que Books, latest edition.

Chinoy, H., et al "XML for EDI : Making E-Commerce a Reality", Paperback , May 2000.

Comer, D., "Internetworking with TCP/IP: Principles, Protocols, Architectures", Prentice Hall, 1988.

Comer, D., "Internetworking with TCP/IP", Two Volumes, Prentice Hall, latest edition.

December, J. and Randall, N., "The World Wide Web Unleased", Sams Net Book, latest edition.

Gibson, W., "Neuromancer", Ace Books, New York, 1984.

Goldfarb, C. "XML by Example: Building E-Commerce Applications", Series on Open Information Management, 1998.

Graham, I., "HTML Source Book", latest edition, Wiley.

Hahn, H., "Internet: Complete Reference", latest edition.

Halasz, F. and Schwarz, M., "The Dexter Hypertext Reference Model", Communications of the ACM, Vol. 37, No. 2, 1994.

Hoff, A., et al, "Hooked on Java; Creating Hot Web Sites with Java Applets", Addison-Wesley, latest edition.

Hunter, D. "Beginning XML", Wrox Press, 2000.

Kador, J., "The Ultimate Middleware", Byte Magazine, April 1996, pp. 79-84.

Krishnamurthy, B., and Rexford, J., "Web Protocols and Practice: HTTP/1.1, Networking Protocols, Caching, and Traffic Measurement", Addison Wesley, 2001.

McGrath, S., "XML by Example : Building E-Commerce Applications", Charles F. Goldfarb Series on Open Information Management), Paperback - June 1998.

Matranga, J., "Understanding BizTalk", Paperback, March 2000.

Nesbitt, K., "Simplify Web Database Access with SI", Internet Advisor, Premiere Issue, 1996, pp. 18-21.

Perrochon, L., "W3 Middleware: Notions and Concepts", Institut fur Informationssysteme, ETH Zurich, Switzerland, 1995.

Philips, P., "Brewing Up Applications with Java", Internet Advisor, January 1996, Premiere Issue, pp. 14-17.

Schulzrinne, H., 'World Wide Web: Whence, Whither, What Next?", IEEE Network, March/April 1996, pp. 10-18.

Stevens, R., "UNIX Network Programming", Prentice Hall, latest edition.

Tittel, E. and James, S., "HTML for Dummies", IDG Books, latest edition.

Webref: http://info.cern.ch/hypertext/WWW/Protocols/HTTP/HTTP2.html - T. Berners-Lee (1994) "HTTP: A Protocol for Networked Information" CERN, IEFT Internet Draft, original version 1991.

2.18 Attachment A: Java and Java Applets

2.18.1 What is Java and Why is it so Hot?

Java is an object-oriented programming language that is playing a unique role in WWW. Although Java is not part of Web, it has gained a unique status for supporting a very diverse array of Web applications. Java is also being used for distributed applications across the Internet (see the sidebar "Distributed Applications With Java"). Due to this reason, we include a discussion of Java in this chapter.

The Java programming language and environment was introduced by Sun Microsystems initially to develop advanced software for consumer electronics. Initially, Sun intended to use C++ for these devices that are small, reliable, portable, distributed, real-time embedded systems. It was found that the problems were best solved by introducing a new language that was similar to C++ but drew heavily from other object-oriented languages such as Eiffel and Smalltalk. The language, initially known as Oak, is now known as Java.

Why is Java so hot? The key is in supporting user interactions with Web pages that use Java. Simply stated, small Java programs, called Java applets, can be embedded in Web pages (these are called Java powered pages). Java powered Web pages can be downloaded to the Web client side and make the Web browsers a powerful user tool. Web browsers at present are relatively dumb (i.e., most functionality lies in Web servers not in Web browsers). Java is changing this. Java applets can run on Java enabled browsers. When users access these pages, these pages along with the Java applets are downloaded to the Web browser. The Java applets run on the Web client side thus making the browser an intelligent component. The Java applets are downloaded to the Web browser site. The user clicks on the Java powered pages where the applets run doing whatever they were programmed to do. There are several implications of this:

- Java applets exemplify "mobile code" that is developed at one site and is migrated to another site on demand. This introduces several security issues but also creates many interesting research opportunities.
- Java applets make Web applications client/server because the Java code can run business logic on the Web client site (i.e., the Web browser houses the first tier).
- The Web screen layout can be changed dynamically based on the user type. A Java program can determine the user type and modify the screen layout.
- Different advertisements can be shown and highlighted to the user depending on the user characteristics (e.g., age, job type, education level, credit history, salary level).
- Access to databases can be invoked directly from the browser instead of invoking a gateway program that resides on the Web server site. The Java program can ask the user to issue a request and then send this request to a remote database. A standard called JDBC (Java Database Connectivity) is being developed to allow Java programs to issue calls to relational databases.
- You can produce graphs and charts dynamically at your browser instead of fetching predefined graphs and images from the Web server (transferring images takes a very long time over the Internet).
- You can run animations, invoke business transactions, and run spreadsheets at your browser site.

Distributed Applications With Java

Java strongly supports distributed applications. If you need to write a Java application where a Java applet on your Web browser invokes another Java application on another machine, then you have the following choices:
- Use the Sun RMI (Remote Method Invocation).
- Utilize the distributed object middleware such as CORBA.

Sun Remote Method Invocation (RMI) allows Java applets to communicate with each other over the Internet. In addition, Sun has added capabilities that allow Java applets to work across a firewall.

CORBA is commercially available from many suppliers such as Iona, Inprise, and IBM. We will discuss

---

CORBA in a later chapter.

Which approach is better? RMI is easier to use for Java-to-Java communications; however, CORBA is supported by numerous vendors. In addition, CORBA supports other languages such as C++.

The main idea is that Java applications can operate very well as distributed applications.

2.18.2 What is a Java Applet?

As stated previously, a Java applet is a small Java program. What is the difference between a Java application and a Java applet? A Java application is a complete, standalone application that uses text input and output. Java applets, on the other hand, are not standalone applications and they run as part of a Java enabled browser. A Java applet contains methods (subroutines) to initialize itself, draw itself, respond to clicks, etc. These methods are invoked by the Java enabled browser. How does a browser know to download Java applets? It is quite simple. A Java powered HTML page contains a tag (the APPLET Tag) that indicates the location of a Java applet. When the browser encounters this tag, it downloads it and runs it. See the sidebar "Downloading and Running Java Applets".

The Java applets are small enough so that they can be imbedded in Web pages but large enough to do something useful. The Java applets are transferred to the Web browser along with everything else imbedded in the Web page (e.g., text, images, video clips). Once transferred to the Web client, they execute on the client side and thus do not suffer from the issues of network traffic between the Web client and Web server. Because these applications run on your client machine, you see a much more natural and efficient execution (imagine running a multimedia application on a remote Web site versus running it on your own desktop).

Due to the popularity of Java applets, many plug-and-play Java applets are already available. Once built, the Java applets can run on many different machines. The Java code is first compiled into byte-codes (byte-codes are machine instructions that are machine independent). The byte-code of the applet is loaded into the browser where it runs efficiently on different machines by using a runtime interpreter. Due to the appeal of Java applet style programming, other programming languages such as C++ and COBOL are beginning to produce byte code that can be invoked by Web browsers (the browsers do not know how the code was created).

Java applets have access to a wide range of libraries that allow Java applets to perform many operations such as graphics, image downloading, playing audio files, and user interface creation (i.e., buttons, scrollbars, windows, etc.). These libraries are included as part of the Java Applet API. This API is supported by all Java-compatible browsers. It is expected that these libraries will grow with them, thus making Java applets even more powerful and diversified.

Downloading and Running Java Applets.

Java browser load process consists of the following steps:
- User selects an HTML page.
- Browser locates the page and starts loading it.
- While loading, it starts to format text.
- It loads graphics if indicated by IMG or FIG tags in HTML.
- Java applets are indicated by an APPLET tag. For example, the tag indicates a Java applet called "Myapplet.class" that is run in a window size of 110 by 100:

```
<APPLET CODE=myapplet.class WIDTH =110 HEIGHT=100>
</APPLET>
```

- The applet code is assumed to be on the same site where the HTML page is.

- Browser loads the indicated class and other needed classes.
- Java "enabled" browsers also keep local classes that may be used by the applets.
- After the applet has been loaded, the browser asks it to initialize itself (init() method) and draw a display area that is used for input/output.

Additional details about Java can be found in the chapter "Object Concepts, Java, and UML" in the Tutorials Module or dozens of Java books available in the book market.

.

3 Distributed Object Technologies: CORBA, Web Services, J2EE, .NET, SOAP, EJBs

Note to the reader: This chapter assumes certain knowledge of object-oriented concepts and technologies. Although the discussion is not very deep and several people have braved through this chapter without knowing very much about objects, you may want to proceed with care. If you are not sure, please review the Tutorial on Object-Oriented Concepts and Technologies in the Tutorials Module before proceeding.

3.1   Introduction

Most of the new applications being developed at present are based on the OO concepts. However, these objects are increasingly dispersed on multiple machines. Consequently, many new applications rely on distributed object middleware to locate, connect to, and communicate with objects that may reside on widely distributed computers. These applications, commonly known as ***EDOC (Enterprise Distributed Object Computing)*** applications, combine two very powerful concepts to meet enterprise needs: object-orientation and distributed computing. The users of these applications interact with objects that may be located locally or on remote machines on the same LAN, within the corporate Intranet, or on the Extranet/Public Internet. Naturally, access of the distributed objects over the Web through "XML Web Services" adds another important dimension to distributed objects (we refer to this as ***OCSI*** to signify the trio of object-orientation, client/server, and Internet technologies). There are many interesting examples of OCSI at present. For example, an online purchasing system can be architected as an OCSI application where a payment object in Chicago, an order processing object in Atlanta, and inventory objects in London and Rome interact with each other over the Web to support global online purchasing. See the Architectures Module of this book for a detailed discussion of OCSI architectures (Figure 3-1 shows a historical evolution).

The purpose of this chapter is to review the distributed object concepts and examine the middleware that enables distributed object applications that follow the OCSI paradigm. After reviewing the basic concepts, the core distributed object technologies such as CORBA and DCOM are reviewed because they laid the foundation of current and future systems. More attention is paid to the more recent industrial developments that are significant in this. First is the interest in business components (large business-aware objects) and component-based architectures with platforms such as Microsoft's .NET and Sun's J2EE. The second is the current attention to XML Web Services standards, also just known as Web Services, that allow applications to be integrated as long as they are Internet-enabled. The core of Web Services is XML messages over standard Web protocols such as HTTP. These industry standards provide a lightweight and widely accepted communication mechanism. Third is the adoption of Web Services by J2EE as well as .NET. Collectively, these developments are combining Web, objects, and distributed computing into powerful platforms for e-business and other applications.

The following questions will guide the discussion in this chapter (this chapter assumes that the reader has a basic understanding of object oriented concepts as discussed in the Tutorial Module):
- What are the key concepts of distributed objects (Section 3.3)?
- What are the emerging standards in distributed objects and what exactly is CORBA (Section 3.4)?
- What is Microsoft ActiveX/ DCOM and how does it fit into the big picture (Section 3.5)?

- What are the developments in J2EE, .NET, and Web Services and how are they inter-related (Section 3.6)?
- What is SOAP and how is it related to the developments in XML Web Services? How does it also relate to distributed objects (Section 3.7)?
- What are Enterprise Java Beans (EJBs) and how are they related to distributed objects (Section 3.8)?

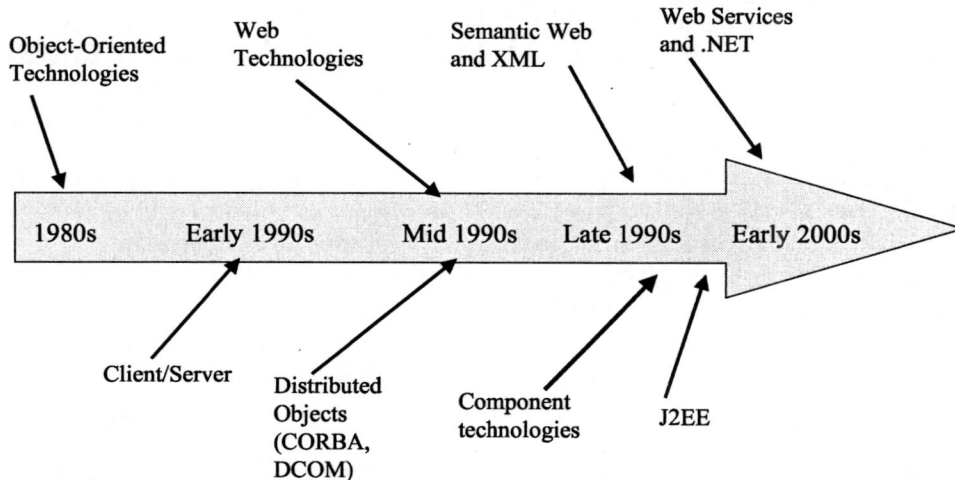

Figure 3-1: Historical Evolution of Distributed Object Computing

---

Key Points

- Enterprise-wide applications can be decomposed and viewed as objects that can reside on different machines. An object on one machine can send messages to objects on other machines thus making the entire network as a collection of objects.
- Interfaces and IDLs (Interface Definition Languages) provide the basic glue for all distributed object computing technologies ranging from older CORBA/DCOM to newer Web Services/.NET/J2EE.
- IDL is used not only to define new services provided by objects, but also to "wrap" existing and legacy systems so that they behave externally as objects.
- The following players are common to all distributed object technologies:
  - **Distributed Objects:** Application objects behave as clients, servers, or both.
  - **IDL:** Objects define their services through an Interface Definition Language (IDL) that specifies the operations to be performed by remote objects. CORBA, DCOM, J2EE, .NET, and Web Services all support IDLs.
  - **Directories:** Object advertise their services through a directory that keeps the IDLs of all operations. Directories serve as "yellow pages" for the objects. CORBA, DCOM, J2EE, .NET, and Web Services all use directories to locate objects.
  - **Object Brokers:** Object brokers allow objects to find each other in a distributed environment and interact with each other over a network. Object brokers are the backbone of distributed object-oriented systems. They essentially provide the "dot" between the object and method in distributed environments. CORBA and DCOM use special brokers but .NET and Web Services use the Internet as a broker.
  - **Object Services:** These services allow the users to create, name, move, copy, store, delete, restore, and manage objects. CORBA and DCOM use special object services but .NET and Web Services use the Internet Services, as much as possible, for this purpose.
  - **Object Invocation Protocols.** Protocols are needed by the brokers to access and invoke objects. CORBA and DCOM use special protocols (CORBA uses IIOP) but .NET and Web Services use the Internet protocols such as HTTP for this purpose.
- Object Management Group (OMG) has defined a suite of standard languages, interfaces, protocols, and services for interoperability of applications in heterogeneous distributed object environments.

- CORBA (Common Object Request Broker Architecture) is an OMG specification for middleware needed to enable distributed object applications. CORBA 2.0,the latest CORBA specification at the time of this writing, includes an extensive array of capabilities and APIs for developing interoperability bridges.
- Microsoft positioned ActiveX and DCOM as a complete environment for components and distributed objects. Microsoft's DCOM and OMG's CORBA share the same goals and provide the same basic functionalities, but there are some "plumbing" differences.
- Business components (large business-aware objects) and component-based architectures with platforms such as Microsoft's .NET and Sun's J2EE are significant developments for distributed object computing.
- XML Web Services standards, also just known as Web Services, allow business components to be integrated as long as they are Internet-enabled. This can lead to global distributed applications.
- Web Services use XML, HTTP, SOAP, UDDI, and WSDL. The most significant aspects of Web Services are XML and HTTP.
  - XML allows definition, verification, and exchange of semi-structured information.
  - HTTP allows objects to be invoked through the firewalls. The inability to penetrate corporate firewalls became the major limitation for CORBA and DCOM.

3.2   Case Study: XYZCorp Investigates Distributed Object Technologies

XYZCorp has bought into object-orientation like everyone else to increase software reuse — most new development is being done in C++ and Java (the company favorite) with a great deal of "interest" in components and business objects. However, it is not clear how to deal with distributed objects and what middleware platform to use. The company invested in adopting CORBA in the late 1990s and felt quite good about itself. But now the ever-unfolding story of Sun's J2EE versus Microsoft's .NET is giving everyone a headache. To complicate life further, Web Services are positioned as the Nirvana. The company does not know how their CORBA strategy fits into all this. In addition, message- oriented middleware is gaining popularity to support loosely coupled enterprise applications.

Frustrated by all this, the company has initiated a technology assessment effort that focuses on distributed object technologies. The advanced technology group in the corporation believes that the distributed object model should be used as the ONLY model throughout the corporation. You have been asked to:
- Investigate the use of distributed object technologies for XYZCorp. For what type of applications is this technology most suitable? Can distributed object middleware do everything needed for this corporation? What can it not handle and why not?
- Is distributed object technology as reflected by CORBA and DCOM much better than the message-oriented middleware? Compare and contrast these middleware technologies in terms of their promises, pitfalls, and application fit (i.e., what types of applications are best supported by these middleware types).
- The company adopted CORBA, but now is not sure if this was the right strategy. In particular, should the company consider SOAP instead of CORBA? Should DCOM be dropped from the picture?
- Show how Web will inter-operate with distributed objects.
- Discuss how the XML Web Services and Microsoft's .Net fits into this picture. Should the company adopt J2EE or .NET to support Web Services?

> The Agenda
> • Distributed Object Technologies
> • CORBA and DCOM
> • Web Services, .NET, J2EE
> • SOAP and EJBs

3.3 Distributed Object Technologies Overview

3.3.1 Concepts

Most of the new applications developed at present are based on the OO concepts. In addition, many legacy applications are being "wrapped" so that they appear as objects to the outside world. However, rarely, if ever, all objects of an application reside on the same machine. It is common to find that the objects of an application will be dispersed on multiple machines. A distributed application can be viewed as a collection of objects (user interfaces, databases, application modules, customers). Each object has its own attributes, and has some methods which define the behavior of the object (e.g., an order can be viewed in terms of its data and the methods which create, delete and update the order object). Interactions between the components of an application can be modeled through "messages" which invoke appropriate methods. In particular, classes and inheritance are extremely useful in modeling applications because these concepts lead to reuse and encapsulation - critical to managing the complexity of distributed systems. For example:

- A customer is defined as a class from which other business classes that define different types of customers can inherit properties.
- An inventory is defined as a class from which other properties of specific inventory items can be inherited.
- A database server is defined as a class from which other vendor specific database servers can inherit properties.
- A network is defined as a class from which other networks inherit properties (e.g., a generic network from which local and wide area networks can inherit properties).

Objects, wherever they reside, are data that can be accessed through methods and support properties such as inheritance, polymorphism, encapsulation, etc. Objects can be clients, servers, or both (see Appendix B for a tutorial on object-oriented concepts). It is quite easy to access a local object in current OO programming languages such as Java and C++. All you need to do is issue the following statement:

```
Object.method (parameters)
```

For example, consider the following object:

```
Object Name   = invoice
Attributes    = customer name, items purchased, price per item, total invoice, etc.
Methods       = prepare, send, review status, update status
```

To prepare an invoice, we say invoice.prepare (parameters for invoice preparation), and to send an invoice, we say, invoice.send (parameters for sending), etc (we are overlooking a few programming details). The "dot" between object name and the method name is of key importance because it tells the compiler to invoke the method of a given object. How can you invoke a method (with associated parameters) on a remotely located object? For example, how can you prepare an invoice object if that object is on a Unix machine in another building? The following fundamental questions arise:

- How can you find (locate) the invoice object in the network?

- How can you send it a message to invoke the "prepare" method?
- How can you pass the needed parameters?
- How can you hide the complexity and heterogeneity of distributed systems from applications?
- How can you recover from the errors?

The distributed object middleware such as CORBA provides answers to these and several other related questions. Before getting involved with details about objects in distributed systems, let us quickly review some of the major concepts. Figure 3-2 shows a conceptual view that will be expanded and refined later. It consists of the following players that are common to all distributed object technologies:

- **Distributed Objects:** Application objects behave as clients, servers, or both.
- **IDL:** Objects define their services through an Interface Definition Language (IDL) that specifies the operations to be performed by remote objects. As we will see, CORBA, DCOM, J2EE, .NET, and Web Services all support IDLs.
- **Directories:** Object advertise their services through a directory that keeps the IDLs of all operations. Directories serve as "yellow pages" for the objects. As we will also see, CORBA, DCOM, J2EE, .NET, and Web Services all use directories to locate objects.
- **Object Brokers:** Object brokers allow objects to find each other in a distributed environment and interact with each other over a network. Object brokers are the backbone of distributed object-oriented systems. They essentially provide the "dot" between the object and method in distributed environments. As we will see, CORBA and DCOM use special brokers but .NET and Web Services use the Internet as a broker.
- **Object Services:** These services allow the users to create, name, move, copy, store, delete, restore, and manage objects. As we will see, CORBA and DCOM use special object services but .NET and Web Services use the Internet Services, as much as possible, for this purpose.
- **Object Invocation Protocols.** Protocols are needed by the brokers to access and invoke objects. As we will see, CORBA and DCOM use special protocols such as IIOP but .NET and Web Services use the Internet protocols such as HTTP for this purpose.

Table 3-1 illustrates the distributed object technologies used in CORBA and Web services. Inclusion of other distributed object technologies (DCOM, J2EE, .NET) to this table is left as an exercise for the reader. Keep in mind that modeling in terms of object-oriented (OO) concepts does not necessarily imply use of object-oriented programming languages such as C++ or object-oriented database managers. It is possible to view systems in terms of OO objects and then implement them in whatever technology makes sense. For example, most systems at present view data as objects but implement the data by using relational databases.

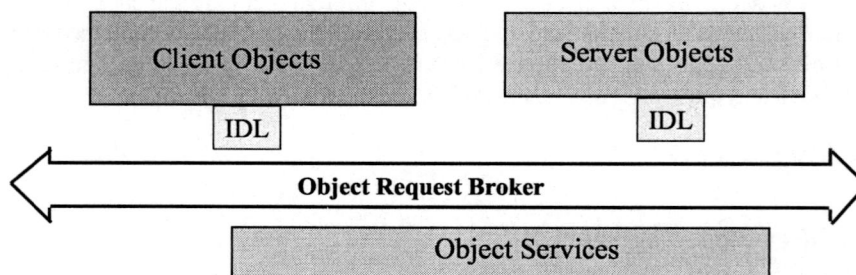

Figure 3-2: The Basic Distributed Objects Model

Due to the interest in object-oriented systems, the elegance with which complex distributed systems can be modeled by using OO concepts, and the appeal of OO technologies in developing new applications ranging from inventory control to network management, many attempts have focused on standardized middleware to support object-oriented distributed systems. The Common Object Request Broker Architecture (CORBA) from the Object Management Group is a prime example of such a standard.

Table 3-1: Distributed Objects in CORBA and Web Services

	CORBA	**Web Services**
Distributed Objects	CORBA Objects	Web Services Components
IDL	CORBA IDL	WSDL
Directory	CORBA Naming Services	UDDI
Object Broker	Object Request Broker	Internet
Object Services	CORBA Services	Web and Internet services such as DNS
Object Invocation Protocol	IIOP	HTTP, SOAP

3.3.2 Distributed Objects: From CORBA/DCOM to Web Services and J2EE

The trend at present is to extend the OO concepts to enterprise-wide distributed applications. Simply stated, distributed objects are objects dispersed across the network and accessed by users. Conceptually, we are talking about decomposing enterprise-wide applications into objects that can be dispersed around different machines on a network. An object on one machine can send messages to objects on other machines, thus viewing the entire network as a collection of objects. When, and if, fully realized distributed objects present a very powerful technology that has the potential of addressing many problems that have plagued the IT community for years (i.e., reuse, portability and interoperability). This is because applications constructed using reusable components that encapsulate many internal details interoperate across multiple networks and platforms.

Support of distributed object-based applications requires special purpose middleware that will allow remotely located objects to communicate with each other. A common mechanism used by such middleware is an object request broker (ORB) that receives an object invocation and delivers the message to an appropriate object. Examples of middleware for distributed objects include OMG's CORBA (Common Object Request Broker Architecture), DCOM (Distributed Computing Object Model) from Microsoft, and RMI (Remote Method Invocation) from Sun. Although, the exact implementations vary (as we will see), they all follow the conceptual view presented in Figure 3-3:

- Each remote object that wishes to provide a service defines its services through an IDL (Interface Definition Language). For example, purchasing and inventory are server objects advertising their services. Each server object specifies its service through an IDL (Interface Definition Language).
- The object request broker (ORB) is the main bus that connects object clients to the object servers.
- The clients use the ORB to locate and invoke needed services. The client uses IDL to invoke a service. For example, the client will use IDL1 for purchasing and IDL2 for inventory checking.

While object-orientation is quite fashionable, the attention has lately shifted to "components" and "business objects" that are large objects containing business functionalities. One of the main reasons for attention to component-based systems is that component-based platforms are commercially available at present. Examples of such platforms are Sun J2EE and Microsoft .NET that we will review later in this chapter (for more information about J2EE and .NET, see the Web sites (www.sun.com) and (http://msdn.microsoft.com), respectively). Figure 3-4 shows a conceptual component-based architecture platform that is a generalization of the Sun J2EE environment and the Microsoft .NET environment. The component-based architecture is composed of several components that can exist at the following tiers:

- Client-tier components run on the client machine.
- Web-tier components run on the Web server to provide server side support.
- Business-tier components run on the business tier and are the "business components" (we will discuss business components later).

- Enterprise system tier software runs on the back-end systems.

These component-based architectures, as we will see, use the distributed object middleware technologies such as IDLs.

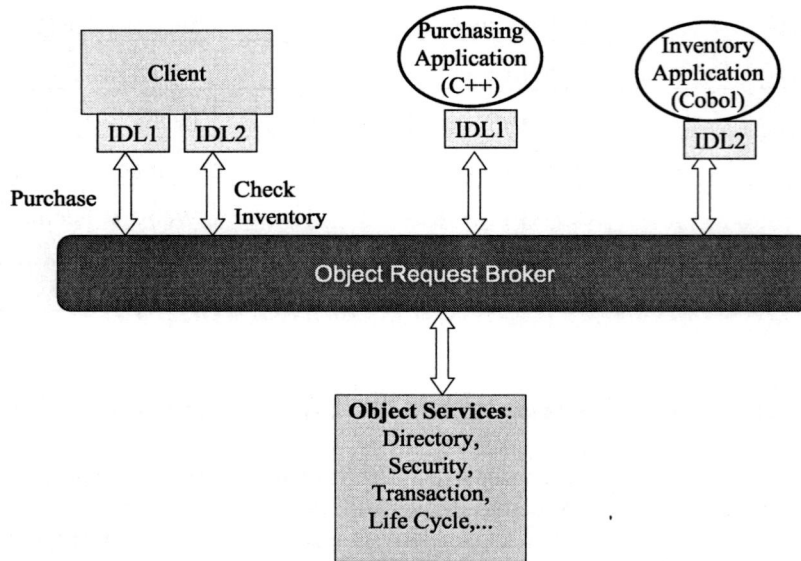

Figure 3-3: Conceptual view of Distributed Object Middleware

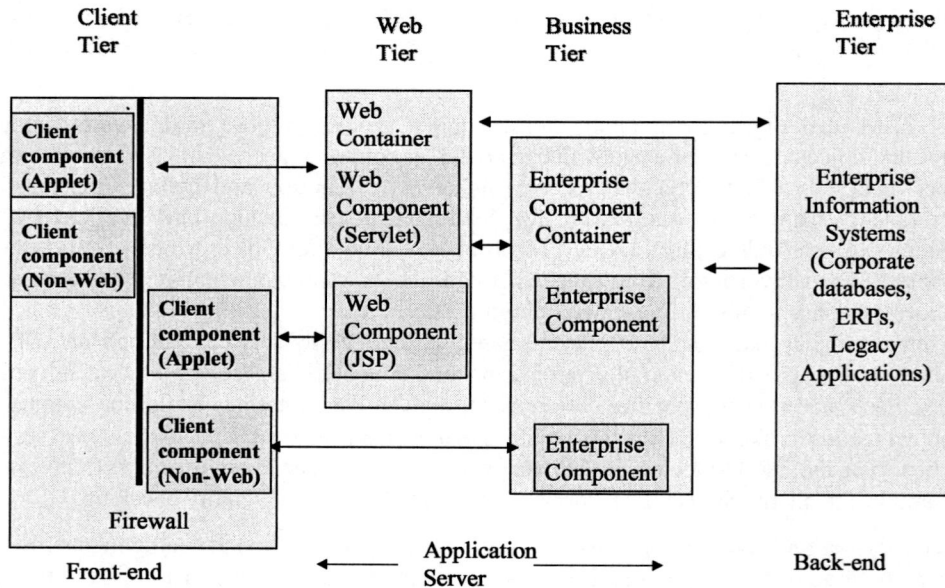

Figure 3-4: A Generalized Component-based Architecture

3.3.3 Interface Definition Languages (IDLs)

3.3.3.1 Interfaces and Interface Definition Language

Interfaces and interface definition languages (IDLs) are at the core of distributed object applications, including the new component-based applications. Simply stated, an interface specifies the API that the clients can use to invoke operations on objects. In particular, an interface describes:

- The set of operations that can be performed on an object.
- The parameters needed to perform the operations.

For distributed object applications, interface definitions are used to advertise the set of operations that an object can provide to prospective clients. Thus, the object's data is accessible only through the interface. Consequently, any server that is encapsulated by its interface can be viewed as an object. Figure 3-5 shows an interface of a simple inventory object that supports two operations: query inventory and update price (a definition of this interface is given in Table 3-2). These operations can be invoked by client programs.

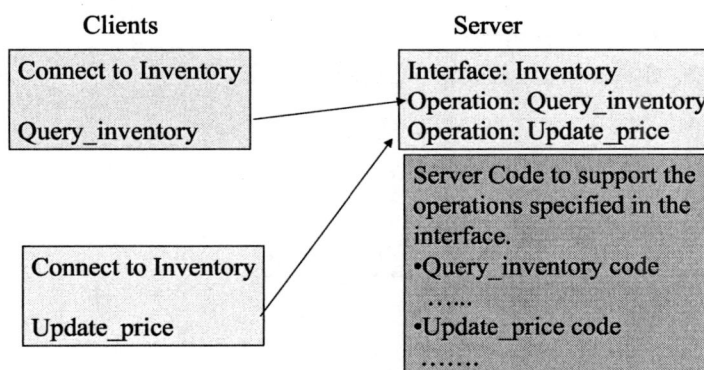

Figure 3-5: Example of an Interface

One or more interfaces may be defined for an object. For example, given an object such as inventory, you may need to define three different interfaces: one for the manager of inventory (i.e., to create, monitor and replenish the inventory), one for the order processing system (i.e., to retrieve and update the inventory), and one for the authorized customers (i.e., to browse through the available products). It is a good practice to design interfaces for different classes of users and to group related operations together. An interface definition includes some or all of the following:

- The interface header that shows an interface name and interface header attributes that uniquely identify the interface. Examples of such attributes are UUIDs (universal unique identifiers) and version numbers of the interfaces.
- Constant and data type definitions that are used to specify data properties (e.g., size) so that clients and servers can exchange data conveniently between different machines.
- A set of operations (methods) and the signatures for each operation. A signature specifies the operation's name, it's arguments, and argument types.

The interfaces are defined by using an interface definition language (IDL). Different middleware products provide IDL compilers that parse the IDL and produce header files and code segments that are used by the client and server programs (we will discuss this in more detail later). For example, CORBA, DCOM, and RMI all provide IDL compilers. In addition, middleware products support utilities and commands to store and retrieve IDLs from interface repositories. Client application developers can browse through these interface repositories to learn about the available server objects and determine the type of operations that can be invoked on an object.

IDLs are declarative languages -- they do not specify any executable code. IDL declarations (e.g., syntax, character types allowed, argument coding, etc.) must conform to the vendor provided IDL compilers. After you create the interface definition using IDL, you compile the IDL file to create header files and "stubs" that are used in building clients and servers. Table 3-2 shows the IDL of a simple inventory system that supports query inventory and update price operations. The syntax used in this example is abstract. We will see actual IDL specifications for CORBA later on in this chapter.

Table 3-2: A Sample Abstract IDL

```
uuid 008B3C84-11c7-8580), version (1.0) /* Header */

interface inventory /* interface name is inventory */

query_inventory (/*The  operation to query inventory */

in char item_id; /* input is item id */

out integer on_hand; /output is on hand */

out integer status )  /*  output status */

update_price ( /*The operation is to update price */

in char item_id;  /* input parameter is item -id */

in integer new_price; /* input: new price */

out integer status )  /*output parameter */
```

3.3.3.2   Types of Interfaces

Interfaces and interface definitions are of two kinds: operational interfaces which contain a set of named operations (i.e., procedures or methods); and stream interfaces, in which communication is organized as a set of linked directional flows. This chapter will focus primarily on operational interfaces. Stream interfaces are used to support distributed multimedia systems. Stream interfaces are used to describe unstructured communications such as voice and video streams in multimedia systems. Stream interfaces can also be used for electronic mail. The basic characteristic of stream interfaces is that they must support continuous data transfers over relatively long periods of time, e.g., real-time playout of video from a remote surveillance camera. In addition, the timeliness of such transmissions must be maintained for the duration of the media presentation. We will pick up the discussion of stream interfaces in a later chapter when we discuss distributed multimedia applications.

Interfaces significantly impact the design of distributed object applications. First, the server object is required to implement at least the operations specified in the IDL, and the client is required to accept at least the set of results generated by the IDL operations. This implies that the server will never respond with a "method/procedure not supported" message to a prospectus client. Second, the clients may not use some of the operations provided by the interface. This implies that the server interfaces can be extended to include more operations without requiring any change to the client. Finally, and most importantly, the "size" of the interface needs to be carefully examined. For example, it is not a good idea to specify an interface that supports 100 operations. In such a case, if one operation needs to be changed, then a new IDL will have to be compiled and all client programs will have to be recompiled (this could be quite irritating). It is best to design a separate interface for each group of users (e.g., one interface for end users, one for the system administrators, etc.).

Interfaces and IDL provide the basic glue for distributed object computing. IDL is used not only to define new services provided by objects, but also to "wrap" existing and legacy systems so that they behave externally as objects. For example, a legacy application written in Cobol could behave as a server object as long as it has an IDL and it provides the operations defined by the IDL. Thus, the "IDL-ized" programs run on top of an ORB without revealing their internal details and work with CORBA gateways to work with non-CORBA systems (see Figure 3-6).

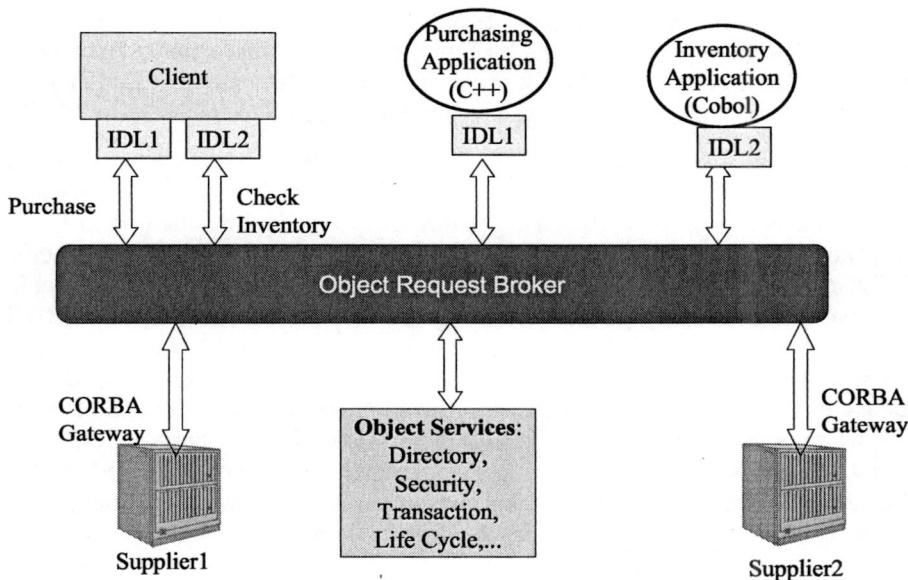

CORBA Gateways convert CORBA calls to non-CORBA

Figure 3-6: Interface Definition Language (IDL) in Action

3.3.4 Components, Business Objects, and Object Frameworks

A very wide range of OO products are commercially available from a diverse array of suppliers. The following three are the most significant because they are at the foundation of J2EE and .NET:
- Components
- Business Objects (business components)
- Object Frameworks

Components and "Applets": Components are high-level "plug and play" software modules that perform a limited set of tasks within an application. Components are essentially objects, also known as "applets", that are recognizable by the users as small applications (i.e., they do not perform internal programming tasks such as initialize internal memory locations). For example, Microsoft Draw is an applet within Microsoft applications. This particular component is high level enough to perform end-user type functions (it draws boxes, arrows, circles, etc.). However, it is not a stand-alone application, it only works with other applications components. Microsoft has many software components for Windows environments that draw, produce charts, perform calculations, etc. Depending on the size of the application, the components may be small or large. Components are very much like objects; however, the emphasis is on recognition by users (many objects are oriented towards programming tasks). Thus, component software can be used as plug and play to build complete applications. Many desktop tools are currently becoming available as components. Examples of typical desktop components are spell—checkers, SQL query builders, print managers (conceptually, each icon on your toolbar can be a separate component).

Business Objects (Business Components): The basic idea of business objects, also known as business components, is that the users can construct large objects that represent the real-world concepts of the business world. Examples of business objects are customer, order, products, and regional office. Business components are larger than components -- components can represent a clock or a calendar but a business component can represent an inventory system. If software could be structured around such objects and other business concepts, then organizations would be able to build software that simulated current business strategy. Moreover, businesses could reuse these objects to build new applications by using the OO paradigm. Business objects started appearing in the marketplace around 1994 when OLE 2.0, OpenDoc, and CORBA-based products started emerging. Since then, OO tools designed to support creation of business objects have appeared from vendors such as Easel and applications that employ business objects have appeared from Sun, IBM, and Microsoft. Business components are at the foundation of "Business Component Factory" [Herzum 2000]. We will discuss business objects in detail in the Architecture Module.

Object Frameworks: Object frameworks are essentially descendents of object-oriented class libraries. Class libraries are collections of predefined object classes that define commonly used presentation, business processing logic, and data management structures and methods. A framework simply defines how given sets of classes are related and arranged for different applications. It is possible to think of frameworks at three levels: foundation classes, middleware frameworks, and application frameworks (or high level frameworks). The foundation classes provide fine-grained data and control statements, I/O functions, GUI structures, memory management functions, and database access functions. The middleware framework covers an extensive set of C/S middleware services such as transaction processing, database access, directory services, telephony, authentication and systems management. The application frameworks, also known as desktop frameworks, provide programmer productivity tools for compound documents, multimedia, groupware, mail, 3D graphics, and decision support applications. An example of commercial object frameworks is the IBM and Taligent object frameworks strategy that is beginning to materialize as products. The objective of this strategy is to create "seas of objects" with object frameworks as the glue to tie these objects into applications. Examples of other players in this market are ParcPlace Systems, Rogue Wave, ILOG, Next, Sun Microsystems, Easel, and others.

These, and other emerging technologies and market segments are leading towards reusable software that can be assembled to quickly build new applications. However, these technologies are introducing new terms and jargon. Due to an ever-growing list of object-oriented "things", many groups are trying to figure out what to do. An example is the Object Management Group (OMG) that has been formed as a non-profit consortium of more than 500 software and systems manufacturers and technology information providers. OMG is specifying a set of standard terms and interfaces for interoperable software by using the object oriented concepts.

Object-Oriented Databases

Object-oriented databases allow storage and retrieval of objects to/from persistent storage (i.e., disks). Object-oriented databases, also known as object databases, allow you to store and retrieve non traditional data types such as bitmaps, icons, text, polygons, sets, arrays, and lists. The stored objects can be simple or complex, can be related to each other through complex relationships, and can inherit properties from other objects. Object-oriented database management systems (OODBMS), which can store, retrieve and manipulate objects, have been an area of active research and exploration since the mid 1980s.

Relational databases are suitable for many applications and SQL use is widespread. However, it is not easy to represent complex information in terms of relational tables. For example, a car design, a computing network layout, and software design of an airline reservation system cannot be represented easily in terms of tables. For these cases, we need to represent complex interrelationships between data elements, retrieve several versions of design, represent the semantics (meaning) of relationships, and utilize the concepts of similarities to reduce redundancies.

OODBMSs and RDBMSs both have their strengths and weaknesses. For example, RDBMSs are very mature and heavily used but cannot handle complex objects well. OODBMSs, on the other hand lack the maturity and ease of use offered by the RDBMSs. A compromise, known as Object-Relational Databases, provides a hybrid solution where relational and object-oriented technologies are combined into a single product. Different vendors use different approaches to Object-Relational Databases. For example, Odaptor

---

from HP uses an underlying relational database with OO front-ends while UniSQL from UniSQL is an OO database that subsumes the relational model.

Time to Take a Break
✓ Distributed Object Technologies
- CORBA and DCOM
- Web Services, .NET, J2EE
- SOAP and EJBs

Suggested Review Questions Before Proceeding

- What are distributed object technologies and why are they important?
- What are the unique features of distributed objects that cannot be found in simple client/server systems?
- What is the role of IDL in distributed object technologies?
- What are the common features of all distributed object technologies?
- What are components and how are they different from objects?

3.4   Common Object Request Broker Architecture (CORBA)

3.4.1   Object Management Architecture

Common Object Request Broker Architecture (CORBA) is a specification proposed by the Object Management Group (OMG) - a non-profit industry consortium formed in 1989 by eight companies with the following goals [Soley 1994]:
- Solve problems of interoperability in distributed systems by using object technology.
- Use de facto standards in object technology and commercial availability of technology.
- Create a suite of standard languages, interfaces and protocols for interoperability of applications in heterogeneous distributed environments.
- Build upon, not replace, existing interfaces.

HP, IBM and Sun were among the original eight members of OMG, which has exceeded more than 800 members ranging from hardware vendors to end users. Interestingly, OMG was formed before any major products were introduced. Most standards bodies are formed to develop standards after products are already in use. For example, ISO/OSI Reference Model for networks was introduced in 1977, almost 5 to 7 years after the introduction of SNA, Decnet, and TCP/IP.

Keep in mind that *OMG produces specifications, not implementations*. Implementations of OMG specifications can be found on over 50 operating systems. OMG solicits new specification proposals through RFI (request for information) and RFP (request for submission) process. Like other standards bodies, the proposals go through a formal evaluation, revision, review, recommendations and approval process.

OMG's first attempt at meeting its goals resulted in an Object Management Architecture (OMA), released in 1990 It was revised in 1992. OMA specified the overall object model for distributed object computing environments, including how objects are defined and created, how client applications invoke objects, and how objects can be shared and reused. The four components of this Management Architecture are (see Figure 3-7):

- **Application Objects**: These are business- aware objects specific to end-user applications. These objects can be pieces of data, software, and user artifacts that can reside on one or many machines. The application objects may be created by an OO language or encapsulated by using a "wrapper" around old systems. Applications are typically built from a large number of basic object classes.

- **Object Request Broker (ORB)**: ORB is responsible for communication between objects. ORB finds an object on the network, delivers requests to the object, activates the object (if not already active), and returns any messages back to the sender. ORB is the backbone of OMA. We will discuss ORB in more detail later.

- **Object Services**: This component supports the request broker by providing services that almost every object needs. These include basic services (finding and invoking objects), thread services (create and manage threads), object life cycle services (create, destroy objects), and naming services (facilitate portable names). Additional services such as event, trading, transactions, and persistence have been added to CORBA services.

- **Horizontal Facilities**: These facilities were initially intended for common services such as user interface, task management, and information management. Examples include e-mail, database access, and compound. However, OMG has found that it was difficult to differentiate between these and CORBA services. At present, OMG has given up on these services.

- **Vertical (Domain) Facilities**: These facilities define the object models and IDLs for a very wide range of industry segments. This is one of the most active areas of OMG with work continuing in domains such as finance, business objects, healthcare, manufacturing, electronic commerce, telecommunications, transportation, and utilities.

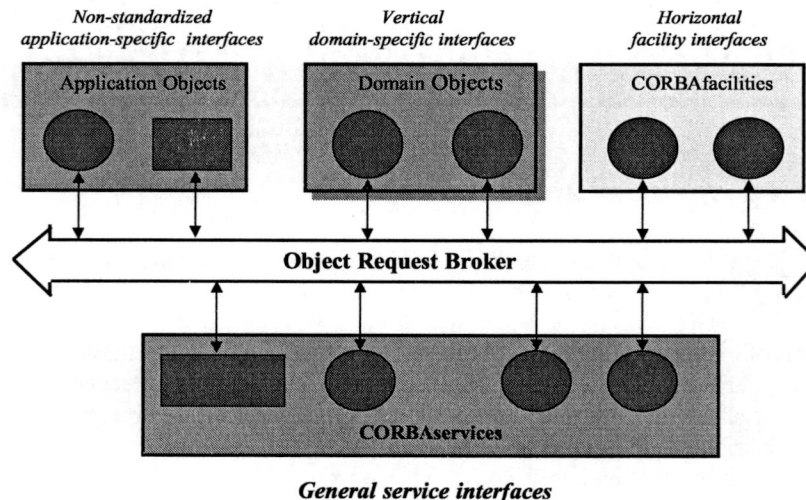

Figure 3-7: Object Management Architecture

It is important to note that the Application Objects, Vertical Facilities, and Object Services are simply categories of objects. Every piece of software in the OMA model is represented as an object that communicates with other objects via the Object Request Broker. These objects were grouped into three broad categories to ease the standardization process.

It is perhaps appropriate at this point to briefly discuss the OMG organization and structure. As shown in Figure 3-8, the OMG consists of an architecture board that oversees the developments of OMG, a Platform Technology Committee that develops the ORB and the Object Services, as well as the Domain Technology Committee that manages the growing vertical industries. Keep in mind that OMG, although well known due to CORBA specification, is actively involved in all aspects of object technologies. For example, OMG has specified the very popular UML (Universal Modeling Language) that is used to represent the models throughout the development of object-oriented systems (see Appendix B for more details on UML). OMG is also developing standards for business objects and component technologies. The adoption process consists of following steps:

Step 1: RFI (Request for Information) to establish range of commercially available software.

Step 2: RFP (Request for Proposals) to gather explicit descriptions of available software. The Architecture Board approves RFPs.

Step 3: Letters of Intent to establish corporate commitment from respondents to the RFPs (this is to assure that the RFP respondents will commit resources to implement technologies).

Step 4: Task Force evaluation & recommendation of the RFPs. Depending on the submissions and subject area, this may be a long, usually a year or more, process. There is also a simultaneous evaluation by Business Committee.

Step 5: Architecture Board consideration for consistency.

Step 6: Board decision based on recommendations from the appropriate Technology Committee & Business Committee.

A fast track process that bypasses some of the steps is also supported to introduce standards quickly. More details about OMG can be found at www.omg.org.

It is perhaps appropriate to comment on OMG's business model. OMG operates in a manner similar to a "non-profit Microsoft" instead of the typical standards bodies such as ISO and ITU. Most CORBA standards go into production within few years, sometimes months (as noted above, a submission to OMG must be accompanied by a "letter of intent" stating the intention to develop a commercial implementation of the standard within one year.) OMG standards rarely starve for vendor implementations because it is a forum in which vendors ask users to set requirements, and users ask vendors for new features.

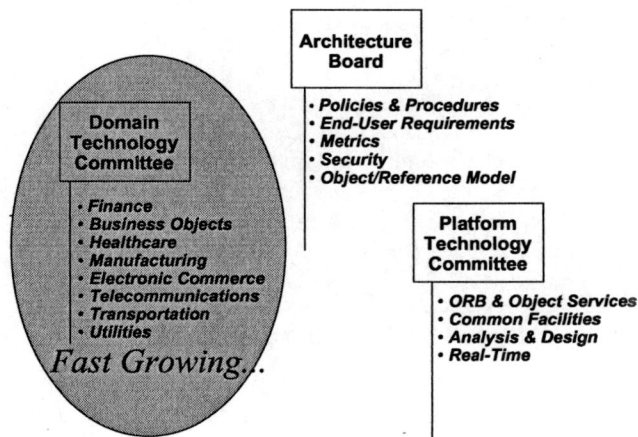

Figure 3-8: OMG Organization

3.4.2 Basic CORBA Concepts

CORBA was introduced in 1991 by OMG to go a step beyond OMA to specify the technology for interoperable distributed OO systems. CORBA specifications represent the ORB technology adopted by OMG and are published as OMG documents.

The key concepts of CORBA are (see Figure 3-9):
- Any object can be a client, server or both. For purpose of description, CORBA uses the C/S model where clients issue requests to server objects. The server objects are called "object implementations" or "servants" because they are the implementations of the invoked object.
- An interface, described in the OMG/ISO IDL (Interface Definition Language), represents contracts between client and server objects. The IDL shows the methods and the parameters being passed through the interface and is the only means of communication between clients and server objects. CORBA requires that every object's interface be represented in OMG IDL. Clients only see the object's interface, never it's implementation. Thus, as long as the interface is the same, you can substitute another implementation of the object – this is intended for plug and play. Program stubs and skeletons are produced as part of the IDL compiling.
- CORBA essentially specifies the middleware services that are used by the objects. A key part of this middleware is devoted to locating a server object, invoking the needed method on the object and returning results. A variety of other services such as naming, threading, lifecycle and event services are also provided.
- All interactions between CORBA objects are mediated by the ORB – clients cannot invoke server objects directly and server objects cannot respond to the clients directly. This requirement transfers all responsibilities to the ORB. Thus, ORB is the "Master. It finds the objects you need, wakes them up, gets them to work on your behalf to produce the results you need, and delivers the results back to you. In addition, if there is a failure, ORB is responsible for failure recovery. ORBs also hide the underlying implementation and system heterogeneity details. What a life it would be without ORBs!

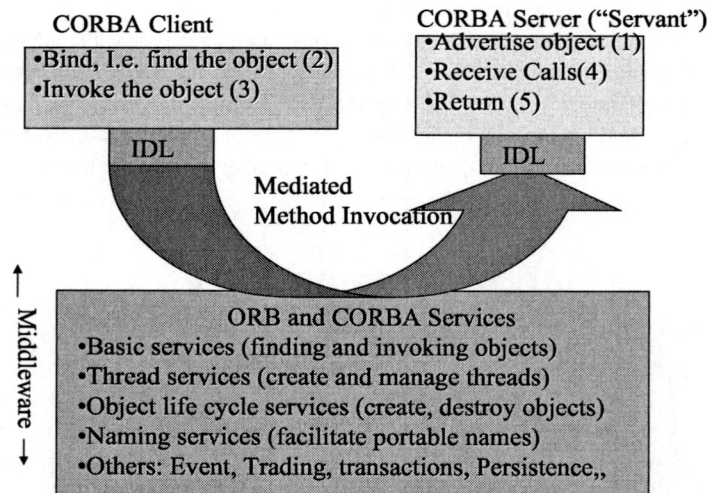

Figure 3-9: A Simple Example of CORBA

Let us now go through a simple flow of Figure 3-9 (we will discuss variants of this model later). First, the server object's interface has to be defined in IDL and the client has to write the code that invokes the server object through this IDL. At run-time, the following steps take place (the step numbers are indicated in the Figure):

1. The server object is started (this is one of the many options as we will see later). It advertises its availability to the ORB that records in its directory the location of the object. The server object then indicates that it is ready to receive calls and waits.

2. The client object issues a "bind" command for the server object (i.e., find server object). The ORB receives this call, locates the server object and returns an object reference to the client.

3. The client uses this object reference to issue the actual call to the server object.

4. The ORB passes this request to the server object that receives the request and processes it.

5. The server object returns the results to the client through the ORB.

The ORB invokes the various services to accomplish this interaction – more about it later.

3.4.3 CORBA Facilities

As defined by the OMG, the ORB provides mechanisms by which objects transparently interact with each other. It enables the objects to establish connections, communicate with one another, make requests, and receive responses. To achieve this, ORB sets up communications links and routes information between objects as needed. It literally provides brokerage services between clients and servers by determining the most efficient way for a client to receive a service and for a server to provide the service. The interfaces to the ORB and the interfaces to the objects built using the ORB are well defined. The underlying implementation of the ORB is not important to the developers building distributed object-oriented applications. Different interfaces can be defined for an object and multiple ORBs can exist in a system. Thus, different client applications can refer to the same object residing on a server but each client application can be given its own interface.

Figure 3-10 shows the architectural components of CORBA and the interfaces/flows between various components. The arrows indicate whether the ORB is called or performs an up-call across the interface. Before discussing the components, let us review some underlying concepts:

▪   **OMG Interface Definition Language (IDL)**: CORBA is built around a single object model embodied in IDL and uses a single specification language, the OMG Interface Definition Language (IDL), to specify the services provided by an object. The parameters needed for each task are specified and compiled using an IDL compiler. Once again, IDL is pure specification, not implementation and enables platform independence. The OMG IDL standard has been stable since 1991. OMG IDL syntax resembles C++. IDL compilers are provided by vendors. CORBA API is also defined in IDL. The IDL itself does not say anything about implementation of an interface, however all CORBA products generate bindings in languages such as Java, C, C++, and Smalltalk. IDL definitions are stored in a public interface directory. Access to this repository can be controlled through access control lists (ACLs). CORBA also specifies language bindings, i.e., mapping of IDL constructs to programming languages.

▪   **Synchronous and Asynchronous Support**: CORBA ORBs initially supported synchronous (i.e., client process is blocked until a reply from the server process is received by the client process) as well as delayed synchronous (i.e., the client process continues work after initiating a request and periodically polls the ORB for the response) communications. The delayed asynchronous model was not used very heavily because it was associated with dynamic binding – a nice but rarely used facility of CORBA (see below). CORBA 3.0 includes messaging services that support a variety of asynchronous communications. CORBA 3.0 also supports publish/subscribe model through its event/notification services. We will discuss CORBA 3.0 in Section 3.4.6. The applications can use synchronous, asynchronous, or publish/subscribe approach depending on application requirements.

▪   **Static Versus Dynamic Binding**: CORBA ORBs allow static as well as dynamic binding between objects. Dynamic binding between objects uses run-time identification of objects and parameters. In one sense, the static and dynamic binding of CORBA is similar to the static and dynamic binding used by SQL. From a developer's point of view, each serves the same purpose (i.e., establishes a link between a client and server object for invoking an operation). However, a developer chooses between these two options depending on how much information is available at compile time. The static binding between objects is based on compile time specification of objects and parameters. Static binding, initially proposed by HP and Sun, is more efficient at run-time because all needed libraries are included at compile time. It is also quite simple (a C call with parameters which specify the object to be invoked, the environment of the object, and any other values needed by the server object). On the other hand, dynamic binding between objects uses run-time identification of objects and parameters. Dynamic binding, initially proposed by DEC (Digital Equipment Corp.), incurs more overhead at run-time but is very flexible (it can be used when some of the information needed to complete an operation is not available at compile time). Dynamic binding needs extensive run time support (i.e. a repository that can be accessed at run time to locate objects). It is particularly useful for applications that are undergoing rapid changes or for a tool to support interactive browsing. The client can use the Dynamic Invocation interface or an IDL stub (determined at compile time).

Editorial comment about dynamic binding: Dynamic binding, although quite appealing in concept has been used very rarely in real life situations. Due to its low use, Minimal CORBA, (a skinny version of CORBA for small applications) has excluded the dynamic feature.

- **General Inter-ORB Protocol (GIOP) and IIOP (Internet Inter-ORB Protocol):** The GIOP is specially designed for ORB-to-ORB communications. It is intended to operate over any connection-oriented transport protocol. Many mappings of GIOP have been specified. The best known is the Internet Inter-ORB Protocol (IIOP) that specifies how GIOP messages are exchanged over a TCP/IP network. IIOP allows a lightweight implementation of CORBA so that CORBA can operate directly on top of TCP/IP and is a required feature of current CORBA implementations.

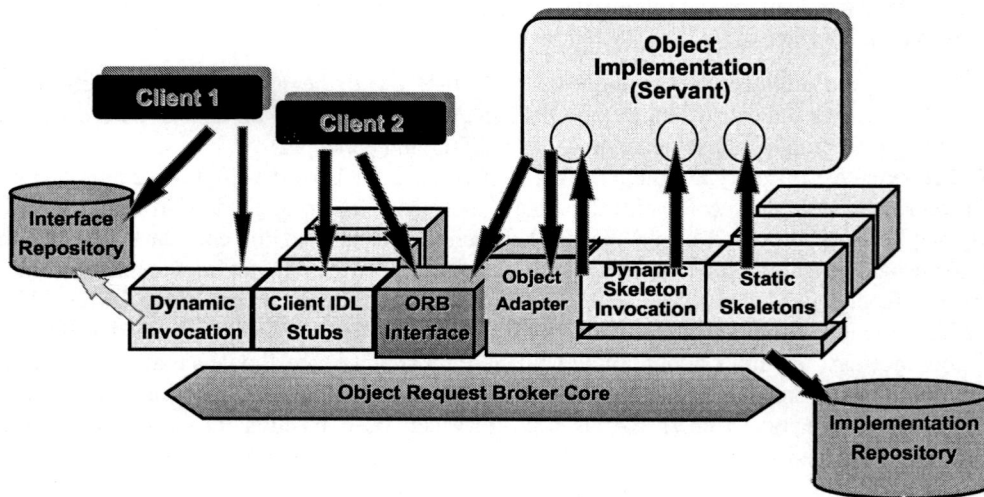

Figure 3-10: CORBA Architectural Components

Let us now go through the CORBA architectural components shown in Figure 3-10 and discuss how they interrelate with each other. Let us start from the left.

Interface Repository: A dynamic representation of available object interfaces is provided in an Interface Repository. This repository represents the interfaces (or classes) of all objects in the distributed environment. The clients access the Interface Repository to learn about the server objects and determine what type of operations can be invoked on an object. With CORBA 2.0, the Interface Repositories provide global identifiers to uniquely and globally identify a component and its interface across multivendor ORBs. This is accomplished through repository IDs. A repository ID is a unique, system-generated, string that is used across Interface Repositories. You can generate repository IDs by using the DCE Universal Unique Identifiers (UUIDs) or via a user-supplied unique prefix that is appended to IDL generated names.

Dynamic Invocation Interface (DII): This interface allows dynamic construction of object invocation. The interface details are filled in by consulting with the Interface Repository and or other run-time sources. By using the dynamic invocation, Client Application 1 can interact with Server Objects (provided descriptions of these Server Objects could be found in the Interface Repository). This component is rarely used.

Client IDL Stubs: The Client stubs make calls to the ORB Core. These precompiled stubs make it easier for the Clients to issue static requests to objects across a network. Client Application 2 uses this option.

ORB Interface: This interface goes directly to the ORB for operations that are common across all objects. This interface consists of a few APIs to local services that may be of interest to some applications. This interface is commonly used by a server object to tell the ORB that it is running and ready to accept calls. The client can also directly interact with the ORB for operations through this interface.

Object Adapters: An object adapter is essentially a scheduler that mediates between the ORB and the object implementations ("servants"). It is responsible for a) generating object references for the called servants, b) activation and de-activation of servants, and c) sending requests to servants. CORBA specifies that each ORB must support a standard adapter called the Basic Object Adapter (BOA). However, BOA was not well specified. To address these issues, CORBA 3.0 has introduced POA (Portable Object Adapter). We will discuss POA in Section 3.4.6.

Server IDL Stub: These stubs, also known as server skeletons, provide the code that invokes specific server methods. These stubs are generated as part of the IDL compilation and are very similar to the client IDL stubs. They provide the interface between object adapters and the server application code. Server Objects use this stub.

Dynamic Skeleton Interface (DSI): The DSI, introduced in later versions of CORBA (CORBA 2.0), provides a run-time binding for servers that do not have IDL generated stubs. These dynamic skeletons can be very useful for scripting languages to dynamically generate server objects. When invoked, the DSI determines the server object to be invoked and the method to be invoked (the selection is based on parameters values supplied by an incoming message). In contrast, the server skeletons generated through compiled IDL are defined for a certain object class and expect a method implementation for each method specified in the IDL. The DSI can receive calls from static or dynamic client invocations.

Object Request Broker (ORB): ORB is obviously at the heart of CORBA. ORB acts as a switch in a CORBA environment — it sets up links between remote objects and routes the messages between objects. Any client object can make a request from a server object through the ORB and any server object can send responses back to the client objects through ORB. We will discuss ORB in more detail in the next section.

Implementation Repository: Implementation details of each interface, including the operating system specific information used for invocation, the attributes used for method selection, and the methods that make up the implementation are loaded into the Implementation Repository. The Implementation Repository can be implemented differently by different vendors. Some implementations of CORBA support IML (implementation mapping language) to describe the implementation details.

3.4.4 Using CORBA – An Example

Let us quickly review the overall process used in building CORBA applications to illustrate the key concepts. A more detailed example with code samples is given in Section ???). The activities involved in developing OO applications in CORBA environments involve the following major activities (see Figure 3-11):
- Create Interface definitions by using OMG IDL.
- Build the server (Object Implementation).
- Build the client application(s).
- Deploy the application.

Create CORBA Definitions: The main activity in this step is the creation of interface definitions in the CORBA IDL format by using a text editor. The IDL statements are compiled by using an IDL compiler. The IDL definitions can be kept in text files or stored in an Interface Repository so that the clients can learn about the server objects and determine what type of operations can be invoked on an object. As stated previously, the interface of an object is used to declare the operations supported by an object. It consists of a collection of the operations and their signatures, i.e., the operation's name, it's arguments, and argument types. For example, the following statements specify the interface for a bank account object in CORBA IDL (we have simplified it somewhat for illustrative purposes):

```
interface bank_account_interf /* interface name is bank_account_interf */
make_deposit  (/*The  operation is make_deposit */
in integer amount_deposited; /* input is amount_deposited represented as an integer */
in integer account_no; /* input is account_no */
out integer current_balalnce ) /*  output parameter is current_balalnce */
make-withdrawal ( /*Operation is  make-withdrawal */
in integer amount_withdrawn; /* input is amount_withdrawn */
in integer account_no; /* input is account_no */
out integer current_balalnce ) /*  output parameter is current_balalnce */
```

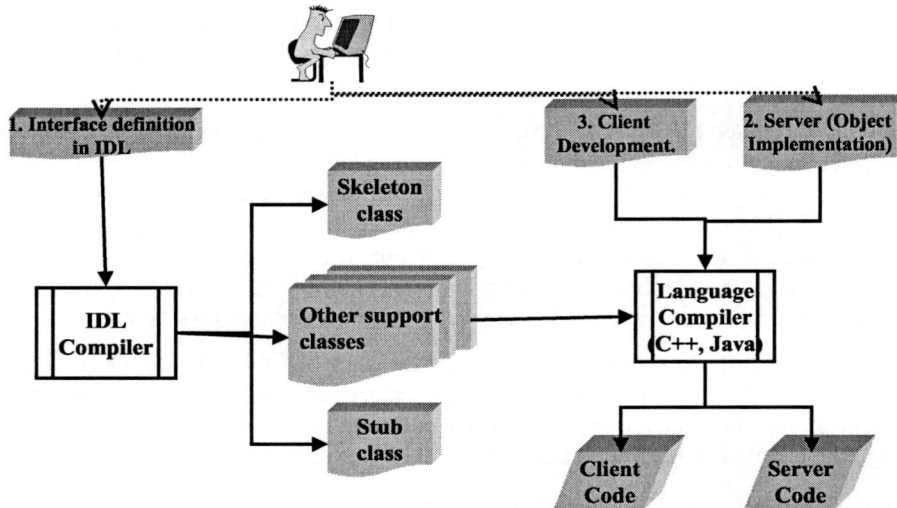

Figure 3-11: CORBA Application Development

The interface statement shows what operations can be performed on the order object. Each interface statement defines an interface and contains the descriptions of the operations (operation signatures).

In addition to IDL, the implementation details of each interface are created. You can use CORBA commands to generate a default implementation description from the interface definition. These implementations are loaded into the Implementation Repository.

After you create the interface definition using IDL, you compile the IDL file to create two very important components for building your application: the client stub and the server skeleton. The client stub and server skeleton are the code templates for building CORBA client and server programs (see Figure 7.8). The client stub is used only to build client programs that use static binding, i.e., the client code is linked with the client stub to form the client application. The client stub is not used to build client programs that use dynamic invocation. The server skeleton is always used as the framework for building the server application, regardless of the invocation type used by the client.

Build the Server (Implement the Object): CORBA servers can be quite complex and diverse. Building of the program servers requires the following steps:

- Generation of server skeletons - The IDL statements are compiled to generate a server skeleton. This compilation also uses the information contained in the IML files. The server skeleton contains method templates that show entry points for all of the implementation methods. The server skeleton also contains the server dispatcher code that makes the implementations and the methods known to the ORB (the dispatcher is called by the Basic Object Adapter). A registration routine is also generated as part of the server code (this routine is called at server start-up).
- Develop server initialization code - Each server initialization needs code to register the implementation, activate the server's implementation, enter a main loop to receive requests, and exit after un-registering and releasing resources. In addition, the server needs routines for creating objects and managing references to these objects. The server skeleton is used to develop this code.
- Develop the methods - The major activity in building a CORBA server is to write the code for the methods that execute the operations. For each method template, you must create the code for the methods. Methods can be implemented as executable code, calls to legacy applications, or scripts to integrate command line interfaces with existing applications.

Build Clients (Static): After a server has been built and registered, clients can be built to invoke the servers. As stated previously, CORBA clients use static invocations (i.e., clients know at compile time the objects and the operations on these objects) or dynamic invocation (i.e., the clients determine at run-time the objects and the operations on these objects). We only discuss static invocation here. The main steps involved in building a static invocation CORBA client are a) generate client stub from IDL or from the interface repository, b) build the client code, and c) compile and link the client.

Deploy and Run the Application: CORBA applications can be packaged and shipped as server only, client only or a collection of clients and servers. To accomplish this, you need to send your IDL, implementation specifications, in addition to the executables. The application is installed and used in a CORBA run-time environment (see Figure 3-12). The IDLs and IML are loaded into the Interface and Implementation Repositories first. Then, the server is installed. At server start-up, it registers itself so that the invoking clients can locate it. The Dynamic Invocation Interface allows dynamic construction of object invocation. The interface details are filled in by consulting with the Interface Repository and/or other run-time sources. The Client IDL Stubs make calls to the ORB using interfaces and make it easier for the Clients to issue static requests to objects across a network. Object Adapters allow an object implementation to access the ORB services. CORBA specifies that each ORB must support a standard adapter called the Basic Object Adapter (BOA). Server Skeletons (Server IDL Stubs) provide the static interfaces to each service supported by the server.

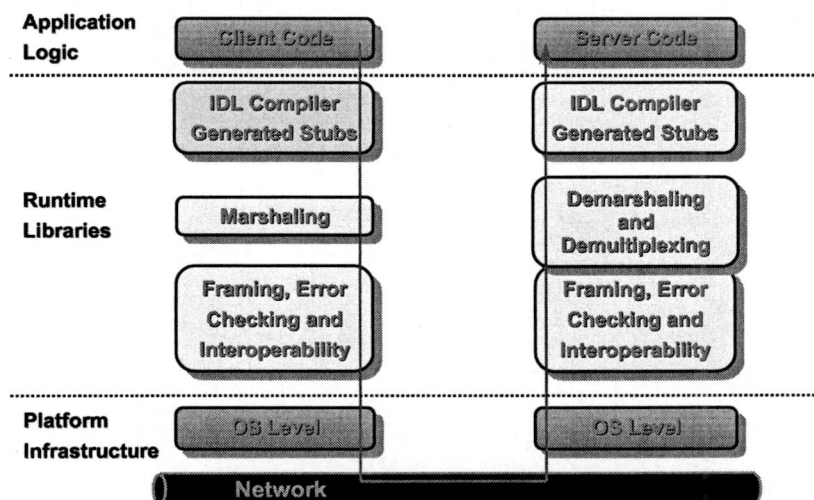

Figure 3-12: Information Flow in a CORBA Deployed Application

---

Script Servers

Some vendors support script servers that use operating system commands in a script (e.g., Bourne shell in UNIX), or command procedures. Building of script servers requires somewhat different steps. First, the implementation must indicate an "activation_type (script)" parameter. In addition, special techniques for handling input-output are needed because scripts are not interactive. Passing information from clients to the scripts also requires calls to special routines. Script servers also have several limitations such as data types, performance restrictions, and object creation. Despite several limitations, script servers are handy tools for quickly developing CORBA applications.

3.4.5 Combining CORBA with Web and XML

Many applications need to combine/integrate CORBA with Web and XML. Perhaps the oldest and the best known method is to invoke CORBA calls from a CGI gateway. Other approaches are:

- Invoke CORBA directly from the Web browsers (Netscape browsers can issue the CORBA IIOP calls).
- Use HTTP as a transport protocol underneath ORBs. A few small companies have implemented this option.
- Use CORBA to interact between Java applets across machines. This option is quite popular at present.

What about XML and CORBA - Well, an XML document can be used as a parameter of IDL. Thus, CORBA can be used as a transport mechanism for XML.

The main idea is to integrate CORBA with Web so that Web browsers can work directly with CORBA objects. Figure 3-13 shows a schematic for the most popular choice (i.e., through Java applets). The Figure shows the 3 major steps: 1) Download the Java applet from the server, 2) load the Java applet, and 3) invoke CORBA calls from the applet. In addition, non browser applications can also call the same server (i.e., as long as the IDL of the CORBA server is known, the Java applet clients or any other client can call the CORBA server. The CORBA server can then invoke the back-end systems.

Please keep in mind that OMG has developed a standard called XMI (XML Interchange) that essentially uses XML as a means to exchange information between UML documents (i.e., XMI flattens UML and then passes it around to different UML sites). This could lead to other ways of integrating CORBA with XML.

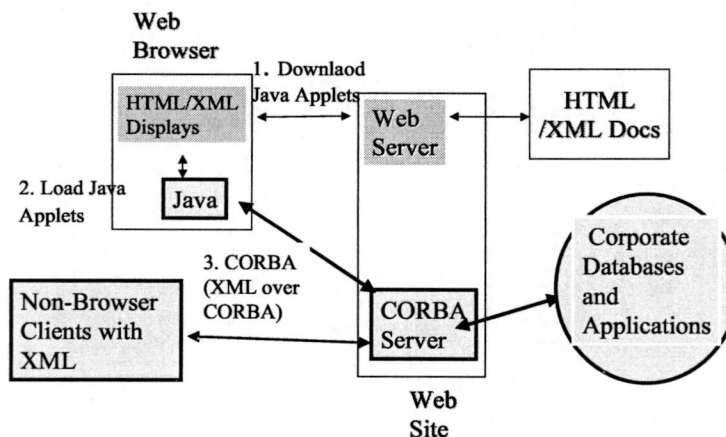

Figure 3-13; Combining CORBA with Web and XML

3.4.6 CORBA 3.0

CORBA has gone through several stages of evolution. It started with specification 1.0 and is at 3.0 at the time of this writing. Initial specifications of CORBA (i.e., CORBA 1.1 and 1.2) did not specify many important services such as security, concurrency, and transaction processing. This had two major consequences. First, the CORBA-based applications were limited in scope (e.g., they provided no security). Second, different vendors chose to plug different services to get going. This has led to CORBA implementations by vendors that do not interoperate with each other (recall that interoperability is the main goal of CORBA!). ORBs from different vendors interoperate with each other only through deliberate efforts and joint agreements between vendors.

CORBA 2.0, introduced in December 1994, addressed many problems by adding many new services. CORBA 2.0 expanded some ORB capabilities -- the Interface Repository expanded and a new interface (Dynamic Skeleton Interface) for servers was added. However, most of the new 2.0 capabilities added have been in the distributed object services of CORBA. Specifically, CORBA 2.0 specifies standards for the following object services (see Figure 3-14):

- Object Naming Service to allow different components to locate each other in a CORBA environment.
- Event Service to support notification to objects for different events.
- Persistence Service for storing components in data stores such as object databases, relational databases and flat files.
- Object Life Cycle Service for creation, modification, and deletion of objects.
- Transaction Management Service to support object-oriented transactions in distributed environments.
- Concurrency Control Service for obtaining and freeing locks.
- Security Service to protect components from unauthorized users.
- Time Service to provide universal timing service.
- Licensing Service to meter the use of components.
- Query Service to provide SQL and OQL (Object Query Language).
- Properties Service to associate properties (e.g., time and date) to components.
- Relationship Service to establish dynamic associations (e.g., referential integrity) between components.
- Externalization Service to get data in and out of a component in streams. This can be used in multimedia applications.

CORBA 2.0 also addressed the problem of ORB interoperability by defining inter-ORB protocols (IOPs) for interoperability of Object Request Brokers. Although the IOPs do not impact application software development (IOPs are too low level for applications), they play a key role for an overall middleware architecture.

CORBA 3.0 is the new kid on the block in the CORBA world. It is built upon CORBA 2.0 and 2.2 and has expanded many existing capabilities plus added new ones. Examples of CORBA 3.0 capabilities are:

- CORBA Messaging
- Real-Time CORBA
- Objects-by-value (OBV)
- CORBA Firewall
- CORBA Component Model
- CORBA Scripting Language
- JAVA-to-IDL/IDL-to-JAVA
- DCE/CORBA Interworking

CORBA 3.0, due to its inclusion/expansion of existing and introduction of new services, is a comprehensive solution for distributed object computing. In fact, CORBA 3.0 has been used as an umbrella term to refer to a suite of specifications which, taken together, add a new dimension of capability and ease-of-use to CORBA.

We will discuss the main features of CORBA 3.0 in the Tutorial Module (see the Chapter "CORBA Technologies – A Closer Look").

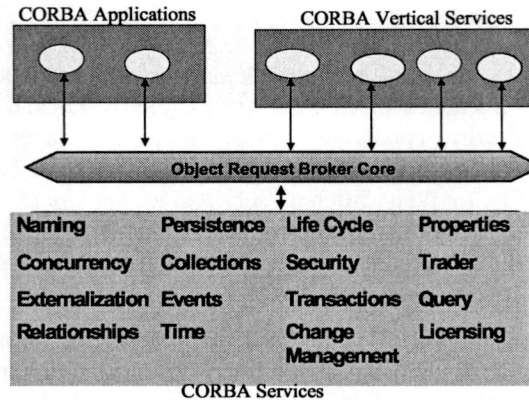

Figure 3-14: CORBA 3.0 Capabilities

3.4.7 CORBA Summary

Object-oriented technologies and techniques have natural applications in distributed systems. Entities in distributed systems can be viewed as objects exchanging messages. OMG was formed to create a suite of standard languages, interfaces and protocols for interoperability of applications in heterogeneous distributed environments. CORBA is an OMG specification for invoking objects in a distributed environment.

Initial specifications of CORBA did not specify many details. However, a wide range of capabilities have been added under the CORBA 3.0 umbrella. In addition, several Domain Task Forces and Platform Special Interest Groups (PSIGs) have been busily working on different aspects of CORBA. Examples of key CORBA developments in CORBA Services, distribution protocols, specialized models, vertical domain facilities, support for analysis and design, and basic object computing model are summarized in the sidebar "Key CORBA Developments".

Many vendors are announcing CORBA compliant software. Examples of a few products are:
- Inprise's Visibroker
- Iona's Orbix
- BEA's M3
- IBM's Object Broker
  - IBM (SOMobjects) - free for OS/2, AIX, Windows
  - PrismTech (OpenBase)
  - ParcPlace (Distributed Smalltalk)
  - TIBCO (ObjectBus)
  - ObjectSpace (Voyager)
  - Objective Interface Systems (ORBexpress) also marketed by ObjecTime
  - Bionic Buffalo
  - I-Kinetics
  - RogueWave (Nouveau)
  - Java RMI over CORBA IIOP

A wide range of free and prototype CORBA implementations are also available. For a list of such products, consult the Washington University at St. Louis Web site (www.wustl.edu/~schmidt/corba-products.html). For a wide range of sources, including test tools, go to http://www.vex.net/~ben/corba/.

Additional details about CORBA are listed in the sidebar "Key Sources of Information for CORBA". The OMG home page (http://www.omg.org) is an excellent source of the recent activities in CORBA.

Although we have concentrated on the object request brokers so far, the concept of brokers is general and is currently being exploited in the message broker architectures (see the sidebar "Message Broker: Another Kind of Broker").

Key CORBA Developments

- **CORBA Services**
  - Naming   - directory service: (svc name) → (svc object reference)
  - Trading   - service discovery: (svc attributes) → (svc name)
  - Event/notification - Producers notify consumers using events
  - Transactions - distributed (2Phase Commit), flat transactional objects
  - Security   - different levels (IIOP over SSL, additionally used)
  - Messaging   - Support asynchronous processing for loosely coupled
- **Distribution protocol**
  - GIOP (Generalized Interorb Protocol) and its mappings (IIOP)
  - Mappings for SS7, ATM
- **Specialized Models**
  - Real-time, Fault-tolerant, Minimum CORBA
- **Vertical Domain facilities (e.g., Telecom)**
  - CORBA to TMN Interworking
  - Wireless CORBA
- **Support for Analysis and Design**
  - UML(universal Modeling Language)
- **Basic Object-Oriented Computing Model**
  - CORBA Components, ISO/OMG IDL and language mappings

Message Broker: Another Kind of Broker

A broker mediates between clients and servers (i.e., instead of a client directly connecting to a server, it first connects to a broker that in turn finds a suitable server). The concept of a broker is independent of the implementation of the broker. For example, the best known implementation of the broker architecture is the object request broker (ORB) as presented in OMG CORBA specification. In CORBA, the ORB mediates the interactions between remote objects. Another type of broker, called a message broker, is being presented as a viable implementation of the broker architecture.

A message broker is not restricted to objects. Instead, it delivers messages between disparate applications, including legacy applications. The underlying technologies used by the message broker may consist of RPCs or MOMs, although MOM does appear to fit this model quite well. The basic idea of a message broker is that it can provide brokerage services asynchronously and support a "publish/subscribe" model. The message broker can also be rule-based, i.e., you specify the rules to be used by the middleware to perform certain actions. Message brokers are at the core of "Enterprise Application Integration" platforms that are commercially available from many vendors such as Active Software, Vitria, and IBM. EAI platforms, based on message brokers, are expected to be a $11 Billion market by the early 2000s. We will discuss EAI platforms in a later chapter.

The Gartner Group proposed and advocated message brokers as key to the future success of distributed

---

computing. The Gartner Group predictions in the mid 1990s that message brokers will be as widespread as database gateways and data warehouses have been correct. See, for example, Bort, J., "Can Message Brokers Deliver?", Applications Software Magazine, June 1996, pp.70-76).

Key Sources of Information for CORBA

- J. Seigal, "CORBA 3.0: Fundamentals and Programming", second edition, Wiley, 2000.
- D.Schmidt, *Overview of CORBA*: http://siesta.cs.wustl.edu/~schmidt/corba-overview.html.
- R.Orfali, D. Harkey, *Client/Server Programming with Java and CORBA*, Wiley 1997.
- T. Mowbray, W. Ruh, *Inside CORBA*, Addison-Weslet 1997.
- T. Mowbray, R. Zahavi, *The Essential CORBA*, Wiley 1995.
- T. Mowbray, R. Malveau, *CORBA Design Patterns*, Wiley 1997.
- J. Farley, *Java Distributed Computing*, O'Reilly 1997.
- The OMG Website: http://www.omg.org.
- "Corba Connections", Comm. of ACM, Special Issue, October 1998.
- http://www.vex.net/~ben/corba/ -- An interesting private Web site that watches CORBA ORB Core Feature Matrix, CORBA services Feature Matrix , and CORBA Vendor Platform Matrix.
- CORBA Business Objects (Workflow).
- Object Management Research in LASER (Pleiade).
- CORBA Web gateway.
- Joint Inter Domain Management.
- Towards a Web Object Model - by Frank Manola.
- Gabriel D. Minton's papers.
- CORBA Design Patterns - by Thomas Mowbray and Raphael Malveau.
- Alan Pope (The CORBA Reference Guide).
- Kate Keahey's Brief Tutorial on CORBA.
- Manfred Schneider's CORBA links.
- CORBA for Linux.
- Segue Software (was Black & White) (SilkPerformer, SilkMeter, SilkPilot, SilkObserver).
- Tom Valesky's Free CORBA page.
- Defense Information Infrastructure - Predicting CORBA Performance.
- Benchmarking some ORBs.
- GNOME - GNU Network Object Model Environment.
- Michi Henning.
- Dominique Benech's COBALT: A KQML-CORBA based Architecture for Intelligent Agents Communication.
- Live Script and Live Repository.

3.5 Microsoft's DCOM (Distributed Component Object Model)

3.5.1 Overview

In March 1996, Microsoft announced its "ActiveX" strategy that integrates the desktop services with the World Wide Web. DCOM (Distributed Component Object Model) serves as a core technology for remote communications between ActiveX components. In the late 1990s, Microsoft positioned DCOM and ActiveX as a complete environment for components and distributed objects in Microsoft environments. Almost everything coming out of Microsoft was based on ActiveX. Later, Microsoft expanded DCOM to COM+. At the time of this writing, COM+ is being phased out in favor of XML Web Services (discussed in the next section).

We briefly discuss DCOM and ActiveX because many current applications are based on this technology. Although ActiveX provides many capabilities, from a distributed objects point of view, the following features are significant (we will see the details in the following subsections):

- All ActiveX components communicate with each other by using DCOM. So a Java applet (an ActiveX component) can call a remotely located Microsoft Word document (another ActiveX component) over DCOM. See Section 3.5.2.
- The Web browser can behave as a container. For example, the Microsoft Internet Explorer can contain components such as Word documents, Java applets, C code, and Excel spreadsheets. See Section 3.5.3.
- Web technologies (browsers, HTML pages Java applets) can be intermixed with desktop tools (spreadsheets, word processors) for distributed applications. See Section 3.5.4.
- Serve facilities such as SQL servers and legacy access gateways can be invoked from ActiveX clients. See Section 3.5.4.

3.5.2 DCOM (Distributed Component Object Model) as an ORB

As discussed previously, ActiveX uses DCOM to provide communications between remote ActiveX components. In this sense, DCOM is the ORB for ActiveX. The basic scenario is that Windows will be a huge collection of ActiveX components and interfaces, with DCOM serving as the ORB. It is expected that all system services will be written as DCOM objects. These and other services can be provided by Microsoft or any third party vendors.

DCOM provides the basic brokerage services for ActiveX. It supports APIs for static as well as dynamic invocation of objects. DCOM uses DCE RPC for interactions between COM objects. DCOM's object model is somewhat limited because DCOM does not support multiple inheritance. In other words, COM supports inheritance through pointers that link different interfaces together. Figure 3-15shows the role of DCOM in ActiveX and Microsoft environments.

The following facilities of DCOM should be noted (see the sidebar "DCOM Versus CORBA" for additional discussion):

- **Interface Definition Language (IDL)**: DCOM uses interfaces that are very similar, in concept, to the CORBA interfaces. An interface defines a set of related functions. The DCOM IDL is used to define an interface, the method it supports, and the parameters used by each method. DCOM IDL can be used to define your own interfaces, in addition to the Microsoft provided interfaces. For example, at the time of this writing, OLE/ActiveX consists of more than 100 interfaces, each supporting about 6 functions. Additionally, more than 100 Win32-style APIs are supported.
- **Object Definition Language (ODL) and Type Libraries**: DCOM supports an Object Definition Language (ODL) used to describe metadata. The interface specifications and metadata are stored in a repository, known as Type Library. Type Libraries are equivalent to the CORBA Interface Repositories.
- **Object Services**: DCOM provides very rudimentary object services at the time of this writing. Examples of the services provided are a basic licensing mechanism, a local directory service based on the Windows Registry, a basic life cycle facility, persistence services for file systems, and a very simple event service called connectable objects. This is in addition to the naming services provided by the Type Libraries. However, the overall ActiveX Platform is expected to support other services such as X.500 directories.

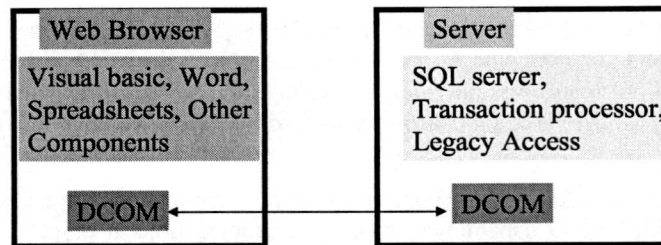

Figure 3-15: DCOM Conceptual View

DCOM Versus CORBA: Similarities and Differences

We will start with the typical disclaimer about technology comparisons, i.e., both technologies are evolving at the time of this writing and consequently the similarities/dissimilarities will also change with time. Our objective is to present, what appears to be, the philosophical and fundamental approaches being used by the two technologies.

At a high level, there are several similarities between CORBA and DCOM. However, several differences appear when you look closely.

Similarities:
- Both are based on the object model.
- Both utilize the interface concept and utilize an Interface Definition Language (IDL).
- Both use static and dynamic calls from clients to servers.
- Both use a repository to locate objects and invoke them (CORBA calls it the Interface Repository and DCOM calls it a Type Library).

Dissimilarities:
- CORBA is a specification but DCOM is an implementation.
- DCOM uses, in addition to IDL, Object Definition Language (ODL), for defining metadata. CORBA uses a single IDL for everything.
- DCOM uses the universal unique ID (UUID), based on OSF DCE, to locate and invoke objects. CORBA does not use UUIDs. It uses object references and repository to locate and invoke objects.
- DCOM uses the OSF DCE RPC as the basic transport mechanism between remote objects. CORBA uses several options such as IIOP (Internet Inter-ORB Protocol) that uses TCP/IP sockets and ESIOP (Environment Specific Inter-ORB Protocol) that runs on top of DCE.
- CORBA only uses connection-based (i.e, TCP) services while DCOM favors connectionless (i.e., UDP) services. DCOM does support TCP connections but it favors UDP for purpose of scaling (do not have to keep track of large number of open sessions).
- CORBA 2.0 has specified a very extensive set of services that include transaction management, security, concurrency control, life cycle, query, etc. In comparison, DCOM services at present are somewhat limited (these are being added through the ActiveX Platform).

Additional discussion about differences between DCOM and CORBA can be found in [Orfali 1996, Foody 1996]. The WWW Consortium held an excellent technical seminar on November 18, 1996, on trade-offs between DCOM and CORBA. Public information discussed in this seminar can be obtained from the Web site (http://www.w3.org).

3.5.3 Web Browsers as Containers of ActiveX Components

An ActiveX component is the basic unit of ActiveX applications. Different components can be combined to develop and deploy new applications. These components may be specifically written for this application or reused from some other project or even purchased off the shelf.

Components by definition cannot survive on their own — they require containers in which to execute. Visual Basic is a common example of a container in the desktop world. Visual Basic applications load needed components from a machine's local disk or a file server. In the Internet World, the Web browsers are a common example of a container — they load Java applets (Java applets are components) and provide an environment to run them (i.e., contain them). Let us focus on Web browsers as containers.

Before ActiveX, Web browsers were primarily serving as containers for Java applets. We have discussed Java applets in Chapter 4. These applets are downloaded from Web servers (embedded in HTML pages) and then the Web browser is used as a container. ActiveX has extended the scope of browsers as containers by allowing ActiveX components to be "contained" by Web browsers. At present, the Microsoft Internet Explorer is the main browser used as an ActiveX container. This can be very useful. For example, the Web browser can now contain spreadsheets, Word documents, and code written in C++, C, Java, or other programming languages. You can build powerful applications that may, for example, supply specialized viewers with the data to be viewed (the viewer and the data is loaded as needed from the network and runs inside the Web browser as a container).

3.5.4 ActiveX Controls – Building Downloadable Web-based Components

Microsoft's ActiveX Controls (formerly called either OLE controls or OCXs) are the special brand of ActiveX components that have been optimized for Internet use. ActiveX controls are, in principle, very similar to Java applets. For example, ActiveX controls, like Java applets, are self-contained pieces of functionality that run inside some kind of container (e.g., a Web browser). Thus, ActiveX controls can be embedded in Web pages and downloaded on demand. However, unlike Java applets, ActiveX controls can be written in various languages such as C, C++, and Java. Unlike Java applets, which are downloaded in a machine-independent format and usually interpreted within the browser, ActiveX controls are binaries. Another difference is that Java applets today are supported primarily by only one kind of container -- the Web browsers. ActiveX controls, on the other hand, are supported by different kinds of containers (e.g., Visual Basic applications).

Developers of downlaodable Web-based applications have two basic choices: Java applets or ActiveX Controls. See the sidebar "Java Versus ActiveX Controls" for discussion.

A plethora of different ActiveX controls already exist in the marketplace. Examples are the controls that implement spreadsheets, data viewing, mainframe connectivity, voice recognition, and the like. Many of these existing controls can be downloaded and executed within an ActiveX-capable browser. Thus, there is an instant supply of available ActiveX components for Web-based applications.

3.5.5 ActiveX Server

The ActiveX Server is based on the Microsoft Information Server (IIS) that is integrated with the Windows NT network operating system. The ActiveX Server includes the Microsoft BackOffice family that includes the Microsoft SQL Server and the Microsoft Systems Management Server. ActiveX Server provides scripting and control facilities to tie into legacy systems or to perform other specialized functions on the server side. The scripting capabilities support PERL, JavaScript and Visual Basic Script.

3.5.6 General Observations and Comments

The facilities of ActiveX have evolved over the years. However, competitors to ActiveX such as CORBA have also matured considerably in the same time period. At present, ActiveX can be combined and "bridged" to CORBA and other technologies. DCOM to CORBA bridges are available from companies such as Iona at the time of this writing. The Iona COM/CORBA bridge provides two-way mapping: it allows DCOM objects to be treated as CORBA and vice versa.

Literature on ActiveX keeps growing. The Microsoft Web site (http://www.microsoft.com) provides access to latest announcements, white papers, and frequently asked questions (FAQs). The book by David Chappell, "Understanding ActiveX and OLE", Microsoft Press, latest edition,is a good overview of the subject matter.

Java Versus ActiveX Controls

Java applets and ActiveX Controls are two valid choices for building downloadable Web applications. The leading browsers, Netscape Navigator and Microsoft's Internet Explorer, support both options. Let us discuss the choice between these two options.

Java applets should be chosen if a component must run on heterogeneous client systems, if the Java security exposures are manageable, and if you are not concerned with the performance limitations of the Java interpretive model (interpreters can be slower than binary code).

ActiveX Controls should be chosen if the component is targeted at Microsoft systems, is needed in a wider range of containers than just Web browsers, and must run as efficiently as possible (ActiveX Controls download binary code).

As expected, both of these models will evolve. For example, "just-in-time" compilers for Java will improve the performance by compiling an applet byte code on arrival. The platform independence issue may disappear because Microsoft is planning to port ActiveX on multiple platforms. Keep in mind that ActiveX Controls also support Java applets (Java environment is modified so that it uses DCOM).

Source: Chappell, D., "Component Software Meets the Web: Java Applets vs. ActiveX Controls", Network World, May 1996.

Combining Distributed Objects with the Web - Let Me Count The Ways

There are several ways to combine distributed objects with Web. Here are the principal ones that use CORBA, OLE/ActiveX, SOAP, and others).

The CORBA route:
- Invoke CORBA calls from a CGI procedure (a script or a subroutine written in C or in any other language) that resides on the Web server. In this case, the CGI procedure is the CORBA client. This is the oldest and most well-known method.
- Invoke CORBA directly from the Web browser. Netscape browsers are beginning to support the CORBA IIOP calls directly. Thus, the Web browser sites behave as CORBA clients.
- Use CORBA to interact between Java applets across machines. This option is currently supported by a few vendors (like Sun).

The ActiveX/DCOM route:
- Invoke DCOM calls from a CGI procedure (a script or a subroutine written in C or in any other language) that resides on the Web server.

- Invoke DCOM calls directly from the components contained in the Web browser (e.g., the Microsoft Internet Explorer). These components may be written in C, C++, Visual Basic, Java or other programming languages behaving as ActiveX Controls and contained inside the browser.

- Invoke DCOM calls from the ActiveX components such as spreadsheets that may invoke Java applets or other components residing on Web servers.

Other routes:
- Use the Sun Remote Method Invocation (RMI) between remotely located Java applets. This technology is very well supported by SunSoft tools but is only restricted, at the time of this writing, to interactions between Java applets only.
- Use HTTP to invoke remote objects. A few small companies have implemented this option by using HTTP underneath ORBs. This option should be used rarely, if at all. We are mentioning it for completeness.

The SOAP Route – The New Way:
- Use XML Web Services and SOAP, the new kid on the block. SOAP is a lightweight protocol for accessing objects over HTTP.

Time to Take a Break
✓ Distributed Object Technologies
✓ CORBA and DCOM
- Web Services, .NET, J2EE
- SOAP and EJBs

Suggested Review Questions Before Proceeding

- What is CORBA and what are its basic facilities and services?
- What is Microsoft's DCOM and what are its basic facilities and services?
- Compare and contrast CORBA with DCOM

3.6 J2EE, .NET, and Web Services – Component-based Platforms

CORBA, DCOM, and RMI were developed in the 1990s. At present, they are all subsumed and, in some cases, replaced by the current component-based platforms that are commercially available at the time of this writing. The two principal contenders at present are Sun's J2EE and Microsoft's .NET. The XML Web Services, introduced in the previous chapter, play a key role in both architectures.

3.6.1 Sun's J2EE (Java 2 Enterprise Edition) Overview

The Java2 Enterprise Edition (J2EE) is a mult-tiered architecture framework proposed by Sun Microsystems. J2EE is a component-based approach to the design, development, assembly, and deployment of enterprise applications. J2EE is not tied to the products and APIs of any one vendor. It is important to note that J2EE is a standard, not a product. J2EE specifications describe agreements between applications and the *containers* in which they run. Sun has collaborated with many vendors of e-Business platforms, such as BEA, IBM, and Oracle, in defining J2EE. The overall J2EE architecture, shown in Figure 3-16 consists of the following components:

- Client-tier components run on the client machine.
- Web-tier components run on the J2EE server.
- Business-tier components run on the J2EE server.
- Enterprise information system (EIS) tier software runs on the back-end systems.

A J2EE application can be configured into two, three or four hardware tiers; however, many J2EE multi-tiered applications are configured as three-hardware-tiered applications. The application components are typically distributed over three different hardware locations. : front-end machines where the clients reside, J2EE application server machines where the Web server and the business logic resides, and the back-end machines where the enterprise database or legacy reside.

J2EE applications, as indicated above, are made up of components. A J2EE component is a self-contained functional software unit that is assembled into a J2EE application with its related classes and files and communicates with other components. J2EE components are written, naturally, in the Java programming language. The main idea is that the J2EE components are assembled into a J2EE application, verified that they are well—formed, in compliance with the J2EE specification, and deployed to production where they are run and managed by the J2EE server. This is all provided and supported by the J2EE platform. J2EE applications use a thin client -- a lightweight interface to the application that does not do things like query databases, execute complex business rules, or connect to legacy applications. Intense operations like these are off-loaded to the middle tier for scalability and performance. The J2EE specification defines four types of components: clienttier components, Web-tier components, business-tier components, and enterprise information system components.

Client-tier components that run on the client machines - A J2EE application can be Web-based or non-Web-based. An application client executes on the client machine for a non-Web-based J2EE application, and a Web browser downloads Web pages and applets to the client machine for a Web-based J2EE application.

Web-Tier Components - J2EE Web components run on the Web server. These components can be either JSP pages or servlets. Servlets are Java programming language classes that dynamically process requests and construct responses. JSP pages are text-based documents that include Java code in HTML documents. What about static HTML pages and applets? These are not considered Web components by the J2EE specification because they are considered as part of the client tier. The Web tier might include a JavaBeans object to manage the user input and send that input to enterprise beans running in the business tier for processing.

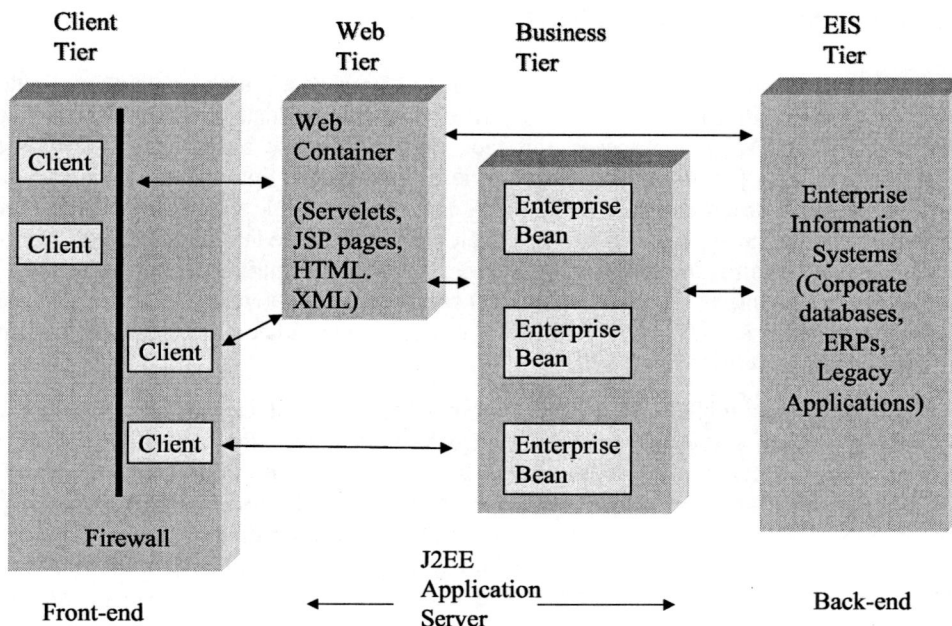

Figure 3-16: J2EE Environment

Business-Tier Components - Business code, which is logic that solves or meets the needs of a particular business domain such as telecom, banking, retail, or finance, is handled by enterprise beans running in the business tier. An enterprise bean receives data from client programs, processes it (if necessary), and sends it to the enterprise information system tier for storage. An enterprise bean also retrieves data from storage, processes it (if necessary), and sends it back to the client program.

Enterprise Information System Tier Components - The enterprise information system tier handles enterprise information system software, and includes enterprise infrastructure systems such as corporate databases, enterprise resource planning (ERP), mainframe transaction processing, purchasing and payment systems, and other legacy information systems. J2EE application components might need access to enterprise information systems to retrieve and process enterprise information.

Reference Implementation and Additional Features - As mentioned previously, J2EE is a specification not an implementation. In addition to the specifications, Sun also ships a reference implementation (RI) of J2EE. Developers write applications to RI to ensure portability of their components. RIs are used for testing purposes and should not be used for production. In addition, vendors that offer J2EE platforms provide specialized features not found in the standard. Some of these features impact portability, such as e-Commerce components, or B2B integration.

To summarize, J2EE has packaged several Java-based technologies that have been developed over the years (e.g., Java applets, Java servlets, JSPs) into a multi-tiered architecture for enterprise wide applications. The most significant aspect of J2EE, from an enterprise computing point of view, is the EJB (enterprise Java Bean) that provides transactional services for corporate applications. We will take a closer look at EJBs in Section 3.8. We will revisit J2EE several times in other chapters of this book. More information about J2EE can be found at the Sun Web site (http://java.sun.com/j2ee).

3.6.2 Microsoft's Dot Net (.NET) Overview

Another popular example of component-based platforms is Microsoft's Dot Net, commonly written as .NET. The Microsoft Dot Net platform includes a family of services and products, built on XML and components. At the core of .NET are *XML Web services* — in fact, .NET is Microsoft's platform for XML Web services. XML Web Services, also just known as Web Services, were briefly introduced in the previous chapter. These Services concentrate on software components that are accessible via standard Web protocols. The main idea is that most of the applications will be developed and delivered through the Web, in particular, the components exchange information through XML over HTTP. In the spirit of components, each XML Web service provides a public interface (called a contract) used to find and invoke the service. In essence, any client or server that can listen and respond to HTTP requests and send and receive XML by using external interfaces can become an XML Web Service.

Keep in mind that Microsoft.NET is a product, whereas J2EE is a standard to which products are written. Microsoft.NET is largely a rewrite of Windows DNA (Distributed Network Architecture), which was Microsoft's previous platform for developing enterprise applications. The underlying component model of XML Web Services implemented in .NET is closely related to the COM/DCOM (common object model) model that is part of DNA. DNA includes many proven technologies such as Microsoft Transaction Server (MTS) and COM+, Microsoft Message Queue (MSMQ), and the Microsoft SQL Server database. The new .NET Framework replaces these technologies, and includes a Web Services layer as well as improved language support.

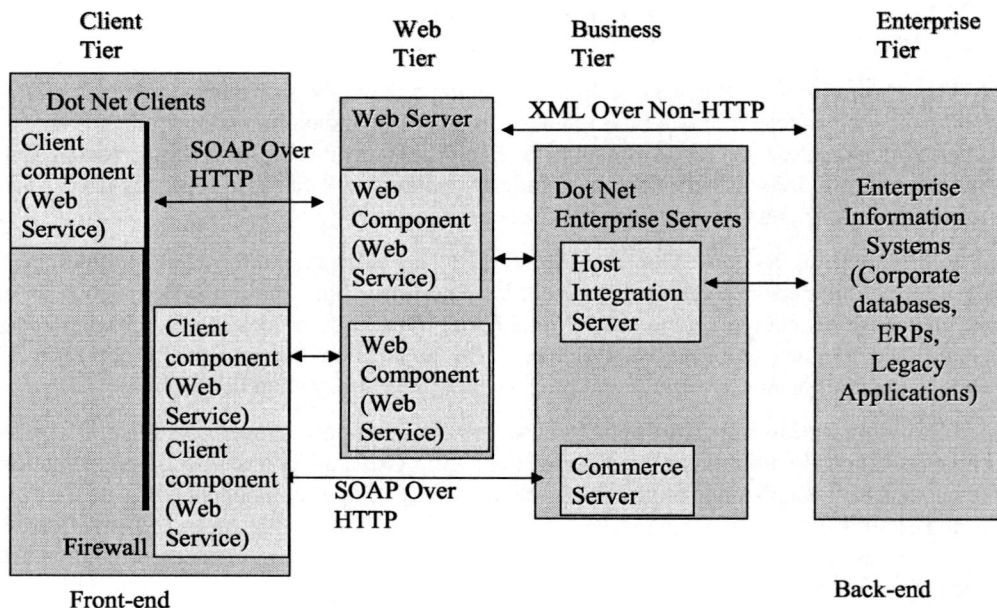

Figure 3-17: Microsoft .NET Architecture

Figure 3-17 shows the overall architecture of .NET (Note that the general architecture of .NET is quite similar to J2EE). It shows how the XML Web Services, shown as Web Services, appear as components in different tiers of the generic component-based architecture. These components communicate with each other by using SOAP (Simplified Object Access Protocol) that can be used to transport XML documents over HTTP. Specifically, Microsoft is building the .NET platform in terms of the following:

.NET Clients: Clients are PCs, laptops, workstations, phones, handheld computers, Tablet PCs, game consoles, and other smart devices that run operating systems such as Windows CE, Windows Embedded, Window 2000, and Windows XP. These clients can house Web Services as components.

.NET Enterprise Servers: The Microsoft .NET Enterprise Servers are intended for enterprise use and have the capabilities to communicate with back-end systems. Examples of these servers are:

- **Microsoft Windows .NET Server** to build, deploy, manage, and run XML-based Web services.
- **Microsoft Application Center 2000** to deploy and manage Web applications.
- **Microsoft BizTalk™ Server 2000** to build XML-based business processes across applications and organizations.
- **Microsoft Commerce Server 2000** for building e-commerce solutions.
- **Microsoft Content Management Server 2001** to manage content for dynamic e-business Web sites.
- **Microsoft Exchange Server 2000** to enable messaging and collaboration.
- **Microsoft Host Integration Server 2000** for bridging to data and applications on legacy systems.
- **Microsoft Internet Security and Acceleration Server 2000** for secure Internet connectivity.
- **Microsoft Mobile Information 2001 Server** to enable application support by mobile devices like cell phones.
- **Microsoft SharePoint™ Portal Server 2001** to find, share, and publish business information.
- **Microsoft SQL Server™ 2000** to store, retrieve, and analyze structured XML data.

Communication Protocols: .NET is built on top of a set of XML-based protocols such as Simple Object Access Protocol (SOAP), Universal Discovery, Description and Integration (UDDI), and Web Service Definition Language (WSDL). These protocols collectively allow Web Services to be described (through WSDL), discovered (through UDDI), and transported as XML messages over HTTP (through SOAP). These services, collectively known as SOAP/XML services, are discussed in Chapter 4 of this Module.

Web Server Sites: Web sites for accessing HTML documents - These sites can also house XML Web Services as components. XML Web Services on Web sites offer a direct means for applications to interact with other applications. XML Web Services applications hosted on Web sites, as well as on remote systems, can communicate via the Internet by using XML and SOAP messages.

Building Block Services: Microsoft is creating a core set of building block services that perform routine tasks and act as the backbone for developers to build upon. The first set of XML Web services are known as .NET My Services (the product formerly code-named "HailStorm"). These services are user-centric -- they use the Microsoft Passport user authentication system to deliver information to users based on preferences they have established.

Tools: Microsoft Visual Studio® .NET and the Microsoft .NET Framework provide a development platform for developers to build, deploy, and run XML Web services. They maximize the performance, reliability, and security of XML Web services.

- **Visual Studio .NET** allows developers to build applications by using Microsoft Visual Basic (of course!), Visual C++, and a new programming language called C# (see below). All languages supported by Visual Studio prior to the release of .NET (except for Java) are still supported by Visual Studio. Visual Studio.NET also provides support for Microsoft's new **C#** language which is semantically equivalent to Java, with just a few minor syntactical differences.
- **The .NET Framework** is an application execution environment that handles essential plumbing chores. The main feature of .NET Framework is language independence (discussed below).

Language Independence Through C#: Microsoft.NET offers language-independence and language-interoperability that is very close to Java concepts. This is a very interesting aspect of the .NET platform. A .NET component can be written, for example, partially in VB.NET, the .NET version of Visual Basic, and C#, Microsoft's new object-oriented programming language. This is how it works. First, the source code is translated into Microsoft Intermediate Language (MSIL or IL). This IL code is language-neutral, and is analogous to Java bytecode. The IL code is then interpreted and translated into a native executable -- the Common Language Runtime (CLR), analogous to the Java Runtime Environment (JRE). The CLR is Microsoft's intermediary between .NET developers' source code and the underlying hardware, and all .NET code ultimately runs within the CLR.

.NET Experience: The .NET experiences are XML Web services built for individuals and for businesses. Some of the products that Microsoft is transitioning into .NET experiences are:

- **Hailstorm** is Microsoft's portfolio of building block Web Services that will be hosted by Microsoft and possibly Microsoft partners. Some Hailstorm Web services will be available on a subscription basis, and others will be free. Information about Hailstorm is available at http://www.microsoft.com/net/hailstorm.asp.
- **Microsoft's Passport** offers an authentication service as a *shared context* so that many other Web Services can depend upon Passport for identity and security credentials. Passport is similar to the Certification Authorities found in PKI (Public Key Infrastructure) systems. Users can store their contextual information (who they are, what they are authorized to do, usernames, passwords, credit card information, etc.) into a single repository that can be shared by multiple Web Services and clients. With shared context, you type this information in once in a passport, and that information is then accessible to all Web services that you choose to give access to that information. The Passport service is now freely available as a Web service-oriented universal identification mechanism through Hailstorm.

The XML Web services, as stated previously, are at the core of .NET. These Services are discussed in some detail in Section 3.7. A great deal of information about various aspects of Web Services is available at present over the Web. An example of the source is the Microsoft site (http://msdn.microsoft.com). We will revisit .NET in other chapters of this book also.

3.6.3 XML Web Services - A Revisit

With XML Web Services, also just known as Web Services, any application can be integrated so long as it is Internet-enabled. The core of Web services is XML messages over standard Web protocols such as HTTP. These industry standards provide a lightweight and widely accepted communication mechanism that any programming language, middleware, or platform can participate in. The main idea of Web Services is that service providers will register themselves in public or private business registries. The registered services will fully describe themselves, including interface structure, business requirements, business processes, and terms and conditions for use. Visit http://www.xmethods.com/ for a listing of some interesting Web services, and links to their accompanying WSDL documents. Consumers of the registered services read these descriptions to understand the abilities of these Web Services and then invoke them. Web Services consist of the following technologies:

- **UDDI** (Universal Description, Discovery and Integration) to provide a directory of services on the Internet. This is conceptually similar to the CORBA/DCOM directory and naming services. More information regarding the UDDI initiative is available at http://www.uddi.org/.
- **WSDL** (XML Web Services Description Language) an XML document that describes the location and interfaces a particular service support. It is conceptually similar to IDL. The Web Services Description Language (WSDL) specification is available at http://www.w3.org/TR/wsdl.
- **SOAP** (Simple Object Access Protocol) through which XML Web Service consumers can send and receive messages using XML. SOAP is conceptually similar to CORBA IIOP. The SOAP specification is available at http://www.w3.org/TR/SOAP/.
- **XML & HTTP** are the core open Internet technologies that are the foundation of XML Web Services, The main source of information for XML and HTTP is www.w3.org.

Web Services are in reality simply XML-based *interfaces* to application and system services and are in fact "Web face lifts" to existing systems. Like many other distributed applications, a Web Service accepts remote service requests, does some processing, and then returns a response. Figure 3-18 shows the steps that take place to develop and use a "loan" service:

1. The provider creates, assembles, and deploys the loan service using the programming language, middleware, and platform of the provider's own choice. It then defines the Web service in WSDL. A WSDL document describes a Web service to others.

2. The provider registers the service in UDDI registries. UDDI enables developers to publish Web services and that enables their software to search for services offered by others.

3. A prospective user finds the service by searching a UDDI registry. The consumer sends a request to UDDI (www.uddi.org) to locate where the loan service is located.

4. UDDI returns the loan service address (www.loan.com/WSDL) that in fact is a link to WSDL.

5. The consumer now issues a call to WSDL to learn how to invoke the loan service (i.e., what method to use, what are the input/output parameters).

6. The WSDL returns a definition of the loan service in WSDL format.

7. The consumer prepares a SOAP message, an XML document, that is sent to www.loan.com over HTTP.

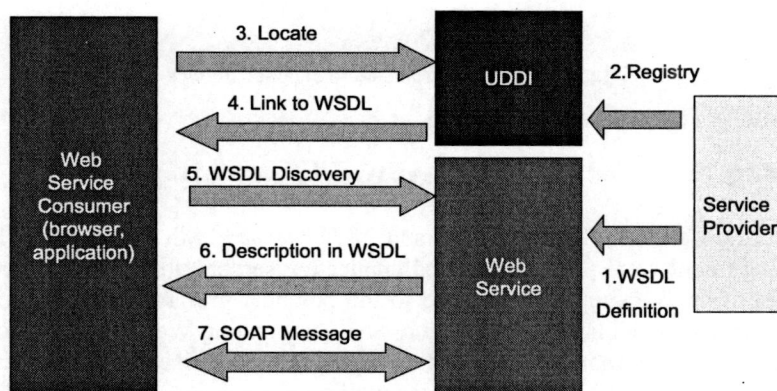

Figure 3-18: XML Web Services in Action

To satisfy this external flow, a number of things happen internally as shown in Figure 3-19. A Web Service contains a Listener that waits for requests. When a request is received, the Listener forwards it on to a component that implements the required business logic. This component might be designed to operate specifically as a Web Service, or it could be some other business component or COM/Java object that the Web Service wants to expose to the outside world. In the latter case, a developer will write some logic that acts as a façade for the Web Service and forwards the request on to the COM/Java object itself. The COM/Java object or other business logic may make use of a database or other data store, accessed using a Data Access layer. As expected, this looks like the classic N-tier architecture in which the Web Service can get its information from a database or another Web Service.

It should be noted that the Web Services core technologies (WSDL, UDDI, SOAP, XML, HTTP) are mainly sufficient for simple Web services. Extended B2B exchanges require an agreed-upon structure for business transactions with multiple steps, backouts, and document flows. These application requirements often stretch the limits of a purely SOAP based implementation. Developments such as **ebXML** (www.ebxml.org) address these issues through a suite of XML specifications and related processes for B2B collaboration and integration. Although there are vendor disagreements on SOAP extensions, ebXML, and service flow descriptions (so what is new!), all major players, including Sun and Microsoft, generally agree that SOAP, WSDL, and UDDI are good things for the future and are working together to establish Web Services standards.

A great deal of information about various aspects of Web Services is available at the Microsoft site (http://msdn.microsoft.com).

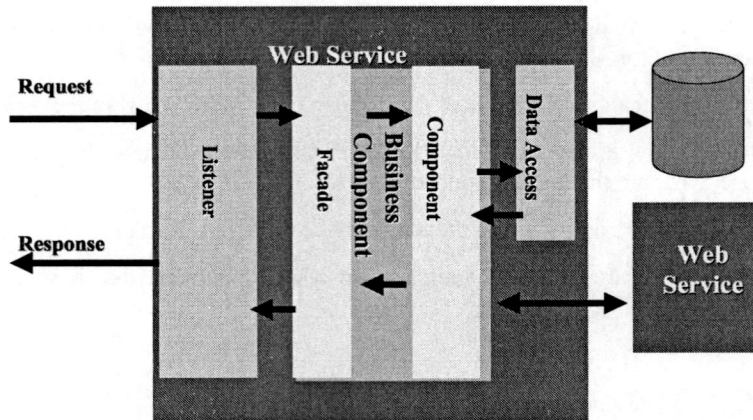

Figure 3-19: Internal Architecture of a Web Service

3.6.4 Combining XML Web Services with J2EE and .NET

The main question is: how do Web Services, J2EE, and .NET interplay with each other? J2EE and .NET are evolutions of existing middleware platforms (called application servers) that have not been used to build large-scale enterprise-wide Web applications. Due to the potential promise of Web Services to provide enterprise-wide or even global applications, both sides are incorporating Web Services into their platforms. In reality, a great deal of 'plumbing' is needed to build Web Services for large-scale transactional applications. Rather than writing all that plumbing yourself, you can write an application that runs within a *container* that provides the transactional services for you. By purchasing the container off-the-shelf, you do not need to be an expert at plumbing. In fact, J2EE and .NET both are providing containers for Web Services.

Microsoft .NET and Web Services: As stated previously, .NET is a product strategy that is largely a rewrite of Windows DNA, which was Microsoft's previous platform for developing enterprise applications. The new .NET Framework replaces many of the DNA technologies with Web Services components – thus, Web Services is a centerpiece of .NET. The developer model for building Web Services with .NET is shown in Figure 3-20.

- The .NET application logic is hosted in Web-tier and business-tier containers. These containers provide the middleware services ("plumbing") needed for enterprise applications. The Web-tier container is a typical Web server with support for the Active Server Pages (ASP.NET).
- The business-tier container supports business processing and data logic and provides transaction, security, and persistence needed for enterprise applications. The business tier of the .NET application is built using .NET managed components. This tier performs business processing and data logic.
- Business partners can connect with the .NET application through Web Services technologies (SOAP, UDDI, WSDL, BizTalk).
- "Thick" clients, Web browsers, and wireless devices connect to Active Server Pages (ASP.NET) that render user interfaces in HTML, XHTML, or WML. Complex user interfaces are built using Windows Forms.
- The business tier connects to databases using Active Data Objects (ADO.NET) and existing systems using services provided by Microsoft Host Integration Server 2000. It can also connect to business partners using Web Services technologies (SOAP, UDDI, WSDL).

Basically, a wide range of front-end and back-end systems can connect to the .NET containers by using Web Services.

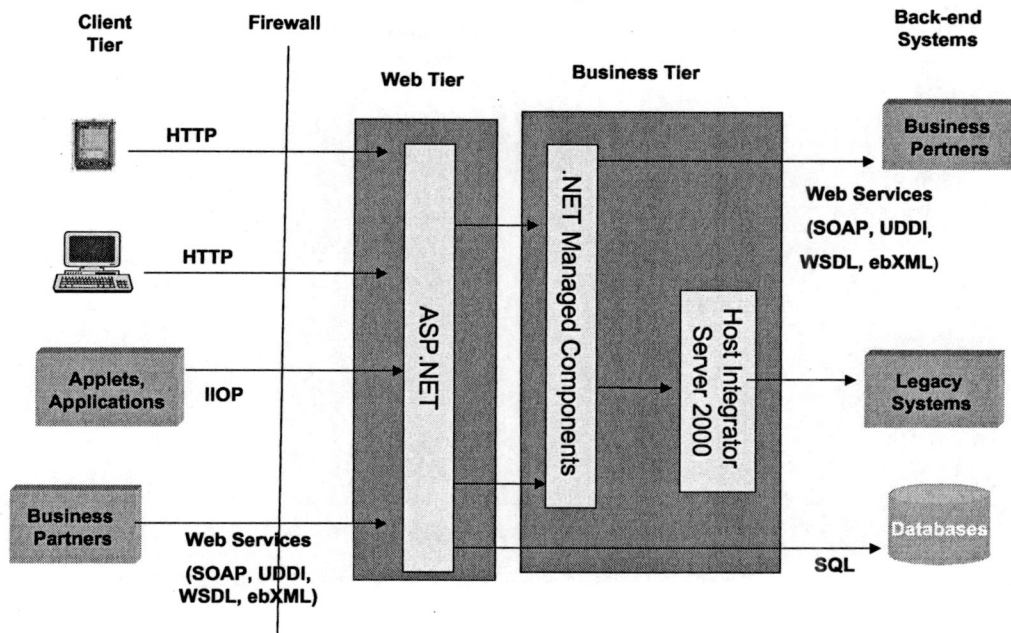

Figure 3-20: Inclusion of Web Services in .NET

J2EE and Web Services: J2EE has mainly been an architecture for building server-side deployments in Java. It can be used to build Web sites, software components, or complete applications. J2EE has been extended to include support for building XML-based Web Services. These Web Services can inter-operate with other Web Services that may or may not have been written to the J2EE standard J2EE Web Services development model shown in Figure 3-21:
- The application logic is hosted in Web-tier and business-tier containers. These containers provide the plumbing needed for enterprise applications. The Web-tier container is a typical Web server that supports the JSP and servlets.
- The business-tier container supports business processing and data logic and provides transaction, security, and persistence needed for enterprise applications. In many J2EE applications, business logic is built using Enterprise JavaBeans (EJB) components. EJBs connect to databases using Java Database Connectivity (JDBC) or SQL/J, or existing systems using the Java Connector Architecture (JCA). It can also connect to business partners using Web Services technologies (SOAP, UDDI, WSDL, ebXML) through the Java APIs for XML (the JAX APIs).
- Web browsers and wireless devices connect to JavaServer Pages (JSPs).
- Applets and "thick clients" connect directly to the EJB layer through the CORBA Internet Inter-ORB Protocol (IIOP).
- Business partners can connect with J2EE applications through Web Services technologies (SOAP, UDDI, WSDL, ebXML). A servlet can accept Web Service requests from business partners.

Thus, a wide range of front-end and back-end systems can connect to the EJB, the main J2EE container, by using Web Services.

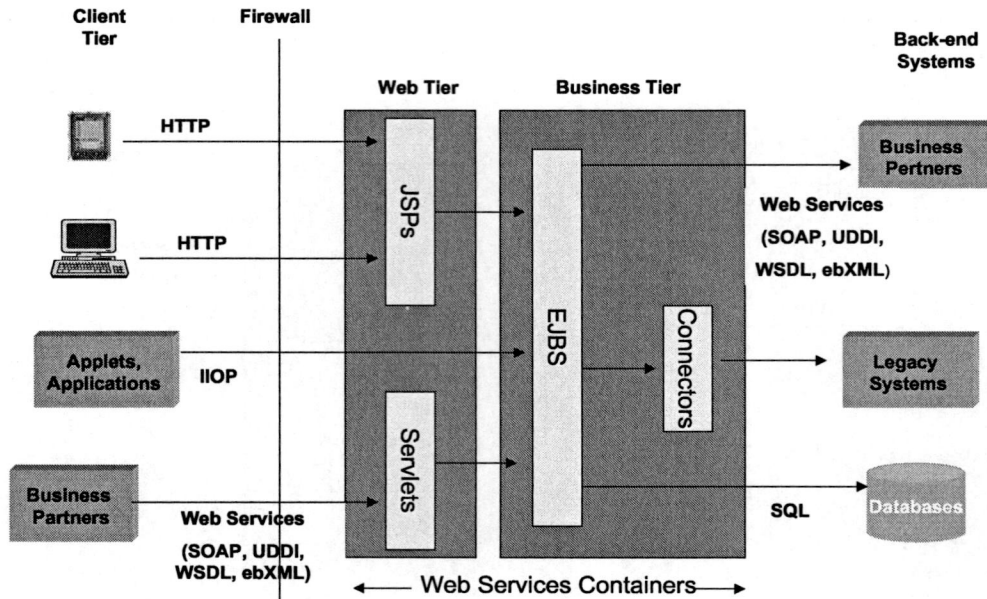

Figure 3-21: Integration of Web Services in J2EE

3.6.5 Comparison Between J2EE and .NET

Comparing .NET and J2EE reminds me so much of the several CORBA versus DCOM comparisons that I performed in the late 1990s for several projects. They use the same overall approach as noted by the similarity of the overall architecture diagrams shown above. However, there are some differences. Table 3-3 captures the main features. Let us discuss a few items.

Difference in Focus: The main idea is that J2EE is a standard and .NET is a product. This is, once again, similar to the CORBA versus DCOM debate that we visited earlier in this chapter (CORBA is a standard while DCOM is a product). The advantage of a standard is that multiple vendors can implement software but the disadvantage is that these implementations may differ. This is the good news and bad news. The good news is that it is a standard and the bad news is that it is a standard! The product, on the other hand can be built and delivered uniformly by the supplier. This also has good news and bad news associated with it. In general, it is better to have a single-vendor solution because it is usually more reliable, interoperable, and less error-prone than a two-vendor bridged solution. One of J2EE's strengths is that it has spawned a great deal of activity in the marketplace, which has resulted in more total functionality than any one vendor could ever provide. In addition, J2EE is platform-agnostic, running on a variety of hardware and operating systems, such as Win32, UNIX, and Mainframe systems. However, J2EE implementations are often not interoperable, due to different vendor solutions. You could, if you wanted, buy J2EE compliant products from large vendors such as IBM, Oracle, and BEA. .NET provides a fairly complete solution from a single vendor--Microsoft. This solution may lack some of the higher end features that J2EE solutions offer, but in general, the complete Web Services vision by Microsoft will find its way into products.

Web Services support: J2EE as well as .NET support Web Services, as discussed previously. J2EE supports Web Services through the Java API for XML Parsing (JAXP). This API allows developers to perform any Web Service operation today through manually parsing XML documents. For example, you can use JAXP to perform operations with SOAP, UDDI, and WSDL. Additional APIs are also under development. Also, more than a dozen SOAP implementations support Java -- almost all are built on J2EE (servlets or JSP). In addition, several UDDI API implementations are available and others are becoming available rapidly. The current releases of Microsoft.NET also enable organizations to build Web Services with automatic generation of Web Service wrappers to existing systems. You can perform operations using

SOAP, UDDI, and SDL (the precursor to WSDL). Visual Studio.NET provides wizards that generate Web Services. It is expected that both J2EE as well as .NET will continue to heavily support Web Services.

Integration with Existing (including Legacy) Systems: An important part of the J2EE vision for integration is the J2EE Connector Architecture (JCA) -- a specification for plugging in *resource adapters* that understand how to communicate with existing systems, such as SAP R/3, CICS/COBOL, Siebel, and so on. If such adapters are not available, you can write your own adapter. In addition to JCA, J2EE provides a set of facilities such as the Java Message Service (JMS) to integrate with existing messaging systems, CORBA for interfacing with code written in other languages that may exist on remote machines, and JNI (Java Network Interface) for loading native libraries and calling them locally. .NET also offers legacy integration through the Host Integration Server 2000. COM Transaction Integrator (COM TI) can be used for collaborating transactions across mainframe systems and Microsoft Message Queue (MSMQ) can integrate with legacy systems built using IBM MQSeries. Finally, BizTalk Server 2000 can be used to integrate with systems based on B2B protocols, such as Electronic Data Interchange (EDI).

Language and Run Time Support: J2EE promotes Java-centric computing, and as such all components deployed into a J2EE deployment (such as EJB components and servlets) must be written in the Java language. To use J2EE, you must commit to coding at least some of your e-Business systems using the Java programming language. Other languages can be brought into a J2EE solution through Web Services, CORBA, JNI, or the JCA, as previously mentioned. On the other hand, .NET supports development in any language that Microsoft's tools support due to the new CLR (with the exception of Java, of course. Microsoft has also introduced its new C# language which is equivalent (with the exception of portability) to Java and is also available as a programming language within the Visual Studio.NET environment. Because of CLR, a single .NET component can therefore be written in several languages. Both Sun J2EE and Microsoft .NET provide runtime mechanisms that insulate software developers from particular dependencies. In addition to XML, Sun J2EE and .NET offer language-level intermediation via the Java Runtime Environment (JRE) and the Common Language Runtime (CLR) respectively.

To summarize, the J2EE versus .NET battle will go on for a while. Both have promises and the marketplace will decide the winner(s). Many articles are being devoted to these differences in the trade journals. Since both approaches are evolving, it is not a good idea to get carried away with minute details. A good white paper that gives a detailed comparison of .NET Versus J2EE can be found at the Middleware Company site (www.middleware-company.com).

Table 3-3: ,NET versus J2EE

Feature	.NET	J2EE
Type of technology Product	Product	Standard
Vendors	Microsoft	More than 30
Web Services Technologies Supported (SOAP, WSDL, UDDI)	Yes	Yes
Web Tier Support	ASP.NET	JSP, Servlets
Business-Tier Support	.NET Managed Components	EJB
Primary Language and Language Independence	C# and Common Language Runtime (CLR)	Java and Java Runtime Environment (JRE).
Database access	ADO.NET	JDBC, SQL/J
Back-end Legacy System Access	Host Integrator Server 2000	Connector
Implicit middleware (load-balancing, etc)	Yes	Yes

Time to Take a Break
✓ • Distributed Object Technologies
✓ • CORBA and DCOM
✓ • Web Services, .NET, J2EE
• SOAP and EJBs

Suggested Review Questions Before Proceeding

- Compare and contrast .NET with J2EE
- What are the Web Services, why they are important, and how are they related to .NET and J2EE?
- How do Web Services work in the J2EE and .NET environments?
- What role does SOAP play in Web Services? Can you use Web Services without SOAP?

Caution: The following two sections have some coding examples. If you are afraid of coding or cannot deal with it, please skip the code segments.

3.7   SOAP – The .NET Foundation Protocol

3.7.1 SOAP (Simple Object Access Protocol) Overview

SOAP is a lightweight and simple XML-based protocol that is designed to exchange information between programs on the Web. Thus, the information exchanged is structured and typed. SOAP specification, currently being worked on by W3C, defines a) the SOAP message format, b) how to send messages, c) how to receive responses, and d) data encoding rules. SOAP can be used in combination with a variety of existing Internet protocols and formats including HTTP, SMTP, and MIME and can support a wide range of applications from messaging systems to RPC. SOAP consists of three parts:
- The SOAP envelope that defines an overall framework for expressing **what** is in a message; **who** should deal with it, and **whether** it is optional or mandatory.

- The SOAP encoding rules that define a mechanism to exchange instances of application-defined data types (e.g., customer name and address).
- The SOAP RPC representation that defines a convention that can be used to represent remote procedure calls and responses.

The SOAP specification also defines how a SOAP message can be carried in HTTP messages either with or without the HTTP Extension Framework (www.normos.org/ietf/rfc/rfc2774).

SOAP concentrates on simplicity and extensibility. Thus, several features, such as distributed garbage collection and objects-by-reference, from traditional distributed object computing are not part of the core SOAP specification. In fact, SOAP is a "wire protocol" which does not include many higher-level services.

Due to space limitations, this is a very short example-based overview of SOAP. Detailed technical information, including the latest SOAP specifications, are listed in the side bar "SOAP References".

3.7.2 Example of SOAP Message

We will use the following example to explain the various parts of SOAP. We will simplify many of the programming details to develop a conceptual understanding. It is assumed that the reader is familiar with XML and HTTP.

In this example, a GetCustomerPhone SOAP request is sent to a Customer service located at www.myserver.com. The request takes a customer name as input and returns a phone number as the SOAP response. The SOAP Envelope element is the top element of the XML document representing the SOAP message. XML namespaces are used to differentiate SOAP identifiers from application specific identifiers. It should be noted that the rules governing XML payload format in SOAP are entirely independent of the fact that the payload is carried in HTTP (i.e., the SOAP message format is independent of the transport).

The following two sidebars show the sample message request and response as two separate HTTP messages with the SOAP message as the payload. The request message asks for the phone number of Joe Peters and the response message returns the phone number (555-2222). If you do not understand everything in this example, do not worry, we will review it as we go along. It should be enough at this point to notice that each message has an envelope (<SOAP-ENV terminated by </SOAP-ENV) that contains a body (<SOAP-ENV:Body> terminated by </SOAP-ENV:Body>). The actual request and response are carried in the SOAP body.

Sample SOAP Message Embedded in HTTP Request

```
POST /Customer HTTP/1.1
Host: www.Customerserver.com
Content-Type: text/xml; charset="utf-8"
Content-Length: nnnn
SOAPAction: "www.myserver.com"

<SOAP-ENV:Envelope
 xmlns:SOAP-ENV="http://schemas.xmlsoap.org/soap/envelope/"
 SOAP-ENV:encodingStyle="http://schemas.xmlsoap.org/soap/encoding/">
 <SOAP-ENV:Body>
    <m: GetCustomerPhone xmlns:m="Some-URI">
      <cname>Peters, Joe </cname>
    </m: GetCustomerPhone >
 </SOAP-ENV:Body>
</SOAP-ENV:Envelope>
```

Sample SOAP Message Embedded in HTTP Response

```
HTTP/1.1 200 OK
Content-Type: text/xml; charset="utf-8"
Content-Length: nnnn

<SOAP-ENV:Envelope
  xmlns:SOAP-ENV="http://schemas.xmlsoap.org/soap/envelope/"
  SOAP-ENV:encodingStyle="http://schemas.xmlsoap.org/soap/encoding/"/>
  <SOAP-ENV:Body>
     <m: GetCustomerPhoneResponse xmlns:m="Some-URI">
        <Phone>5555-2222 </Phone>
     </m: GetCustomerPhoneResponse >
  </SOAP-ENV:Body>
</SOAP-ENV:Envelope>
```

3.7.3 The SOAP Message Exchange Model

SOAP messages are essentially one-way transmissions from a sender to a receiver, but as illustrated in the example above, SOAP messages are often combined to implement the request/response model. SOAP implementations can be optimized to exploit the unique characteristics of particular network systems. For example, the SOAP response messages can be delivered as HTTP responses, using the same connection as the inbound request.

Regardless of the transport protocol (e.g., HTTP, CORBA) that carries SOAP messages, the messages are routed along a "message path", which allows for processing at one or more intermediate nodes in addition to the ultimate destination.

A SOAP application receiving a SOAP message MUST process that message by performing the following actions in the order listed below:
1. Identify all parts of the SOAP message intended for that application.
2. Verify that all mandatory parts identified in step1 are supported by the application for this message and process them accordingly. If this is not the case, then discard the message. The processor MAY ignore optional parts identified in step 1 without affecting the outcome of the processing.
3. If the SOAP application is not the ultimate destination of the message, then remove all parts identified in step 1 before forwarding the message.

The recipient of SOAP messages understands the exchange protocol being used (e.g., RPC, MOM, etc.) and many other semantics necessary for correct processing. For example, certain applications will understand that a particular <getCustomerPhone> element signals an RPC request while another application may infer that all traffic directed to it is encoded as one-way messages.

3.7.4 SOAP Messages - Envelopes, Headers and Body

All SOAP messages are encoded using XML. A SOAP message is an XML document that consists of a mandatory SOAP envelope, an optional SOAP header, and a mandatory SOAP body (see Figure 3-22).

Envelope: The Envelope is a mandatory part of SOAP messages and defines **what** is in a message; **who** should deal with it, and **whether** it is optional or mandatory. An Envelope is the top element of the XML document representing the message. A SOAP message MUST have an Envelope element associated with the "http://schemas.xmlsoap.org/soap/envelope/" namespace. If a message is received by a SOAP application in which the SOAP Envelope element is associated with a different namespace, the application MUST treat this as a version error and discard the message.

Header: The Header is a generic mechanism for adding features to a SOAP message without prior agreement between the communicating parties. SOAP defines a few attributes that can be used to indicate who should deal with a feature and whether it is optional or mandatory. Typical examples of extensions that can be implemented as header entries are authentication, transaction management, payment, etc. An example is a header with an element identifier of "Transaction", a "mustUnderstand" value of "1", and a value of 22, i.e., you are telling the receiver to understand a transaction with value 22. This would be encoded as follows:

```
<SOAP-ENV:Header>
  <t:Transaction
   xmlns:t="some-URI" SOAP-ENV:mustUnderstand="1">
     22
  </t:Transaction>
</SOAP-ENV:Header>
```

The SOAP mustUnderstand global attribute is used to indicate whether a header entry is mandatory or optional for the recipient to process. The value of the mustUnderstand attribute is either "1" or "0". If a header element is tagged with a SOAP mustUnderstand attribute with a value of "1", the recipient of that header entry either MUST obey the semantics and process correctly to those semantics, or MUST fail processing the message. In other words, if this transaction is not processed, then an error condition is raised.

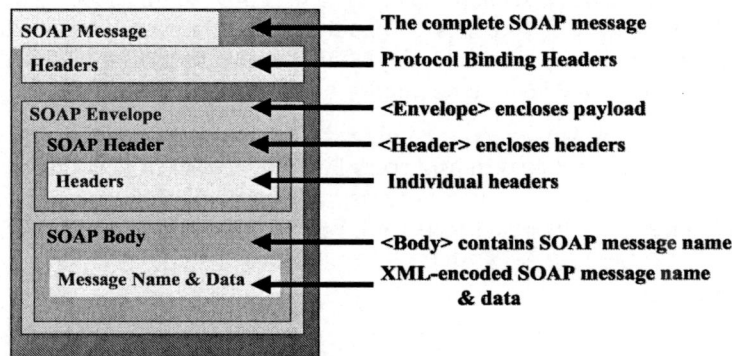

Figure 3-22: SOAP Message Structure

Body: The SOAP Body element provides the mandatory information intended for the ultimate recipient of the message. As shown in the previous example, the Body element is encoded as an immediate child element of the SOAP Envelope XML element. If a Header element is present, then the Body element MUST immediately follow the Header element, otherwise it MUST be the first immediate child element of the Envelope element. The SOAP Body may contain a Fault element to carry error and/or status information within a SOAP message. It can contain fault codes such as Versionmatch and Mustunderstand errors. In the example above, the Body carried the request as well as the response in two different envelopes.

3.7.5 SOAP Exchange Protocols

SOAP messages can be transported over HTTP or other C/S exchange protocols. In most cases, SOAP over HTTP is getting more attention. Carrying ("binding") SOAP over HTTP combines the flexibility of XML with the simplicity and richness of HTTP. SOAP naturally follows the HTTP request/response message model such as:

- SOAP request parameters are passed in a HTTP request.
- SOAP response parameters are returned in a HTTP response.

This shows that the semantics of SOAP are mapped to HTTP semantics -- carrying SOAP over HTTP does not mean that SOAP overrides existing semantics of HTTP.

It is important to mention the SOAPAction HTTP request header field that can be used to indicate the intent of the SOAP HTTP request. The SOAPAction header field can be used by servers such as firewalls to appropriately filter SOAP request messages in HTTP. An example of SOAPAction that passes Hello to amazon.com is:

SOAPAction: "http://www.amazon.com/Hello"

SOAP can also be used with RPC. This is a more general case of SOAP. To make an RPC method call, the following information is needed:
- The URI of the target object (the RPC server)
- A method name
- The parameters to the method
- Optional header data

By using this approach, you can invoke a CORBA or other server that uses RPC at its core.

3.7.6 SOAP Security and Interface with WSDL

SOAP builds on HTTP Security (it supports HTTPS and X.509 certificates). The developers and IT administrators choose which methods to expose explicitly. SOAP does not pass application code, so the issues of mobile code security do not come into play. SOAP is also firewall-friendly (i.e., firewalls can be programmed to handle SOAP traffic) and is type safe.

WSDL (Web Service Description Language) is a uniform representation for services -- it is similar to IDL. WSDL is Transport Protocol neutral as well as Access Protocol neutral (it is not restricted to SOAP). For Web services, WSDL describes schema for data types, call signatures (message), interfaces (port types), endpoint mappings (bindings), and endpoints (services). WSDL is used to construct the SOAP messages.

3.7.7 SOAP Summary

SOAP has gained popularity steadily since Microsoft announced it as the foundation technology for its Windows XP platform. The SOAP specifications have been submitted to W3C. Microsoft has developed many toolkits in this area (e.g., the Microsoft SOAP Toolkit 2.0, SOAP for windows XP, and SOAP extensions for Visual Basic). Other extensions worth mentioning are SOAP Perl from soaplite (www.soaplite.com). For additional sources of information, see the sidebar on SOAP References. For a list of growing number of books in this area, consult your favorite booksite such as www.amazon.com.

SOAP References

SOAP Specification: URL: http://www.w3.org/TR/SOAP/
SOAP Developer Resources at http://msdn.microsoft.com/soap/

SOAP Resources at http://msdn.microsoft.com/xml/general/soapspec.asp
SOAP articles from a business and technical perspective at the site
http://www.soapWebservices.com/articles/

3.8 EJBs (Enterprise Java Beans) – The Foundation of J2EE

3.8.1 Enterprise Components - The EJB (Enterprise Java Bean) Architectures

An *enterprise component* is a component that is specifically designed for object-oriented enterprise applications. Simply stated, an enterprise component resides on the server to provide plumbing needed for transaction processing and access to back-office systems. As compared to a *component* that can be developed to deliver a service such as a clock, an *enterprise component* is developed to deliverbusiness services such as payment systems, inventory management, and order processing. Thus, the enterprise components need abilities to handle transactions, multiple user sessions, persistence, and back-end application access.

Figure 3-23 shows how enterprise components reside between the Web tier and enterprise resources. Typically, business code that solves or meets the needs of a particular business domain such as banking, retail, or finance, is handled by enterprise components. Enterprise components receive requests from client programs, process it (if necessary), and send it to the enterprise information systems. An enterprise component also receives data from enterprise databases, processes it (if necessary), and sends it back to the client program.

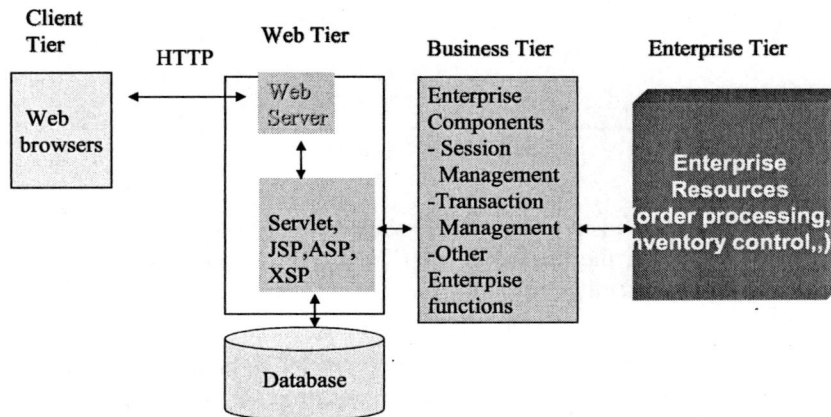

Figure 3-23: Enterprise Components Residing Between Web Tier and Enterprise Resources

An enterprise component centric architecture extends the component-base in several ways. The main idea is that the enterprise data is maintained by enterprise components. In addition, the sessions with clients are handled by enterprise components. This design provides flexibility, manageability, and separation of developer responsibilities.

Enterprise Java Beans (EJBs) are perhaps the most well-known examples of enterprise components. EJBs come in the following flavors:

- **Session Beans**: A session bean represents a transient conversation with a client. When the client finishes executing, the session bean and its data disappear. Session beans hold client specific business logic; therefore, a session bean executes on behalf of a single client and cannot be shared among multiple clients. Session beans can be state-full (they maintain state with the client) or stateless.
- **Entity Bean**: An entity bean represents persistent data stored in a database. If the client terminates or if the server shuts down, the bean "plumbing" services ensure the entity bean data is saved. It represents an object view of data stored in persistent storage or an existing application. The bean wraps the data as an object so that it can be reused in different applications. For example, an entity bean representation of a customer can be used in personalization, order management, and marketing.
- **Message-Driven Bean:** A message-driven bean allows a business component to receive JMS (Java Message Services) messages asynchronously. This is a new bean that was introduced to combine

features of a session bean and a Java Message Service (JMS) message listener. JMS is a messaging facility that supports a variety of messaging paradigms such as message queuing and publish/subscribe.

3.8.2 EJB Containers and Servers

The EJBs themselves contain the business logic and do not worry about any plumbing (e.g., handling multiple sessions, doing transaction processing) needed to run the EJBs. This plumbing is provided by the EJB environment through EJB containers and servers (see Figure 3-24).

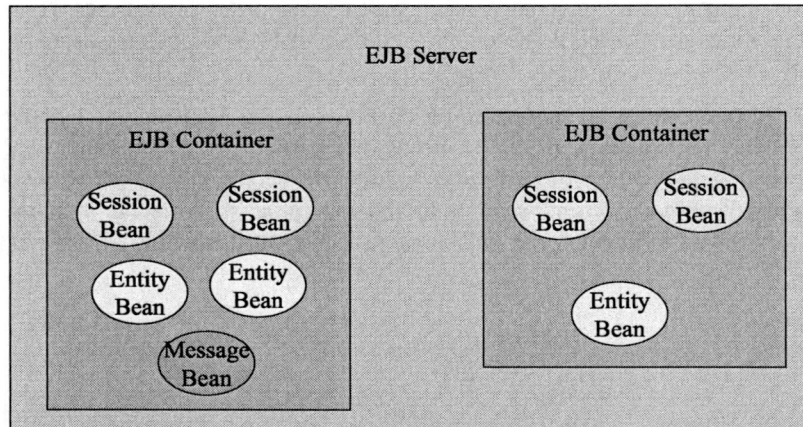

Figure 3-24: EJB Environment

EJB Servers: These servers, like many other servers such as Web servers, handle requests from clients (EJB clients) and connect them to the needed EJBs. EJB servers are commercially available from Sun (Jboss), BEA (BEA EJB server) and other vendors.

EJB Containers: These containers actually house the EJBs (very much like applets are housed by Web browsers). An EJB container provides the actual plumbing needed to create new instances of new EJBs, connecting them to the clients through the EJB servers, connecting them to back-end databases, providing logic for transaction management, etc. In some sense, EJB containers are similar to CORBA BOAs (Basic Object Adapters) that create instances of CORBA objects, locate them, manage them, etc.

Although it is technically incorrect, many people use the term "container" and "servers" interchangeably. As shown in Figure 3-24, one EJB server houses one or more containers that in turn manage one or more EJJBs in the form of entity, session, or message beans.

EJBs are at the core of the component-based application platforms such as Sun's J2EE and Microsoft's .NET.

Many books have been published on EJBs. Perhaps the best source is the Java.sun.com Website. In particular, this Website provides tutorials and blueprints on J2EE (e.g., http://java.sun.com/j2ee/tutorial/ and http://java.sun.com/j2ee/blueprints/).

3.8.3 Entity Versus Session Beans – The Highlights

Entity beans differ from session beans in several ways. Entity beans are persistent, allow shared access, have primary keys, and may participate in relationships with other entity beans. Here is a quick highlight.

Persistance: Persistence indicates that the entity bean's state exists beyond the lifetime of the application or the J2EE server process. There are two types of persistence for entity beans: bean-managed and container-managed. Bean-managed persistence means that you write the calls that access the database. Container-managed persistence eliminates this need -- the EJB container automatically generates the necessary database access calls.

Primary Key: Each entity bean has a unique object identifier. A product entity bean, for example, might be identified by a product number. The unique identifier, or primary key, enables the client to locate a particular entity bean.

Transaction Management: The EJB container provides transaction management. This is important because entity beans may be shared by multiple clients and those clients might want to change the same data. You do not have to code the transaction statements in the bean--the container marks the transaction boundaries (start transaction, end transaction, etc.) for you.

Relationships: An entity bean may be related to other entity beans. For example, in a purchasing enrollment application, the `CustomerEJB` and `ProductEJB` beans would be related because customers buy products. You implement relationships differently for entity beans with bean-managed-persistence and those with container-managed-persistence. With bean-managed persistence, you write the code to implement the relationships. As expected, with container-managed persistence, the EJB container takes care of the relationships code.

3.8.4 An Example

Let us go through an example of accessing a remote customer database by using EJBs. This example is a simplification of the example given in the Architecture Implementation Chapter of the Architecture Module. The steps involve:

- **Remote interface definition** that advertises the methods (services) provided by the EJB. This is very similar to building an interface definition in an IDL (Interface Definition Language).
- **Bean class** that implements the business logic of the EJB. The bean class contains the methods that are advertised in the remote interface. In reality, the bean class can be a session or entity bean.
- **Home interface** that initializes the bean and defines methods for creating, deleting, and finding the beans.

Remote Interface for Customer EJB: The following code simplified segment shows the remote interface (it shows the two methods (create_cust and view_cust):

```
package customer_paxkage;

public interface customer_interf extends javax.ejb.EJBObject {

public create_cust (object customer_obj)

public view_cust (char cust-id)

}
```

Bean Class for Customer EJB: The major activity in building an EJB application is to write the code for the two methods (create_cust and view_cust): that are shown in the remote interface. Methods can be implemented as executable code, calls to legacy applications, or scripts to integrate command line interfaces with existing applications. Methods can be written to directly invoke SQL database accesses. For example, the following pseudo code to access the customer relational table can be added to the create_cust and view_cust methods:

```
public class Customer_Bean {

create_cust  (customer_obj, status);

/* code for inserting a row in SQL table for a customer */

/* .. include other code */



view_cust (cust-id, customer_obj, status);

exec sql;

select  cname,  caddress,  balance  from  cust_table  where
c_id=:cust_id;

end sql;

/* code for storing cname, caddress, balance into an object
*/

}
```

Home Interface for Customer EJB: The following code shows the needed home interface:

```
public interface customer_home extends javax.ejb.EJBHome {

 public find_by_primary_key (customer_key pk)

          throws FindException, RemoteException;

}
```

To deploy an enterprise bean, you need to: :
- **Build a Deployment Descriptor**: A Deployment Descriptor describes what classes make up a bean and how a bean should be managed at run-time. Most EJB server products at present provide wizards to build a Deployment Descriptor.
- **Create a JAR file**: A JAR (Java Archive) file is a platform independent file format for compressing, packaging, and delivering several files together. Based on ZIP file format, the JAR file format is a very convenient way of packaging and delivering software -- create a JAR file of all the classes, interfaces, implementation modules, and run-time instructions and send them to the receiver. For the Customer EJB application, you create a JAR file that consists of the classes, the interfaces, and the Deployment Descriptor.
- **Create Database Tables**: You also need to create the database tables for entity beans. For example, a customer table should be created for the customer EJB.

These steps are typically aided through the EJB server wizards. These wizards walk you through various choices and generate a run-time system that will operate in the chosen vendor environment such as BEA. Details of these steps are vendor specific and are beyond the scope of this book.

After customer EJB has been built and deployed in an EJB server, clients can be built to invoke this EJB. The clients will locate and connect to the EJB server, and then create instances of EJBs for interactions. To locate the server, the client uses JNDI (Java Network Directory) services. JNDI is an API for directory and naming systems. The actual directory may be any directory. The method getInitialContext() is used to connect to an EJB server through JNDI.

After coding the client, it is compiled, linked and debugged using the EJB environment compilers and tracing facilities.

3.8.5 Design Issues in Building EJB Applications

3.8.5.1 Model-View-Controller

A variety of techniques are being used to employ EJBs to build flexible architectures. Flexibility is provided by using a data, presentation, and business logic architecture in which these three functions are separated. The J2EE literature refers to this as MVC (Model-View-Controller) architecture. This architecture, under whatever name, allows for a clean separation of business logic, data, and presentation logic. As expected, this architecture also enables content providers and application developers to focus on what they do best. Figure 3-25 shows how an MVC architecture can be implemented to represent data, presentation, and business logic. This figure also shows how you can use JSP pages, servlets, and JavaBeans components (entity beans, session beans) to implement this architecture.

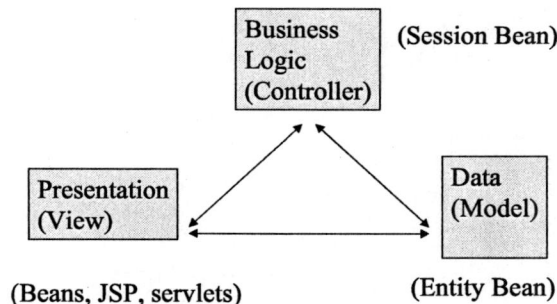

Figure 3-25: Model-View-Controller Architecture

This architecture separates the logic driving the application (controller) from the presentation logic (view) and from data presented to the user (model). This design is similar to the design in the previous section, except that a central controller receives all requests and coordinates the activities of other parts. Now let us explore each part of the MVC architecture:

- **Model** - The model represents the data on which an application is based. The data is typically held in databases. In an EJB-centric application, enterprise beans hold the data needed by the application. All modifications to the data occur thorough events sent to the EJB controller.
- **View** - A view presents the model data for a specific type of client. This allows enterprise applications to support a number of different views (e.g., Web view, cellular phone view, Visual Basic view) from the same model. The view for a Web application consists of server page (*SP) files, which have sole responsibility for displaying the model data. It is important that *SP pages only contain code related to the display of model data.
- **Controller** - The controller maintains the data in the model and ensures that the data presented by the view is consistent with the corresponding model. To design a controller, a Web application developer

can use a front component to receive all requests and then invoke needed JavaBeans components and enterprise beans to get the job done.

3.8.5.2   Controller Design

The most crucial aspect of building an enterprise component-based application is design of a controller. The controller is made up of many components responsible for taking data posted in an HTTP request and converting it into an event to update the model data. Figure 3-26 shows a conceptual design of the controller. It can be seen that the controller consists of front component, request processor, Web controller, and EJB controller. As shown in this figure, the controller components can reside in Web server tier or the EJB tier. This figure also shows the flow of an HTTP request from an HTTP client to the controller mechanism. As mentioned before, all requests from HTTP clients go to a front component. The requests are then sent to the request processor, which converts them to events and then sends the events to the Web controller. The Web controller acts as a proxy and sends the event to the EJB controller, which processes the event and updates the model data maintained by the enterprise beans accordingly.

All business logic is handled by the EJB controller and enterprise beans. The EJB controller returns a set of changed models to the Web controller. The Web controller then sends the model update events to the respective views. The views then contact the enterprise beans that they mirror and update their data from the enterprise beans. The JavaBeans components do not change any data; they only read the model data contained by the enterprise beans when they receive the model update notification.

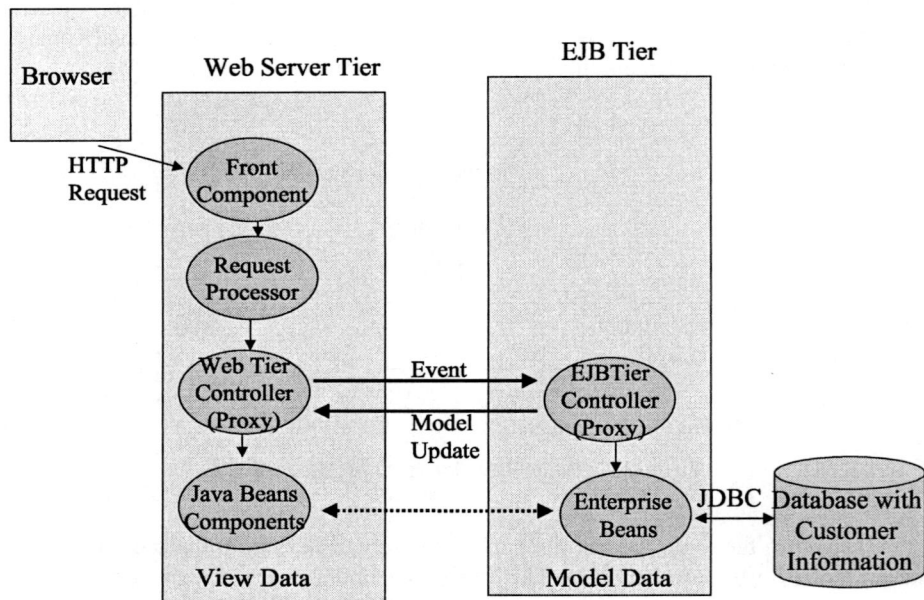

Figure 3-26: Controller Design Example

3.9   XYZCorp Case Study: Hints and Partial Solutions

- For a high tech company like XYZCorp, use of distributed objects is almost natural.
- At the time of this writing, distributed object technologies have many promises but they are getting competition from very loosely coupled paradigms such as MOM.
- The following table can be used to compare and contrast distributed object technologies with other middleware. Completion of this table is left as an exercise.

	CORBA	Web Services (SOAP, WSDL)	MOM
Suitability to problem			
Diversity of platforms			
Openness (standards)			
Performance			
Scalability			
Flexibility			
Others			

- The main issue for several organizations in the late 1990s was to determine whether CORBA or DCOM should be chosen as a middleware for distributed objects. At a high level, CORBA is more suitable for heterogeneous computing environments consisting of PCs, UNIX, and mainframes. DCOM is designed for Windows and Windows NT environments. Obviously DCOM is developed and supported by Microsoft. CORBA products are supported by many vendors such as Iona, Inprise, IBM, HP, DEC and Sun. At present, similar arguments are being presented in J2EE (based on standards) versus .NET. Some things never change.

- The investment in CORBA is quite safe if you adopt J2EE because it supports CORBA. However, if you have chosen DCOM in a big way, .NET is a much more natural choice.

- Different approaches can be used to integrate distributed objects, especially CORBA, with Web. Examples are invoking CORBA calls from a CGI gateway, invoking CORBA directly from the Web browser, using HTTP as a transport protocol underneath ORBs, and using CORBA to interact between Java applets across machines. The following diagram can be used to establish a strategy for integrating Web with OO. Perhaps the most natural way will be to use the Web browsers that invoke CORBA objects directly (this technology is currently just becoming state of the market as we go to press). You can add or build a separate diagram for ActiveX.

- Web Services with SOAP provide a very promising way to integrate applications by using XML and HTTP. Since both J2EE as well as .NET support Web Services, adoption of Web Services for future applications seems to make sense. Should the company adopt J2EE or .NET to support Web Services is a choice that depends on the current investment. Since XYZCorp has invested heavily in CORBA, and uses Java very heavily, adoption of J2EE may be more natural.

3.10 Summary

Object-orientation (OO) has a great deal of promise in reducing the complexity of C/S applications. The primary standard for distributed OO systems is OMG's CORBA. CORBA is a very powerful and important specification for distributed object-oriented applications. Microsoft has chosen to adopt ActiveX/DCOM/COM+ for enterprise-wide distributed object computing over the Internet/Intranet. An important aspect of the current work is to combine distributed objects and XML with the Web through the XML Web Services. In this case, SOAP could be a direct competitor to CORBA.

3.11 Problems and Exercises

1) Compare and contrast CORBA with DCOM/COM+ and Web Services. Can you identify classes of applications for which you would choose one versus the other?

2) Extend Table 3-1 to include other distributed object technologies (DCOM, J2EE, .NET).

3) Does CORBA directly support inheritance and polymorphism? Justify your answer with examples.

4) Suppose you have been given the responsibility of managing compound documents in a medium-sized (around 3000 employees) organization. Will you choose OLE or OpenDoc? Justify your answer.

5) Review the OMG home page, the Microsoft home page, and the OpenDoc home page on the Internet. Note the most recent activities in the last two months.

6) Many people feel that CORBA is dead, especially because of the popularity of SOAP? What do you think? Support your answer through research.

3.12 Additional Information

A great deal of information on distributed objects and Web Services is becoming available over the Internet. For developments in distributed objects, the best source is the OMG site (www.omg.org) and the best source for additional information about Web Services is the W3C site - www.w3.org. Due to the popularity of web services (WS) , many magazines such as eAI Journal (www.eaijournal.com) and Data Management Review (www.dm.com) are devoting complete sections to WS. Special web sites such as **Web Services** Architect (www.webservicesarchitect.com) and **Web Services** industry portal (www.webservices.org/) are also fully operational. You can access recent developments by using Web surfing tools such as Google or AltaVista.

Acharya, R., "EAI: A Business Perspective", eAI Journal, April 16, 2003

Britton, C., "IT Architectures and Middleware: Strategies for Building Large, Integrated Systems", Addison-Wesley, 2000

Chang, Y., et al, "An Object Transaction Service Based on the CORBA Architecture", International Conference on Distributed Platforms, Dresden, Feb. 1996.

Chappell, D., "Understanding OLE and ActiveX", Microsoft Press, latest edition.

El-Rewini, H. and Lewis, T., "Distributed and Parallel Computing", Prentice Hall, 1997.

Farooqi, K., Loggripo, L., and Demeere, J., "The ISO Reference Model for Open Distributed Processing: An Introduction", Computer Networks and ISDN networks, July 1995, pp. 1215-29.

Foody, M., "OLE and COM Versus CORBA", UNIX Review, April 1996, pp. 43-45.

Friday, A.; Blair, G.S.; Cheverst, K.; Davies, N., "Extensions to ANSAware for Advanced Mobile Applications", International Conference on Distributed Platforms, Dresden, Feb. 1996.

Gothale, A. and Schmidt, D., "Measuring and Optimizing CORBA Latency and Scalability Over High Speed Networks", Proceedings of the International Conference on Distributed Computing Systems, May 27-30, 1997.

Hayes, F. and Faden, M., "A Move to Unite OLE and CORBA", Open Systems Today, Sept. 5, 1994, page 1.

Hemming, M., "Binding, Migration, and Scalability in CORBA", Communications of ACM, Oct 1998, pp.62-72.

Herzum, P. and Sims, O., "Business Component Factory", Wiley, 2000.

Horn, C. and O'Toole, A., "Distributed Object Oriented Opproach", International Conference on Distributed Platforms, Dresden, Feb. 1996.

Hubert, R., "Distributed Object Technology in EDS", International Conference on Distributed Platforms, Dresden, Feb. 1996.

Konstantas, D., "Migration of Legacy Applications to a CORBA Platform: A Case Study", International Conference on Distributed Platforms, Dresden, Feb. 1996.

Koschel, A. and Leibfriend, "Experiences in using the CORBA implementation DSOM", International Conference on Distributed Platforms, Dresden, Feb. 1996.

Lee, J., Siau, K., and Hong,S., "Enterprise Integration with ERP and EAI",   Communications of the ACM Feb 2003

Lerner, et al, "Middleware Networks: Concept, Design and Deployment of Internet Infrastructure", Kluwer Academic Publishers; 2000

Lykins, D, "Enterprise Wars; J2EE vs. .NET", eAI Journal, Jan. 2002

Minton, G., "Programming with CORBA", UNIX Review, April 1996, pp. 29-39.

Millikin, M., "DCE: Building the Distributed Future", Byte Magazine, June 1994, pp. 125-134.

Mowbray, T., and Zahavi, R., "The Essential CORBA", John Wiley, 1995.

Myerson, J.," The Complete Book of Middleware", Auerbach Publications, 2002

Nicol, J., et al, "Object Orientation in Heterogeneous Distributed Computing Systems", IEEE Computer, June 1993. pp. 57- 67.

Orfali, R., and Harkey, D., "Java and CORBA", John Wiley, 1998.

Orfali, R., Harkey, D., and Edwards, J., "The Essential Distributed Objects Survival Guide", John Wiley, latest edition.

Orfali, R., Harkey, D, and Edwards, J., "Client/Server Survival Guide", John Wiley, latest edition.

Otte, R., Patrick, P., and Roy, M., "Understanding CORBA", Prentice Hall, 1996.

Rosenberry, W., Kenney, D., and Fisher, G., " Understanding DCE", O'Reilly & Associates, 1993.

Rosa, N.S.; Cunha, P.R.F.; Sadok, D.F.H. "A Methodology for Realization of LOTOS Specifications in the ANSAware", International Conference on Distributed Platforms, Dresden, Feb. 1996.

Rymer, J., "Distributed Object Interoperability", Distributed Computing Monitor, Seybold Group, Vol. 10, No. 3, Boston, March 1995.

Rymer, J., "Buisness Objects", Distributed Computing Monitor, Patricia Seybold Group, Jan. 1995.

Schimdt, D., Evaluating Architectures for Multithreaded Object Request Brokers", Communications of ACM, Oct. 1998, pp. 54-61.

Serain, D., and Craig, I., "Middleware: Practitioner Series", Springer-Verlag, 1999

Schurmann, G., "The Evolution from Open Systems Intercoonection (OSI) to Open Distributed Processing (ODP)",Computer Standards and Interfaces, Vol. 17 (1995) pp. 107-113.

Seigal, J., "CORBA 3.0: Fundamentals and Programming", second edition, Wiley, 2000.

Seigel, J., "OMG Overview: CORBA and the OMA in Enterprise Computing", Communications of ACM, Oct. 1998, pp. 37-43.

Semich, W., "What's the Next Step After Client/Server?", Datamation, March 15, 1994, pp. 26-34.

Senivongse, T.; Utting, I.A., "A Model for Evolution of Services in Distributed Systems", International Conference on Distributed Platforms, Dresden, Feb. 1996.

Shan, Y., Earle, R., and McGaughey, S., "Objects on the Server", Object Magazine, May 1995, pp. 49-54.

Soley, R., "Role of Object Technology in Distributed Systems", published in "Distributed Computing", edited by R. Khanna, Prentice Hall, 1994.

Soley, R., "Standards for Distributed Platforms", International Conference on Distributed Platforms, Dresden, Feb. 1996.

Steinder, M., Uszok, A. and Zielinski, K., "A Framework for Inter-ORB Request Level Bridge Construction", International Conference on Distributed Platforms, Dresden, Feb. 1996.

Tibbits, F., "CORBA: A Common Touch for Distributed Applications", Data Communications Magazine, May 21, 1995, pp. 71-75.

Vinoski, S., "New Features for CORBA 3.0", Communications of ACM, Oct. 1998, pp. 44-53.

4 Enterprise Data and Transaction Management

© - Amjad Umar

Prerequisite: The reader of this chapter is expected to have some background in database technologies at the level of the Database Tutorial Chapter in the Tutorial Module. Please browse through the said tutorial before proceeding. Otherwise, you may find this material to be bitter and dense.

4.1   Introduction

Enterprise Data (also known as Corporate Data) is the information that is used or created by a corporation in conducting business and is shared across the business processes of the corporation (see Figure 4-1). Enterprise data of contemporary EB organizations resides on a variety of platforms (PCs, UNIX, MVS) in a variety of formats (relational databases, catalogs, IMS databases, object-oriented databases, HTML documents, XML documents, indexed files, word processing files, powerpoint files, spreadsheets, or design diagrams). In addition, this data is inherently distributed (exists at more than one computer) in the following two manners:

- Distribution without replication (e.g., price information in Chicago, customer file in New York)
- Distribution with replication (e.g., price information in Chicago as well as in New York)

Retrieval, modification, and management of enterprise data, in whatever format it exists, where ever it exists, and in whatever number of copies it exists, is the focus of this chapter. In particular, we concentrate on the role of Web and XML technologies to retrieve and manipulate mission critical distributed data (with and without replication). Section 4.3.2 gives a quick overview of Web and XML in modern enterprise data and transaction management. Middleware that manages the access and modifications of enterprise data, typically distributed and replicated, adds another layer on top of the basic C/S protocols (e.g., RPCs, RDAs, and MOMs). This concept is defined in Section 4.3. A highly desirable goal of this middleware is data location transparency (access and manipulation of remotely located data without knowing the location of the data in the network). After the overviews, the issue of distributed data access is addressed in sections 4.4 through 4.6. A wide range of technical and administrative challenges span data distribution and replication. A great deal of research literature has been published to address these challenges since the mid 1970s. We will primarily attempt to answer the following questions in this part of the chapter:

- What are the characteristics of distributed file processing (Section 4.4)?
- How can remote databases be accessed and what is the role of the remote SQL standards such as ODBC/JDBC and DRDA (Section 4.5)?
- What is distributed query processing (e.g., distributed joins) and how does it relate to heterogeneous and federated databases (Section 4.6)?

After discussion of distributed data access, the issue of distributed transactions is addressed in Sections 4.9 through 4.12. Simply stated, a transaction is a group of statements that must be executed as a unit. For example, a transaction may be a group of SQL statements that transfer funds from one bank account to another (these statements must be executed as a unit because if the funds have been debited from one account, then they must be credited to the other). Transaction processing is at the core of e-commerce today but has existed in the form of on-line transaction processing (OLTP), since the early 1970s. Mainframe-based transaction managers (TMs) such as CICS and IMS-DC/IMS-TM have matured over the years to provide high performance and reliable service. The main question is how to process transactions in Internet environments? C2B and B2B E-commerce over the Internet is an active area of work (i.e., how users purchase goods and how funds and goods are transferred between business entities over the Internet). The key technical problem is: how do you update related data that may be stored on different machines? Currently, the approaches to distributed transaction processing fall into the following categories:

- TP-Less, i.e., do not use any transaction management considerations (we discussed this approach in the previous chapter).
- TP-Lite, i.e., use database procedures to handle updates.
- TP-Heavy, i.e., use a distributed transaction manager to handle updates.

Why is there a difference in opinion? Why can we not use the same OLTP philosophy and approaches that have worked for a number of years? To answer these and other related questions, we will first introduce the key transaction concepts and then discuss the special issues and emerging standards of distributed transaction processing (Section 4.9). This discussion will give you an idea of the complexities of TP-Heavy and why everyone is not jumping on this bandwagon. We will then discuss, in Section 4.10, the data replication servers that provide periodic data synchronization instead of the instantaneous synchronization used by the distributed transaction processors (TP-Heavy). Section 4.11 discusses the trade-offs between using data replication servers versus the instant update synchronization protocol (known as two phase commit) used in TP-Heavy solution. Eventually, Section 4.12 discusses the trade-offs between TP-Less, TP-Lite, and TP-Heavy for distributed transaction processing. In general, TP-Lite may serve many applications' needs; however, TP-Heavy must be considered for large mission critical applications. Keeping this in mind, we consolidate the distributed data access and distributed transaction management into a single framework to highlight the wide range of technical issues and approaches involved (Section 4.13 and 4.14). We conclude this chapter by reviewing examples of commercially available products in this area.

This chapter assumes a working knowledge of database technologies and SQL at the level described in Appendix C tutorial.

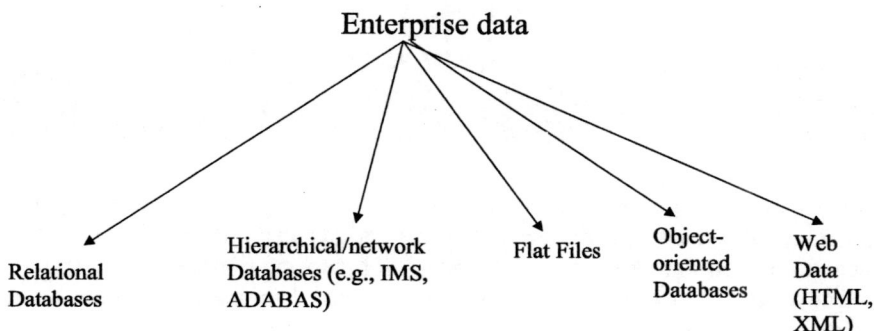

Figure 4-1: Enterprise Data

Key Points

- Enterprise data of contemporary EB organizations resides on a variety of platforms in a variety of formats and is inherently distributed (exists at more than one computer).
- A wide range of middleware services is available to access, manipulate and update enterprise data.
- The Simple SQL Middleware is very commonly used to provide access to a single SQL server.
- Distributed Query Processing middleware is used to join tables located on different sites.
- Heterogeneous and Federated Databases in Network Environments is an area of considerable academic research.
- The Open Database Connectivity (ODBC) API from Microsoft has become a de facto API standard for accessing remotely located heterogeneous databases.
- Distributed Relational Database Architecture (DRDA) from IBM has become a de facto exchange protocol standard for accessing DB2 data.
- Many SQL Gateways are commercially available from database vendors such as Oracle, Sybase, and Informix.
- A great deal of current research is focusing on object-oriented multi-database systems where multiple, autonomous and, possibly, heterogeneous databases are accessed through an OO "view integrator".
- The approaches to C/S transaction processing fall into the following categories: TP-Less, TP-Lite, and TP-Heavy.
- Data replication servers are used in conjunction with TP-Lite and thus, play a vital role in managing replicated data due to their flexibility and due to the limitations of two-phase commit.
- Message-oriented middleware (MOM) can also provide a light-weight mechanism for distributed transaction processing.
- A Distributed Data and Transaction Management System (DDTMS) as a C/S middleware that is concerned with the management of distributed data (files plus databases with certain degree of replication) and distributed transactions.
- DDTMSs attempt to include heterogeneous data located at heterogeneous computers, interconnected through heterogeneous networks.
- Standards play an important role in the operability and portability of DDTMS. For example, ODBC, DRDA, and ISO Remote Database Access (RDA) standards for database access, and the ISO Transaction Processing (TP) and the X/Open Distributed Transaction Processing (DTP) standards are worth noting.
- Future work will focus on object-oriented distributed transactions where an object invocation will enforce the ACID properties.

4.2 Case Study: XYZCorp Establishes a Data and Transaction Processing Strategy

The financial information systems (FIS) department is very unhappy about how financial data is being managed and processed in the company. Due to mergers and acquisitions, the financial data is dispersed around the company. FIS folks are interested in a strategy for data and transaction processing that supports access to authorized users but maintains data integrity in an ever-changing environment. A corporate data management group has gotten into action and has identified the following key questions:

- Which of the financial data should be considered as corporate data? Why?
- What data will be duplicated if any?
- Should we choose TP Lite or TP-Heavy for financial data? Are their models to help us choose as a solution approach?
- What are the factors to be considered in choosing distributed data and transaction management middleware?

- Where does XML fit into this picture?

The group that supports online purchasing heard of this initiative and is also nterested in participating in this effort. The company is pushing to support online purchasing. The web architecture people so far have focused on front-end (i.e., how will the users access the purchasing system). The main question is how the databases involved in online purchasing (customer information, price files, product catalogs, inventory database) will be allocated and processed. The current situation is that massive file transfers (some lasting more than 8 hours) have to run at night to synchronize different files needed to support online purchasing. They want the corporate data management group to address the following questions:

- Can client/server architectures reduce the massive file transfers?
- How, specifically, will the databases be allocated? A database may be allocated to the corporate office, to a regional office and/or the local offices, or partitioned (master database on one computer, read-only copies on others).
- What are the specific product names that will be used in this architecture (with URLs)?

While working through these details, you should take the following information into account:

- You can assume that all queries shown above are issued from all sites at almost the same frequency.
- Assume that the databases are relational tables; however, different sites use different databases. The mainframe uses DB2, regional sites use Oracle, and local sites use Microsoft SQL Server.
- Information should be available to authorized users to print customized reports, perform spreadsheet analysis and exercise decision support software for greater insight.
- Facilitate new applications and new approaches to existing applications easily.
- Provide different local processing (especially at overseas offices) .
- Consider the cost of implementation and security while allocating information.

The Agenda
- Basic Concepts
- Distributed Query and Transaction Processing
- TP Lite versus TP Heavy
- Consolidation and Evaluation

4.3 Distributed Data and Transaction Management Concepts

4.3.1 Review of Basic Concepts

Figure 4-2 shows a typical centralized computing environment with a *file management system* which manages flat files, a *database management system (DBMS)* which manages the access and manipulation of a database, and a *transaction management system (TMS)* which manages the interactions between the users and the DBMS. Let us briefly review these components.

A *data file*, also called a "flat file", consists of a collection of records such as text statements, HTML statements, C program statements or graphic data. Conceptually, a *database* is a collection of logical data items in which the granularity of a logical data item may be a file, a record, or an arbitrary collection of data fields. A *database management system (DBMS)* is a software package that manages the access and manipulation of a database by multiple users. Specifically, a DBMS (1) manages logical representations of data, (2) manages concurrent access to data by multiple users, and (3) enforces security and integrity controls of a database. The tutorial in Appendix C gives more details about database technologies and SQL, a common database access language. A *query* is a sequence of operations (data access and manipulation commands) that display information but do not transform the state of a system. In essence, queries are read-only. Queries can be simple (e.g., display all customers living in Michigan) or complex (e.g., queries involving joins between 10 or more relational tables). A *transaction* is a sequence of operations (data access and manipulation commands) that transform one consistent state of a system into a new consistent state. Transactions are atomic, they either happen in entirety or do not happen at all ("all or nothing"). For example, transferring money from one account to another account is a transaction. The terms node, computing site, or site refer to a computer in an enterprise that participates in enterprise data management (e.g., to store data, to serve as an end-user access point).

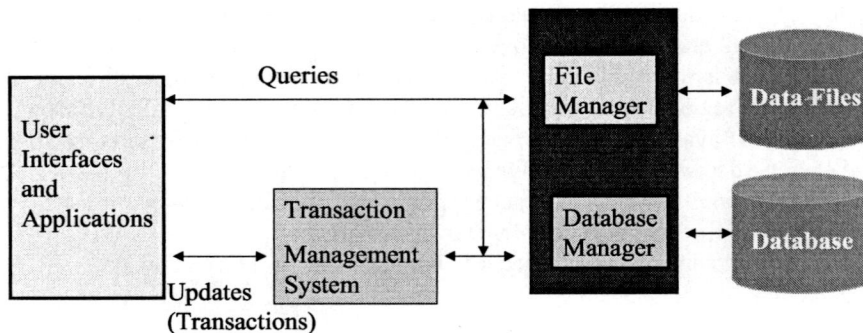

Figure 4-2: Conceptual View of Data and Transaction Management

4.3.2 Role of Web and XML in Enterprise Data and Transaction Management

Web and XML are playing a key role in modern enterprises from two points of view. First, the Web data is an important part of enterprise data that is growing rapidly. Second, Web provides a powerful mechanism for accessing and manipulating enterprise data, in particular relational databases. Figure 4-3 shows the role of Web in data and transaction management. Note that this view adds three building blocks to the previous view shown in Figure 4-2: Web data, Web browser, and Web server.

Web data for enterprise use consists of HTML documents, XML documents, XML DTDs, XML schemas, and "clickstreams" (capture your clicks as you walk through web pages). This data is a rich source for data mining (we will discuss this issue in a later chapter). The following developments at W3C (World Wide Web Consortium) are of particular importance:

- **Document Object Model (DOM)** converts the HTML and XML documents into a database that can be accessed and manipulated through a DOM API. This API allows you, for example, to scan all customer records in an XML document and determine those customers who live in Chicago.
- **Resource Description Facility (RDF)** allows you to describe all the Web data (who created what documents and where is the document stored, etc). In addition, RDF allows you to create site maps (i.e., how are your HTML and XML documents accessed at your site).
- **XML query languages** are designed to query XML documents. An example is ,XQL. XQL resembles the XSL (XML stylesheet language). One simply describes the types of "nodes" to look for using a simple pattern modeled after directory notation. For example, book/author means find author elements contained in book elements.

Web access to databases is provided through a Web Gateway that translates the browser requests to database calls and then translates the query response to HTML pages. The gateway can also invoke a transaction manager, if needed. Different approaches to build Web Gateways have been used. The first generation gateways allowed a user to enter a search text to a Web server. The gateways formatted the results of the query and sent them back as plain text. Since then, a considerable commercial activity in this field has occurred and many Web Gateways for relational databases and other systems have been configured and deployed on the Web. These gateways use technologies that range from simple CGI programs to sophisticated servlets and Enterprise Java Beans. We will discuss the Web Gateways in more detail in Section 4.7.

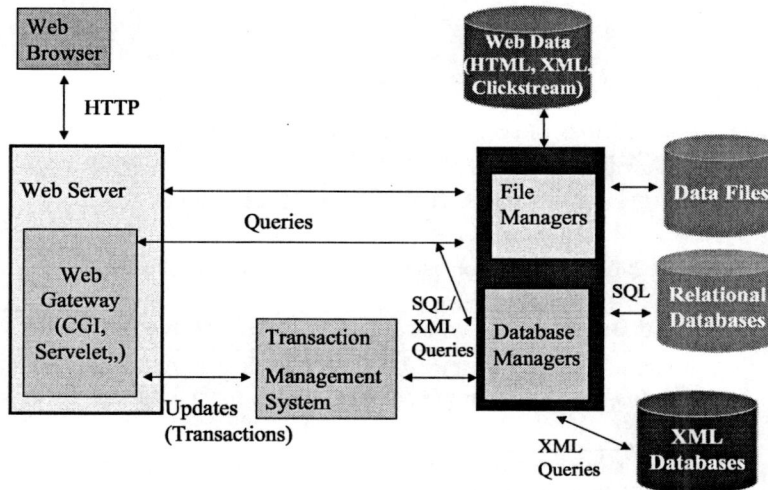

Figure 4-3: Web-based Data and Transaction Management

Let us now turn to the database managers that can access relational as well as XML databases. Figure 4-4 shows an expanded view of this module. This module receives XML as well as SQL traffic (retrievals plus updates). For some time, the only choice was to store everything in RDBMS. Thus, all XML documents were converted into relational tables and then processed through SQL. Many of the currently available RDBMS, such as Oracle 9i and SQL server 2000 allow you to return the results of an SQL query as an XML document. However, a new breed of "native" XML databases have become commercially available that allow direct storage and retrieval of XML information. Examples of these databases are Tamino and XDB. The database managers must be able to access the relational as well as XML databases.

A generic data access module for XML (XML Processor) is shown in Figure 4-4. The figure shows two options for XML. In the first option, we are storing data in RDB. The XML Processor provides the mapping that is needed between XML structure and RDB structure. As stated previously, some new DBMS (XML-enabled databases) such as SQL Server 2000 and Oracle 9i have some built-in functionalities that can make this task easier. This option requires XML to RDB translation. However, the main advantage is that SQL can be used to view, access, manipulate, and update XML data stored in RDBs. The second option is to store data in native XML format. In this case, no translation between XML and RDB is needed. We need to view, query, manipulate and update the native XML documents. In other words, something like SQL is needed so that XML documents can be treated as databases. The native XML databases provide such capabilities.

Naturally, questions about XML native and RDB comparison arise. Table 4-1 compares and contrasts the RDBs with XML Native Databases in terms of database capabilities such as data types, handling primary keys, relationships, etc. Detailed discussion and analysis of this topic will be given a later chapter.

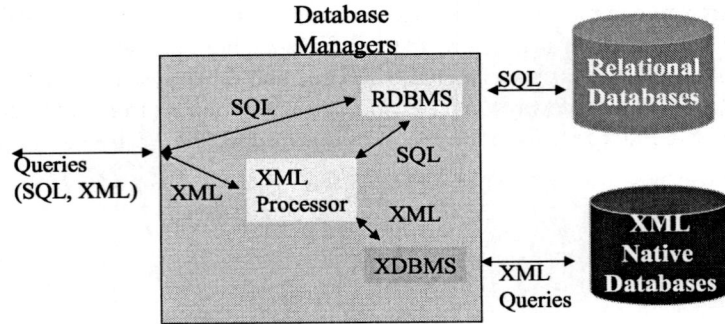

RDBMS = Relational Database Management System
XDBMS =   XML Database Management System ("Native")

Figure 4-4: Accessing Relational and XML Databases

Table 4-1: Table Comparison between XML and Relational databases

	Relational Database	**XML Native Databases**
Data storage	Data is stored in tables, arranged in columns, and stored in binary form.	Data is stored as text file in hierarchical form delimited by tags.
Primary key	Data in one table can be uniquely identified by primary key.	Elements (with no text) can be considered the equivalent of a table and an element can be identified by an ID attribute.
	Primary key may consists of one or more attributes.	There can't be more than one ID attribute for one element.
Relationship	Tables are related through foreign keys.	Elements can be related to other elements using IDREFs / attributes *or* Through containment of one element in another.
	Foreign keys allow two-way navigation.	IDREFs allow one-way navigation i.e., from the referencing elements and not from the referenced element.
Meta data	Supported	Meta data is specified in text files like DTD or XML Schema. XML Schema supports strong data typing and other constraints.
Views	Supported	Supported
Data and data structure	In RDBMS, structure and data are distinct and once we define structure, we need not mention it again and again while entering new data.	XML documents are verbose; whenever we enter new data we have to mention the tags. So the structure element of the document is repeated.
Querying Capabiliti es	Well developed and reliable through SQL	XML documents can be queried through diverse querying languages like XQL and XML Query that are being developed. Still under development

4.3.3 Distribution Data Access Management: What and Why?

Distributed data is data, in whatever format it exists, that resides on more than one computer. For example, in a medium-sized organization, customer information may be stored in an MVS-DB2 database, price information may exist in a UNIX Oracle database, inventory information may reside on a Microsoft (MS) SQL Server, and sales information may be dispersed among many desktop spreadsheets. Data can be distributed in the following two manners:

- Distribution without replication (unique data distribution) - In this case, only one copy of data D exists in an enterprise. For example, customer information exists only on MVS-DB2 and price information exists only on a UNIX Oracle database server.
- Distribution with replication (duplicate distribution) - In this case, more than one copy of data D exists in an enterprise. For example, customer information may exist on MVS-DB2 as well as a regional UNIX Oracle database server.

Figure 4-5 shows a conceptual view of distributed data in an enterprise where the customer information is uniquely assigned while the parts information is partially replicated.

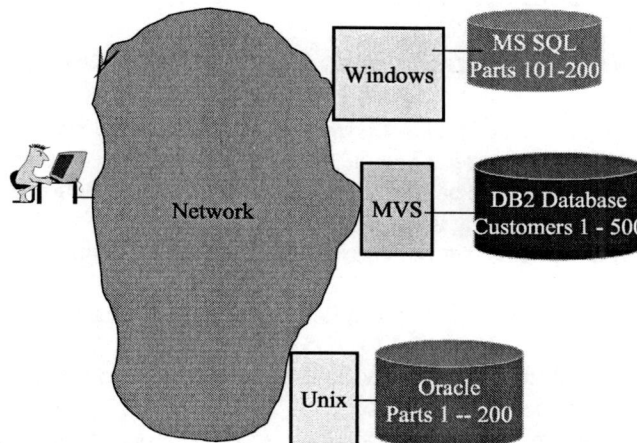

Figure 4-5: Example of Distributed Data

Data distribution and replication offers many advantages, but at the same time it introduces several unique technical as well as management challenges. For example, data distribution and replication:

- Allow users to exercise control over their own data while allowing others to share some of the data from other sites.
- Save communication costs by providing data at the sites where it is most frequently accessed.
- Improve the reliability and availability of a system by providing alternate sites from which the information can be accessed.
- Increase the capacity of a system by increasing the number of sites where the data can be located.
- Improve the performance of a system by allowing local access to frequently used data.

However, data distribution and replication:

- Introduce challenging technical issues of update synchronization, failure handling, and distributed transaction management (we will discuss these issues in more detail later in the next chapter).
- Increase complexity of the system and introduce several management challenges especially when geographical and organizational boundaries are crossed.
- Make central control more difficult and raise several security issues because a data item stored at a remote site can always be accessed by the users at that remote site.

- Make performance evaluation difficult because a process running at one node may impact the entire network.

May deteriorate the overall performance of older private wide area networks (WANs) that suffer from the "SUE" factor (slow, unreliable, expensive) as pointed out by Gray [Gray 1987]. Conceptually, this problem should not exist in the broadband wide area networks that operate at 100 Mbps or higher (however, these networks could get congested too).

Due to these advantages and disadvantages, data distribution and replication trade-offs must be evaluated carefully. These trade-offs are discussed in the chapter "Data Architectures" in [Umar 1997]. Ideally, Distributed Data and Transaction Management middleware, introduced in the next section, should be available to maximize the benefits of distributed data and hide the underlying complexities from the end-users.

It is important to distinguish between a distributed database and a distributed database manager. A distributed database contains information, usually business aware, that is physically distributed to several computers and a distributed database manager is a software package (or a collection of software modules) which manages distributed databases. An example of a distributed database is a customer database that may be partitioned and distributed to several regional customer sites for quick access. The same customer information may appear at more than one site (duplicated). An example of a distributed database manager would be an Oracle DDBM, which gives an end user a single database view of the customer database.

4.3.4 Distributed Data and Transaction Management Overview

A *distributed data and transaction management system (DDTMS)* is middleware responsible for managing all data (files plus databases) and the operations on the data in a distributed computing environment. The primary objective of a DDTMS is a transparency of data location and transaction execution. Specifically, a DDTMS attempts to provide the following levels of transparency:
- Location transparency: Data items can be retrieved from any site without the user having to know the site.
- Replication transparency: If one copy of a data item is updated, then all other copies are also updated (synchronized).
- Distribution transparency: A transaction may be decomposed and routed to different sites to access distributed data without the knowledge of a user.
- Failure transparency: If a site fails, a DDTMS will access the desired data from a different site, if possible, without the knowledge of a user. The DDTMS will also assure that the transactions maintain database consistency in the face of failures.

A DDTMS is a collection of software modules which provides management of the following (see Figure 4-6):
- Distributed files
- Distributed databases
- Distributed transactions

The taxonomy shown in Figure 4-6 shows the functions performed by the three components of a DDTMS: distributed file managers, distributed database managers, and distributed transaction managers. This view assumes that a DDTMS provides access and manipulation of all data, which may be in "flat" data files or in integrated databases in a network. A *distributed file manager (DFM)* is responsible for providing transparent access, manipulation and administration (e.g., security) of data files that are located at different computers in the network. The SUN Network File Services (NFS) system can be viewed as a DFM. Section 4.4 describes these services in more detail. A *distributed database management system (DDMS)* provides transparent access, manipulation and administration of remotely located databases in a network. For example, an Oracle DDMS allows a user to query relational databases located at many computers as if they were at one computer. A DDMS may perform a diverse array of functions. Conceptually, a DDMS supports the following major functionalities:

- **Single-site remote database access (SRDA)** provides access to a single remote database per query. Thus, if a join is needed between two tables at two different sites, then the user will have to issue two queries, bring the results back to the local site, and then perform the joinhimself/herself. We will describe SRDA in Section 4.5.
- **Distributed query processing (DQP)** provides transparent read-access, manipulation and administration of remotely located databases in a network. This is an extension of SRDA where a user issues one query that can join tables located at multiple sites. For example, an Oracle Distributed Database Manager allows a user to query relational databases located at many computers as if they were at one computer. These services cannot be used to update databases. We will describe DQP in Section 4.6.

A ***distributed transaction manager (DTM)*** coordinates the execution of a single transaction across multiple systems. DTM is responsible for assuring concurrency (i.e., simultaneous access) and commitment control (i.e., the transaction must be completed properly or entirely withdrawn in the event of a failure). Examples of DTM are BEA Tuxedo, NCR Top-End and Transarc Encina. Section 4.9 describes DTM services in more detail.

We should note that Figure 4-6 presents a conceptual framework for studying and analyzing the access and manipulation of data in distributed computing. However, many commercially available products overlap the functionalities shown in Figure 4-6. For example, many commercially available DDBMs include some of the DTM functionalities.

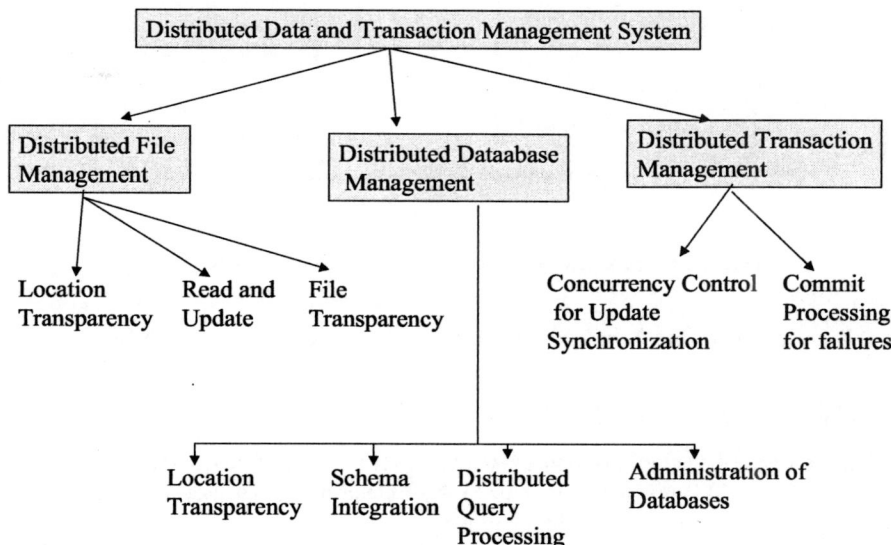

Figure 4-6: Taxonomy of Distributed Data and Transaction management Systems

Figure 4-7 shows a conceptual view of DDTMS and depicts how a DDTMS interacts with and interrelates to the following components:
- Applications that generate the queries (e.g., SQL statements).
- Local Data Management Systems (LDMSs) which perform the functions described in Section 4.3.1.
- Remote Communication Interfaces (RCIs) for sending/receiving messages across a network. RCI may use the basic C/S protocols such as remote procedure call (RPC), remote data access, and message-oriented middleware (MOM), or network dependent protocols such as TCP/IP Sockets, LU6.2, NetBIOS, etc.
- Network services transport the messages between sites. The network services may include, if needed, network gateways to convert network protocols (e.g., TCP/IP to SNA).

- Global directories show the location of data in the network. For example, Figure 5.3 shows two global directories that show that data table d1 is located on computer C1 and data table d2 is located on computer C2.

Although not shown in Figure 4-7, the modules can be configured as clients and servers. The client modules can exist at locations where an application generates a query and the DDTMS plans and monitors its execution. The server modules exist where the data resides. This model does not imply that all computers must have both client as well as server modules of a DDTMS.

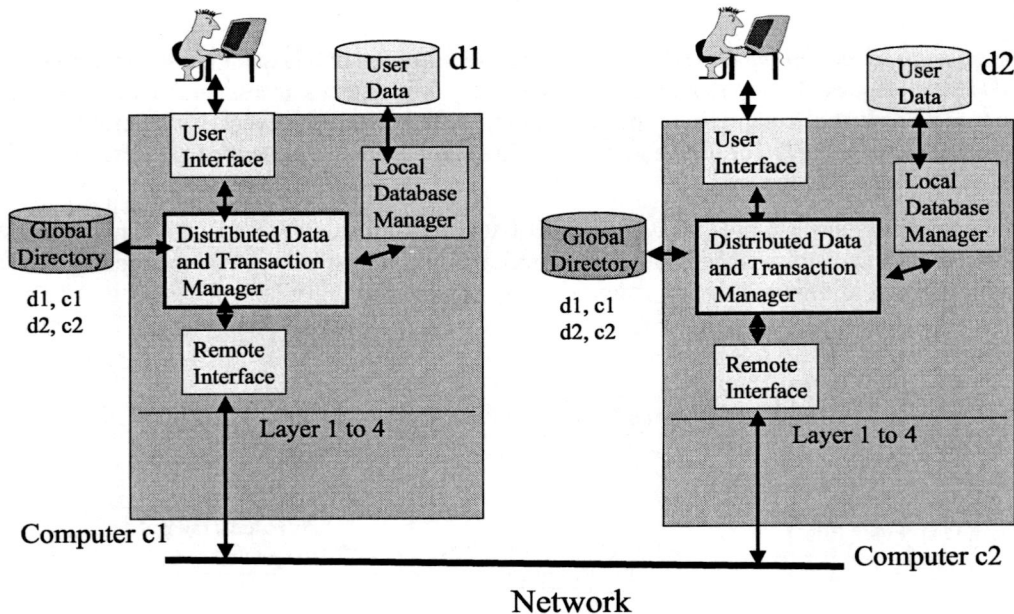

Figure 4-7; A Conceptual Model of Distributed Data Management

Let us explain this conceptual model through an example. Consider the following SQL query issued by a user application at computer C1:

SELECT name, address FROM Employees

Let us assume that the Employees table is located on computer C1. In this case, DDMS will parse this query, determine that the data is at C1, and pass the query to the LDMS at C1. However, if the Employees table is at computer C2, then the following steps will take place:

- DDTMS will determine, through a global directory, that the Employees table is on C2.
- DDTMS will issue requests for read locks on the Employee names and addresses at C2 (this step is bypassed if locking is not supported).
- The RCI module will prepare and send the SELECT statement over to C2 by using whatever C/S protocols are used between C1 and C2.
- The RCI at C2 will receive the message and send it to the DDMS modules at C2 (DDMS operates as a server scheduler in this case).
- DDTMS will pass this request to the LDMS at C2 for actual execution of the request.
- DDTMS will receive the results of the SELECT statement and pass them to RCI for sending back to C1.
- RCI will send the results of the SELECT statement back to C1.
- RCI at C1 will receive the results and pass them back to DDMS.
- DDTMS will free locks held, if any, and send the response back to the application to display the results to the user.

Let us now consider a few variations. If the Employee table exists at more than one computer, then the DDMS must find the optimal site. Now, if the Employee table exists at more than one computer but it needs to be updated (say through an SQL Update statement), then the DDTMS module would invoke a commit protocol (we will discuss this in transaction management) to guarantee the integrity of the database. Next, if the databases at C1 and C2 are from two different vendors (e.g., Oracle on C1 and IBM DB2 on C2), then the DDTMS modules at the two nodes may perform the functions of a "database gateway" by translating the data exchange protocols between the two vendors (this gateway may reside on a separate machine; Sybase Omni Server Gateway is such an example).

We will review the various algorithms and techniques used in these modules in the balance of this chapter.

4.4 Distributed File Processing

Distributed file processing (DFP) allows transparent access and manipulation of remotely located files. DFP supports open, read, write, and close of remotely located files from application programs and/or human users. It may provide access to a complete file or to a portion of a file across a network. Typically, DFP services include:

- Selection and de-selection of a remotely located file for access.
- Creation and deletion of remote files.
- Read and modification of remote file data and attributes (e.g., change a file's name).
- Control of the concurrency functions through locking/unlocking.
- Security from unauthorized access.

These services are provided by distributed file managers. Most of the distributed file managers are currently implemented as client-server systems in which each requester of a remote file service acts as a client which routes the file access commands to appropriate file servers in the network. File servers allow several users to share the same files, provide backup/recovery of shared files, allow users and the files to move around the network without retraining, and support diskless workstations. Available distributed file managers support the above stated functionalities at varying degrees. Examples of the distributed file managers are IBM's Distributed Data Manager, the Andrews File System developed at Carnegie-Mellon, and SUN's NFS (Network File Services) system. An extensive discussion of file server issues can be found in [Doeppner 1997, Svobodova 1984].

4.5 Single-site Remote Database Access: The Simple SQL Middleware

4.5.1 Overview

Figure 4-8 illustrates the single-site remote database access (SRDA). As stated previously, this capability allows clients to access remote databases that are dispersed among several sites of an enterprise. However, each client call, typically an SQL query, can only refer to database tables at one site. This capability provides several benefits to the end-users -- the databases can be moved around but the users can still access them remotely. For example, a corporate data warehouse can be housed on an Oracle server and be accessed by a variety of SQL-based decision support clients throughout an organization.

The SRDA capability is currently available as "simple SQL middleware" from a wide range of DBMS vendors (see Figure 4-9). SQL requests are sent to the remotely located SQL servers and the results are sent back to the clients. A large number of vendors (e.g., IBM, Informix, Sybase, Oracle, Microsoft) are developing SQL database servers that handle SQL calls from clients (e.g., applications and/or off -the-shelf end user tools) and respond with results. SQL-based C/S environments are naturally biased toward the remote data access (RDA) paradigm discussed in a previous chapter. Let us go through the key components of this environment.

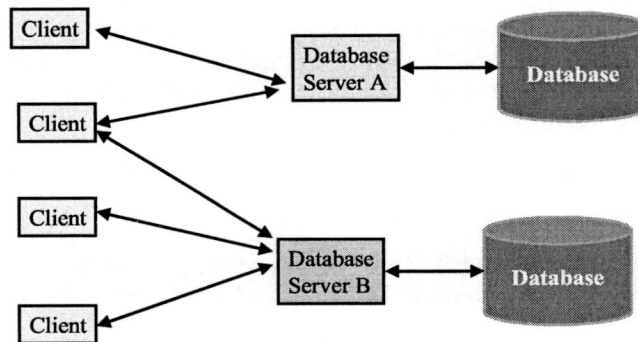

Figure 4-8: Single-site Remote Data Access

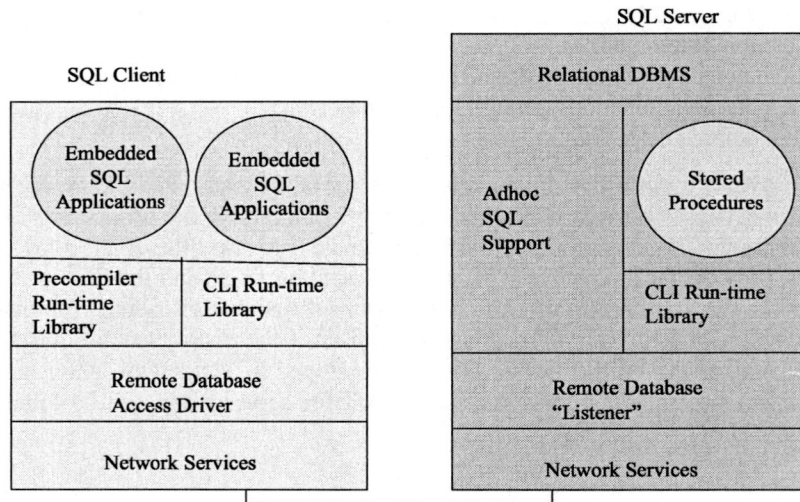

CLI = Command Level Interface

Figure 4-9: A Typical SQL-based C/S Environment

4.5.2 SQL Clients

SQL clients issue SQL calls to remote databases from applications, or end-user tools. SQL, with variations, is the standard query language for relational databases and is also being used to access non-relational databases. The client does not need to know the data types, lengths, and location. It just sends requests to retrieve the data by issuing an SQL query. For example, a client may issue the following SQL queries:

SELECT NAME FROM EMPLOYEE;

SELECT NAME, ADDRESS, SALARY, AGE FROM EMPLOYEE WHERE AGE > 30;

SELECT NAME, SALARY, AGE FROM EMPLOYEE WHERE AGE > 30 AND SALARY < 30000;

The first SQL query lists names of all employees; the second query lists names, addresses, salaries and ages of all employees older than 30; the third query is similar to the second query with an additional condition (salary < 30000). Note that the client request does not specify where the employee data table is located. This information is supplied by the remote database access middleware. Each client machine loads the middleware "data drivers" that accept the SQL calls from users or application programs and converts these calls into network messages that are sent to the server. This middleware also receives, interprets, and converts the responses from the server.

The SQL client has many choices such as the following:
- Dynamic versus Static SQL - Dynamic SQL allows an application to generate and execute SQL statements at run-time while static SQL is precompiled.
- Embedded versus Command Level Interface SQL - Embedded SQL allows programmers to place SQL statements into programs written in a standard programming language such as C or Cobol (these languages are known as host languages). Call Level Interface (CLI) for SQL consists of a library of function calls that support SQL. To submit an SQL request, the SQL statement is placed in a text buffer and the buffer is passed as a parameter in a function call. The error information is indicated by status codes.
- Single statement versus stored procedures - A client can send individual SQL statements or invoke a stored procedure (a set of SQL statements) at the server.

SQL middleware may support one or more of these options. For example, Microsoft's Open Database Connectivity (ODBC) supports the CLI interface, Informix supports embedded SQL, and most support stored procedures.

4.5.3 SQL Servers

The SQL servers, also known as SQL engines, provide secured access to shared relational databases. These servers provide varying degrees of SQL support (the SQL extensions for stored procedures, triggers, rules, etc.). Many SQL servers serve as front-ends to non-relational databases (i.e., they receive SQL calls and convert them to whatever form is needed by using database drivers). Examples are the Information Builder's EDA/SQL and Ingres SQL-object server. The SQL servers have the following architectures:
- Process-per-client, i.e., each database client has its own process address space. This architecture has been used by Informix and DB2/2.
- Multithreaded architecture, i.e. all clients share the same address space. This architecture is used by Sybase and Microsoft SQL Server.
- Hybrids, i.e., clients are given separate processes in the beginning but are multithreaded after execution starts. This approach is used in Oracle Servers.

Most of the SQL servers have been developed since the late 1980s. Initially developed for LANs, this technology has also moved to MVS mainframes. Although most SQL servers are designed around the standard bare-bone SQL, each vendor adds extensions to SQL to enhance performance. It is the responsibility of the user to choose extensions judiciously. An SQL server maintains a dictionary that describes the format and relationships of data (data schema). Some servers provide dictionary facilities for valid data ranges and display formats (YYMMDD or YY/MM/DD). Due to their origin, many SQL servers have been installed on LAN server machines. Different vendors support SQL servers on different computing systems that use different communication protocols with different performance and dictionary options.

At present, most SQL servers run on PCs, UNIX workstations, minicomputers, and mainframes interconnected over Token Ring, Ethernet, and packet switching networks operating under TCP/IP, SNA, and Novell Netware. They also provide different levels of scalability (i.e., as an application grows, a user can migrate from a small server to a large server). Examples of some of the available servers are: Oracle Server, Microsoft SQL Server, IBM DB2 Server. Interesting developments in this area have been the Microsoft "Component SQL Servers" strategy for selling 300 million SQL Servers for NT at very cheap prices [Semic 1994]. The implication of this strategy is that inexpensive SQL Servers could be used to run copying machines, cash registers, and office phones (the 300 million server strategy is based on the assumption that the 11 million places of business in the United States will buy about 30 cheap SQL Servers).

Many database servers may cooperate with each other to manage distributed databases. These servers, called the distributed database servers, coordinate the client access to individual database servers, where each database server manages its own database. We will discuss this topic in more detail in Section 4.6.2.

4.5.4 Remote Data Standards: ODBC/JDBC and DRDA

The standards for distributed data access fall into two broad categories:
- API standards that allow client applications to be portable from one vendor environment to another vendor environment as long as the same API is used. Microsoft ODBC and SQL Access Group's Command Level Interface (SAG) CLI) are examples.
- Exchange protocol standards that allow database servers from vendor X to interoperate with clients from vendor Y. ISO Remote Database Access (RDA) and IBM's DRDA are examples of interoperability standards.

We will first review the ODBC API due to its current popularity. However, other emerging APIs are also discussed. We then focus our attention to two main exchange protocols: IBM's DRDA and ISO's RDA.

The Role of Standards: An Example

Sometime ago, I was involved in a client/server project that required installation of a server on an IBM mainframe from a vendor (let us call it vendor X). The server was to allow access to DB2 and other databases from different clients. After a great deal of effort, we had the server installed and were happy to notice that we could support client programs, from the same vendor, on several workstations around the enterprise.

During the pilot project, we discovered that another group had purchased a C/S application from a vendor (let us call it vendor Y) that also needed access to the same DB2 database. It seemed simple enough: let us allow the vendor Y application to access the DB2 database through our server from vendor X.

The answer was a disappointing "No way".

The reason was that the vendor X server did not understand the client calls from vendor Y. Both of these vendors supported proprietary exchange protocols.

Our choice was to install yet another server on the mainframe from server Y (you can end up with 10 servers for 10 types of clients).

Ideally, open exchange protocols could allow server X to be called from clients from vendors Y, Z or others. This could happen if, for example, all vendors used ISO RDA, or something similar.

What about open APIs? The open APIs would allow a client to use the same call to access different databases. For example, a client program that retrieves data from vendor X server could also retrieve data from vendor Y server without any reprogramming. Microsoft's ODBC has become a default open API standard.

(Source: Umar, A., "Object-Oriented Client/server Environments", Prentice Hall, 1997).

4.5.4.1 Open Database Connectivity (ODBC) and Java Database Connectivity (JDBC)API

The Open Database Connectivity (ODBC) is an application programming interface (API) introduced by Microsoft that allows C programs to access databases by using SQL. The ODBC API is a Call Level Interface (CLI). By using this API, a single application on a desktop can access remote databases under different DBMSs (e.g., Informix, Oracle, Sybase). The same ODBC calls are used by application programmers to access relational databases of different vendors. ODBC relies on data drivers to convert the ODBC calls to different database formats. For example, Informix data drivers are needed to access Informix databases, and Oracle data drivers are needed to access Oracle databases, etc.

Java Database Connectivity (JDBC) API was created by JavaSoft (www.javasoft.com), a Sun Microsystem company, to allow Java programs to access remote SQL databases in a manner similar to ODBC. JDBC is based on the same Call Level Interface (CLI) that is used in ODBC. Thus, if you know ODBC, learning JDBC should be no problem. For the purpose of this chapter, we will not distinguish between ODBC and JDBC.

A programmer can create an ODBC/JDBC application without knowing the target DBMS. Users can add drivers to the application after it has been compiled and shipped. At development time, the application developer only needs to know the ODBC/JDBC calls to connect to a database, execute SQL statements, and retrieve results.

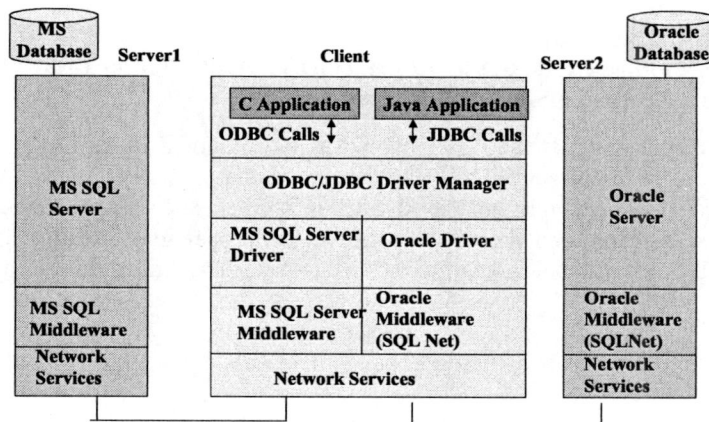

Figure 4-10: A Sample ODBC/JDBC Environment

Figure 4-10 shows a sample ODBC/JDBC environment in which an application accesses an Oracle and an MS SQL database. The main components of ODBC/JDBC are:

- Application: Performs business-aware logic and calls ODBC/JDBC functions to submit SQL statements and retrieve results. Specifically, it performs the following tasks: – Requests a connection with a target database. It specifies the target database name and any additional information needed to make the connection.
  - Passes one or more SQL statements by placing the SQL text string in a buffer.
  - Processes the produced result set or error conditions.
  - Ends each transaction with a commit or rollback.
  - Terminates the connection after the target database is not needed.
- Driver Manager: Loads drivers on an as-needed basis for the applications. The Driver Manager, provided by Microsoft, is a dynamically-linked library (DLL). In addition, to loading drivers dynamically, the Driver Manager also performs the following:
  - Maps a target database name to a specific Driver DLL.
  - Processes several ODBC initialization calls.
  - Validates the parameters and sequences of ODBC calls.
- Driver: Processes the ODBC/JDBC function calls, modifies them to the target database format (if needed), submits the SQL statements to the target database, receives the results, and presents the results to the application. Drivers are DLLs that implement the function calls. If an application needs to access three target databases from three vendors, then three drivers will be needed. Different vendors, such as

Q&E, have developed ODBC/JDBC drivers for different target databases. In many cases, "ODBC/JDBC driver suites" are available for accessing dozens of target databases.

- Target Database Middleware: the database needed by the applications and the associated middleware. This database may be located on the same machine as the application, or may be located on a remote machine connected through a network. Depending on the availability of drivers, ODBC can support a very wide range of target databases from different DBMS suppliers. Examples of the supported drivers are for Oracle, Ms SQL, Informix, and Sybase databases.

ODBC/JDBC uses the SQL syntax based on the X/Open and SQL Access Group (SAG) SQL CAE specification. The API provides the following:

- A library of function calls that allow an application to connect to a target database, execute SQL statements, and retrieve results.
- Facilities to explicitly include strings containing SQL statements in source code or construction of strings at run-time.
- A standard set of error codes.
- A standard way to connect and log on to a target database.
- A standard representation for data types.
- Use of same object code to access different DBMSs.
- Conformance levels for the ODBC/JDBC API and ODBC/JDBC SQL to assure that driver developers do support the same function calls and SQL statements.

To send an SQL statement, the statement is included as an argument in an ODBC function call. This statement is independent of the target DBMS (the drivers do the conversion). The ODBC function calls include a set of "core" functions that are based on the X/Open and SAG Command Level Interface specification. Extended functions are provided to support additional functionality such as asynchronous processing and scrollable cursors. Examples of the typical ODBC/JDBC function calls are:

SQLConnect

SQLExecute

SQLFetch, and

SQLDisconnect.

The ODBC/JDBC drivers come in two flavors: single-tier and multi-tier. The single-tier drivers include ODBC processing plus the data access software, while the multi-tiered drivers separate the data access code from ODBC/JDBC processing (see Figure 4-11). In essence, the multi-tiered drivers facilitate the use of a data access gateway and are more suitable for large-scale implementations (all data access code is localized in a data access gateway). For example, the ODBC/JDBC to DB2 gateway shown in Figure 4-11 uses a multi-tiered driver.

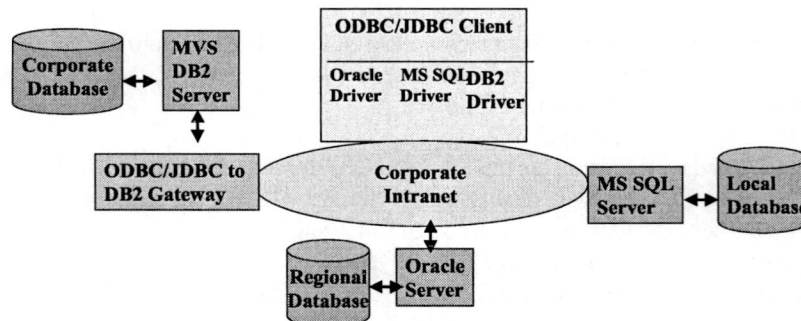

Figure 4-11: ODBC in Enterprise Networks

4.5.4.2 Distributed Relational Database Architecture (DRDA): An Exchange Protocol

Distributed Relational Database Architecture (DRDA) is IBM's long-term strategy for distributed relational databases in an enterprise. Introduced as part of the IBM System Application Architecture (SAA), it specifies the exchange protocols and conventions that govern the interactions between database clients and a database server. DRDA protocols and conventions support the following four levels of database transactions:

- Remote request: one SQL command to one remote database.
- Remote unit of work: many SQL commands to one remote database (this represents a remote transaction).
- Distributed unit of work: many SQL commands to many databases, but each command accesses one database (i.e., no joins across databases).
- Distributed request: many SQL commands to many databases but, each command can access multiple databases (i.e., joins across databases and sites are allowed).

DRDA supports dynamic as well as static SQL. In addition, later versions of DRDA have included support for stored procedures. It requires APPC (APPC can run over SNA or TCP/IP networks by using the IBM AnyNet feature). DRDA supports two-phase commit (see discussion on transaction management), provides common diagnostic return codes (based on SQL-92 standard) and recommends the use of SAA SQL (a subset of SQL-92).

Initially positioned as the standard for all relational databases, DRDA has become a de facto standard for access to DB2 databases. By using DRDA, clients from different DBMS vendors can access DB2 data. The access to DB2 is provided through a DRDA gateway that translates the different DBMS protocols to the DRDA exchange protocol. Figure 4-12 shows a conceptual view of a DRDA gateway that allows Oracle clients to access DB2 data. The Oracle client can query the DB2 database just like the Oracle database. The DRDA gateway converts the Oracle calls to DB2 calls. To DB2, the Oracle client appears as another DB2 client. DRDA gateways are commercially available from a multitude of vendors such as Informix, Oracle, and Sybase-Microdecisions. The main advantage of DRDA is that it does not require any server on the mainframe to access DB2 data (DRDA support is included as part of DB2).

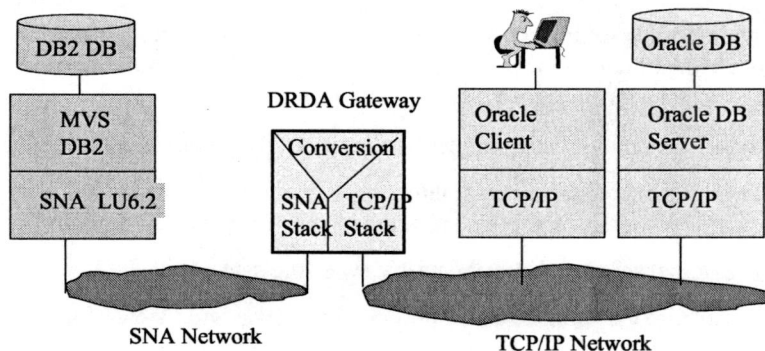

Figure 4-12: Conceptual View of a DRDA Gateway

Time to Take a Break
- ✓ Basic Concepts
- Distributed Query and Transaction Processing
- TP Lite versus TP Heavy
- Consolidation and Evaluation

Suggested Review Questions Before Proceeding

- What is enterprise data and enterprise data management? Give examples.
- What is distributed transaction management? Give examples.
- What is remote SQL middleware and how does it support remote data access?
- What is the role of XML and Web in the modern data transaction management environments? Give examples.

4.6 Distributed Query Processing and Distributed Database Servers

4.6.1 Overview

Distributed query processing (DQP) is concerned with providing transparent and simultaneous read access to several databases that are located on, perhaps, dissimilar computer systems. For example, an end user can issue a single SQL query that joins three different tables (customer table, inventory table and price table) located on three different computers (see Figure 4-13). The specific functions provided by a distributed query processor are (these functions can be used as a checklist to compare, evaluate and select different DQP products):

- Schema Integration: A global schema is created which represents an enterprise-wide view of data and is the basis for providing transparent access to data located at different sites, perhaps in different formats. A schema shows a view of data. In a DDBM, the data may be viewed at different levels, leading to the following levels of schema (see Figure 4-14):

  - The local internal schema represents the physical data organization at each machine.

  - The local conceptual schema shows the data model at each site. This schema shows a logical view of data and is also referred to as the logical data model.

  - The external schema shows the user view of the data.

  - The global conceptual schema shows an enterprise wide view of the data. This schema is also referred to as the corporate logical data model.

- Location Transparency: This provides transparency of data access and manipulation. The database queries do not have to indicate where the databases are located. The queries are decomposed and routed to appropriate locations. If more than one copy of data exists, then an appropriate copy is accessed. This allows the databases to be allocated at different sites and moved around if needed.

- Table Fragmentation: A relational table can be fragmented (partitioned) and dispersed over the network without any changes to the end user queries. For example, a customer table T can be partitioned into fragments t1, t2, t3, say by customer numbers (e.g., t1 has customer 1 to 100, t2 has customers 101 to 200, etc.). Let us assume that t1 was allocated to computer c1, t2 to c2, and t3 to c3. To retrieve information about customer number 135, the end user would issue the following SQL query:

SELECT * FROM T WHERE cust_number = 135;

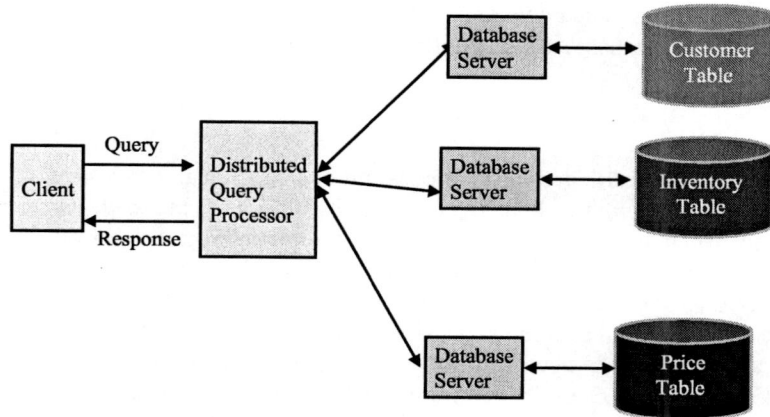

Figure 4-13: Distributed Query Processing

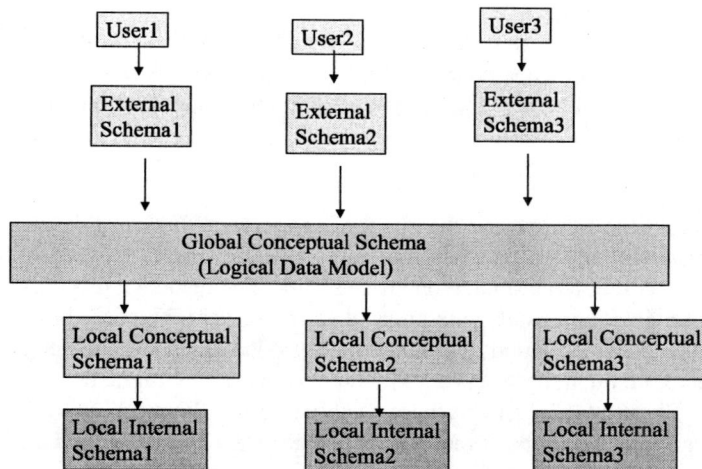

Figure 4-14: Views (Schemas) in a Distributed Database

Note that the SQL query is against table T and not the fragment t2.

- Multiple vendor support: Distributed query processing should allow a user to transparently access information from multiple vendor DBMSs (i.e., a user should be able to join tables supported by Informix, Oracle, Sybase, and DB2). This capability is currently available from some vendors (e.g., Sybase Omni Server allows joins between Sybase, DB2, and other non-Sybase tables; Oracle provides similar capabilities).
- Multiple data format support: Distributed query processing should allow users to perform SQL joins between relational as well as non-relational data sources. Many products such as IBM's InfoHub and Information Builder's EDA/SQL provide these capabilities.
- Multiple site support: Of course, distributed query processing should allow queries to data at different sites (this is the whole idea!).
- Administration Facilities: These facilities are needed to enforce global security and provide audit trails.

Distributed query processing support for all these functions is a non-trivial task. It is not easy to provide schema integration and perform efficient joins between data stored in multiple formats, at multiple sites, under the control of multiple vendor products. We are postponing the technical discussion of these issues, along with other knotty issues of distributed transaction processing, to next chapter where we will consolidate all the issues of distributed data retrieval and update into a single framework. A brief overview of supporting heterogeneous databases, called multidatabases, is given in the next section.

4.6.2 Distributed Database Servers

The reader should recall that distributed query processing is a functional component of a distributed data manager and not a stand-alone product. Due to the popularity of SQL database servers, distributed database servers are becoming available to provide distributed query processing, among other, functionalities. A distributed database server coordinates the client access to individual database servers, where each SQL database server manages its own database over a LAN or WAN. Consider an example where three databases d1, d2 and d3 reside on three different computers under the control of three database servers (see Figure 5.8). Let us assume that a client needs to access information from the three databases. The client can issue the following three queries (D1, D2, D3 are data tables in databases d1, d2, d3, respectively):

SELECT a1, a2 FROM D1

SELECT a3, a4 FROM D2

SELECT a5, a6 FROM D3

Each query will be sent to the appropriate server. After these queries have been executed, the client application may need to combine the responses for further analysis. Let us assume that the client application needs to join (combine) the attributes a1, a2,…., a6 from the three databases based on a given criteria. The client issues an SQL statement of the form:

SELECT a1, a2,..., a6 FROM D1, D2, D3 where [condition]

In this case, who is responsible for the join: the client or the servers? If one of the three database servers is responsible for coordinating the join between databases residing under the control of several database servers, then this server becomes a distributed database server. The responsibilities of a distributed database server become more complex if some data is duplicated across servers. The distributed database server must essentially address all the aforementioned distributed query processing functions. It is possible to designate one server to be the distributed database server, which coordinates the interactions between several "local" database servers (see   Figure 4-15). In this case, a three-tiered client-server system is used. The user application client issues the database calls that are received by the distributed database server. This server now acts as a client and issues requests to the standalone database servers.

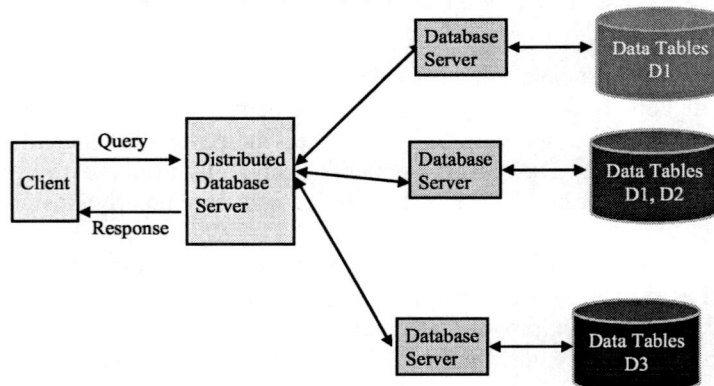

Figure 4-15: Distributed Database Server

How are distributed database servers different from distributed file servers such as NFS? A database server has all the capabilities of a database manager while a file server has the capabilities of a file manager. Specifically, NFS cannot be used for accessing databases, and NFS does not include any capabilities to manage duplicate data. Database servers are more complex than file servers because they include typical

DBMS capabilities such as maintaining the integrity of a database under security and consistency constraints, different views of data, record level locking, automatic logging, failure handling and data dictionary.

4.6.3 Heterogeneous and Federated Databases in Network Environments

Heterogeneous databases are of great practical significance because many real life distributed databases are from different vendors, using different data models, and are accessed through a combination of LAN database servers and WAN database servers. For example, a general problem for a DDBM is to provide transparent access to the business, engineering, and manufacturing databases that may be stored on UNIX workstations, MVS mainframes, or PCs and that are interconnected through LANs, TCP/IP and SNA networks. Database heterogeneity in a network can take several forms:

- Databases may support heterogeneous data models (hierarchical, network, relational, or object-oriented).
- Different query languages may be used in different databases (for example, different languages are used to access different object-oriented databases).
- Database management systems may be provided by different vendors.
- Computing platforms may be heterogeneous (microcomputer databases, minicomputer databases, and mainframe databases) operating under heterogeneous operating systems (UNIX, MVS, Windows).
- Networks may be heterogeneous (LANs, WANs, TCP/IP, SNA).

Several terms are used to refer to heterogeneous database systems. For example, heterogeneous databases are also known as multi-database systems (MDBS). An MDBS is an integrated distributed database system consisting of autonomous DBMS's that existed before integration. Yet another term used in this context is a federated database system. An FDBS is a collection of cooperating but autonomous component databases that are controlled and coordinated by a Federated Database Management System (FDBMS). A significant aspect of FDBMS is that the component databases may operate independently as heterogeneous systems but still participate in a federation. We will use the terms heterogeneous, multidatabase and federated database synonymously, although some differences exist (see [Litwin 1990] for discussion).

The basic feature that distinguishes these databases from the distributed databases discussed in the previous section is the notion of transparency. It is almost impossible to provide complete transparency in heterogeneous databases because a complete global data schema is difficult to create. In fact, the lack of global data schema is the main distinguishing feature between heterogeneous and integrated distributed databases. Figure 4-16 shows three different levels of heterogeneity from a global schema point of view.

In the integrated distributed database approach shown in Figure 4-16a, a single global schema is created which is used by all users and application programs. The local internal schema represents the physical data organization at each machine, the local conceptual schema shows the logical view of data at each site and the external schema shows the user view of the data. As discussed previously, the global conceptual schema shows an enterprise wide view of the data. A global schema is created from the local schemas of the local databases. In practice, global conceptual schemas in large organizations are rarely achieved due to social and organizational factors.

In a heterogeneous distributed DBMS, a partial global schema may exist or it may not exist at all. Figure 4-16b shows the partial global schema (GCS) approach in which only portions of the local conceptual schemas are used to build the GCS. The GCS may contain, for example, the most frequently accessed corporate data. The users can issue queries either through their own external schema or through the GCS. This approach is used in the "tightly coupled" federated databases [Sheth 1990]. The FDBMS may provide an integrated view of the data included in the GCS where the user issues a query in a "global" query language against the partial GCS.

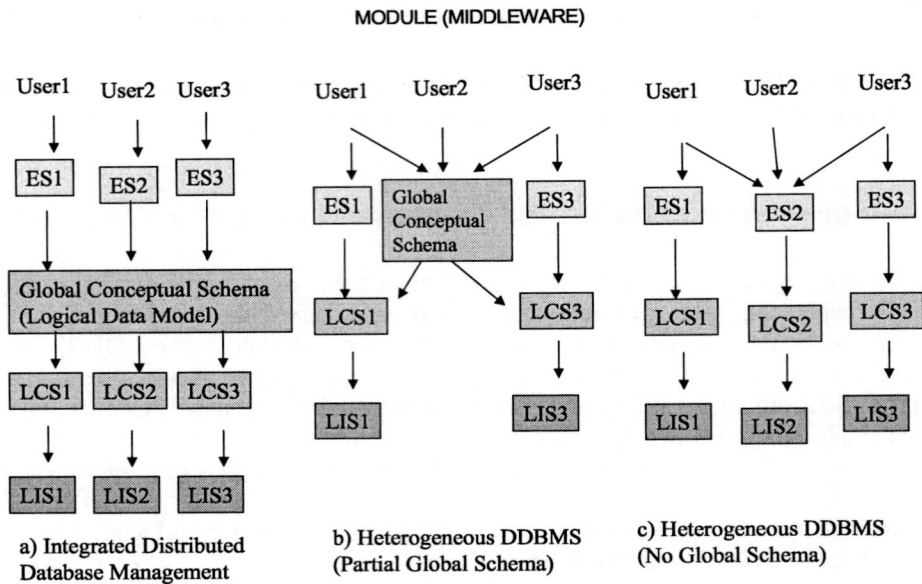

ES= External Schema, LCS= Local Conceptual Schema, LIS=Local Internal Schema

Figure 4-16: Different Models of Distributed Databases

Figure 4-16c represents the approach in which no global conceptual schema exists. This approach is used in some multidatabase systems with very diverse schema (the "loosely coupled" FDBMS). One approach to accessing such a database is a special multi-database language thatallows users to define and manipulate autonomous databases. This language has special capabilities such as logical database names for queries, same definitions in different schema, etc. A DDBM may loosely couple the component DBMSs by providing a user interface which presents the various databases in a menu created directly from the local schemas (GCS is not used). The user may have to know the name, the local schema, and the query language of the individual databases.

Most DBMS vendors at present provide some heterogeneous DDBMS capabilities. For example, Sybase as well as Oracle allow remote joins between DB2 and Sybase and Oracle, respectively. Most of the research at present is focusing on object-orientation in multidatabase systems.

4.7 Web-based Data Access

4.7.1 Web Query Processing and XQL (XML Query Language) – XML as a Database

Web query processing has been an area of active work for several years. At present, many products are commercially available that accept queries from a web browser and send them to relational databases by using ODDBC/JDBC drivers. Some research is also going on in this area. The following references are a sample:

- Haritsa, J., et al, " Distributed Query Processing on the Web", ICDE 2000.
- Pardon, G., Alonso, G., "CheeTah: a Lightweight Transaction Server for Plug-and-Play Internet Data Management", pp.210-219, VLDB2000.
- Diao, Y., et al, "Toward Learning Based Web Query Processing", pp.317-328, VLDB2000.

Most of the current work in web query processing has been directed to XML. Several XML query languages have been introduced such as XQL and XML Query. Let us look at one for the purpose of illustration.

XQL is designed specifically for XML documents. It is a general-purpose query language, providing a single syntax that can be used for queries, addressing, and patterns. XQL is a notation for retrieving information from a document. The information could be a set of nodes (e.g., XML elements), information about node relationships, or derived values. The result of a query could be a node, a list of nodes, an XML document, an array, or some other structure.

XQL uses "context" for queries. A 'context' is the set of nodes against which a query operates. To understand the concept of context, consider a tree containing nodes. Asking for all nodes named 'X' from the root of the tree would return one set of results. Asking for the set of nodes named 'X' from a branch in the tree would return a different set of results. Thus, the results of a query depend upon the context against which it is executed. There are a variety of ways that applications might specify the input context of a query. XQL allows a query to select between using the current context as the input context and using the 'root context' as the input context. A query prefixed with '/' (forward slash) uses the root context. The following examples illustrate XQL:

- /author will find all author elements within the current context.
- //author will find all author elements anywhere within the current document.

More information about XQL and XML Query can be found at the W3 consortium (www.w3.org).

4.7.2 Web Access to Relational Databases - The Web Gateways

4.7.2.1 Overview

Web access to relational databases is provided through a Relational Gateway that translates the browser requests to SQL calls and then translates the query response to HTML pages. Since the first relational gateway developed for Oracle databases at CERN in 1992, a large number of relational gateways have been announced from a variety of vendors. In essence, a relational gateway should support all functions typically provided by an RDBMS plus access from Web. Specifically, the functional requirements should include the following:

a) Ability to develop Web applications which access new or existing relational databases. This means that the application developers need support for:

– Simple queries, repeated queries (intermediate results), nested queries.

– Automatic temporary saving of intermediate query results.

– Embedded SQL support.

– Stored procedure invocation.

– Remote procedure calls.

b) Ability for users to do ad hoc browsing and reporting. This includes ad hoc, form-based SQL access.

c) User interface capability (i.e., display results in forms, produce pie charts and forms such as produced by report writers).

d) Support for access and integration of results from multiple databases.

Different approaches to satisfy these requirements have been used. The first gateway allowed a user to enter an SQL expression as a search text to a WWW-server. It formatted the results of the query and sent them back as plain text. Since then, a considerable commercial activity in this field has occurred and many relational gateways have been configured and deployed on the WWW. Many gateways focus on retrieval of data using simple SELECT statements while more sophisticated relational gateways have started to appear.

4.7.2.2   Technical Considerations

The key technical problem in designing relational gateways is that the transaction protocols in HTTP and in SQL are quite different. SQL is not limited to a single transaction when accessing a database. In a typical session with a DBMS, the user performs many transactions. A typical SQL server transaction allows for interaction a number of times before an eventual COMMIT statement is issued and the session is finished.

The most general role of the relational gateway program is to establish a connection between the client and the DBMS, so that information can be passed in both directions. When there is a mismatch between the HTTP interaction protocol and the SQL interaction protocol, the gateway also has to mediate between the protocols in order to maintain consistency on both sides. In practice, the main purpose of relational gateways is to mediate between the two protocols.

Simple database gateway implementations use the single HTTP transaction (i.e., connection, request, response, close) for database access. This somewhat limits the interaction with the DBMS. For example, no interaction with the user is allowed to continue a query based on intermediate results. A sophisticated relational gateway program, such as discussed by [Bjorn 1995], can accept multiple users at the same time and maintain user integrity by managing a session number for each user. The session number, provided by the DBMS, is unique for each user. The connection between the server and the browser is broken several times, but each time it is re-established. The session number, which is appended to the URL (along with the current page), allows the relational gateway to verify the user. Neither user name nor password is passed, so there is no additional security risk involved. From a database point of view, sessions are not the same as transactions. For example, multiple transactions with the DBMS can occur in one session.

Initial Web relational gateways invoke relational database functionalities on the Web server by using CGI. These gateways typically present an HTML FORM to the user, the user fills in the FORM, this form invokes a CGI script which generates SQL and interfaces with the DBMS. The response from the DBMS is converted to HTML and returned to the Web browser. A FORM contains some fields where the user enters data in a structured way, a button to submit the form (which simulates submitting a form to an office or similar in the real world), and a button to erase the user's input so that the form can be used again. The CGI gateways can be configured as:

- CGI Executable - A database application program is executed as a CGI executable itself; thereby, forking the application process for every request.
- Application Server - A database application program runs as a daemon process. A CGI executable just dispatches the request rather than accessing the DBMS engine.

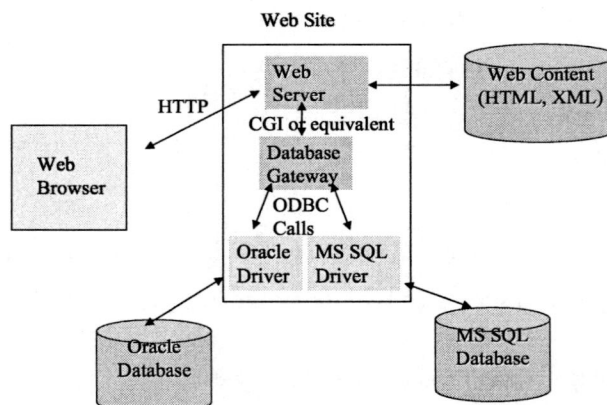

Figure 4-17:   Web Access to Heterogeneous Data

Figure 4-17 shows an example of Web access to heterogeneous relational databases through a database gateway residing at the Web site. The database gateway is a CGI program, a Servlet, a JSP (Java Server Page) or something similar (e.g., ASP) that can be invoked by a Web server. The database gateway contains ODBC calls to access Oracle, MS SQL, and other databases. The main advantage of using ODBC in this case is that you can use one database gateway to access any ODBC client databases. Otherwise, you will need one gateway for Oracle, one for MS SQL, one for Informix and one for Sybase.

4.7.2.3 Support for Repeated and Nested Queries

In a nested query, one (or more) SELECT statement(s) occur within another SELECT statement. It is not an easy task to build a GUI that handles the nesting of SELECT statements. Many relational gateways do not support this approach. They allow the user to repeatedly query the database using intermediate results or combinations of intermediate results with other parts of the database. This is possible because all results of a SELECT statement produce a new table which in turn can be queried, and so on. The use of repeated queries is an attempt to somewhat capture the power of nested queries while at the same time maintaining a simple and clean graphical user interface.

Nested versus repeated queries have performance trade-offs. Repeated queries introduce extra work to explicitly save the results of each SELECT statement into a view (or a new table if the DBMS does not support views). Most systems avoid this, because of the overhead involved. However, the intermediate saving is needed to ensure that results do not get lost when time-out errors occur. In other words, by providing necessary time-out error handling, you get a mechanism for providing repeated queries at no extra cost.

4.7.2.4 Handling Time-Outs

The time-out issues for each protocol must be dealt with. The HTTP time-out problem stems from limitations inherent to the HTTP protocol; whereas, the SQL server time-out is a "garbage cleaning" feature we must provide since there is a possibility that the user is not on-line any longer to terminate his connection with the DBMS.

HTTP Time-Out: The time-out period for the HTTP protocol depends on the settings for the WWW-browser, but a time-out much longer than 1 minute destroys the illusion of interactivity which is very important to the Web users. This means that the relational gateway should contact the database and receive a reply which it can pass on to the server within that minute, or else there is no guarantee that a connection to the browser is still maintained between the browser and the WWW-server. For simple queries, one minute is certainly sufficient, but as the complexity of the commands sent to the DBMS increases, as well as the number of simultaneous users, the likelihood that some tasks will not be accomplished within one minute increases drastically.

At the time when the query completes, two scenarios are possible:
- The connection to the browser has not timed out. In this case, the result is passed back through the gateway to the user's Web browser screen.
- The connection to the browser has timed out. In this case, the result is available in the temporary table and all the user has to do is go back to the previous screen of the browser and SELECT all columns of the temporary table. If the user does not reconnect, the gateway automatically finishes the session with the DBMS as described below.

To make sure that data can be returned in all circumstances, even when loads are very high, some relational gateways also offer the option of returning results by mail instead of on-screen.

SQL Server Connection Time-Out: The relational gateway program establishes and keeps a session with the DBMS independent of whether a user is currently connected to the WWW-server or not. However, the gateway must have an ability to end the session even if the user does not connect again. The relational gateway allows the system administrator to set a connection time-out period between one and 999 minutes. When the time-out occurs, the gateway ends the session with the DBMS. If at that time, there is a VIEWxxxxxx table corresponding to the session, it will be erased. Eventual mail results are always e-mailed to the user before the session terminates.

4.7.2.5 Observations and Comments

The fundamental problem with supporting SQL access from programs over Web is that SQL is conversational (i.e., an SQL statement from a program returns a cursor that is used by programs to "fetch" different rows of the table that has been returned to the programs). Thus, if a program requires multiple interactions within a transaction, then the Web gateways have to maintain cursor positions. Many relational gateways establish their own sessions with the database server and mediate between the single interaction HTTP protocol and the protocol of the database server, which inherently support the sequence of interactions.

Relational gateways should support insertion and deletion of tables and columns, addition and deletion of data, and simple as well as repeated queries. Furthermore, to ensure delivery of query results, temporary tables as well as a mail reply option should be implemented. The gateway also should automatically log out users after a period of time specified by the system administrator. The user's password should be only passed through the gateway once, when the user logs in. However, since the password at that time is passed openly, some form of secure HTTP must be used or otherwise a security risk is incurred. However, once the first connection has been established, only session numbers can be passed back and forth and no additional security risk is incurred.

What is a Transaction Database?

Transaction databases (TDBs) (also known as transaction-oriented databases and transaction-based databases) support organizational activities, i.e., organizations use them to store the information they require to carry out their business. TDBs provide support analysis of organization's activities for improvement and/or streamlining its performance. The main properties of TDBs are:

- The information is in a state of change.
- Changes occur as transactions.
- Data can be found quickly and is not duplicated.
- The interrelationships between data items are stored in the database.
- The properties and method of storage of data is internal to the database.

Historically, TDBs have been constructed by using flat files, hierarchical databases, network databases, and relational databases. OODBMSs and active databases are the future of deploying TDBs. Not surprisingly, most TDBs at present are based on the relational DBMSs from vendors such as Oracle, Sybase, and Informix. For example, SunWorld Online describes results of an April 1996 survey that indicates that 35 percent of the respondents indicated that Oracle is the primary engine for transaction databases (Sybase and Informix follow at 21 percent and 19 percent, respectively). The same survey indicated that the largest transaction database that most respondents (40%) develop or manage is in the range of one to five gigabytes; a few (20%) deal with larger TDBs that are in the range of 20 to 100 gigabytes.

Transaction Databases as Data Warehouses

Although TDBs are mainly intended, as stated previously, to support transactional activities, these databases can serve as very useful sources for populating data warehouses. For example, in an insurance company, a transaction database may keep all the insurance claims processed. This is naturally a very rich source for a 'claims" data mart that can be used for decision support and can be mined to discover interrelationships between different claims and different user populations and geographical areas.

In the same vein, transaction databases in EC can be used for data warehouses. In particular, the purchase log that shows what items were purchased by whom in an EC environment is a rich source for data warehouses. A transaction database that keeps track of all purchases made in an organization can be created easily by capturing the purchases when a customer clicks on the "purchase" icon after filling his/her shopping cart. This TDB, if loaded in an RDBMS, can be used for a sophisticated analysis of user buying habits and negotiating prices with the merchants. You can also embark on data mining of the purchase log to discover associations and relationships between customers, projects, items, and suppliers.

The catalogs that maintain the product information, in effect, are data warehouses that support the decisions of purchasing through browsel and analysis. These databases are not typically TDBs unless you store inventory information in the catalogs (inventory update can be treated as a transaction). A catalog can be viewed as a data warehouse especially if it is a consolidated catalog of many suppliers to provide a consistent look and feel to catalog reviewers.

What is the best approach to support data warehouses in EC? Are there any special considerations that need to be taken into account? As a starting point, an RDBMS should do the job, but EC applications increasingly use graphics and in some cases, may need to store multimedia information. Object relational and universal databases are good candidate technologies.

4.8 XYZCorp Case Study: Partial Solution 1

Let us address the data duplication and access aspects of the online purchasing problem. Here are some general guidelines:

- The inventory data is updated frequently, so it should be allocated carefully. Many companies keep inventory data at two levels: local (regional) and master (corporate). The users should be able to get the local inventory first and access the corporate if not available locally.
- The price and customer data can be replicated because it is not updated frequently.
- A virtual catalog is used for products where multiple physical catalogs give the end-user a single catalog view. This is an extension of the portal idea ("data portal").
- Keeping the data at different sites but accessing it through C/S middleware (e.g., ODBC) can reduce the cost of massive file transfers.
- The most common middleware technology for accessing heterogeneous remote databases is ODBC/JDBC.
- Increased use of XML to transfer information between business partners is an area of vibrant growth. The XML "documents" can be exchanged by using almost any middleware technology (e.g., email, HTTP, CORBA). Due to the popularity of Web Services, transporting XML over SOAP may turn out to be the most common approach (see the previous chapter).

Suggestion: We are now ready to jump into distributed transaction management. It may exercise different parts of your brain. Before proceeding, you may want to take a break.

4.9 Distributed Transaction Management – The TP-Heavy Approach

4.9.1 Overview of Transaction Management Concepts

Let us now turn our attention to data modification that is typically accomplished through a transaction manager. The concept of a transaction originates from the field of contract law [Gray 1981, Walpole 1987] in which each contract between two parties (a transaction) is carried out unless either party is willing to break the law. From a business and end-user point of view, transactions occur at two levels: customer to business and business to business (see Figure 4-18). In computer science, a transaction is defined as a sequence of data operations (read, write and manipulation commands) that transform one consistent state of the system into a new consistent state [Eswaran 1976]. Examples of business transactions are: electronic transfer of money from one account to another, update of an inventory database, and purchasing a ticket electronically. To accomplish these business transactions, computer transactions are executed. Examples of the computer transactions are a group of database operations (e.g., SQL statements) that need to be executed as a single unit, a program with embedded SQL statements that updates one or more relational tables, and a Cobol program that modifies indexed files [Ozsu 1999].

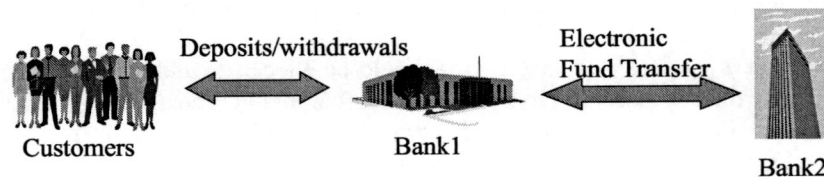

Figure 4-18: Transaction Example: Customer to Business and Business to Business

4.9.1.1 The ACID Properties

A transaction has four properties, known as the ACID properties:

Atomicity: A transaction is treated as a single unit of operation; either all the transaction's actions are completed, or none of them are. This is also known as the "all-or-nothing property". If a transaction completes all of its actions successfully, then it is said to be committed.

Consistency: A transaction maps one consistent (correct) state of the database to another. Informally, consistency is concerned with correctly reflecting the reality in the database. For example, if a company has 500 employees, then a database consistent with this reality should also show 500 employees. The notion of a consistent state is highly dependent on the semantics of the database. A set of constraints, called semantic integrity constraints, is used to verify database consistency.

Isolation: A transaction cannot reveal its results to other concurrent transactions before commitment. Isolation assures that transactions do not access data that is being updated (temporarily inconsistent and incomplete during the execution of a transaction).

Durability: Once completed successfully (committed), the results of a transaction are permanent and cannot be erased from the database. The DBMS ensures that the results of a transaction are not altered due to system failures (transactions endure failures).

Detailed discussion of the ACID properties for transactions can be found in [Gray 1993, Ozsu 1999]. The implication of the ACID properties for transaction management is as follows:

Serializability (Concurrency Control): This allows transactions to execute concurrently while achieving the same logical result as if they had executed serially. Concurrency control allows multiple transactions to read and update data simultaneously, and includes transaction scheduling and management of the resources needed by transactions during execution. Transactions can be scheduled serially ("single-threaded") to minimize conflicts or in parallel ("multi-threaded") to maximize concurrency.

Commit Processing: This allows commitment of transaction changes if it executes properly and removal of the changes if the transaction fails. The transactions usually "bracket" their operations by using "begin transaction" and "end transaction" statements. The transaction manager permanently enters the changes made by a transaction when it encounters the "end transaction" statement; otherwise, it removes the changes. Transaction managers also log the results of transactions on a separate medium so that the effects of transactions can be recovered even in the event of a crash that destroys the database.

Although the ACID properties as well as the serializability and commit processing implications are important, it has been argued that all these properties amount to atomicity and serializability [Triantafillou 1995]. This is a pragmatic view that greatly simplifies the discussion of transaction processing.

4.9.1.2 Transaction Models

Transactions may be classified into the following broad models:

- **Single-site versus multiple-site (distributed) transactions**: The transactions may be restricted to a single site (e.g., one database server) or it may span many sites. We will discuss distributed transactions in the next section.

- **Queued or conversational transactions**: In queued transaction processing, such as found in IMS-DC, arriving transactions are first queued and then scheduled for execution. Once execution begins, the transaction does not interact with the user. In conversational transaction processing, such as found in CICS, the transactions interact with the outside world during execution.

- **Short (flat) or long (workflow) transactions**: Short, also known as flat, transactions start with a "begin transaction" instruction and end with a "commit transaction" or "abort transaction" instruction. Flat transactions are all or nothing at all activities (you cannot commit a portion of a flat transaction). Long duration transactions (also known as Workflows, Sagas and Flexible Transactions) consist of a sequence of distributed or queued transactions to perform a multitude of activities that may span several business units of an organization. Long transactions may be constructed by chaining or nesting individual transactions. These transactions cannot be typically satisfied by a single transaction (distributed or queued). A special case of long transactions is massive batch updates. These transactions are typically handled by providing a series of "synch points" at which all the changes made are committed (e.g., a synch point after every 100 hundred updates).

4.9.1.3 Transaction Managers

A transaction manager (TM), also known as a transaction processing monitor (TP monitor), specializes in managing transactions from their point of origin to their termination (planned or unplanned). The TM facilities are traditionally integrated with the DBMS facilities, as shown in Figure 4-19. This allows database queries from different transactions to access/update one or several data items. However, some products only specialize in TM with special focus on handling thousands of OLTP users. These TMs provide a variety of monitoring, dynamic load balancing, process restarts, and priority scheduling capabilities. Under the control of a sophisticated TM, a transaction may be decomposed into sub-transactions to optimize I/O and/or response time. Examples of commercially available TMs are IBM's CICS, Transarc's Encina, and BEA Tuxedo. It is not always possible to find separate TMs in commercial products. In some systems, TM facilities are embedded in communication managers, operating systems and/or database managers. In particular, most RDBMS vendors at present provide some TP facilities, known as TP-Lite (see Section 4.12).

An introduction to TMS facilities is given in the book [Ozsu 1999]. A detailed classification of transaction processing systems can be found in [Leff 1991].

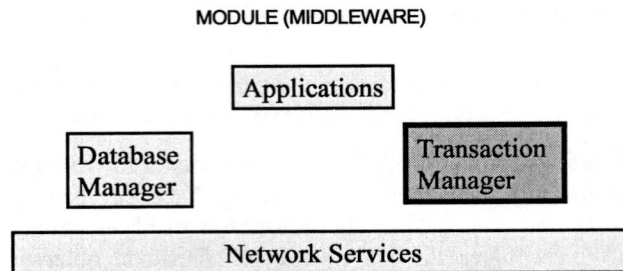

Figure 4-19: Conceptual View of a Transaction Manager

4.9.2 Distributed Transaction Processing Concepts

Distributed transaction processing (DTP) allows multiple computers to coordinate the execution of a single transaction. This occurs when the data needed by a transaction resides at many computers. Atomicity of a transaction is of key importance - all the activities performed on different computers by a transaction must be completed properly or entirely withdrawn in the event of a failure in the network, application code, and/or computing hardware. A distributed transaction manager (DTM), a collection of software modules, is responsible for distributed transaction processing. Transactions in a DTM are known as distributed (also known as multi-site) transactions that access data at several different sites. A distributed transaction consists of several local (also known as single site) transactions which access data at one site.

4.9.2.1 Distributed ACID

Each distributed transaction is treated as a single recoverable unit and must pass the "ACID" (atomicity, consistency, isolation, and durability) test. Consequently, the main responsibilities of a DTM are as follows:

- **Atomicity** of transactions through commit processing for failure handling and recovery.
- **Serializability** of transactions through update synchronization and concurrency control.

It is important for different sites to reach commit agreement while processing sub-transactions of a global transaction. The most widely used solution to this problem is the two-phase commit (2PC) protocol that coordinates the commit actions needed to run a distributed transaction. When a transaction issues a COMMIT request, the commit action is performed in two phases: prepare for commit and then commit. If a failure occurs in the prepare phase, then the transaction can be terminated without difficulty; otherwise, all sub-transactions are undone. Two-phase commit will be discussed in Section 4.11.1. Two-phase commit has been implemented in many systems and is also included in the ISO Transaction Processing (TP) standard.

Many algorithms for update synchronization and concurrency control have been proposed and implemented since the mid 1970s. Most algorithms used in practice are variants of two-phase locking (2PL), which allows a transaction to lock the resources in first phase and unlock in the second phase after performing reads/writes. Algorithms are also used to resolve distributed deadlocks that occur when transactions wait on each other. A review of these algorithms can be found in [Umar 1993 Chapter 6].

4.9.2.2 Distributed Transaction Models

Figure 4-20 shows a few basic models of distributed transactions. In case of remote transactions, the client submits (ships) the request to execute the transaction on a remote system. The remote transaction either commits or aborts, independent of the requesting system. In case of commit coordination, the requesting site manages the execution of the transaction across multiple sites. The protocol used in this case is two-phase commit. Serial execution moves the coordination from one site to the next to complete a multi-site transaction.

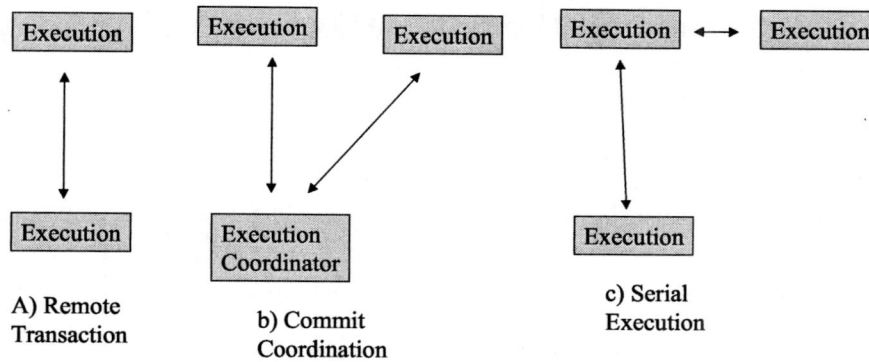

Figure 4-20: Models of Distributed Transactions

These three basic models can be combined to produce many other DTP models for long running (workflow) distributed transactions. In addition, the activities performed on different systems can be coordinated as queued or conversational transactions. In queued DTP, the transaction managers at different sites queue the incoming transactions and then execute them later, thus allowing for organizational boundaries and control between systems. In conversational DTP, the transaction managers interact with each other directly through the communication network. Note that queued DTP is not suitable for commit coordination (Figure 4-20b) because the sending site can only communicate with other sites through queues. Queued model does work quite well for remote and serial transactions.

It is important to briefly discuss read-only distributed transactions. This happens due to the following reasons:

- Updates issued by transactions did not modify any records (e.g., telephone number was changed to what it originally was).
- Updates were issued, but did not occur due to violations of integrity constraints or programmed triggers.
- Read-only distributed transactions process more quickly and incur minimal overhead.

4.9.2.3 Distributed Transaction Managers: The TP-Heavy Approach

A distributed transaction manager (DTM) is responsible for the execution of a distributed transaction from its beginning to its end and is in charge of ACID in a distributed environment. Thus, a DTM must address numerous technically challenging issues such as concurrency control in distributed environments, update synchronization, and data integrity after failures in a distributed environment. Due to the complexity of DTMs, they are referred to as "TP-Heavy". Research in distributed transaction management has been actively pursued for heterogeneous databases for several years [Pu 1991, Soparker 1991]. Although detailed technical discussion of these topics is beyond the scope of this book, we will review the key technical challenges and approaches in Section 4.13 and suggest additional sources of information.

Examples of DTM products are Microsoft's Transaction Processor, NCR's Top-End, BEA's Tuxedo and Transarc. It is expected that in the future more products will become available and products will operate across PCs, UNIX and MVS environments. In addition, these products will conform to the ISO and X/open standards for distributed transaction management. We discuss these standards next. Some interesting references in this area are:

- Vogler, H., and Buchmann, B., "Using Multiple Mobile Agents for Distributed Transactions". CoopIS 1998: 114-121.
- Weikum, G., "Review - Atomicity versus Anonymity: Distributed Transactions for Electronic Commerce". ACM SIGMOD Digital Review 1:(1999).
- Ram, P., Do, L., and Drew, P., "Distributed Transactions in Practice".SIGMOD Record 28(3): 49-55 (1999).

4.9.3 Standards for Distributed Transaction Processing

Standards are needed for DTP for the following reasons:
- Interoperability of two TMs from two different vendors to provide DTP services. For example, allow Tuxedo, CICS and Encina to interoperate with each other.
- Interoperability of TMs with database managers so that a TM from vendor X can interoperate with database managers from vendors Y and Z. For example, allow CICS to work with Informix, Oracle, and Sybase databases.

To respond to these requirements, two open standards for distributed transaction processing are under active development:
- The X/Open Distributed Transaction Processing (DTP) Model.
- The ISO Transaction Processing (OSI TP) standard.

Figure 4-21 and Figure 4-22 show two different views of the relationships between these two standards. Conceptually, each computer system has a transaction processing environment consisting of four components: the applications (APs), the resource (database) managers (RMs), the transaction managers (TMs), and the communication resource managers (CRMs). X/Open defines the interfaces between the four components at each computer. The OSI TP protocol is used between two distributed transaction managers (possibly from two different vendors) to communicate with each other via the communication resource managers. Let us briefly review these interfaces (the standard APIs).

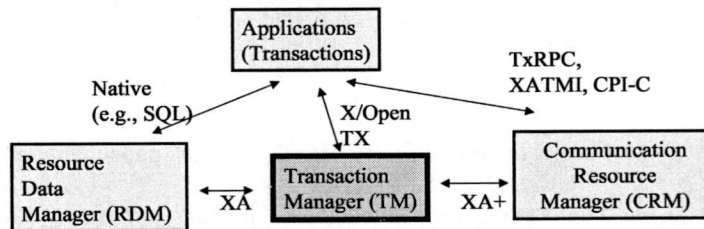

Figure 4-21: Standards for Distributed Transaction Processing (Single System View)

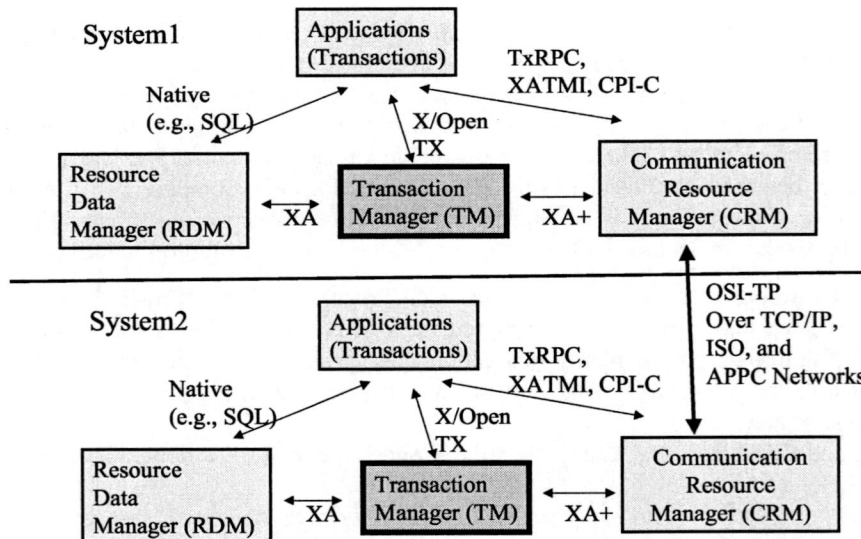

Figure 4-22: Standards for Distributed Transaction Processing (Multiple System View)

The X/Open DTP defines the following application program interfaces:
- XA is the API between the transaction manager and database systems. For example, a TM issues an xa_prepare, xa_commit, and xa_rollback to perform a two-phase commit.

- TX is the API between application programs and the transaction manager. For example, an application program issues a tx_begin command to start a transaction.
- "Native" calls, e.g., SQL, are issued from the transaction to the resource managers.
- XA+ is the API between a transaction manager and a communication resource manager. This API is used by a TM to communicate with a TM on another computer through the CRM.
- Many application-to-CRM APIs are being developed. Examples are the TxRPC (transactional RPC based on DEC's Remote Task Invocation technology), CPI-C (a peer-to-peer API used in the IBM APPC environments), and XATMI (a Tuxedo Application/Transaction Management Interface).

OSI TP is primarily used between CRMs at different sites to provide global transaction control. OSI TP is a layer 7 application service element (ASE) designed to work with other layer 7 OSI ASEs such as:
- Commitment, Concurrency and Recovery (CCR), a two-phase commit protocol.
- Association Control Service Element (ACSE), an association/release protocol.
- User-ASE(s), a user-defined ASE that performs functions such as data transfer.

OSI-TP is a synchronization protocol between transaction managers (TMs). It does not provide data transfer and relies on the User-ASE(s) for data transfer. The protocol allows different levels of coordination between TMs; examples are "none" and "commitment". The coordination level "commitment" provides two-phase commit functionality through the CCR. The coordination level "none" bypasses this functionality and can be used as a starting point in distributed transaction management.

The X/Open DTP is evolving and other standards are being considered (for example, the standards for queued distributed transactions are under consideration). X/Open DTP has been widely accepted by the DBMS as well TM vendors. With standardization of XA, XA+ and other APIs mentioned above, multivendor DBMS products that support X/Open DTP can participate in global transaction coordination. .

Time to Take a Break
- ✓ Basic Concepts
- ✓ Distributed Query and Transaction Processing
- • TP Lite versus TP Heavy
- • Consolidation and Evaluation

Suggested Review Questions Before Proceeding
- What are the main issues in distributed query processing and how do the distributed database servers support this type of processing?
- How does distributed query processing work in the Web environments and how do the XML query languages help?
- What is a transaction and what are the key issues in processing transactions?
- How does transaction processing work in a distributed environment?
- Discuss some transaction processing standards with examples

4.10 Data Replication Servers – The TP-Lite Approach

Distributed transaction managers (DTMs) were an active area of academic and industrial work in the 1980s and early 1990s. DTMs use a "TP-Heavy" approach to maintain the ACID properties in a distributed environment. In the mid 1990s, the notion of "Data Replication Servers" became popular for managing replicated data by using a "TP-Lite" approach. The basic difference is that instead of updating replicated data in real-time (the DTM TP-Heavy approach), the replicated data is updated periodically (e.g. once an hour) by using a replication server (the TP-Lite approach). We will examine this issue in Section 4.11. This section presents an overview of the main concepts, defines the main terms, outlines the key technical considerations, suggests a generic architecture of Replication Servers and presents a framework that can be used to analyze and evaluate various vendor offerings.

4.10.1 Overview

Data replication is concerned with copying data completely or partially to multiple sites. The main advantage of replication is that the data is stored where it is used most often. In addition, replicated data can be accessed from alternate sites. Replication improves the read performance and data availability, but can degrade the update performance due to the need to synchronize replicated copies. Depending on the business needs, data may be replicated to support operational processing or informational processing. Here are some examples of data replication:

- Price information is replicated at all stores to speed up the checkout counter processing. The price information may be completely or partially replicated.
- Skeleton customer information (e.g., customer name, account number, credit limit) is kept at all different stores to speed up the order processing. Complete customer information is kept at a central site.
- Data warehouses containing portions of data from operational systems are constructed by many enterprises to support decisions in marketing and business planning.
- Detachable computers (e.g., mobile computers) are not always connected to the data source and therefore, typically keep redundant data. Detachable computers usually extract needed data and store it on their local disk for access while operating in a detached mode.

Data may be replicated for the following reasons [White 1994, Triantafillou 1995]:

- Distribute data to where it is used to improve performance, e.g., the price file.
- Data may be replicated to improve data availability.
- Data may be copied to detachable computers for off-line processing.
- Data from different decentralized servers or detachable clients may be integrated into one copy.
- Data is extracted from multiple operational databases and loaded/replicated into a data warehouse.
- The database on some platforms may have better tools for application development and/or administration. Thus, it may be quicker and cheaper to develop and maintain new applications around the replicated data on new platforms.
- Some platforms may provide better and easier data access and manipulation tools.
- Data may be replicated during a gradual migration period.

However, data replication can be an expensive and time-consuming activity that must be carefully coordinated. In particular, the issue of keeping the replicated data synchronized with master/primary data is of key importance.

4.10.2 Definitions and Technical Considerations

4.10.2.1 Data Replication Servers

Data Replication Servers, or just Replication Servers, manage replicated data and attempt to maximize the benefits of data replication by minimizing the costs and risks associated with replication. In essence, a

Replication Server provides software components that replicate the changes being made at one site to other sites. The three main logical components of a Replication Server are (see Section 4.10.3 for more details):

- Data extractor that captures the data being changed.
- Replication manager that knows the sites where the replicated copies are and sends the changes to the appropriate sites.
- Data synchronizer that actually applies the changes to the replicated copies.

4.10.2.2 Read-Only versus Updateable Data

Data replication is based largely on the notion of primary versus secondary copies of data:

Primary (Updateable) Copy: This copy can be read as well as updated by the end users. In many practical cases, there is only one primary copy of a given data object (a data object can be a relational table, a set of data records, or a set of data fields) that is assigned to a particular site (primary site). However, the primary copy of data object d1 may reside on site s1, while the primary copy of data object d2 may reside on site s2 (e.g., primary copy of prices may be in Chicago, but the primary copy of customers may be in New York).

Secondary (Read-Only) Copies: Each primary copy may have one or more secondary copies at other sites (secondary sites) that are read-only. The users of the secondary copies perform updates by submitting a special update transaction that updates the primary data. The changes in the primary data are reflected in the secondary copies periodically (asynchronously) or in real-time (synchronously).

This division of data into read-only and updateable data objects provides many benefits. In some cases, the read-only copies are referred to as "snapshots". The notion of snapshots was first proposed by Adiba and Lindsay [Adiba 1980]:

" The point of the snapshot concept is that many applications - probably a majority - can tolerate or may even require data as of some particular earlier point in time".

Read-only copies are particularly useful for decision support applications; however, they introduce serious performance problems for applications that require on-line updates. If only one primary updateable copy is maintained, then all updates must be directed to this primary site. However, if multiple updateable copies are kept, then the multiple copies must be synchronized through locking mechanisms to avoid update conflicts [see the discussion on two-phase commit versus replication in Section 4.11).

4.10.2.3 Initial Replication

The data is initially replicated by using one of the following methods:

Full Copy - The source data tables are copied completely (dumped) to target locations. Example is price files.

Subset Copy - Segments of a table are copied to different sites. For example, the customer information may be partitioned by regions and sent to regional offices for their use.

Merged Copy - Data from different tables (or table fragments) is copied to populate one or more target tables. For example, a data warehouse may be populated by extracting and merging information from different operational databases.

Enhanced Copy - The target data is extracted, cleaned up, consolidated, and summarized before loading into a target database. This type of copying is typically used to establish data warehouses.

4.10.2.4 Update Synchronization (Transaction versus Periodic)

Update synchronization, also known as update propagation, refers to making all copies of data reflect the same values (i.e., if one copy is updated, then the others must be also updated). The main challenge in data replication is to keep the replicated data consistent with each other. A significant body of technical literature has been published to propose solutions that minimize the performance degradation due to data synchronization [Barghouti 1991, Bernstein 1987, Gray 1993, Triantafillou 1995]. At the highest level, the solutions fall into two categories:

- Transaction level synchronization schemes: These schemes are based on the assumption that if one copy of data is updated, then all other copies must be updated before the transaction terminates. If this cannot be accomplished, then the transaction must be aborted. These schemes are used by the contemporary distributed transaction managers. The synchronization is transparent to the end users. The core technique used in these schemes is two-phase commit (see Section 4.11.1).
- Periodic synchronization schemes: The transaction updates the primary copy and then terminates. Other copies are updated through replication servers (an off-line process) periodically (based on time and/or events).

Since the late 1980s, a great deal of industrial attention has been paid to periodic data replication techniques and tools. This is in sharp contrast to the extensive theoretical work accumulated in transaction level update synchronization algorithms since the early 1970s. The trade-offs between the two approaches are discussed by [McGoveran 1994]. We will review these trade-offs in detail in Section 4.11. At this point, let us use a simple example of detachable computers to illustrate the basic trade-offs. Detachable computers (e.g., mobile laptop computers) are not always connected to the data source and therefore, typically keep redundant data for quick local data access. However, for such systems, data synchronization has to be asynchronous because the detachable computers do not know when other copies of data are being updated. In these cases, the typical periodic data synchronization technique used is:

- The detachable computer calls a data server to access the latest copy of data.
- The data server receives the request and then disconnects the detachable computer (this is done to save connection time while the server goes out and tries to find the needed data).
- The data server finds the needed data and calls the detachable computer.
- The data server downloads the data and then disconnects the detachable computer.

4.10.2.5 Data Refreshing versus Incremental Updating

Data refresh means that the data is re-created from scratch every time it is synchronized. In essence, this is similar to the initial load discussed above (i.e., the target databases are scratched and reloaded with new data). This method is very simple but is not suitable for large databases that may require several hours to reload.

Incremental updates mean that the changes (deltas) to one data copy are applied to other copies of data. In other words, only the changed data values are sent to the secondary copies. Incremental updates should be considered for large databases that require frequent synchronizations. This method is also known as update propagation. Incremental updating is more complicated than data refresh because it requires:

- A change capture program that only extracts data that has changed.
- An incremental updater that updates only those data records that have changed.

4.10.3 General Architecture of Replication Servers

Figure 4-23 shows a set of logical components of a generalized Data Replication Server. In essence, a data replication server provides software components that replicate the changes being made at a primary site to one or more secondary sites. These logical components are customized and specialized by different vendors depending on how the data is initially loaded, how it is synchronized (refreshed or incrementally updated), whether the replicated data is read-only or updateable, how the data changes are captured, and how frequently the data is synchronized.

4.10.3.1 Data Extractor

The data extractor component is responsible for selection (capture) of needed data from the primary databases. Entire database may be selected for refresh or only deltas (i.e., data changes) may be captured. Data captures for refresh is straightforward, but requires considerable effort for delta captures. The delta captures can be achieved through a variety of techniques such as the following:

- Capture the data changes from the logs. The capture program continuously monitors the logs, and extracts the needed changes. This technique is commonly known as "log scraping".

- Use database triggers, commonly available in RDBMSs, to capture the changes. The triggers can be set for times (e.g., 6 p.m. every day) or other events such as whenever a new order arrives.
- Employ programmatic captures from the database. A capture program scans the source databases and selects data based on predefined business rules. The capture logic is application dependent and not part of the replication server. An example of a business rule is: "extract all data since yesterday 5 p.m. on the highest sales in the southwestern region of the company".

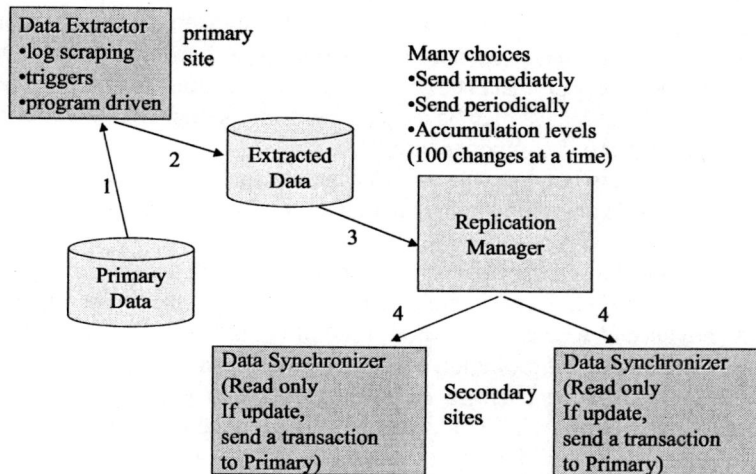

Figure 4-23: Data Replication Server Architecture

There are many trade-offs between these approaches. The log scrapers are off-line processes and do not interfere with the operation of the system. The triggers provide more flexibility but require extra programming effort. The specialized data capture programming gives maximum flexibility to the end-users, but can be an expensive undertaking.

The data extractor component may also transform the primary data into the secondary data formats, if needed. This includes conversions of data formats and data models (e.g., IMS to RDBMS). Many data replicators convert data to ASCII format and/or transform it into a target data load format. For most of the data replications, the need for extensive data conversion may not exist because the same data in the same format may be replicated at several sites (e.g., customer information at multiple sites). However, some applications such as data warehousing require considerable transformations such as data consolidation (unification of different values), summarization, and derivation (generation of new fields).

4.10.3.2 Replication Manager

This component is the heart of the data replication server. It receives the data from the primary site(s) and transmits it to the appropriate secondary site(s). The replication manager may itself reside on the primary site(s), on a separate "replication server machine", on secondary site(s), or on a combination. Associated with the replication manager is a directory which shows what data is to be extracted, where it is to be sent (i.e., the secondary site(s)), how frequently the extracted data is to be sent to the secondary site(s), and if the sent data is to be applied immediately or delayed.

The replication manager usually includes an administrative module that enables users to define, generate, initialize, and customize the various replication server components. Examples of the administrative functionalities are:

- Generation of data extraction and conversion programs.
- Specification of the primary and secondary sites for the replicated data items.
- Specification of the parameters to govern the operation of various components.

The administrative functionality can be provided through a GUI operating from a desktop. The generated programs can run on a desktop or on the primary data site. The administrative facilities may also include scripting languages to ease the burden of operating and administering a Data Replication Server.

4.10.3.3 Data Synchronizer

This component is responsible for transmission of captured data from the primary site to the secondary site(s) and resultant data load/update at the secondary site(s). The secondary data may be replaced entirely with the new data (refreshed) or it may be updated selectively to reflect changes (deltas). In many data replication servers, a staging area is created on the primary sites to store the captured data. Data synchronizers employ remote data transfer service such as bulk data transfer or interactive data exchanges depending on how quickly the secondary data is to be synchronized. Depending on the amount of data to be transmitted and loaded, special techniques may be used to speed up the transmission/load process (e.g., bulk database load). Typical options for this component are:

- Establish client/server sessions between the primary and secondary sites to apply the updates in real time as they become available or employ bulk data transfer for batch update processing (e.g., end of day processing).
- Resolve conflicts, if applicable. Many older replicators allowed updates of primary copy only, thus no conflict resolution was needed. Newer replication servers (e.g., the latest Oracle Replicator) are beginning to add "advanced" features that allow multiple copies to be updated based on a conflict resolution scheme. Typical conflict resolution schemes are based on time stamps (i.e., if copy A is being updated but copy B has more recent changes, then A is not updated and the request is sent to copy B).
- Broadcast the data to all secondary sites simultaneously or serialize the updates one secondary site at a time.
- Lock all secondary sites when they are being updated to assure that all secondary sites have the same copy of data or ignore this locking.
- Apply updates immediately when they are received at the secondary sites or perform bulk updates periodically.
- Use bulk load utilities and/or SQL load for RDBMSs.

4.10.3.4 Framework for Analyzing/Selecting Data Replication Servers

Several data replication servers are becoming commercially available from a diverse array of vendors. Here is a partial list of data replication servers, listed alphabetically:

- IBM Data Replication Toolset (Data Refresher, Data Hub, Data Propagator)
- Oracle Replicator
- Prism Warehouse manager
- Sybase Replication server
- Trinzic Infopump and InfoHub
- Praxis Omni Replicator

Some of these servers are oriented towards data warehousing while the others are intended for distributed transaction processing. It is beyond the scope of this book to discuss these and other data replication products. However, the generic architecture presented in the previous section can be used as a basis to analyze, evaluate, and select the most appropriate data replication tools. For example, the generic architecture can be used to analyze the data replication servers based on the following factors:

- Type of primary data sources
- Type of secondary sites (read-only or update)
- Mechanism to capture data changes (e.g., log scrapers versus triggers)
- Data refresh and/or delta update capabilities
- Real-time versus periodic batch update synchronization
- Conflict resolution options

Table 4-2 shows the factors that can be used to analyze/evaluate data replication servers. These factors are presented in terms of the logical architectural components presented in the previous section. Table 4-2 can be used as a basis for generating questions that can be included in a request for proposal (RFP).

Table 4-2: Analysis Matrix For Data Replication Servers

Evaluation Factors	Product1	Product2	Product3
Extraction capabilities ▪ Primary data supported (e.g., IMS, DB2, Oracle, Sybase) ▪ Ability to select records/fields from primary databases ▪ Method of data extraction (log scraping, triggers, programs ▪ Any data conversions performed			
Server management/administration capabilities ▪ Automatic extraction/conversion of code generation capability ▪ Quality of code generated ▪ Completeness of code generated ▪ Efficiency of generated code ▪ Ease of use (user GUI interface, training requirements) ▪ Data dictionary capability (ties to data dictionaries) ▪ Productivity aids (e.g., generation of scripts, JCL created)			
Update synchronization capabilities ▪ Client/server sessions between the primary and secondary sites or bulk data transfers ▪ Broadcast the data to all secondary sites or serialize ▪ Lock all secondary tables (or rows) when they are being updated or ignore this locking ▪ Apply updates immediately when they are received at the secondary sites or perform bulk updates periodically ▪ Use bulk load utilities and/or SQL load for RDBMSs			
Operability (environment needed for tool operation, e.g., PCs, UNIX workstations)			
Vendor maturity (strength of company, market position, etc.)			
Replication server maturity (product reliability, product direction)			
Product support (based on other client feedback and customer service contracts, technical support, help desk support)			

4.11 Two -Phase Commit ("TP-Heavy") Versus Data Replication Servers ("TP-Lite")

Implementation of algorithms for failure handling of distributed transactions is an expensive undertaking. Two-phase commit (2PC) and Data Replication Servers are two different approaches to guarantee integrity of distributed data under failures. Two-phase commit as well as Replication Servers have some trade-offs. Due to the academic and industrial activity in two-phase commit and the widespread availability of Replication Servers, a careful analysis of the trade-offs between using two-phase commit-based algorithms versus using Replication Servers is essential for several practical situations.

The reader should keep in mind that both issues are transparent to the end users. The discussion in this section is intended for a general understanding of the issues and approaches that should lead to improved strategies for the overall architecture.

4.11.1 Two-Phase Commit

Two-phase commit is the principal method of ensuring atomicity of distributed transactions. For a single-site transaction, updates are made permanent when a transaction commits, and updates are rolled back if a transaction aborts. However, a distributed transaction may commit at one node and abort at another. For example, update completes at node n1 and fails at n2. A transaction, distributed or not, may terminate abnormally due to two reasons: "suicide", indicating that a transaction terminates due to an internal error like a program error, or "murder" to indicate an external error like system crash [Gray 1979]. It is the responsibility of two-phase commit software to remove all changes made by a failing transaction from all nodes so that the transaction can be re-initiated. For atomic actions to be recoverable, the following two conditions must be met:

- Updated objects are not released until the action is completed.
- The initial states of all objects modified by the action can be reconstructed through the use of a log.

The two-phase commit protocol adheres to these conditions and coordinates the commit actions needed to run a transaction. When a transaction issues a COMMIT request, a series of actions are initiated. These actions are divided in the following two distinct phases:

Phase 1 (Prepare): This phase is preparatory, the commit is not actually carried out in this phase. The participating sites in this phase record enough information in the logs so that a transaction can be rolled back or committed, if needed. The specific steps in this phase are:

1. The "commit global coordinator" (the initiating node) sends a PREPARE message to all cohorts (commit coordinators running on nodes participating in the execution of this transaction).

2. Each cohort logs enough information so that it can roll back or commit the transaction.

3. Each cohort sends one of the following responses to the global coordinator:

"prepared" - the modified data has been prepared for commit or rollback.

"read-only" - no data on the node has been modified, so no prepare is needed.

"abort" - the node cannot successfully prepare.

4. The global coordinator waits for a reply from all cohorts.

5. If all cohorts indicate "prepared", then the next phase is initiated; if any cohort indicates "abort", then the entire transaction is rolled back at all sites; if a cohort indicates "read-only", then that cohort is bypassed from commit processing (this expedites the two-phase commit processing).

Phase 2 (Commit): If all cohorts respond "prepared" and/or "read-only", then the initiating site (global coordinator):

1. Writes COMMIT entry into the log.

2. Sends a COMMIT message to each cohort.

3. Waits for positive response from each cohort. If no response, then write abort message and terminate the transaction/

4. Writes a complete entry in log and terminates.

The key problem in two-phase commit is failure of the global coordinator (i.e., the originating node fails during commit processing). In addition, two-phase commit causes tremendous delays and "discomfort" in an unreliable environment (it is tough to succeed in two-phase commit if any cohort fails for one reason or another!).

The protocol described here shows the basic two-phase commit processing. A great deal of intricate processing takes place at the originating node and cohorts (see [Gray 1993] for details). Two-phase commit (2PC) has been implemented in several systems with some variations to deal with different failure conditions. In general, two-phase commit is offered by DBMS vendors as automatic (i.e., totally done on behalf of application developers) or programmatic (i.e., 2PC subroutines provided to application developers for customized usage). An extensive discussion of the reliability issues for no data replication, data replication, full replication, and network partitioning is given by [Garcia-Molina 1987].

4.11.2 Trade-offs Between Two Phase Commit and Replication Servers

Two-phase commit (2PC) and Data Replication Servers are two different approaches to guarantee integrity of distributed and replicated data under failures. The fundamental difference between these two approaches is the transaction versus periodic propagation of updates (update synchronization).

Transaction level update synchronization, as discussed in Section 4.10.2.4, is the basis of 2PC. In this synchronization scheme, a distributed transaction is treated as an atomic action and thus, all updates must be synchronized during a distributed transaction or the entire transaction must be rolled back. This is the basic reason for the somewhat complicated steps of 2PC. Periodic update synchronization, on the other hand, synchronizes updates after completion of a transaction. This approach, used in the commonly available Data Replication Servers, does not respect the boundaries of distributed transactions (i.e., data is synchronized after a transaction has completed).

Both approaches have certain advantages and disadvantages. 2PC has the following major pluses and minuses:

+ All updates are simultaneously available to end-users.

+ Guarantees atomicity of a distributed transaction.

+ Fully transparent to end-users.

+ Many improvements have been introduced to increase robustness, flexibility, and efficiency.

- Chances of failures are high in unreliable systems (transactions abort too many times).

- Takes too long if many copies of data exist (too many cohorts).

- Creates difficult situations if the global commit coordinator (the originating site) fails during 2PC.

- Does not allow many customizations and complicated application rules (e.g., retry prepare if cohort responds with "abort", apply an update after certain time).

Owing to these limitations of 2PC, Replication Servers are becoming a viable alternative for many organizations. However, the periodic update synchronization scheme used in many Replication Servers also has some pluses and minuses:

+ Very flexible (can be configured for different situations such as events, time, triggers, etc.).

+ Can offer additional capabilities (i.e., conversion and transformation of data).

+ Can be used for large and occasionally unreliable networks.

- Requires a primary/secondary copy (this paradigm may not fit some applications). This restriction is being removed in modern replication servers by introducing conflict resolutions that are based on rules or manual intervention.

- Some notion of global time must be maintained to assure that updates are synchronized at certain times.

Owing to these trade-offs, some systems provide transaction as well as periodic update synchronization. For example, several Replication Servers allow transactional update synchronization that employs 2PC.

The following guidelines are suggested to the users of 2PC and Replication Servers [McGovern 1993]:
- Keep data replication as minimal as possible. Large number of replicates can cause serious problems in 2PC as well as Replication Servers.
- If data must be synchronized as a transaction, then keep the number of copies small and use 2PC.
- If concurrency requirements outweigh "subsecond" data integrity requirements (i.e., data can be synchronized periodically) then use Replication Servers.
- If the network and nodes are unreliable, then use Replication Servers.

Extensive discussion of this topic can be found in [Schussel 1994, Gray 1993, Garcia-Monila 1987].

4.12 Distributed Transaction Processing: TP-Less, TP-Lite, TP-Heavy

In distributed environments, approaches to handle transactions (data update) vary widely due to the wide range of configurations (small PC LAN-based systems versus large systems involving multiple mainframes), query versus update traffic (ad hoc SQL queries versus massive updates), vendor offerings (database vendors versus TP vendors), and user/developer background (PC users/developers versus mainframe users/developers). The approaches being used at present fall into the following categories:
- TP-Less, i.e., do not use any transaction management considerations.
- TP- Lite, i.e., use database procedures to handle updates.
- TP-Heavy, i.e., use a transaction manager to handle updates.

Another approach, somewhere between TP-Lite and TP-Heavy (perhaps TP-medium), is becoming increasingly popular due to the growth in messaging-oriented middleware (MOM). See the sidebar "Running to MOM for Distributed Transaction Processing".

4.12.1 TP-Less

In this case, the database and file management capabilities for retrieving and updating data are used. For example, some relational database vendors treat each SQL statement as a transaction. Thus, each SQL select, update, insert, and delete is treated as a unit of consistency. However, a group of SQL statements are not combined into a transaction that must be committed or aborted. Similarly, in file systems, each file read and update is treated by the users as a transaction (there is a potentially serious problem here because many file systems do not provide the capabilities to treat each file I/O as a transaction).

TP-Less is currently being used heavily in small C/S environments with PCs and UNIX machines. In particular, this approach is favored heavily when all data needed by the users is on one SQL server. TP-Less has the advantage of being efficient and inexpensive (no additional overhead and software is needed). However, it has several limitations. First, it cannot be used when some data is in flat files (the ability of file managers to provide ACID properties should be examined carefully). Second, related updates cannot be grouped together as a transaction. Finally, all data must reside on one site (TP-Less may use a data replication server to handle duplicate data on multiple sites).

4.12.2 TP-Lite

TP-Lite goes a step beyond TP-Less by implementing each transaction as a stored procedure. Recall that a stored procedure is a collection of SQL statements that are performed as a unit. A user can define, for example, a set of SQL statements that update a customer account and store them in a database management system as a stored procedure that is invoked from different programs that need to update customer account information. Any updates that need to be performed together and any retrievals that are dependent on these updates can be imbedded in a stored procedure. In addition, stored procedures can enforce any additional integrity and security restrictions. TP-Lite capabilities are provided by most RDBMS vendors such as Informix, Oracle, and Sybase (basically, any vendor that supports stored procedures is in the TP-Lite business).

TP-Lite is mainly the invention of database vendors to provide some transaction management capabilities. This approach, when combined with data replication servers to synchronize replicated data, appeals to many C/S application developers. TP-Lite is being widely used to manage transactions in C/S environments where the data resides on a single SQL server. TP-Lite is better than TP-Less (it supports a group of SQL statements as a transaction), but it does not provide any global transaction control. In addition, TP-Lite cannot be used to handle transactions that need access to data stored in flat files (stored procedures are the domain of database vendors).

Running to MOM for Distributed Transaction Processing

Message-oriented middleware (MOM) is gaining popularity for many applications, including light-weight implementations of distributed transaction processing (DTP).

MOM, discussed in detail in a previous chapter, allows an application A to put a message on a queue that is later picked up by application B (or C and D) to process asynchronously. A queue can be a print stream or any intermediate file. This simple approach can be used to link existing applications very easily without modifying any code at either side (i.e., redirect the output of application A to a disk queue and redirect the input of system B to the same disk queue). This approach does not require the additional software development on either side (you do not need a client that issues an RPC and a server that receives, parses and dispatches processes). This also eliminates the need for staff training on both sides.

The main appeal of MOM for DTP is that the queue messaging can be transactional (i.e., MOM can make sure that only one message is transferred and that automated rollback recovery is available). This is a very familiar territory for mainframe-based transaction managers such as IMS (IMS has been using queued messages since the 1970s).

MOM providers such as IBM, DEC, Peer Logic and Covia Technologies are actively pursuing this opportunity.

4.12.3 TP-Heavy

TP-Heavy uses a separate TM to manage transactions in C/S environments. As discussed previously in this chapter, these TMs maintain the ACID properties of transactions that may span many database servers (i.e., they support DTP). For example, they allow PCs to initiate complex multi-server transactions from the desktop. TP-Heavy systems support the DTP functions discussed earlier in this chapter (i.e., global concurrency control, distributed two-phase commit, failure handling). More importantly, TP-Heavy systems are not restricted to database transactions -- they manage all data (flat files, databases, and queues). Examples of TP-Heavy products for C/S environments include CICS, Encina, Tuxedo, and Top End.

TP-Heavy has the obvious appeal since it takes transaction management seriously. TP-Heavy is essential when transactions involve data stored in multiple formats on multiple sites. However, TP-Heavy may be too "heavy" for small C/S applications that need access to data stored on a single SQL server.

4.12.4 Trade-offs Between TP-Lite and TP-Heavy

It appears that TP-Lite as well as TP-Heavy have certain pluses and minuses in C/S environments (TP-Less is too restricted for most serious business applications). The following questions should be asked by an application developer before deciding on TP-Lite versus TP-Heavy:

- In what format is the data stored (databases, flat files)? If the data is stored in multiple databases and flat files, then TP-Lite is not suitable (database procedures only work in RDBMS environments).
- How many SQL servers does the data reside on? If the application needs to update and commit data that is stored on multiple servers, then TP-Heavy should be used (database procedures cannot participate with other database procedures in a distributed transaction).
- What is the requirement for data synchronization? If the data synchronization interval is periodic, then a TP-Lite solution combined with a data replication server may be useful to handle updates against replicated data.
- What are the requirements for performance and load balancing? TP-Lite solutions with database procedures are much faster, on the surface, than the TP-Heavy solutions that require synchronization between sites. But, TP-Heavy solutions provide many sophisticated procedures for dynamic load balancing, priority scheduling, process restarts, and pre-started servers that are especially useful for large-scale production environments. These features are the main strength of TP-Heavy products because many of these products have been used over the years to handle thousands of transactions in production OLTP (on-line transaction processing) environments.

In general, small C/S applications are being deployed by using TP-Lite, while large mission critical C/S applications, especially the ones that were "downsized" from mainframe OLTP environments, are using TP-Heavy. In the meantime, many PC LAN-based applications are quite happy with TP-Less.

Time to Take a Break
- ✓ Basic Concepts
- ✓ Distributed Query and Transaction Processing
- ✓ TP Lite versus TP Heavy
- Consolidation and Evaluation

Suggested Review Questions Before Proceeding

- What are replication servers and how do they process distributed transactions?
- What exactly is two phase commit and how does it work?
- In what situation a replication server (TP-Lite) solution works better than two phase commit (TP-Heavy)?
- What are the tradeoffs between TP-Less, TP-Lite, and TP-Heavy? Explain through examples.

4.13 Distributed Data and Transaction Management: A Consolidation

Let us go back to the notion of a Distributed Data and Transaction Management System (DDTMS) that is responsible for managing all data (files plus databases) and the operations on the data (queries, updates) in a distributed computing environment. Figure 4-24 shows a conceptual view of DDTMS and depicts how DDTMS interacts with and interrelates to the following components (note the similarity between this model and the distributed data management model described in the previous chapter):

- Applications (transactions), which generate the queries/transactions (e.g., SQL statements).
- Local Data and Transaction Management Systems (LDTMSs), which manage access and update of local data.
- Remote Communication Interfaces (RCIs) for sending/receiving messages across a network. RCI may use the typical C/S protocols such as remote procedure call (RPC), remote data access, and message-oriented middleware (MOM).
- Network services, which transport the messages between sites. The network services may include, if needed, network gateways to convert network protocols (e.g., TCP/IP to SNA).
- Global directories that show the location of data and other servers in the network. For example, Figure 4-24 shows two global directoriesdisplaying that data table d1 is located on computer C1 and data table d2 is located on computer C2.

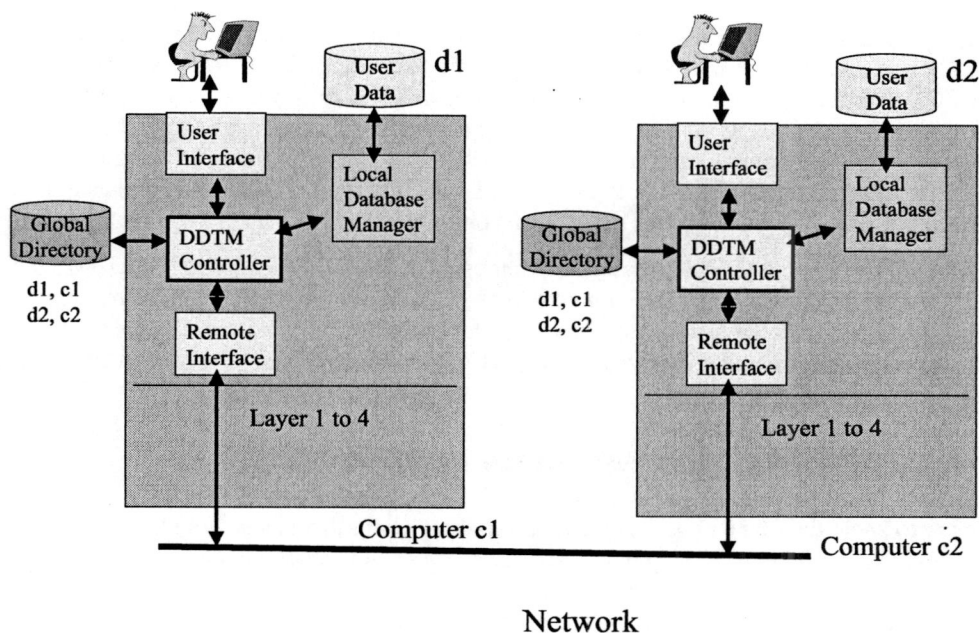

Figure 4-24: A Conceptual Model of DDTMS

A DDTMS performs a diverse array of functions. A DDTMS designer encounters the following main challenges:

- Global data definition and translation, i.e., how to provide view integration.
- Global directory allocation, i.e., where to place the global directories.
- Distributed file processing (DFP), i.e., how to provide transparent access, manipulation, and administration (e.g., security) of data files that are located at different computers in the network (we covered this topic in the previous chapter).

- Single-site remote data access and distributed query processing (DQP), i.e., how to provide transparent read-access and query processing of remotely located databases in a network (we covered this topic in the previous chapter).

Distributed transaction processing (DTP), i.e., how to coordinate the execution of a single transaction across multiple systems and how to assure concurrency (i.e., simultaneous access) and data integrity (i.e., the transaction must be completed properly or entirely withdrawn in the event of a failure). We have discussed DTP earlier in this chapter.

These challenges are briefly reviewed and the key approaches to meet these challenges are outlined. A more detailed technical discussion of these topics can be found in [Umar 1993, chapter 6].

4.13.1 Global Data Definition and Translation Challenges

The target data may be stored in homogeneous (e.g., all relational) or heterogeneous data sources (e.g., IMS, DB2, indexed files, OODBMS). A common global schema is needed to parse the queries against these data sources. The global schema shows all the data in the network and shows where the data is located. The problem of global schema design is straightforward if all the data sources are homogeneous, but is nontrivial in a network with heterogeneous databases. In such cases, the key challenges are:

- How do you define the data?
- Where is the query translated (originating node or target node)?

At present, most DDTMS (Distributed Data and Transaction Management Systems) use SQL for schema definition and manipulation [Richter 1994, Ozsu 1999]. This is primarily due to the popularity of SQL. In most cases, SQL is used to issue queries against non-relational databases and even flat files. For example, EDA/SQL from Information Builders Incorporated uses SQL to access more than 35 data sources including IMS, DB2, Sybase, Oracle, ADABAS, VSAM files, Focus files, etc. [Bland 1993]. Similarly, IBM's Data Joiner uses SQL to define views and join information stored in DB2, IMS, VSAM, Sybase, Oracle and other ODBC compliant data sources. In almost all cases, the query is translated from SQL to the target format at the target computers. The query translation is typically accomplished through "database drivers" that translate SQL to other formats (e.g., SQL to IMS Data Language calls). The interested reader is referred to [Oszu 1999, Sheth 1990, Litwin 1990] for more details on this topic.

The reader should note that SQL is not adequate to represent the OODBMS queries (OODBMS data model is far richer than the relational model that can be expressed in SQL). On the other extreme, it is difficult to use SQL for the legacy databases and file structures that are not in common use. For example, although many SQL drivers exist for popular file systems such as VSAM, these drivers do not exist for older and less popular flat files.

4.13.2 Global Directory Allocation (Name Services) Challenges

It is customary to show the [data, node assigned] pair in the global schema and store the global schema in a global directory. Due to the number of global directory accesses, it is crucial to allocate the global directory carefully. The directory allocation problem can be treated as a file allocation problem (FAP) where a file F is allocated to N nodes to minimize a given objective function. For example, Chu [Chu 1976, Chu 1984] has studied the directory allocation problem as a FAP. The following trade-offs can be observed:

- If the directory is at a central site, then the communication cost is high because every transaction will need to access the central site to locate data.
- If the directory is at every site, then the update cost will increase due to duplicate directory updates.
- A common approach used in small networks is to store the directory at a central node with the following processing rules:
- Search the local directory at the arriving node.
- If not found, then search the directory at the central site.

Many other approaches for directory allocation are conceivable. For example, instead of one centralized directory, many "regional" directories may be established where each directory shows the location of data within a subnet (see [Ozsu 1999, Bernstein 1987] for details).

4.13.3 Distributed File Processing Challenges

The DDTMS challenge is to integrate the access and manipulation of remotely located flat files with databases. In other words, the end user should not know if the target data being accessed is in a flat file or a relational database. As mentioned previously, SQL has become a de facto standard to provide this end-user transparency. This capability is currently included in many commercially available products (e.g., IBM's Data Joiner and IBI's EDA/SQL). The reader should once again note that integration of older file systems into DDTMS is a non-trivial task because off-the-shelf products for remote processing of such file systems are not readily available. Most commercially available products are targeted towards heavily used file systems such as IBM's VSAM (Virtual Sequential Access Method).

4.13.4 Distributed Query Processing Challenges

The technical challenge is to develop an access strategy to minimize communication cost (or response time). In practice, the most important pragmatic issue is how to do the joins between remotely located tables. Joins between remote sites can cause a considerable amount of communication traffic. For example, a remote join between an N row table and an M row table can theoretically cause NxM network messages (imagine remote joins between tables with millions of rows!). A technique known as a semi-join has been proposed to optimize remote joins by sending only the necessary data between computers to perform a join [Bernstein 1981 JACM]. Simply stated, a semi-join consists of the following steps for joining R1 and R2 on attribute A:

- Relation R1 is projected on attribute A, giving R1'. In other words, R1' is the column A of R1.
- R1' is transmitted to R2 and joined with R2, giving R2'. In other words, only one column of R1 is transmitted to R2 site. The join is performed at the destination site and not over the network. This significantly reduces the network traffic.
- R2' is transmitted to R1 and joined with R1, giving the final join. In other words, only a small fraction of R2 is transmitted, once again reducing the network traffic.
- In addition to remote joins, the following distributed query optimization algorithms issues need to be considered:
- Where do you access the data if duplicate copies of data exist? In most cases, the nearest copy of data is accessed.
- What paradigm should be used to access the remotely located data? A query may send ad hoc SQL or invoke remotely located procedures to access the remote databases. We have discussed this issue under the remote data access (RDA) and remote procedure call (RPC) paradigms.
- How do you utilize the trade-offs between slow networks (e.g., WANs) or slow computers (e.g., congested systems)? Many query optimization algorithms have been published in the literature for slow networks (these algorithms minimize communication and maximize use of CPU) and for fast networks (these algorithms maximize communication traffic and avoid CPU utilization).
- How should the joins be performed between heterogeneous data sources (e.g., joins between RDBMSs from two different vendors, join between RDBMS and a flat file)?The solution for this problem is currently to use ANSI SQL for joins. As stated previously, this solution is currently state of the market.

More details about these topics can be found in [Umar 1993, Ozsu 1999, Ceri 1984, Hevner 1979].

4.13.5 Distributed Transaction Processing Challenges

Database consistency/concurrency and data integrity to handle failures of distributed transactions are the two key challenges.

4.13.5.1 Database Consistency/Concurrency

Concurrency control coordinates simultaneous access to shared data. The problem of concurrency control in centralized DBMSs is well understood and one approach, called two-phase locking, has been accepted as a standard solution for a long time [Eswaran 1976]. However, concurrency control in distributed systems is an area of considerable activity with few accepted solutions. This is due to three main complicating factors:

- Data may be duplicated in a DDTMS, and consequently, the DDTMS is responsible for updating the duplicate data.
- If some sites fail or if some communication links fail while an update is being executed, the DDTMS must make sure that the effects will be reflected on the failing node after recovery.
- Synchronization of transactions on multiple sites is very difficult because each site cannot obtain immediate information on the actions currently being carried out on other sites.

Due to these difficulties, over 50 concurrency control algorithms have been proposed in the past, and still continue to appear. Literature surveys have shown that most algorithms are variants of two-phase locking and time-stamped algorithms [Bernstein 1987, Bernstein 1981 ACM]. However, several algorithms do not fall into any category. A review of these algorithms can be found in [Umar 1993]. For a very detailed discussion of concurrency control algorithms, refer to [Oszu 1999, Bernstein 1997].

The reader should note that most of these algorithms assume a transaction level update synchronization interval (i.e., updates to one database must be synchronized with all other copies before a transaction terminates). As we saw in the discussion of Replication Servers, many organizations have found that a periodic (e.g., once an hour or once a day) synchronization interval is an adequate pragmatic solution instead of the expensive and complicated concurrency control algorithms.

4.13.5.2 Failure Detection and Transaction Recovery

As stated previously, when a transaction commits, all transaction updates are permanent, but if a transaction aborts, updates are rolled back. In DDTMS, a transaction may commit at one site and abort at another due to failures in the network and/or the computing sites. For example, an update at node n1 completes, but fails at n2 because of disk failure at n2. The common approach used is two-phase commit (2PC) discussed previously in Section 6.6.

An extensive recovery system for distributed database management systems was first proposed by Gray [Gray 1979] and implemented in System R. This system consists of the following four protocols (the approach used in System R has been used widely as a generic solution):

- Consistency locks: This means that each transaction must be well formed and two-phase. A transaction is well formed if it locks an object before accessing it, does not lock an already locked item, and unlocks each locked item before termination. A transaction exhibits two-phase behavior if no objects are unlocked before all objects are locked. Transactions using 2PL are automatically well formed and two-phase.
- DO-UNDO-REDO log: This is an incremental log of changes to the databases that record the before/after images of each update during the transaction processing (DO operation). This log also allows removal (UNDO) of a failed transaction's updates and reapplication (REDO) of the successful transaction's updates in the event of a database crash.
- Write-ahead log: This protocol consists of writing an update to a log before applying it to the database.
- Two-phase commit: This protocol coordinates the commit actions needed to run a transaction. When the transaction issues a COMMIT request, then a "commit coordinator" initiates the two-phase commit process we have discussed previously.

For comprehensive failure handling in distributed environments, the concurrency control techniques are combined with consistency control for failure handling and time-out for deadlock resolution into a single algorithm of distributed transaction management. For example, the two-phase locking, two-phase commit and time-out algorithms are combined into a single concurrency and consistency control algorithm of a potential DDTMS.

Implementation of sophisticated algorithms for failure handling is an expensive and time-consuming undertaking. Replication Servers are becoming a viable alternative for many organizations because two-phase commit does not behave very well when data is updated at many sites and when the network is unreliable (see the discussion in Section 4.10). Due to the widespread availability of Replication Servers, and the many additional features (e.g., conversion) offered by these servers, a careful analysis of the trade-offs between using two-phase commit-based algorithms versus using Replication Servers is needed (see Section 4.10).

4.14 A Distributed Data and Transaction Management Evaluation Framework

A DDTMS can be configured and implemented by using a variety of approaches discussed in the previous section. At a high level, we can categorize DDTMS in terms of the following major capabilities discussed in the previous section:
- Global data definition and translation capabilities
- Global directory allocation capabilities
- Distributed file processing capabilities
- Distributed query processing capabilities
- Distributed transaction processing capabilities

These capabilities depend on the choices of appropriate techniques and algorithms to address the challenges discussed in the previous section. For example, one DDTMS may not include any distributed file processing capabilities, another may only provide distributed query processing, while a third may provide distributed transaction processing capabilities only through periodic update synchronizations.

Another dimension to evaluating DDTMS products is the type of environment in which the distributed and replicated data needs to be managed (we can add other dimensions also such as the business drivers, etc.). Let us use the following variables as a starting point to represent the target-operating environment:
- Homogeneous versus heterogeneous data sources - The data sources may all be RDBMSs from the same vendor or may be widely heterogeneous.
- Network control (central, distributed) - One node may be designated to coordinate all DDTMS interactions or the interactions may be peer-to-peer.
- Number of copies allowed in a network - There may be a single, two (one at a central site, one at a local site), and more than two replicated copies.

Table 4-3 shows a simple two-dimensional framework to categorize the complexity of data distribution and replication management decisions and to help the managers evaluate appropriate products. The rows of Table 4-3 reflect the various capabilities (e.g., global database definition, global directory allocation, distributed transaction processing). The columns of Table 4-3 show five environment configurations based on the environment variables (e.g., data sources, network control, level of replication). The configurations shown in Table 4-3 show the complexity range of a user environment. The simplest implementation of a DDTMS is for configuration 1 (homogeneous, centrally controlled, unique data allocation). It is most difficult for configuration 5, when the data sources are widely heterogeneous, there is no central control, and the data can be replicated at several sites. This is why many products support configurations 1 and 2, and very few support configuration 5. Let us review the entries in Table 4-3.

As shown in Table 6.2, the first configuration is straightforward to support due to the following reasons:
- Database definition and translation are not difficult because all data sources are relational (SQL can be used everywhere).
- Directory allocation is not difficult because the central site can be used to house the global data directory.
- Distributed file processing capability is not required because all data is housed in relational databases.

- Distributed query optimization is simple because data is at unique sites and the algorithms do not need to find the "nearest" data site for optimal results.
- Distributed transaction processing capability is also not difficult. Specifically, database consistency/concurrency control is relatively simple because data is not duplicated and update synchronization is not needed. Failure handling is also simple because there is no need to synchronize updates after failures.

In summary, configuration 1 is quite simple to implement and can be supported easily by a DDTMS product. Consequently, several commercially available DDTMSs from vendors such as IBM, Oracle, Informix and Sybase support this configuration. For example, most systems support relational DBMS, assume some level of centralized control and allow limited or no data distribution. Remote procedure call (RPC) and remote data access (RDA) paradigms are supported by many C/S middleware products to directly access the data where it resides. This approach allows a single application to access many databases (i.e., program P can access table T1 on node n1 and T2 on node n2).

Configuration 2 is somewhat more difficult to implement because of the database consistency/concurrency, distributed query optimization, and failure handling has to deal with limited data duplication. This configuration is also supported by many vendor products (the key database vendors such as IBM, Oracle, Informix and Sybase support this option).

Configuration 3 becomes more difficult to implement because the number of options in database consistency/concurrency, query optimization and failure handling increase due to many copies of data in the system. In this case, two-phase commit may not be suitable especially if a large number of duplicated copies are allowed. Data Replication Servers may be more suitable for this configuration (and also for the later configurations).

Configuration 4 becomes even harder to implement because the directory allocation is complicated due to many sites where the data can exist. Configuration 5 is the most difficult configuration to support because many choices and trade-offs exist at all levels; consequently, it is not supported by many vendor products.

The main point is that organizations should strive to stay with configurations 1 and 2, if possible, by controlling the level of data replication and data heterogeneity.

DDTMSs have moved from research to commercial products. However, the differences between the research results and commercial availability need to be understood. Evaluation of commercial DDTMS is difficult due to the discrepancies between promised versus available facilities. In general, the complexity of the DDTMS to be developed depends on the options supported (requirements to be satisfied). It is easier to develop DDTMS, which supports single copy and homogeneous data sources. The difficulties encountered in implementing DDTMS must be carefully weighed against the advantages of DDTMS over centralized systems. For several applications, it may still be better to provide a centralized database or use a single copy DDTMS after all of the costs for query processing, concurrency control, and failure management have been taken into account.

Table 4-3: A Framework for Evaluation of DDTMS Facilities

	Global data definition	Global directory allocation	Distributed file processing	Distributed query processing	Distributed transaction processing
Config. 1: . Homogeneous data sources . No data duplication . Centrally controlled network	Not difficult (use SQL)	Allocate directory to central site	Not applicable	Not difficult (use remote joins)	Not difficult (no need for update synchronization)
Config. 2	Not difficult (use SQL)	Allocate directory to central site	Not	Moderate difficulty (use of an	Moderate difficulty (need for

			applicable	alternate copy)	synchronizing two copies). Can use 2PC.
. Same as config 1 . One copy can exist at central site					
Config. 3 . Same as config 2. . Several copies can exist at other sites	Not difficult (use SQL)	Allocate directory to central site	Not applicable	Optimization difficult (choice between many alternate copies)	Very difficult (need for synchronizing many copies). 2PC may not be adequate
Config. 4 . Same as config 3. . No central control	Not difficult (use SQL)	Directory cannot be allocated to central site	Not applicable	Optimization difficult (choice between many alternate copies)	Very difficult (need for synchronizing many copies). 2PC may not be adequate.
Config.5. Same as config 4. . Heterogeneous data sources (e.g., heterogeneity with OODBMS, old flat files)	Many difficulties (cannot use SQL for OODBMS)	Directory cannot be allocated to central site	Many difficulties with older files	Optimization difficult (choice between many alternate copies)	Very difficult (need for synchronizing many copies). 2PC may not be adequate.

4.15 Examples of Distributed Data and Transaction Management

In the TP-Heavy family, products such as Transarc's Encina. AT&T's Tuxedo and IBM's CICS are worth noting. CICS is currently available on platforms such as MVS, AIX, OS/2, OS/400, Windows NT, and HP-UX. Tuxedo is also being ported to almost all UNIX platforms. Standards are playing an important role in the C/S TP products. Most of these products support the XA and XA+ interface so that a given TP monitor can interoperate with many database managers and communication managers (see Section 4.9.3 for a discussion of XA and XA+). However, the following three application to communication resource manager APIs are being developed:

- TxRPC (transactional RPC): This API is based on DEC's Remote Task Invocation technology.
- CPI-C: This is a peer-to-peer API used in the IBM APPC environments.
- XATMI: This is a Tuxedo Application/Transaction Management Interface.

For TP-Lite, several data replication servers are commercially available from a diverse array of vendors. Examples are IBM Data Replication Toolset (Data Refresher, Data Hub, Data Propagator), Oracle Snapshot, Prism Warehouse Manager, Sybase Replication server, Trinzic Infopump and InfoHub, and Praxis Omini Replicator. Some of these replicators are used for data warehousing while the others are intended for distributed transaction processing.

BEA Systems currently supports a distributed transaction processor on top of CORBA. See the web site (www.Beasys.com) for details. The following two sidebars show CORBA and DCOM based transaction services.

CORBA-based Object Transaction Services (OTS)

CORBA (see the sidebar on CORBA) from the Object Management Group (OMG) includes specifications for object transaction services (OTSs). These services are based on the X/Open Distributed Transaction Reference Model. However, this model has been extended to handle distributed objects by way of the following two improvements:
- The XA interface (this specifies the APIs between the transaction managers and the database managers), and the TX

interface (this specifies the APIs between the transaction managers and applications) have been specified by using a set of CORBA interfaces defined in IDL.

- All inter-component communication is mandated to be via CORBA method calls on instances of these interfaces.

In addition, the OTS is fully compatible with X/Open compliant software. The OMG enforces this compliance by requiring that the OTS be able to import and export transactions to and from XA-compliant resource managers and TX-compliant Transaction Managers, respectively. To handle concurrency control, the OMG has introduced the OCCs (Object Concurrency Control Service) specification that provides locking support to facilitate resource sharing among concurrently executing objects. In addition, the OMG has specified nested transactions, as an optional part of the OTS, to insulate a global transaction from partial failure of some of its constituent operations.

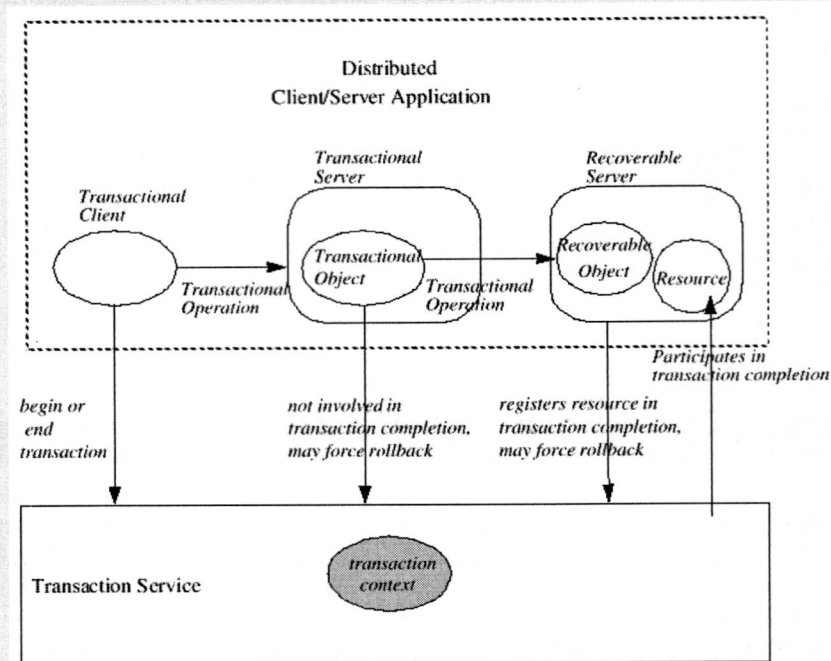

Figure 4-25: Conceptual View of Object Transaction Service

Figure 4-25 shows a conceptual view of OTS. The OTS is a CORBA service that mediates between the CORBA applications to ensure that the updates to databases are performed atomically within the scope of a transaction. For example, if application A and B are part of a transaction that needs to update a database, then the OTS is called by the participating applications to initiate a transaction, register the databases and other resources that participate in the transaction, coordinate the updates, and rollback any changes made in case of a failure.

Microsoft Transaction Server (MTS) Versus Sun EJBs

Microsoft has introduced the Microsoft Transaction Server (MTS) as a component-based programming environment for developing, deploying, and managing Internet/Intranet transaction-based applications. MTS 1.0, released in December 1996, ran on Windows NT 4.0 and accommodated both Windows NT and Windows 95-based clients (with DCOM support) for transaction processing. Since 1996, many MTS has been updated several times to run in different windows environments.

Because of its component-based application development model, MTS encourages the breakdown of application logic into ActiveX components that can be built using any of the development tools such as Visual Basic, Visual C++, Visual

J++, Cobol, or .NET Framework. These components are installed into the MTS runtime environment. Once installed in the MTS environment, these components can be invoked from HTML browser clients and Win32 clients. A browser client invokes the MTS ActiveX components using any Internet server (including the Microsoft Internet Information Server) and a Win32 client invokes MTS ActiveX components using DCOM (Distributed Component Object Model). The MTS itself provides the infrastructure for transaction coordination across systems, system resources such as processes and database connections, initiates and controls transactions, enforces security, and provides administrative tools. In addition, MTS provides a set of dispatchers that interact with IBM mainframe CICS and IMS transactions, OLE transactions, and X/Open XA (this could be used as an interface with the CORBA-based OTS). Figure 4-26 shows a conceptual view of MTS.

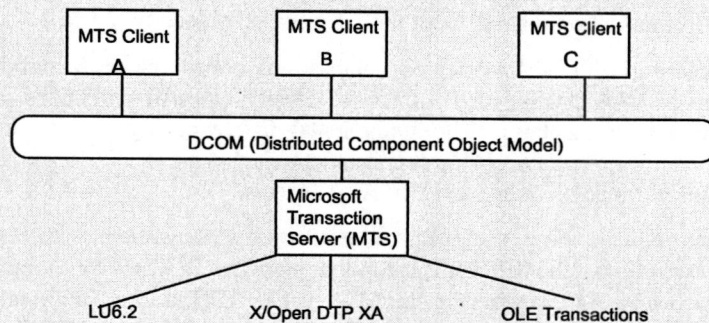

Figure 4-26: Conceptual View of Microsoft Transaction Server (MTS)

MTS competes with Sun's Enterprise Java Beans (EJBs) to provide transaction services for distributed objects (we discussed EJBs in the previous chapter). While MTS provides transaction services for COM objects, EJBs provide similar services for Java beans (Java objects) that can be invoked through CORBA or Sun's RMI (Remote Method Invocation). Besides that, the general architecture of Enterprise JavaBeans is very similar to MTS. Both systems host objects that are being managed – an EJB container provides hosting capabilities that are similar to the MTS Executive for MTS. In addition, both MTS and EJB rely on a transaction coordinator that is responsible for ensuring that all operations in a transaction are successful or that none of them are. Many white papers comparing different features of MTS versus EJBs can be found at the Sun and Microsoft sites, along with the usual commercials.

4.16 State of the Art: Object-Orientation in Transaction Management

Object-orientation in transaction management has been an area of considerable academic and industrial investigation. The Spectrum Reports on Open Transaction Management, August 1993 and May 1994, are early examples (consult the Spectrum home page at http://www.aladdin.co.uk for information about more recent reports). Broadly speaking, object-orientation in transaction management exists at the following levels:

- Object-oriented transaction programming
- Transaction processing with distributed objects
- Transaction processing with object-oriented databases

Object-oriented transaction programming simply accounts for programs written in an object-oriented programming language (e.g., C++, Smalltalk) to perform the transaction operations (i.e., commit, rollback).

This approach is in principle the same as any other transaction programming and is currently state of the practice and state of the market. After all, C++ programs can be used in Encina and Tuxedo environments. From a transaction processing point of view, no complications are introduced.

Transaction processing with distributed objects is concerned with performing ACID operations between objects across machines. This introduces many complex issues. In particular, messages exchanged between objects can carry transaction semantics. For example, if an object sends a message to a remote object, then operations such as concurrency control and recovery may be needed between the distributed objects. The traditional object models do not take this type of processing. Specialized middleware is needed for transaction processing with distributed objects. The Object Management Group (OMG) has been considering transaction processing with distributed objects as a service for its Common Object Broker Architecture (CORBA). CORBA has specified an Object Transaction Management service and a Concurrency Control service as part of CORBA Object. These two services are expected to boost industrial products to support transaction management with distributed objects.

Transaction processing with object-oriented databases is concerned with introducing TP-Heavy type of operations on top of OODBMSs. Most of the TP-Heavy types of operations are currently available on relational and hierarchical databases. The fundamental difference is that unlike older DBMSs that provide read and write operations, the OODBMSs support methods that are rich in semantics. Most of the research in OODBMS has concentrated on query and modeling aspects.

From an industry point of view, the issue of transaction management with distributed objects is being divided between two camps: the Microsoft camp that manages DCOM-.NET objects and the Sun camp that supports the Java beans. As discussed in the MTS versus EJB sidebar, both use similar approaches with different implementations (so what is new!). Due to the popularity of XML, the issue of processing transactions by using XML is also becoming increasingly important with more attention being paid to Web Services transaction processing.

4.17 XYZCorp Case Study: Partial Solution 2

On the financial data allocation, the following information may be useful:
- Most of the financial data can be considered as corporate data (it is shared by multiple people for business use).
- Only a very small portion of financial data should be duplicated.
- The DDTMS evaluation model discussed in Section 4.15 can be used to evaluate the various trade-offs. TP-Lite should be used where possible. This represents Case 2 or 3 of the DDTMS evaluation model (these two cases are quite suitable for many real-life situations).
- The following factors can be used to evaluate DDTMS middleware:

   a) General Considerations
   - Distributed File Services
   - Distributed Database Support
   - Distributed Transaction Processing
   - Replication Servers

   b) Detailed Considerations
   - Data translation
   - Directory design
   - Update synchronization
   - (TP-Lite, TP-Heavy)
   - Distributed query optimization
   - Failure Handling
   - Network Support
   - Operating Systems Support

- Vendor Information (Company size, Staying power, Current installed base, Level of support, price options)

4.18 Problems and Exercises

1) What are the key challenges in data and transaction processing and why there is no agreement on a common approach?

2) What are the main functions provided by a DTP (TP-Heavy)? How do these functions differ from a local transaction manager?

3) Define the following standards and describe their role in DTP.

    ISO TP   . X/Open DTP   . XA+   . XA

4) 4. In your own words, when is it better to use a replication server versus two-phase commit?

5) Use the framework introduced to analyze a replication server. What changes/extensions would you recommend to the framework?

6) Develop a decision table that shows the trade-offs between TP-Lite, TP-Less, and TP-Heavy.

7) List the architectural components of the DDTMS architecture in which the following problems are addressed: concurrency control, commit processing, global schema generation, deadlock detection, distributed query processing, RPCs.

8) Explain the role of XML in the modern data and transaction management situations.

4.19 Additional Information

We have attempted to give an overview of an area that continues to grow. A more theoretical coverage of DDTMS can be found in [Umar 1993, Chapter 6]. The following books are recommended for additional details:

- Elmagarmid, A., "Database Transaction Models for Advanced Applications", Morgan Kaufmann Publishers, 1992.
- Bernstein, P. A., Hadzilacos, V., and Goodman, N., "Concurrency Control and Recovery in Database Systems", Addison Wesley, 1987.
- Bernstein, P.A., and Newcomer, E. "Principles of Transaction Processing for the Systems Professional", Morgan Kaufmann, 1997.
- Gray, J. and Reuter, A., "Transaction Processing: Concepts and Techniques", Morgan Kaufmann Publishers, 1993.
- Ozsu, M. and Valduriez, P., "Principles of Distributed Database Systems", 2nd edition, Prentice Hall, 1999.

The interested reader can find additional information in several journals and conference proceedings such as:

- ACM Transactions on Database Systems
- ACM SIGMOD International Conferences
- IEEE Intern. Conferences on Data Engineering
- International Conferences on Very Large Databases
- International Conference on Distributed Computing
- IEEE Transactions on Knowledge and Data Engineering
- Spectrum Reports (http://www.aladdin.co.uk)
- Standish Consulting Group Reports
- Database Programming and Design
- Data Management Review

Bernstein, P.A. and Goodman, N., "Concurrency Control in Distributed Database Systems", ACM Computing Surveys, Vol.13, No.2, June 1981, pp.185-222.

Bernstein, P.A. and Chiu, D.W., "Using Semi-Joins to Solve Relational Queries", JACM, Jan. 1981.

Brett, C., "The Rise of Messaging Middleware: The Decline of DOLTP", Spectrum Report on Open Transaction Management, Last updated: Jan. 1996. (http://www.aladdin.co.uk).

Britton, C., "IT Architectures and Middleware: Strategies for Building Large, Integrated Systems", Addison-Wesley, 2000

Bukhres, O., and Elmagarmid, A., "Object-Oriented Multidatabase Systems", Prentice Hall, 1996.

Cardenas, A.F., "Heterogeneous Distributed Database Management: the HD-DBMS", Proceedings of ??? Need rest of reference

Chu, W.W., "Performance of File Directory Systems for Data Bases in Star and Distributed Networks", 1976 NCC, Vol. 45, 1976.

Doeppner, T.W. Jr.: "Distributed File Systems and Distributed Memory", The Computer Science and Engineering Handbook 1997: 1851-1969.

CICS, "Customer Information System: Concepts and Facilities", IBM Manual, 1995 (ask for latest release).

Date, C.J., "An Introduction to Database Systems", Fifth edition, Vol.1 and Vol. 2, Addison Wesley, Latest edition

Date, C.J., "Twelve Rules for a Distributed Database", InfoDB, Vol. 2, Nos. 2 and 3, Summer/Fall 1987.

Diao, Y., et al, "Toward Learning Based Web Query Processing", pp.317-328, VLDB2000.

Elmagarmid, A., "Database Transaction Models for Advanced Applications", Morgan Kaufmann Publishers, 1992.

ENCINA, "Encina for Open OLTP", Transarc Corportaion publication, 1995 (ask for the latest edition).

Garcia-Molina, H., "Performance of Update Synchronization Algorithms For Replicated Data in a Distributed Database", Ph.D. Dissertation, Stanford University, June 1979.

Garcia-Molina, H., Abbot, R.K., "Reliable Distributed Database Management", Proceedings of the IEEE, Vol. 75, No. 5, May 1987, pp601-620.

Gorton, I., "Enterprise Transaction Processing Systems: Putting the CORBA OTS, Encina++ and Orbix OTM to Work", Addison Wesley; 2000

Gray, J., "Notes on Database Operating Systems", in Operating Systems: An Advanced Course, Springer-Verlag, N.Y. 1979, pp.393-481.

Gray, J., "The Transaction Concept: Virtues and Limitations", Proceedings of Conference on Very Large Databases, Sept. 1981, pp. 144-154.

Hansen, M. and Follette, J., "Getting in Front of Lotus Notes Replication", Business Communications Review, May 1995.

Haritsa, J., et al, " Distributed Query Processing on the Web", ICDE 2000.

Hevner, A.R., and Yao, S.B., "Query Processing in Distributed Database Systems", IEEE Transactions on Software Engineering, Vol. SE-5, No. 3, May 1979.

Hevner, A.R., 'A Survey of Data Allocation and Retrieval Methods for Distributed Systems', School of Business and Management Working paper # 81-036, Univ. of Maryland, Oct. 1981.

Hevner, A.R., and Yao, S.B., "Querying Distributed Databases on Local Area Networks", Proceedings of the IEEE, May 1987, pp.563-572.

Peterson, D., "The Great Debate: OLTP vs. RDBMS", Business Communications Review, May 1995.

Lef, A. and Pu, C., "A Classification of Transaction Processing Systems", IEEE Computer, June 1991, pp.63-76.

Leinfuss, E., "Replication Synchronizes Distributed Databases Over Time", Software Magazine, July 1993, pp. 31-35.

Lerner, et al, "Middleware Networks: Concept, Design and Deployment of Internet Infrastructure", Kluwer Academic Publishers; 2000

Lyon, J., et al, "Transaction Internet Protocol (TIP)", Technical Report draft-lyon-tip-nodes.02.txt, Tandem and Microsoft, February 1997.

Mack, S., "Sybase to Address Update Problems", Infoworld, November 16, 1992.

McCord, R. and Hanner, M., "Connecting Islands of Information", UNIX Review, May 1987.

Myerson, J.," The Complete Book of Middleware", Auerbach Publications, 2002

Ozsu, M. and Valduriez, P., "Principles of Distributed Database Systems", 2nd edition, Prentice Hall, 1999.

Ozsu, M. and Valduriez, P., "Distributed Database Systems: Where Are We Now?", IEEE Computer, August 1991, pp. 68-78.

Pardon, G., Alonso, G., "CheeTah: a Lightweight Transaction Server for Plug-and-Play Internet Data Management", pp.210-219, VLDB2000.

Pu, C., Leff, A., and Chen, S., "Heterogeneous and Autonomous Transaction Processing", IEEE Computer, Dec. 1991, pp. 64-72.

Ram, P., Do, L., and Drew, P., "Distributed Transactions in Practice". SIGMOD Record 28(3): 49-55 (1999).

Schlack, M., "Key to Client/Server OLTP", Datamation, Appril 1, 1995. pp. 53-56.

Schussel, G., "Database Replication: Playing Both Ends with the Middleware", Client/Server Today, November 1994, pp. 57-67.

Serain, D., and Craig, I., "Middleware: Practitioner Series", Springer-Verlag, 1999

Sheth, A.P., and Larson, J.A., "Federated Database Systems for Managing Distributed, Heterogeneous, and Autonomous Databases", ACM Computing Surveys, September 1990, pp.183-236.

Spectrum report, "The Changing Shape of Open Transaction Management", Vol. 7, report 3, August 1993.

Triantafillo, P. and Taylor, D., "The Location-Based Paradigm for Replication: Achieving Efficiency and Availability in Distributed Systems", IEEE Transactions on Software Engineering, January 1995.

Tuxedo, "Transaction Processing withTuxedo", UNIX Systems Laboratories Publication.

Umar, A., "Distributed Computing and Client/Server Systems", Prentice Hall, Revised 1993.

Vogler, H., and Buchmann, B., "Using Multiple Mobile Agents for Distributed Transactions". CoopIS 1998: 114-121.

Weikum, G., "Review - Atomicity versus Anonymity: Distributed Transactions for Electronic Commerce". ACM SIGMOD Digital Review 1: (1999).

White, C., " Data Replication Techniques, Tools, and Case Studies", DB/EXPO, New York, Dec 6-8, 1994.

Wolfson, O., "The Overhead of Locking (and Commit) Protocols in Distributed Databases", ACM Trans. on Database Systems, Vol. 12, No. 3, Sep. 1987, pp. 453-471.

Yu, C., and C. Chang, "Distributed Query Processing", ACM Computing Surveys, vol. 16, no. 4, pp.399-433, Dec. 1984.

Zimowski, M., "DRDA, ISO RDA, X/Open RDA: A Comparison", Database Programming and Design, June 1994, pp. 54-61.

5 Middleware State of the Practice, Market, and Art

5.1 Introduction

General purpose middleware services discussed in this module are used widely and are an area of continuing research. This chapter summarizes the following key developments:

- State of the practice information to show the approaches/products that are being actually used by organizations. See Section 5.2 for illustrative case studies and examples.
- State of the market information to show commercial availability of the products. See Section 5.3 for a brief review of commercial-off-the-shelf (COTS) products.

- State of the art approaches, which capture the trends and research directions. See Section 5.4 for research notes and trends.

A quick review of all three aspects in this chapter is intended to present a realistic view of the subject matter.

5.2 State of the Practice: Short Case Studies

5.2.1 Middleware State of the Practice – General Observations

Different types of middleware services are being used at present to support distributed applications in modern digital enterprises. The Web and XML technologies are naturally quite popular to support a wide range of Web applications. As we all know, use of the Web is growing at a phenomenal rate. At present, most of the Internet traffic is generated by Web users. What are people doing with the Web? Here is an incomplete sampling:
- Surfing the Web for a variety of personal reasons
- Visiting corporate Web sites
- Buying items on-line
- Printing maps and driving directions
- Checking weather before travelling
- Bargain hunting for hotels and travel tips
- Advertising of products and services
- Job hunting
- Researching and conducting literature surveys
- Collecting case study information

Our main interest is in using the Web for e-business. For e-business, the Web users must be able to easily access corporate information and support business applications. The corporate information is stored in data stores such as flat files (e.g., text files, graphic data), indexed files (e.g., VSAM), relational databases (e.g., Informix, Oracle, Sybase, DB2), IMS databases, and the like. Web browsers are designed for displaying HTML files. However, a large proportion of corporate information does not exist in HTML files. For example, corporations typically keep customer information, product information, inventory information, and many other critical pieces of information in relational databases.

In addition to Web, commonly used middleware at present includes primitive middleware such as terminal emulation, email and file transfer; basic client/server middleware for remote procedure call (RPC), queued messages, and remote data access (RDA); and distributed data management middleware such as database gateways for remote joins. In many cases, organizations pick and choose between these individual packages and "assemble" their own middleware environments to best suit their needs. For example, many organizations use terminal emulation, bulk data transfer, email, and remote SQL middleware (e.g., ODBC drivers). Distributed technologies such as CORBA are being used frequently. Middleware to access distributed data and process transactions is also being used widely.

The following short case studies illustrate the state of practice for use of middleware in different organizational settings. A large number of case studies about different uses of middleware can be found in Web sites and trade magazines. Here are some examples with the usual disclaimer (many sites change their mind about what they publish and where it is published on the site -- so they are somewhat volatile):
- www.xml.org - A large repository of examples of using XML and Web
- www.microsoft.com/net/use/casestudies.asp - Microsoft site showing several case studies of XML Web services and .NET
- www.bea.com - BEA's Web site -- has many examples and case studies
- http://www-4.ibm.com/software/Webservers/commerce/ - IBM site for ecommerce -- shows examples
- http://www.oracle.com/applications/ - Oracle Web site for Oracle products and how they are being used in different industries

- www.sun.com -- many pointers and links to a wide range of examples and case studies for using J2EE and Java technologies in different industry segments
- www.middleware.com - several pointers to case studies and examples
- www.omg.org - pointers to examples of how the distributed object technologies such as CORBA are being used in the industry
- www.w3.org - pointers to examples of how some of the Web standards are being used
- Information Week magazine (www.informationweek.com) publishes many case studies and examples of IT on a regular basis. Many of these examples illustrate how middleware technologies are being used in the industry.

5.2.2 J.D. Edwards Uses Messaging Services

Many companies use email systems – a basic messaging system that sends email back and forth. But current messaging systems have some capabilities for collaboration and group communications. Here is an example of how Microsoft Exchange is being used in one organization.

J.D. Edwards is a large enterprise software supplier that employs more than 6,000 employees in 50 offices worldwide. The company decided to move to a single infrastructure based on Microsoft Exchange Server and Microsoft Outlook. The decision to migrate to Exchange reduced the associated support and training costs. Many groups within J.D. Edwards have benefited from Exchange Server. For example, the Training Group uses Exchange, in concert with the company's intranet, to communicate the availability of in-house training and "distance learning" opportunities to their employees. The Training Group also uses the Exchange calendar to manage its training schedules.

J.D. Edwards also uses the Public Folders feature of the Outlook and Exchange platform extensively. For example, the company uses Public Folders to support many IT project management efforts. In order for a project manager to track the progress of their job, custom forms were developed within each project folder. The primary benefit of public folders was ease-of-use for J.D. Edwards. The company's executives can utilize Public Folders to gather and organize meeting agenda items, helping them to more easily manage daily business activities. In addition, company employees use Public Folders for classified ads. They use their Public Folders to buy and sell personal items and for other activities, thus reducing related e-mail traffic and providing them with a tangible benefit.

J.D. Edwards also has developed a number of applications for Exchange. One example is the Web-based discussion applications that employees access through the company's intranet and through Outlook. J.D. Edwards plans to use the Instant Messaging feature of Exchange 2000 Server in conjunction with discussion applications. This feature will allow users to find out whether colleagues are online, then instantaneously send short text messages to each other without server-to-server communication. The company also plans to develop Unified Messaging applications on this platform.

Source: http://www.microsoft.com/net/business/casestudies.asp, Posted: April 18, 2001

5.2.3 Web Technologies at Procter and Gamble

Procter & Gamble Co. (P&G) is a large international company that specializes in consumer goods such as soaps, detergents, and cosmetics. P&G typically doubles its sales every decade. But due to competition, it is having trouble sustaining this goal. The company is turning to Internet and Web technologies to increase sales and generate new revenues, reduce inefficiencies of its supply chain, and establish new relationships with consumers. P&G has launched several Web sites to promote its products and uses its main corporate Web site (PG.com) to link to numerous other subsites devoted to P&G products. In this sense, PG.com serves as the P&G portal that points to other sites such as Tide and Mr. Clean, and vice versa. The Web sites provide a variety of services and help to consumers such as offering on-line advice on how to remove stains, create custom gift packages using P&G products, . and design their own custom-blended cosmetics. PG.com also invites visitors to send new product suggestions to the company. By using the Web to interact with customers, P&G has cut its marketing research costs by 50 to 75 percent.

P&G's management is also using the Web to loosen things up within the organization and to encourage employees to be more creative and take more initiative. Internal intranets such as InnovationNet.com and MyIdea.com allow employees to publicize their ideas for improving the company and to exchange reports and contact other people working on similar problems. P&G also instituted a collaborative planning, forecasting, and replenishment (CPFR) system to slash inventory and cycle time. CPFR shares sales forecasts with its retailers such as Kmart, Target, and Wal-Mart in the United States and overseas. The system automatically orders items to replenish inventories, if needed, and automatically notifies companies about exceptions such as dramatic drops in sales. Early tests showed that the CPFR system helped P&G reduce inventory by 10 percent and cycle time (the time required to get a product from the assembly line to the retailer's shelf) by 10 percent. Sales increased by 2 percent as well, because P&G was able to use the information in the system to take immediate actions to prevent out-of-stock items.

Sources:
- Laudon, K., and Laudon, J., "Management Information Systems", 7th edition, Prentice Hall, 2002
- Kayte VanScoy, "Can the Internet Hot-Wire P&G?" Smart Business Magazine, January 2001

5.2.4 The Chemical Markup Language (CML) – XML in the Chemical Industry

CML (Chemical Markup Language) is a new approach to managing molecular information in the chemical industry. It covers disciplines from macromolecular sequences to inorganic molecules and quantum chemistry. It supports a hierarchy for compound molecules, reactions, and macromolcular strucures/sequences. CML is based strictly on SGML. The CML DTD is available at: http://www.xml-cml.org/dtd/cml1_0_1.dtd . The CML Schema is available at: http://www.xml-cml.org/dtd/cml1_0_1.xsd .

CML has already been used to manage documents and information in:
- Macromolecular Sequence
- Macromolecular Structure
- Spectra
- Organic Molecules
- Publishing
- Quantum Chemistry
- Inorganic Crystallography
- Hypertext (HTML)
- Databases
- Terminology
- Regulatory processes
- Molecular databases

CML provides "lossless" transmission of information: aspects of the encoded data can be selected and processed without loss of the remainder. It is machine-independent so that data can be transferred between different operating systems and machine architectures. CML supports and interfaces with developments such as Java, C++ and CORBA. Most current molecular formats are limited in the information they contain. Few can hold both 2- and 3-D coordinates simultaneously. CML represents a superset of current approaches and information can be transferred between applications without loss. CML has support for atom- and bond-based stereochemistry that is not normally explicitly available.

A CML system may require these components:
- Direct output: It should directly convert the output of programs to XML and CML.
- Editors: An editor allows users to edit a CML file.
- Molecular Legacy Converters: Such as MDLMolfile, SYBYL MOL2, SMILES
- Theochem Legacy Converters: Such as MOPAC, Gaussian, GAMESS
- Spectral Legacy Converters: Such as SQZed, DIF, DUP
- CML-SAX : A SAX parser for CML.
- CML-DOM: A DOM parser for CML. A API called CMLDOM has been implemented.

- Chemical functionality and transformations
- Chemical search/query: It should support the search and query in CML files.
- Layout: It will create a 2D layout if coordinates are not present.
- Geometry calculation: It will calculate geometry for atoms and groups.
- Display: Both display 2D and 3D.

Available software for CML:
- CMLDOM-JS: A Javascript implementation of the main components of CML.
- SELFML-JS: This (Javascript) tool reads one or more SELFML files and displays them, including the emedded CML describing the compounds
- CMLDOM-J: A complete Java implementation of the CML-DOM, extensible to further refinements of CML.
- JUMBO3-J: A Java browser for any document containing CML elements including 2D and 3D displays.
- Chimeral: Working examples of large CML-based documents and scientific articles which use an XSLT stylesheet component library and applets for viewing.
- JME: JME (Java Molecular Editor) is an editor used to create a CML-aware 2D chemical structure.
- JMVS: This is a Java3D-based CML-compliant molecular visualiser.
- JChemDig and JchemAgent: Web-based robots, which can traverse a remote Site, identify chemical content based on chemical MIME types and create a CML-based database of these files, including derived metadata.
- JChemValidate: An online resource for converting to and digitally signing CML documents.

CML is a powerful tool for molecular information. It provides a machine independent data representation, an interface to different databases, and lossless data transmission. It is a successful example of using the Web technology in other fields.

5.2.5 Dun & Bradstreet Use of XML – A Case Study

Dun & Bradstreet (D&B) provides information about businesses to its customers. Businesses buy this information to make informed business decisions, to build relationships with their customers, suppliers, and business partners The D&B information includes business-to-business credit, marketing, purchasing, receivables, management, and decision-support services. A customer might use D&B information to assess credit and risk, assess a supplier's overall financial and operational performance, understand the current status of key suppliers as well as their future outlook, and gather articles (culled from hundreds of nationwide sources) about newsworthy events relating to suppliers. To provide accurate and complete information in a timely manner, D&B maintains one of the world's largest business information databases. This database holds information about businesses around the globe, including more than 53.8 million companies in 200 countries, and can contain as many as 1,500 data elements for any given company. D&B obtains this information from many diverse sources, including:
- Public utility companies
- Federal bankruptcy filings
- The office of the U.S. secretary of state
- The U.S. Postal Service
- More than 2,500 state filing agencies
- Daily newspapers, publications, and electronic news services

The D&B database consists of hundreds of millions of pieces of data, ranging from trade styles to trade experiences to financial statements. Because D&B gathers information from an increasing number and variety of global sources, the company needed a way to adapt to different systems quickly and easily. At the same time, D&B wanted to make information easily available, thus reducing barriers for existing and potential customers. D&B also wanted to increase the value of its information by making it available in a format integrated with a customer's existing business processes. In the past, D&B developed systems for customers to use D&B data, but D&B wanted to shift this role to customers, both to allow them more flexibility in building solutions and to save D&B the expense of building solutions for each customer.

D&B chose XML as a significant part of their solution for several reasons. First, XML is an open specification, thus it is easy for customers to build applications. Second, XML offers substantial benefits over EDI in terms of easier deployment, moderate learning curve, and rapid adoptability. Finally, XML aligns many protocols, platforms, hosts, and structures for D&B and allowed D&B to make its business global -- a highly desirable feature.

D&B selected the Web Methods B2B Solution (www.Webmethods.com) as the basic platform. The B2B Solution is designed to enable organizations with legacy applications and diverse data to convert different protocols and formats to XML. It also facilitates real-time data exchange between XML and HTML documents. The B2B Solution, shown in Figure 5-1, consists of several components. The B2B Developer and B2B Integration Server are tools for building the application and interface and facilitating the flow of information. To facilitate integrating data from many sources, including databases, ERP applications, and EDI systems, Web Methods developed a technology called the Web Interface Definition Language (WIDL). WIDL[1] is an XML application that simply consists of a DTD. The DTD defines an interface definition language that can be used to extract data from an HTML page and convert it to XML, thus separating the data from its presentation. B2B Developer is a set of visual tools used by developers to assist in creating applications and data access interfaces. The B2B Integration Server coordinates and facilitates information flow between applications and Web sites. Data can be exchanged between applications and Web sites. B2B Solution also allows applications to access other applications across the Internet. It permits applications to access data embedded in Web pages.

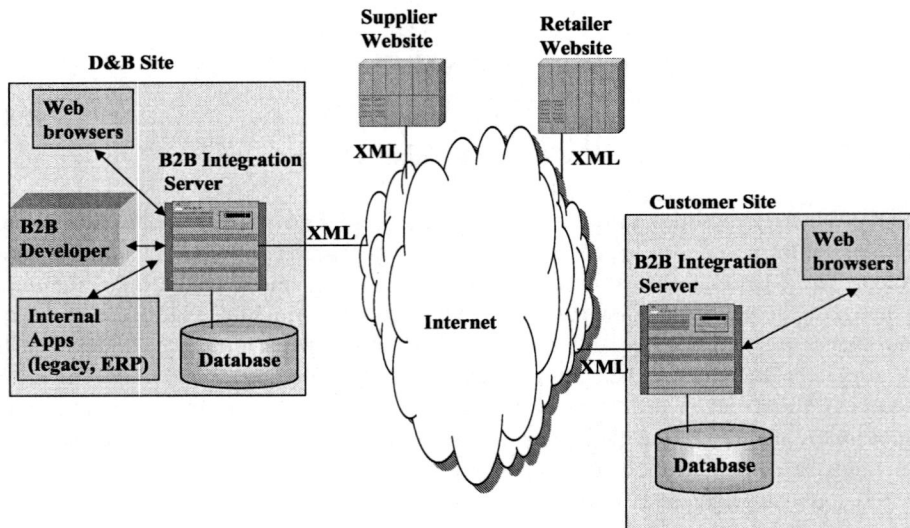

Figure 5-1: D&B Solution

For D&B, the B2B Integration Server is the central integration point for internal and external applications to communicate transparently by using XML. The B2B Integration Server obtains data from various D&B sources, integrates it, and presents it to a user via the Internet. XML is key to the solution as it uses HTTP to transport XML documents. Using HTTP ensures that the XML data can move through firewalls.

Key Points: This case study depicts how XML can enable a corporation to solve a business problem, transform the way it does business, create new opportunities, and open new markets. The case study describes how XML can be used as the glue to pull together a number of disparate systems.

Sources:

---

[1] WIDL is very similar, in concept, to the CORBA IDL.

- "Mastering XML", Premium Edition by Chuck White, Liam Quin and Linda Burman, Sybex © 2001
- www.D&B.com

5.2.6 Dollar Rent a Car and Trans World Entertainment Corp Use Web-XML

Dollar Rent a Car Inc. uses XML Web services to conduct business online with its disparate business partners. Dollar used an easily re-usable interface for their XML-based system that transforms the information to different formats for different users by using XSL. Dollar Inc. is able to re-adapt that interface (reused 4 times) with very little additional technical effort, and at the same time, increase their marketing presence – contributing to their bottom line in terms of sales. Thus additional business opportunities can be easily exploited without too many technical hurdles.

In the case of Trans World Entertainment Corp. (TWEC), where the commodity is videos and CDs, TWEC provided their customers with unique, customized Web experiences on their visits by using XML. The company also increased brand recognition and interactions through its Web site. TWEC extracted master product catalog data and pushed the customized contents to in-store kiosks, Web sites, and viewing stations, based on user profiles. This provided a highly effective user viewing experience.

Source: http://www.microsoft.com/net/business/casestudies.asp

5.2.7 Distributed Objects Examples – Short "Snippets"

At the time of this writing, CORBA, OLE, ActiveX, and OpenDoc are widely state of the practice with many implementations. The examples include work since the mid 1990s. Here is a small sample of case studies (new and old):

- **Capitol One Financial Corporation.** The business problem for Capitol One Financial Corporation was to build a system that would be able to process daily transactions for over 10 million cardholders. The application relied on Orbix, IBM's MQSeries messaging software for delivery between system components, and Transarc for transactional capabilities.
- **Telcordia Technologies.** Many large scale software systems known as "operation support systems" were converted to CORBA in the late 1990s. These systems download Java applets from the Web server to the Web client at startup. The Java applets are CORBA clients that issue calls to a CORBA server to access remote databases and back-end systems.
- **Charles Schwab & Company.** The business problem of Charles Schwab was to create an on-line system to access research information and trade. This was created through the use of CORBA/IIOP-compliant objects that allowed developers to quickly access an object to change a business rule dynamically. The result was the launch of SchwabLink Web, a Java-based extranet that conforms to CORBA and Internet Inter-ORB Protocol standards, in 1998.
- **Exante Health.** This group designed and developed an Internet-based product set for the integration of information within enterprises and with external business partners in the healthcare industry. The project used technologies such as JAVA, CORBA (Visigenic), Oracle RDBMS, and ActiveX.
- **ABB Engineering.** CORBA has been used in ABB corporation to build new applications and to integrate legacy applications. The lessons learned include advantages of distributed object technologies over conventional techniques.
- **Chase Manhattan Bank.** The business problem of Chase Manhattan was similar to Schwab. Chase Manhattan wanted to rollout Web-based banking services. The complication was that this would span across multiple business and consumer units. Java and CORBA technologies were used to tie several systems together. The result was a Website that could be used for the bank's wholesale banking service, the consumer-based home banking service, and mortgage application service.
- **Credit Suisse.** The business problem for Credit Suisse was that there were various diverse platforms, operating systems and development environments. The bank wanted to integrate the bank's systems. To accomplish this, CORBA from IONA Technologies was used. The result was an integrated enterprise solution for Credit Suisse.

- **Wells Fargo Bank.** Wells Fargo desired to view a customer's entire bank relationship using the existing systems. CORBA standards, was used to integrate various source applications. The result was a Customer Relationhsip System that was built within three months.

In addition, several examples of integrating Activex/OLE and CORBA can be found in the industry. Boeing Aerospace, for example, used OLE/Activex at client side and CORBA at the back end in several applications. Several other case studies describe how some legacy systems have been migrated to CORBA. For example, a large manufacturing company in Switzerland built a CORBA-based interoperability layer between several heterogeneous legacy systems that included CAD-CAM and very large Fortran programs.

The ISG (international systems group) Web site (www.isg-inc.com/Case_Studies.htm) has several case studies that show how object-oriented technologies such as CORBA have been used in various industries. To gain some insights, a detailed CORBA development example of a simple inventory system is discussed in the CORBA chapter of the Tutorial Module.

Sources:
- http://ids.csom.umn.edu/faculty/kauffman/courses/8420/Projects/Machart/corcases.htm
- www.isg-inc.com/Case_Studies.htm

5.2.8 Bank Boston: Using Distributed Objects for Software Infrastructure

BankBoston has 100 offices in North America and does business in 23 countries worldwide. The bank wanted to build some sophisticated analytical applications that would be initially rolled out to internal customers on trading floors all over the globe. The databases and other server components of the application would remain centralized, but remote offices would have access over the intranet. After this, the Public Internet access to the same applications for customers and trading partners would be provided. The idea was to build "customer-addictive tools" that would be given out, free of charge, to the bank customers. Although no business is transacted with these applications, they can help build loyalty.

BankBoston relies heavily on CORBA to build complex applications that are tied to a single platform or a single CPU. The company is using a five-tier architecture. Each tier can be a server dedicated to a specific function, improving overall system performance. For example, a component that must perform a million calculations in three seconds would be assigned to a particularly high-end server, while other servers would perform more routine tasks. A Java user interface provides rich analytic graphics, while remaining as thin as possible. The application featured a Sybase database, TIBCO publish-and-subscribe middleware for real-time data feeds, a C++ application on a Solaris server, and a C++ client on SunOS workstations. A Web version of the application substituted a Java applet for the SunOS client, making the user interface available on a variety of operating systems, without changing the back end. It added Iona Technologies' Orbix for CORBA translation on the server and included the Java version, OrbixWeb, in the applet. The applet also incorporated Sitraka's Java components for displaying charts and tables. The Java applets were sued instead of ultra-thin client based on HTML because once the applet loads, it can continue generating charts based on new data rather than relying on the server to provide new images.

Source: http://www.scl.com/products/sitraka/stories/jclass/bostonbank.html

5.2.9 MITRE Corporation - The DISCUS Data Interchange System

Mitre corporation developed a Data Interchange and Synergistic Collateral Usage System (DISCUS) that integrates multiple legacy application systems. The conceptual architecture of DISCUS, shown in Figure 5-2, is based on an object request broker that receives requests from multiple applications and accesses some databases. The information from one database is converted to another by using translators that are built as part of the project. The end users of this system are primarily information scientists who require accesss to multiple forms of information: text, images, maps, and relational data. This information needs to be accessed by a variety of legacy applications that include Map front-ends, image processing, and other tools/applications. The system uses CORBA (Common Object Request Broker Architecture) for accessing remote data.

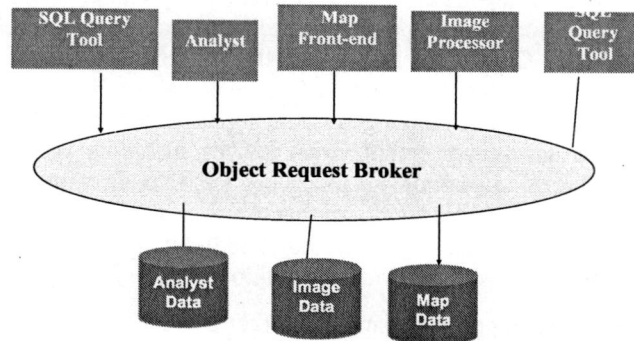

Figure 5-2: DISCUS Data Interchange System

5.2.10 XML Web Services at MSNBC.com to Reach New Markets

MSNBC is a cable and Internet joint venture of Microsoft and NBC News. It has been the number-one news site on the Internet since January 1999, according to Media Metrix. With normal traffic of nearly 3 million unique users a day—spiking to 7 million users when major news breaks—the site provides content produced by MSNBC correspondents located around the globe, stories from NBC News, and third-party content acquired from other major news sources that include Newsweek, the Washington Post, and the Wall Street Journal.

Distribution of information is, naturally, a key component of the MSNBC.com business model. Headlines and abstracts are exchanged heavily between partner sites and MSNBC.com on a daily basis. MSNBC extends its reach by placing headlines on other sites and driving viewers back to MSNBC.com for the rest of the story. The main problem is that integrating new partners requires additional code for each new partner. The hundreds of lines of additional code for new partners adds further complexity to a code base that is becoming unmanageable. Consequently, it became cost prohibitive to service all but a select few partners, thus leaving a huge untapped market with hundreds of potential distribution partners that could not be served.

To meet these challenges, MSNBC.com redesigned its solution to integrate distribution partners using XML Web services. By using XML Web services, MSNBC.com can now integrate and service a completely new class of distribution partners without having to worry about the delays and development costs associated with custom integration efforts. By implementing XML Web services using the Microsoft .NET platform, MSNBC.com claims to have reduced the lines of code needed to service distribution partners by roughly 80 percent. This was done by building generic XML Web services that are exposed by publishing an interface. Once these interfaces are published, the new partners can access the headlines and display it on their site in a manner that lets them retain their own look and feel. The company simply makes changes in one place and all partners can take advantage of it. This translates to an enormous reduction in the amount of development resources required to support all the new devices being introduced into the market. XML Web Services has given MSNBC.com a reusable and cost-effective way to service partners of all sizes. In addition to reducing costs associated with integrating new partners, this has greatly improved the company's ability to implement new features and accommodate new types of devices. The solution is built around Microsoft .NET Framework.

Sources:
- www.msnbc.com

- http://www.microsoft.com/servers/evaluation/casestudies/MSNBC.asp, Posted July 27, 2001

5.2.11 Expedia Uses .NET for Travelers

Expedia.com is a well known awarding-winning online travel agency that provides travelers with a variety of services and information. The company operates Expedia.com, an online travel service in the United States with localized versions in Canada, Germany and the United Kingdom. Expedia.com provides a combination of air, car and hotel booking, vacation package and cruise offers, destination information and mapping, and personalized planning and booking services for its customers. Although Expedia had the ability to push important travel information to numerous devices, including Web-enabled cell phones and PDAs, they recognized the value of creating device independence. Expedia wanted to write the information once and then deliver it to different devices without having to rewrite the information for each device. Expedia also wanted to tie information into a user's existing buddy list and calendar, eliminating the need for customers to reconstruct their contact lists and schedules within Expedia.

To enhance the users' experience, Expedia is using Microsoft .NET Passport. By using Passport service, Single Sign-in is enabled and provides a method for authenticating users that eliminates redundant log-on procedures. With Passport's authentication service, combined with Notification service, a user can choose to receive alerts to their desktop, a cell phone, PocketPC or any other wired or wireless device. As more .NET My Services become available, Expedia hopes to provide users with access to their contact lists through Contacts service. This will give users the ability to automatically send notifications of flight plans to people on their contact list. Expedia also plans to use the .NET Calendar for users to populate their calendar with their itinerary.

XML Web services and .NET Platforms are allowing Expedia.com to transform travel itineraries into communication centers—allowing travelers to pick distinct notification settings for different members of their buddy list. Expedia will enhance the PC user's experience with features like desktop notification, and support for mobile users. By separating the content from the delivery mechanism, the foundation of XML Web services, Expedia will save valuable development time. Expedia uses the following Microsoft .NET services

- .NET Passport
- .NET Alerts
- .NET Contacts
- .NET Calendar

Sources:
- www.expedia.com
- http://www.microsoft.com/servers/evaluation/casestudies/expedia.asp

5.2.12 US Army Uses J2EE for Traffic Management

The U.S. Army Military Traffic Management Command (MTMC) provides global surface transportation services to meet national security objectives. Its Freight Systems Division (FSD) is responsible for supporting the procurement of commercial freight transportation services for the Department of Defense. As part of the U.S. Army's continuing quest to modernize its business practices, the FSD has implemented a series of time- and cost-saving measures. In particular, the FSD decided to overhaul its shipment systems to use just-in-time logistics, resulting in reduced stockpiles of raw materials and finished components. This FSD also needed to establish new relationships with material vendors and transportation companies who would agree to deliver goods only as needed.

Sun Professional Services developed an e-commerce and EDI Global Freight Management (GFM) system by using the J2EE technology. GFM supports the procurement and logistic efforts of more than 3,000 traffic managers in 800 FSD locations across the country. With the implementation of the GFM system, the FSD expects a) an increase in user productivity as new shipment transactions can be completed in less than three minutes, b) to interface with multiple carriers through a single Web browser-based interface, strengthening its control of shipping processes, and c) a complete return on investments within 18 months due to productivity improvements.

Sources: http://dcb.sun.com/practices/casestudies/

5.2.13 Distributed Data Management Examples

A very large number of examples and case studies can be quoted that illustrate different aspects of distributed data management middleware. Let us go through a few.

Figure 5-3 shows an example of Web access to heterogeneous relational databases through a CGI gateway. The CGI gateway invokes ODBC/JDBC drivers to access Oracle and MS SQL server databases. The main advantage of using ODBC/JDBC in this case is that you can use one gateway to access different types of databases. Otherwise, you will need one gateway for Oracle, one for SQL Server, and one for Sybase (if needed).

Figure 5-4 shows a general heterogeneous environment in which DB2, Oracle and MS SQL databases exist. One client can access these three databases by using different ODBC/JDBC drivers.

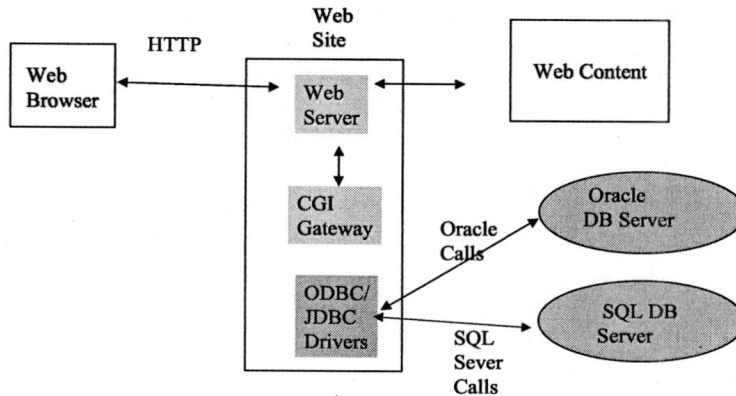

Figure 5-3: Web Access to Heterogeneous Relational Databases

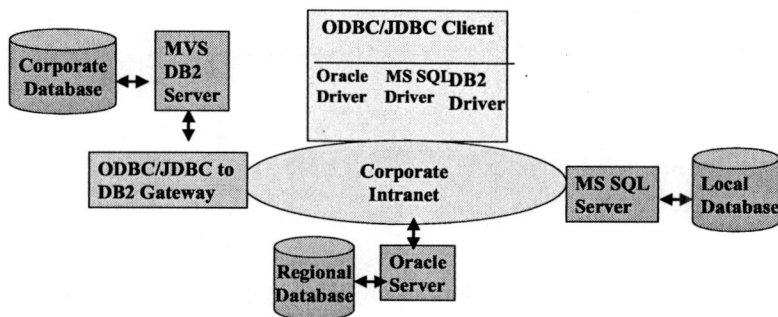

Figure 5-4: Example of Heterogeneous Database Access

5.2.14 Distributed Transaction Management Examples

The following examples and case studies illustrate different aspects of distributed transaction management. Many examples indicate the work in the mid 1990s because many new projects in distributed transactions appeared in that time period.

Encina Example. Figure 5-5 shows an example of an Encina distributed transaction environment (www.encina.com). In an Encina environment, computing nodes fall into three broad categories:

- Encina secure nodes where the Encina application servers run. An application server receives Encina client requests and processes them, typically after interacting with resource managers (DBMSs). The secure nodes are basically "trusted computers" (typically restricted access operating in physically secure areas) that require a high level of reliability, security, and performance. The secure nodes house the Encina Toolkit.
- Encina public nodes where the Encina clients reside. The public nodes can be desktop computers that do not require a high level of reliability, performance or security. The public nodes house Encina client libraries (the libraries that are used to develop Encina clients).
- Non-Encina nodes are typically mainframes or other systems that are not running Encina. These systems are accessed by Encina applications through the Encina PPC component.

Figure 5-5 shows three subnets that are interconnected to each other. The first two subnets are contained in an "Encina Monitor Cell" that is under the control of Encina Monitor. The Encina Monitor Cell consists of a collection of Encina public and secure nodes (the following figure shows 3 secure nodes and 4 public nodes). Different application servers and resource managers (e.g., database managers) can be allocated to the 3 secure nodes and accessed from the 4 public nodes. To provide monitoring of a cell, each cell consists of one cell manager. In addition, each node (secure plus public) is assigned a node manager.

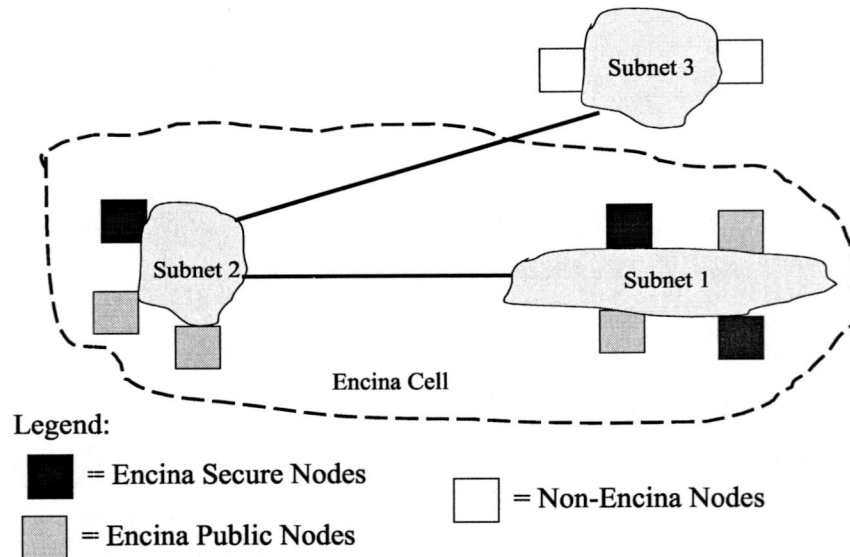

Figure 5-5: Encina Example

Case Study -- An Object Transaction Service. Many distributed transaction management systems at present are not based on object-oriented technologies. An early example of distributed transaction management service over CORBA was reported by [Chang 1996]. Each transaction in this system is treated as an object, thus object invocations need to adhere to ACID properties. At the time of this writing, CORBA (discussed in the next chapter), is finalizing the object transaction management services over CORBA. It is expected that we will see many similar efforts in the future.

Case Study – CICS Transaction Processing with Teradata. Abbey National Share Registration System represents an interesting, albeit somewhat dated, example of processing CICS transactions against a separate database computer housing Teradata databases (source: Spectrum Open Transaction Management Report, August 1993). This project required addressing the lack of the two-phase commit procedure within the Teradata environment when working with the CICS transaction management (TM) environment. It should be noted that CICS TM environments support two-phase commit between different MVS machines. However, what can be done if one partner, in this case Teradata, does not support two-phase commit. To address this, the Abbey National Share Registration System was designed so that it needs to commit as infrequently as possible to ensure that an entire transaction is a complete unit of work (i.e., no intermediate checkpoints). In addition, most data was kept in the Teradata machine, minimizing the need for distributed data management (thus reducing the need for two-phase commit).

Case Study – Using Data Replication for Transaction Processing. Data replication needs to be planned to support distributed transaction processing. An example of the planning process used at CIGNA, a large health insurance company, follows. The replication planning includes building a replication architecture (how data moves between applications and replicated databases), network architecture (physical layout and data rates), information requirements (e.g., response time requirements), scheduling (e.g., when replicated data will be synchronized), and change management (e.g., changes in the underlying technologies).

5.3 State of the Market: Products

5.3.1 Middleware State of the Market

State of the market for the middleware services is cluttered with hundreds of off-the-shelf products that are discussed regularly in trade magazines such as Web Week, Computerworld, Object Magazine, Datamation, and Database Programming and Design. In addition, analysis of products are published regularly by consulting organizations such as Gartner Group, Forrester Research, Seybold Group, and the Yankee Group. Let us quickly scan the state of the market for the key building blocks for application engineering/reengineering (middleware, networks, databases, and operating systems). Off-the-shelf middleware software is currently available from a very large number of providers.

The growing number of commercially available middleware products should be seriously considered before undertaking in-house development. In most cases, it is better to develop applications which utilize the commercially available middleware. It is generally better to use the high level protocols and services, if available, to reduce the application complexity. The exceptions to these general guidelines are real-time applications. For these applications, it may not make sense to incorporate a heavy weight middleware that adds significant overhead and imposes platform restrictions (e.g., if the middleware runs on PCs only, then the application is restricted to PCs). In such cases, it may be better to use the network calls (e.g, TCP/IP sockets) for remote interactions.

The middleware services have evolved, and continue to evolve, since the early 1990s. Each evolution has added more functionality and made it easier to engineer/reengineer the applications. A Gartner report in 1999 identified more than 100 suppliers of middleware services. For example, basic middleware products are widely available in the marketplace. Middleware for Web is being provided by many large organizations such as Microsoft and IBM, and almost innumerable small enterprising firms. Many vendors at present provide distributed object middleware such as CORBA and Microsoft is marketing it's ActiveX/DCOM products. A great deal of attention is being paid to XML Web Services, J2EE, and .NET. In addition, distributed data management middleware services such as remote SQL gateways are available from database vendors such as Oracle, Sybase, Informix, and IBM. Distributed transaction processing middleware is available from companies such as IBM, Transarc and AT&T. We will review the state of the market in these areas in later sections.

5.3.2 Basic Middleware State of the Market

Middleware to support RPC, RDA and QMP has been commercially available since the mid 1990s. In addition, many management and support services are also being included in off-the-shelf products. Here is a brief synopsis of state of the market.

Remote Procedure Call (RPC)-based middleware is widely available in UNIX, MVS and PC environments. Here are some examples of RPC products:

- Open Software Foundation's RPC (variants of this RPC have been included in several products such as Microsoft DCOM)
- SUN RPC system
- Netwise RPC
- Novell Netware RPC
- Information Builder's EDA/SQL RPC
- IBM TCP/IP RPC
- OSI RPC

Remote Data Access (RDA) products are currently heavily supported by the "database server industry". Simply stated, a database server houses a database and controls user access to the database from local as well as remote users that submit SQL queries. Many SQL database servers are commercially available on desktops (e.g., Microsoft Access and Microsoft SQL Servers), mid-range computers (e.g., Oracle Database Servers, IBM DB2 Database Servers) as well as mainframe systems (IBM MVS DB2 Servers). While ODBC and JDBC are common remote SQL middleware in the desktop and midrange computers, the IBM DRDA (Distributed Relational Database Architecture) is a popular approach for accessing mainframe DB2 databases from clients operating in UNIX and PC environments. An interesting historical note is that many popular SQL database servers of the 1990s such as Gupta, Sybase, and Informix have virtually disappeared from the marketplace.

QMP is supported by MOM (message oriented middleware) suppliers. MOM products have been getting serious vendor attention since 1993. Interest in MOM is fueled by the dramatic increase of detachable computers and the application requirements that need loosely coupled asynchronous behavior. Although many MOM products exist in the industry, MQSeries from IBM appears to have the majority (expected to be about 70%) of MOM share. Sun's Java Messaging Services (JMS) is also a popular product.

Directory and Security Services. The directory services are mainly gravitating towards LDAP (Lightweight Directory Access Protocol) with many LDAP products from Microsoft, IBM, Netscape and others. A variety of security products are available commercially (see the security chapters in the Management Module).

5.3.3 Web State of The Market

The marketplace for Web middleware is exploding with a bevy of products from suppliers large and small. Here is a small sampling of some of the products.

- Microsoft has actively pursued the Microsoft Internet Strategy which includes an Internet Information Server (an HTTP server in Windows environment), an Internet Explorer (a Web browser), an Internet Assistant for MS Word Windows (an HTML editor for MS Word), a Web development tool (MS Frontpage), a Media server (video and audio server with support for HTTP), a Merchant Server (an Internet server for electronic commerce), and many others.
- Netscape has also developed a wide range of Web products that go beyond the basic browser and server. Examples of the products include the Netscape Commerce server for electronic commerce and a variety of tools for Java development on the Web such as FastTrack to support Java and Java Script (see the Netscape home page for more information).
- Sun has also become a major player by announcing several products that support Java in a Web environment. Examples include Java Virtual Machines (JVMs) for numerous browsers, Remote Method Invocation (RMI), and the J2EE environments.

- A large number of Web gateways are currently available to provide Web access to relational databases and other non-Web resources. Older Web gateways use CGI while the newer ones use Servlets, JSP, and ASP. For a sampling of products, just search the Internet by using "relational gateway" as a search parameter on a search engine of your choice (e.g., Alta Vista or Google).

5.3.4 XML Web Services State of the Market

Although there is still some activity in the basic Web technologies, most of the current attention is being paid to the family of XML products and XML Web Services. Major players in this market segment are the three usual suspects (Microsoft, IBM, and Sun). Microsoft's .NET platform is based on XML Web Services and Sun's J2EE interfaces with XML Web services quite well also. IBM is also fully supporting the XML Web Services with several products in this area. The best sources of information on products in this area are the Web sites of these companies.

In addition to the major players, several other companies are also fully supporting XML Web Services and building products around this standard. An example of such a company is Tibco (www.tibco.com) that has rolled out an extensive platform for storing, accessing, and manipulating XML documents. Another example is XML Global Technologies (www.xmlglobal.com) that is building XML Web Services platforms. The company's core products are GoXML™ Foundation and GoXML™ Central. GoXML Foundation is an XML-based data integration platform with search, transformation, and database components. GoXML Central is an XML-based platform that enables participation in global electronic marketplaces. It supports ebXML, UDDI, and other Web service protocols.

5.3.5 Distributed Objects State of the Market

In distributed objects, the state of the market can be discussed in terms of three different developments: a) the "traditional" distributed object technologies such as CORBA, Miscrosoft DCOM/Activex, and Sun RMI (Remote Method Invocation), b) evolution of business components, and c) combining Web with distributed objects and business components.

The traditional middleware products in the market to support distributed objects fall into two broad categories:
- Individual products for CORBA, DCOM/ActiveX, and RMI.
- Interoperability products between CORBA, DCOM/ActiveX and RMI.

CORBA-based products in the 1990s became available from many vendors. Examples are the Distributed Systems Object Model (DSOM) from IBM, Distributed Objects Everywhere (DOE) from SUN, ObjectBroker from Digital, and Orbix from Iona Corporation. However, the CORBA market has gone through a major consolidation with only a handful of CORBA survivors such as Orbix from Iona (www.iona.,com) and Visibroker from Borland (www.borland.com). Support for these CORBA products is available on Windows, various UNIX versions, IBM OS/400, and MVS. DCOM/ActiveX products are, understandably, currently available from Microsoft on Windows and on Unix (supposedly). DCOM/ActiveX has been the platform for distributed object computing for Microsoft since 1997 and has very strong support. RMI was introduced by Sun to allow Java programs to talk to each other across different machines. RMI so far has found limited applications and is primarily supported by Sun (obviously).

Interoperability between DCOM/ActiveX, and CORBA is achieved through gateways. A few CORBA/DCOM gateways have been introduced in the marketplace. For example, Iona's Orbix provides two-way gateways between CORBA and DCOM/Activex that allow a DCOM object to be viewed as a CORBA object and vice versa. Such gateways are proprietary but could become open because OMG, with Microsoft's concurrence, has issued an RFP for a two way CORBA/COM gateway.

The object-oriented industry has evolved from simple objects to business components. Microsoft has many software components for Windows environments that draw, produce charts, perform calculations, etc. These components can be used as plug-and-play modules to build complete applications. Many desktop tools are currently available as components. Examples of typical desktop components are spell-checkers, SQL query builders, print managers (conceptually, each icon on your toolbar can be a separate component). The basic idea of business objects, also known as business components, is that the users can construct large objects that represent the real-world concepts of the business world. Examples of business objects are customer, order, products, and regional office. Business objects started appearing in the marketplace around 1994 when OLE 2.0, OpenDoc, and CORBA-based products started emerging. Since then, OO tools designed to support creation of business objects have appeared from vendors such as Easel and applications that employ business objects have appeared from Sun, IBM, and Microsoft. A commonly known example of business component is Enterprise Java Bean by Sun. We will discuss business objects in detail in the Architecture Module.

CORBA, DCOM, and RMI were developed in the 1990s and many of the component-concepts were developed in the same time period. At present, they are all subsumed and, in some cases, replaced by the current distributed component-based platforms that allow business components to be defined, discovered, and invoked over the Web. The two principal contenders at present are Sun's J2EE and Microsoft's .NET. The XML Web Services play a key role in both architectures. We have discussed these platforms in Chapter 2 of this module.

5.3.6 Distributed Data and Transaction Management State of the Market

5.3.6.1 Distributed Data Management State of the Market

A plethora of off-the-shelf products provide the distributed data management functions discussed in this module. These products appear as SQL middleware for distributed data access and SQL gateways to translate protocols between different databases.

SQL gateways exist for two reasons. First, to allow SQL clients from vendor X to interoperate with the SQL servers from vendor Y (for example, Sybase Omni Server allows Sybase clients to access Informix, Oracle and DB2 databases). Thus these gateways are used in the Proprietary API and completely proprietary middleware categories discussed in the previous section. Second, to allow SQL clients to access non-SQL databases (e.g., the EDA/SQL from Information Builder, Inc.). Figure 5-6 shows a conceptual view of a typical SQL server.

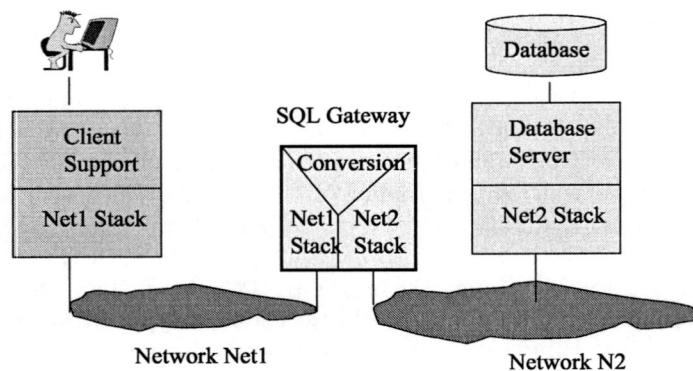

Figure 5-6: Conceptual View of SQL Gateways

Many vendors such as Oracle, Microsoft, and IBM currently support SQL gateways. The gateway software makes a remote database look like a local database to the client applications and tools. The SQL request can be submitted as ad hoc, through a command level interface, or embedded in a programming language such as C. Typically, these gateways are suitable for ad hoc SQL queries only with little or no support for remote stored procedures and procedure calls. To provide access to legacy data that is stored in non-relational databases such as IMS, some database gateways provide "SQL-to-IMS" converters which cast SQL calls to IMS database access calls. This data translation is usually accomplished at the target database server machine through data translators (for example, IBI's EDA/SQL provides many translators at the target machines that convert SQL calls to IMS and other non-relational data sources). However, the quality of these gateways must be examined thoroughly before enterprise-wide heavy usage (there are many intricate performance issues in translating SQL to non-SQL formats).

The main advantage of SQL database gateways is their flexibility and end-user control. However, these gateways assume that:

- the database schema is known and can be understood by the end-users
- the target databases are based on relational database technologies (SQL to non-relational formats has some performance and functionality limitations)

The database gateways raise many network and system performance issues (e.g., size of SQL results sent over the network is unpredictable, gateways can be security as well as performance bottlenecks). In addition, the database gateways can be expensive (in the range of $200K for mainframe based systems). Most of the existing database gateways provide read as well as update to single hosts. The capabilities for distributed query processing among the same vendor databases are also available. However, distributed query processing between multiple vendors and distributed transaction processing support is sparse.

An interesting example is the DRDA (Distributed Relational Database Architecture) gateways from IBM. These gateways convert client calls to DRDA. As stated previously, DRDA is a de-facto standard for DB2 access. More than 20 vendors have announced DRDA support. Another example is the EDA/SQL Gateway. This gateway from Information Builders Inc. translates the SQL to access more than 30 data sources in relational as well as non-relational formats. EDA/SQL uses a proprietary SQL API and client/server middleware (called the API/SQL and EDA/Link, respectively) to access IMS, DB2, Informix, Oracle, Sybase, Focus, Adabas and many other data sources stored on MVS, UNIX, and Windows Platforms. The EDA/SQL gateway provides numerous translators that convert EDA SQL to other SQL variants and non-SQL formats.

5.3.6.2   Distributed Transaction Processing - State of the Market

Distributed transaction management solutions are roughly clustered into two families of products: the TP Heavy products and the TP Lite products.

In the TP Heavy family, products such as Transarc's Encina, AT&T's Tuxedo and IBM's CICS are worth noting. We have discussed Encina in the previous section. IBM has adopted the strategy of "CICS on everything". CICS is currently available on many platforms such as MVS, AIX, OS/2, OS/400, Windows NT, and HP-UX. Tuxedo is also being ported to almost all UNIX platforms.

Standards are playing an important role in the C/S TP products. Basically, most of these products support the XA and XA+ interface so that a given TP monitor can interoperate with many database managers and communication managers. However, the following three application to communication resource manager APIs are being developed:

- TxRPC (transactional RPC). This API is based on DEC's Remote Task Invocation technology,
- CPI-C. This is a peer-to-peer API used in the IBM APPC environments,
- XATMI. This is a Tuxedo Application/Transaction Management Interface.

With the major C/S transaction processing products becoming available on almost all platforms, you have to decide whether to standardize on a product or to standardize on standards.   It might be appropriate for small environments to stay within the offerrings of a single product. But for large scale organizations that need distributed transaction processing across many platforms, it is best to stay within standards.

For TP-Lite, several data replication servers are commercially available from a diverse array of vendors. Examples are IBM Data Replication Toolset (Data Refresher, Data Hub, Data Propagator), Oracle Snapshot, Prism Warehouse Manager, Sybase Replication server, Trinzic Infopump and InfoHub, and Praxis Omini Replicator. Some of these replicators are used for data warehousing while the others are intended for distributed transaction processing.

5.4   State of the Art: Trends

5.4.1   State of the Art: General Trends

As businesses continue to face the pressures of flexibility, quick turnarounds, and efficiency, the need to provide flexible and portable applications for inter as well as intra enterprise work will grow. The need for middleware to quickly enable such applications will also grow accordingly. The following general trends in general purpose middleware are worth noting:

- Middleware will continue to become more sophisticated by extending the scope of local services to distributed environments so that users and applications can perform the same actions across networks that are typically performed on local machines. For example, the research in distributed operating systems is attempting to provide an operating system across networks.
- Standards will play an important role because without standards each new middleware component will add more complexity. Consortia such as W3C, X/Open and Object Management Group that are attempting to introduce standards into industrial products will continue to play a significant role.
- As middleware services become more popular, some middleware services will shift down to database managers, network services and operating systems. This could reduce the number of separate middleware products.
- The notion of client/server paradigm could be outdated due to the emergence of many new situations in which processes cooperate with each other as peers without any clients or servers. The object oriented systems, especially CORBA, are moving in this direction.
- The trend toward higher level object oriented services and protocols which are independent of the underlying network architectures will continue. The notion of object-oriented message systems will continue to be increasingly popular. In these systems, all clients and servers will be treated as objects which exchange messages. The format of the messages will be independent of the location of the objects.
- More off-the-shelf software will become available for "zero-programming" client/server applications. At present, many decision support applications which access remotely located SQL databases without any programming are state of the market and practice. Other off-the-shelf client/server applications in manufacturing, finance and human resource management are also becoming available from database vendors. This trend will continue.
- The issue of high level APIs will gain more importance as more middleware layers are introduced with a proliferation of APIs. High level APIs should give a programmer a uniform object invocation for accessing objects. The invocation method should internally issue an RPC, RDA or any other call.
- The middleware vendors will continue their efforts to provide transparency at the following levels (the first two levels are already achievable):
  - End user transparency, i.e. the end user does not know what parts of an application are running where
  - Developer transparency, i.e., the developers do not have to know where their code will run (e.g., code portability)
  - Manager transparency, i.e., the managers do not have to know if one system or many systems need to be managed
- More off-the-shelf compound middleware platforms that package domain specific middleware services for different applications will become more prevalent. Examples of these platforms, known as "application servers", are mobile application servers and ecommerce servers. We will discuss application servers in detail in the Platforms Module.
- Next generation middleware is becoming more intelligent and adaptive to respond to different survivability requirements (see Section 5.4.4).

The three-tiered architecture shown in Figure 5-7 is a common scenario at present. In this scenario, the Web browsers are used as the primary entry point for users to access all resources. Web middleware is used as a front-end to access Web resources over the public Internet or private Internet (Intranet). The middle tier houses Web resources, i.e. the databases and the programs that can be directly accessed/invoked from Web clients (e.g., HTML pages, Java applets). Web browsers are increasing their capabilities to directly access more and more resources (e.g., invoking CORBA calls from Web browsers). The middle tier will continue to grow as more databases and applications can be directly accessed from the Web browsers.

The middle tier is also serving as a gateway to the back-end non-Web (mostly legacy) resources. The back-end non-Web resources are accessed from the middle tier by using the traditional middleware such as remote SQL, screen scrapers and file transfers. As the back-end resources become more OO (either through object wrappers or migration), the communication between the middle and third tier can increasingly use the distributed object model. The middle tier can serve as a transition gateway to gradually migrate the legacy resources to employ the distributed object middleware. This marriage of object orientation with Web is a very promising direction that is currently the foundation of Web services, .NET, and J2EE. A more detailed view is presented in Figure 5-8.

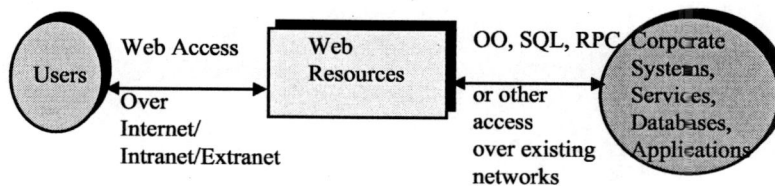

Figure 5-7: Emerging Scenario- High Level View

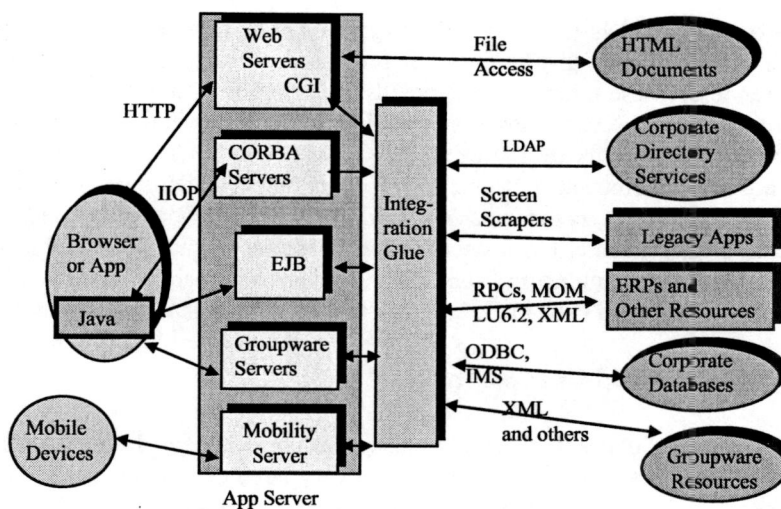

Figure 5-8: Emerging Scenario - Detailed View

5.4.2 Middleware for Real-time Enterprises

Many small and large organizations are adopting the real-time enterprise model where the business activities monitors (BAMs) manage the business in real-time instead of monthly and weekly reports. Real-time enterprises, discussed in Chapter 1 of the Overview Module under the general heading of Next Generation

Enterprises, typically use the publish-subscribe model for real-time business activity monitoring. In a publish/subscribe model, shown in Figure 5-9 , the messages are "published" into a "channel". For example, a supply chain management system can publish events to trigger alerts if packages will not arrive at their destination as expected. Real-time enterprises can define critical business activity metrics such as number of new online-orders and the number of customers dropping a service as events on a "business activity" channel. The subscribers are the BAMs that monitor and respond to these events and alert the management for appropriate action. BAMs can appear as management consoles with green, yellow and red icons (the GE model as described in Chapter 1 of the Overview Module) or can just send emails to the appropriate managers.

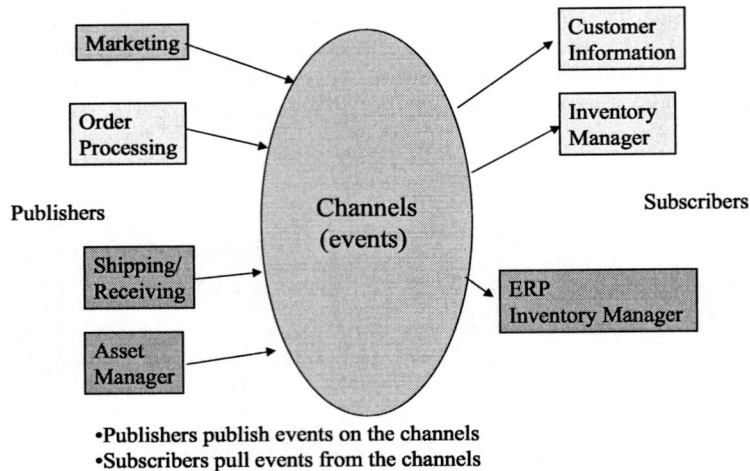

• Publishers publish events on the channels
• Subscribers pull events from the channels

Figure 5-9: A Publish/Subscribe Model

The "publish and subscribe" models for real-time enterprises can be developed by using different type of middleware services. At the time of this writing they are based on XML, JMS, J2EE (Java 2 Enterprise Edition), and Web Services. These middleware standards are being used to exchange information between applications in real-time through events. Providers publish important events as XML messages and the consumers subscribe to these events by retrieving these messages. Sun's JMS (Java Message Service) platform, which blends Java and messaging technology for building Web Services is becoming a key player in pub-sub. By using the JMS API, companies can build XML Web Services for event-based BAMs. As discussed in chapter 1 of this module, many decisions are made in various steps of the publish-subscribe paradigm such as pull versus push, number of subjects and channels to manage, and handling large number of subscribers. These decisions need to be made based on the nature of business activities being monitored.

5.4.3 Middleware for Grid Computing

Simply stated, grid computing consists of several clusters of computers at different sites that are tightly interconnected through very fast networks, behaving as a very large computing system. For example, the National Science Foundation (NSF) TeraGrid Project is building a transcontinental supercomputer with extremely high computing capabilities. It consists of clusters of high-end microcomputers at multiple sites (the Argonne National Laboratory outside Chicago, the University of Illinois at Urbana-Champaign, Caltech in Pasadena-CA, and the University of California-San Diego) that are being networked together very tightly so that they behave as a single supercomputer. This "virtual computer" will be eight times faster than the most powerful academic supercomputer available today. This computational power will enable scientists to address the computationally intensive tasks in medicine, climate modeling, and defense.

Development of middleware for grid computing is an active area of research and development. Most of the work is directed towards peer-to-peer (p2p) communications instead of the client/server middleware services currently in vogue. An interesting example is the Globus Project (www.globus.org) that is developing middleware and other technologies needed to access and manage resources in widespread locations. A Globus Toolkit is commercially available. The following projects are also worth noting (see the links for details):

- www.jxta.org -- Jxta Peer to Peer Network
- www.cs.virginia.edu -- Legion Project at University of Virginia
- datafarm.apgrid.org -- Grid Datafarm
- www.mithral.com/projects/cosm/ -- The Cosm P2P Toolkit
- www.gridbus.org -- The Gridbus

For additional details on grid computing, visit the **Grid Computing** Technology Centre (GCTC) (www.gridcomputing.com) and the Global **Grid** Forum (www.gridforum.org) web sites.

5.4.4 The Next Generation Middleware – Possible Research Directions

We have studied various aspects of middleware so far. Let us now recap and discuss some future areas of research.

Basically, middleware enables rapid and cost effective development of distributed applications. Although it is possible to build applications directly on top of hardware, OS and network protocols without using any middleware services this is extremely tedious, error-prone and costly over system life-cycles. However, currently existing COTS middleware packages have several limitations. In essence, middleware must satisfy the needs of two very demanding masters: applications that reside above the middleware and networks that exist below the middleware. Both masters are evolving rapidly and impose ever-changing requirements on middleware (see Figure 5-10). This is especially true for the current US Government initiatives such as Internet2 (www.internet2.org), Next Generation Internet (www.NGI.org) and a very large number of network technologies and applications being developed in the private sector.

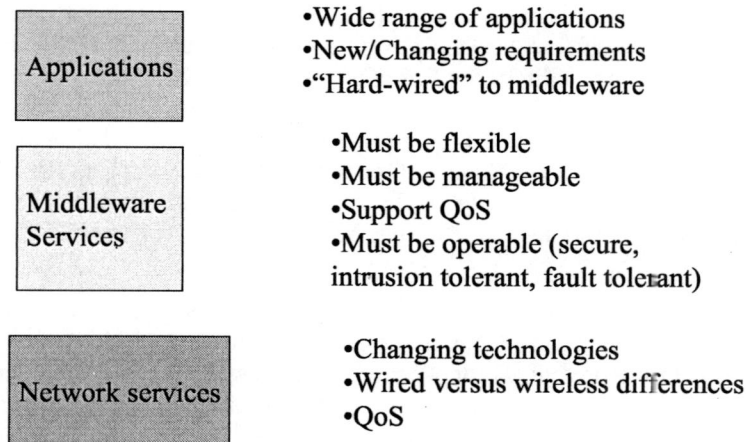

Applications	•Wide range of applications •New/Changing requirements •"Hard-wired" to middleware
Middleware Services	•Must be flexible •Must be manageable •Support QoS •Must be operable (secure, intrusion tolerant, fault tolerant)
Network services	•Changing technologies •Wired versus wireless differences •QoS

Figure 5-10: Middleware Challenges

The middleware solutions so far have been point solutions in that each middleware package is targeted towards specific types of networks and applications. For example, some middleware services are developed for object-based applications, others for message-oriented applications, some for wireless and others for wireline. In particular, the dependence of enterprise applications on middleware is an area of major re-engineering costs. Consider, for example, the situation at Telcordia Technologies. In the early 1990s, they developed their applications by using homegrown middleware. In the early 1990s, OSF/DCE became popular and so many applications were re-engineered to become OSF/DCE compliant. But in the late 1990s

CORBA became more popular and thus the OSF/DCE applications were re-engineered to become CORBA compliant.

At present, loosely coupled publish-subscribe-based applications are gaining popularity for enterprise-wide integration. So the now CORBA-compliant applications are being targeted for yet another major re-engineering effort. A similar situation exists for wired versus wireless applications. The wireless applications need to be redesigned for wired versus wireless services. This application re-engineering to keep pace with middleware services is an expensive and futile effort that must be addressed in the future systems. In addition, the current COTS middleware packages are very inflexible and sorely lack any QoS specification and enforcement mechanisms. Also, these COTS packages cannot adapt themselves to the power/CPU/memory requirements of the mobile devices.

It is essential to re-think the middleware situation at present and develop fundamentally new approaches Towards this end, *Next Generation Middleware* is needed that combines several concepts: intelligent compensating middleware, adaptable and reflective middleware, formal models, and a middleware integration factory (see Figure 5-11).

a) Intelligent Compensating Middleware (ICM). This activity should concentrate on how new functionalities can be plugged into the *existing COTS* middleware. This activity should focus on:
- Development of a common API that will make applications middleware unaware so that a change in middleware does not require re-engineering of applications.
- Allowing various COTS middleware packages to be called from this API internally. This will allow new middleware services (say for new type of network capabilities such as IP multicast) to be introduced without changing the applications. This approach should plug-in missing features to existing COTS middleware through "intelligent compensation". This will allow new features such as more efficient routing to be added seamlessly to existing COTS middleware.

Initial work on developing ICM for intrusion tolerance is reported in [Umar 2001].

b) Adaptive and reflective middleware (ARM). This activity should attempt to:
- Facilitate adaptive and reflective middleware (ARM). ARM is middleware whose functional or QoS related properties can be modified either statically or dynamically [Schmidt 2001]. For example, ARM could include new QoS capabilities dynamically and could adapt for wireless versus wireline communications at runtime.
- Develop new interceptor technologies that go beyond the current interceptors as they exist in CORBA or "exits" as they are supported in Message Oriented Middleware such as IBM's MqSeries. This technology is of fundamental importance to the future middleware services because new facilities should be pluggable into the middleware. This may be an extension of [Filman 2000].

c) Formal Models and Algorithms. This activity should develop:
- A conceptual framework for classifying and representing middleware. This model will take a component view of middleware and attempt to formalize the interrelationships between business service components (BSCs) that represent the applications, Middleware Service Components (MSCs) that represent the middleware services, and Network Service Components (NSCs) that represent the network services. In addition, middleware will be classified in terms of services for locating and establishing connections, for exchanging information, for enforcing security, and for managing/monitoring the system resources. This can be based on the work by Umar and Missier [Umar2000, Missier 2001].
- Different algorithms that will be designed to provide adaptivity and QoS features in middleware. These algorithms will consider network and user dynamicity, and migration of mobile code with different network properties such as unicast, anycast, multicast etc. These algorithms could be imbedded in the ICM and/or ARM.

d) Middleware Integration Factory. There is a need to automate middleware integration as much as possible. A "factory" could be envisioned that:
- Generates the integration glue between new and existing middleware services (e.g., generates the adapters that can be used to integrate new middleware services with existing COTS middleware).
- Provides an environment to test the integration of new and existing middleware services.

- Generates – eventually -- fundamentally new middleware services and adapts existing middleware without impacting the applications or the underlying networks.

This factory could allow integration glues, test scripts, and new middleware services to be generated quickly. Research in formal taxonomies of middleware is needed to build such factories.

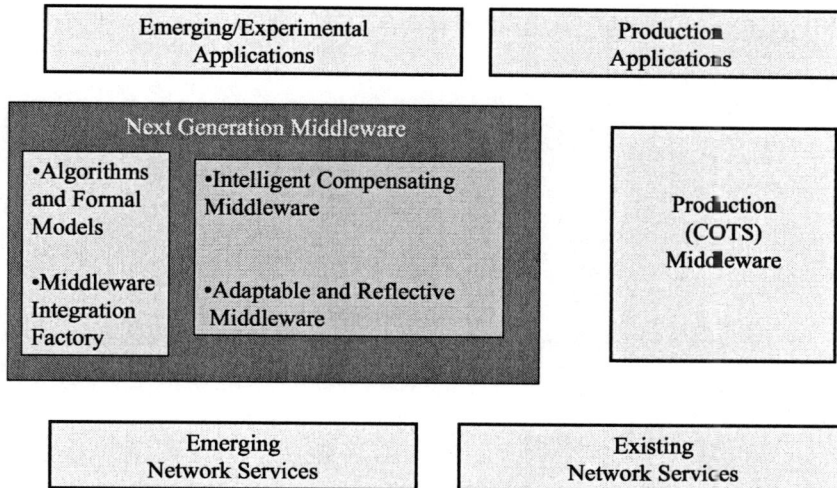

Figure 5-11: Next Generation Middleware - The Big Picture

5.5   Exercises

1) Survey the current literature and find additional case studies that reflect middleware state of the practice.

2) Survey the current market literature and find additional state of the market products to update the middleware state of the market.

3) Survey the current research literature and find additional research topics that reflect middleware state of the art. In particular, evaluate middleware services for real-time enterprises.

5.6   References

Chang, Y., et al, " An Object Transaction Service Based on CORBA", International Conference on Distributed Platforms, Dresden, March 1996

Filman, R., et al, "A CORBA Extension for Intelligent Software Environments", NASA Research Report, NASA Ames Research Center, Mottfield, CA, 2000.

Missier, P. and Umar, A., "Representing Knowledge about Modern Software Architectures", Accepted for publication IFIP International Conference on Knowledge-based Systems (April 2001).

Schmidt, D., "Adaptive and Reflective Middleware Systems", Presentation, DARPA/ITO, 2001.

Schmidt, D., et al, "Towards Adaptive and Reflective Middleware for Network-Centric Combat Systems", CrossTalk, Nov. 2001

Umar, A. Ghosh, R. Zbib, F Anjum, "ICM External Architecture", DARPA Report, Data Item: A002, Work Completed under the Project "A Comprehensive Approach for Intrusion Tolerance Based on Intelligent Compensating Middleware", BAA00-15, February 2001.

Umar, A., A. Ghosh, R. Zbib, F Anjum, "Intrusion Tolerant Middleware", DARPA Information Security Conference and Expo (DISCEX), June 2001.

INDEX

Note: This is the index of this module only. For a detailed table of content and a master index of the entire handbook, visit the website (www.amjadumar.com)

Printed in the United Kingdom
by Lightning Source UK Ltd.
9562200001B